An Introduction to the Study of Mysticism

An Introduction to the Study of Mysticism

Richard H. Jones

Published by State University of New York Press, Albany

© 2021 State University of New York

All rights reserved

Printed in the United States of America

No part of this book may be used or reproduced in any manner whatsoever without written permission. No part of this book may be stored in a retrieval system or transmitted in any form or by any means including electronic, electrostatic, magnetic tape, mechanical, photocopying, recording, or otherwise without the prior permission in writing of the publisher.

For information, contact State University of New York Press, Albany, NY
www.sunypress.edu

Library of Congress Cataloging-in-Publication Data

Name: Jones, Richard H., 1951– author.
Title: An introduction to the study of mysticism / Richard H. Jones.
Description: Albany : State University of New York, [2021] | Includes bibliographical references and index.
Identifiers: LCCN 2021035255 (print) | LCCN 2021035256 (ebook) | ISBN 9781438486338 (hardcover : alk. paper) | ISBN 9781438486321 (pbk. : alk. paper) | ISBN 9781438486345 (ebook)
Subjects: LCSH: Mysticism.
Classification: LCC BL625 .J66 2021 (print) | LCC BL625 (ebook) | DDC 204/.22—dc23
LC record available at https://lccn.loc.gov/2021035255
LC ebook record available at https://lccn.loc.gov/2021035256

10 9 8 7 6 5 4 3 2 1

Contents

Preface		vii
1	What Is Mysticism?	1
2	Types of Mystical Experiences	9
3	Mystical Paths	25
4	The Diversity of Mystical Knowledge-Claims	32
5	The Interaction of Experience and Culture in Mystical Knowledge	51
6	Approaches in the Study of Mysticism	63
7	Themes in the History of Mysticism	77
8	Psychological, Sociological, and Cultural Approaches to Mysticism	97
9	The Scientific Study of Mystical Experiences	111
10	The Relation of Mysticism and Science	129
11	Are Mystical Experiences Cognitive?	147
12	Mysticism and Language	169

13	Mysticism and Morality	187
14	Comparative Approaches to Mysticism	207
15	Theological Approaches to Comparative Mysticism	224
16	The Importance in Studying Mysticism Today	231
Notes		237
References and Further Reading		263
Index		291

Preface

Interest in meditation is exploding today. In November 2014, *Time Magazine* hailed the "mindfulness revolution" on its cover. Mysticism, however, has fallen into general disrepute. The first definition that the *Oxford English Dictionary* gives the word in its latest edition reflects the popular view of mysticism today: "Frequently derogatory. Religious belief that is characterized by vague, obscure, or confused spirituality; a belief system based on the assumption of occult forces, mysterious supernatural agencies, etc." The negative connotations of "mysticism" were set in the seventeenth century when the term was devised: it was first used in English to criticize religious groups seen as overly "enthusiastic" in their devotion, such as the Quakers and Shakers (and thus not properly British). Many people today think mysticism is the "essence" of religion or the most "authentic" religiosity, but theologians in Western religions also criticize it as a distortion of religion that leads only to heresy, antinomian behavior, and a negative impact on society. In the end, many theists agree with G. K. Chesterton's well-known disparagement of "mysticism" as "starting in mist, ending in schism, with 'I' in the middle." In academia, its study has become unfashionable in religious studies, philosophy, and the social sciences. In philosophy today, about the only time the term comes up is when disparaging an opponent's reasoning—"Oh, you are a mystic!" accompanied by a dismissive wave of a hand. Cognitive scientists in neurology and psychology are interested in meditation and drug-enabled mystical states of consciousness but only for learning more about how the brain works. Members of the health sciences and psychotherapists are also becoming interested in meditation and psychedelic drugs for their possible effects on limited aspects of our physical and psychological well-being. But scientists are not interested in whether the resulting mystical experiences provide knowledge that enables a person to lead a life more in tune with reality.

In such circumstances, why bother studying mysticism itself? But if we move from treating "mysticism" as a vague general cultural term of derision to restricting its scope to phenomena surrounding certain types of experiences occurring in altered state of consciousness, there are good reasons to study it. If mystical experiences are unique mental states, as neuroscientists are now suggesting, then studying such experiences would be valuable to gain data on the nature of consciousness or at least the operation of the brain. In addition, mystical experiences would then present the possibility that they provide genuine unique insights into reality should be seriously examined. If some mystics in fact experience a transcendent reality, that would be momentous—such experiences would present a challenge to naturalistic beliefs concerning what is fundamentally real on experiential grounds rather than metaphysical or theological speculation. Philosophers thus should address the issue of the possible validity of mystical claims, rather than immediately dismissing them unexamined on grounds of naturalistic metaphysics, and people outside of academia also should take notice. Even without that possibility, people interested in religion or other cultures and eras should be interested in the roles that mysticism has played throughout history in different cultures, including today. Theologians make religious judgments on the status of mystical claims in their own tradition and in others, but it is the role of scholars in religious studies to lay out the world's mystical traditions without such judgments. Determining that everything connected to mysticism is unique to each culture and era or that there are cross-cultural or even universal phenomena in mysticism would be significant. Matters such as these make the scholarly study of mysticism important, even if the academia study of mysticism may be limited because of the nature of mystical experiences themselves and the incompleteness of the historical record. So too, there is still much to learn about both how the brain operates during mystical experiences and also the social and psychological aspects of the lives of mystics.

On a personal level, there are also good reasons to study mysticism. Mysticism is not a matter of simply adopting certain *beliefs*—it is a matter of *experience and how one lives*. People who have had spontaneous mystical experiences or drug-enabled experiences or who meditate may well wonder about the nature of such experiences and should want to know the issues surrounding them and how others have dealt with them. Outside of that context, the study of the practices and ideas of the world's mystics may lead to enlarging one's worldview or may affect one's values or at least may lead to examining one's own beliefs and values. The religious may be interested in the mystics of their own tradition and also in seeing what mystics of other traditions believe and how they live. Moreover, these experiences occur spontaneously more commonly among the general population than usually supposed—they are not limited to monastics or others who have devoted their lives to a mystical way of life or who have taken psychedelic drugs. And with the practice of meditation among a growing segment of the general population, these experiences have taken on a more prominent presence in our culture today than in the recent centuries in the West. Thus, even people who have not any type of mystical experience or have not experienced awe and wonder at the world may want to know more about mystical experiences.

With that being said, being familiar with mysticism should be part of any well-rounded person's education. A good place to start, I hope, is the overview of today's principal approaches to the study of mysticism provided. This book sets forth definitions of "mystical experiences" and "mysticism," along with descriptions of their general nature (chapters 1–5); overviews of the different current approaches to the study of mystical experiences and mysticism (chapter 6) and of the general themes in the world's major mystical traditions (chapter 7); introductions to the different current social and psychological approaches, including gender studies (chapter 8); an introduction to the neuroscientific study of meditators and participants in psychedelic drug studies (chapter 9); a comparison of mystical and scientific knowledge in light of New Age beliefs (chapter 10); and introductions to the major analytic philosophical issues (chapters 11–13) and to comparative approaches in religious studies and theology along with postmodern objections (chapters 14–15). Popular misunderstandings of the nature of mysticism as stipulated here are also pointed out along the way.

But be prepared to step out of your comfort zone: studying mysticism involves altered states of consciousness, examining lives transformed by a single momentary experience, and such claims as that something can exist but not be ultimately real, that paradoxes are acceptable and even necessary, that what is experienced is ineffable, that the enlightened are beyond good and evil, and that one ascends to a reality by delving inward.

— 1 —

What Is Mysticism?

The first issue is getting a handle on what phenomena should be considered "mystical." The vagueness of the word and the generally negative attitude toward it in our culture has led to the term being used for a wide range of phenomena generally looked down upon today: magic, hallucinations, miracles, speaking in tongues, anything occult or esoteric, paranormal powers and experiences, anything supernatural or otherworldly, anything theological or spiritual, anything nonscientific in nature, any obscure belief, any thinking or speculation deemed unintelligible or irrational or not based on evidence, or anything with a hint of "New Age" thought about it—in short, anything academics today generally deem flaky.

History of the Word "Mystical"

But the sense of the term "mysticism" within academia is more limited and connected to certain experiences. The adjective "mystical" arose in connection to Greek mystery (*mysterion*) cults to describe certain knowledge (*gnosis*) and rituals to be kept from the uninitiated—*mystikos*, meaning "hidden" or "secret," from a root *muo*, meaning "to close the mouth and eyes." The *mystes* were the initiates into the mysteries. Christians adopted the term "mystical" to refer to mysteries such as the presence of Christ's body in the Eucharist or the church as the "mystical body of Christ," and fairly early on ended the idea of initiates. Later it referred to hidden meanings within the Bible, in addition to the text's literal sense. In the fifth century, a Syrian Neoplatonist Christian monk writing under the name Dionysius the Areopagite advanced the idea of "mystical theology" as an understanding of the Bible informed by experiences of God. By the twelfth century, when Bernard of Clairvaux first referred to the "book of experience," the "mystical" allegorical meanings of biblical passages that Christian contemplatives expounded were ultimately based on their experiential knowledge of God—in the words of Bonaventure, "the mind's journey into God."[1] "Mystical theology" then meant a *direct awareness of God*, not the scholarly enterprise of theology in the modern sense. Thomas Aquinas (1225–1274) wrote in his *Summa Theologica* that there are two ways to know God's will: speculative thought and "an affective and experimental knowledge of divine beauty—one experiences within oneself the taste of God's gentleness and the kindness of his will." Jean Gerson (1363–1429) captured the sense of mysticism in that period: "Mystical theology is experiential knowledge of God realized through an embrace of unitive love." The principal form of mystical writing up until the late Middle Ages was exegetical exposition of the hidden mystical meaning of biblical passages. Only the adjective "mystical" existed until the seventeenth and eighteenth centuries, when the nouns "mystic" and "mysticism" were invented as spirituality was becoming separated from general theology and the sciences were becoming separated from philosophy. Romanticism and American transcendentalism reacted to the generally negative view of mysticism in modern times.

The medieval experiential slant set mysticism on a path that led scholars in the modern era to see it in terms of individuals and their *personal experiences*, not in terms of Christian doctrines and institutions. In short, mysticism became psychologized in the modern era. This was cemented by William James in his *Varieties of Religious Experience*. However, there is still no agreement on what experiences were deemed mystical—William Ralph Inge in 1899 listed twenty definitions of "mysticism" and six of "mystical theology" (1899: 8). William James delineated four phenomenological characteristics of mystic experiences: transiency, passivity, noetic quality, and ineffability (1902 [1958]: 292–94). But the term "mysticism" remained connected to the idea of "union with God." Evelyn Underhill's classic definition of mysticism is "the art of union with Reality" ([1915] 1961: 23). At the end of his career in 1947, Inge considered mysticism to be a matter of "communion with God, that is to say with a being conceived as the supreme and ultimate reality" (1947: 8). He saw mysticism as the essence of Christianity, but many others at the time still saw it as incompatible with Christianity or any theism.

"Mystical Experiences"

Some scholars today would still restrict the label "mystical" to Christianity, since that is where the term arose, and "mystical experience" to only "union with God." For others, "mystical" has become a comparative category for phenomena in other religious traditions related to any experience of overcoming a sense of separation from a fundamental reality upon which the everyday realities depend for their existence. Thus, for many the term "mystical experience" has been separated from its original context of Christian doctrines and expanded to cover all experiences in all cultures that are free of a sense of being a reality separate from whatever realities are deemed "fundamental" or "ultimate" or "more real" than ordinary phenomena—a god, a nonpersonal transcendent reality such as Brahman or consciousness, one's true transcendent self (the *purusha* of Samkhya-Yoga or *jiva* of Jainism), or the beingness of the natural realm that exists prior to our conceptualizations.

But not all "experiences of God" are deemed mystical: visions, voices, and even ordinary prayers may be experiences of God, but they do not have the feel of an unmediated contact with a fundamental reality—that is, a *direct awareness* of a reality that overcomes any sense of separation, otherness, or duality, although one type of experience may fade into another. Visions, like sense-experiences, involve a duality of the experiencer and what is experienced—experiencers see beings or symbols and receive verbal or other information. If visions are not veridical, they are a strictly internal occurrence, but they still seem to involve seeing something external—the felt phenomenological content seems like a perception. But in mystical experiences our normal sense of being a separate "self" within the phenomenal world—a self-contained entity that has experiences, controls the body, and remembers things that happened to it in the past—is broken down, as are the barriers that our conceptualizing mind sets up to carve up the phenomena we see in the world into manageable segments. There is then a sense of the connection of apparently separate realities or the realization that we have always been a more fundamental reality than we normally think.[2] Our sense of a "self" or "ego" separate from the rest of phenomenal reality and our division of what is observed into separate entities is so integral to our normal states of consciousness that the elimination of such divisions alters our consciousness. Thus, direct access to what is deemed fundamentally real is not possible through the ordinary cognitive processes or ordinary mental states of our experiencing and thinking but only through radically altered states of consciousness (ASCs).[3]

In sum, mystical experiences give an immediacy with no sense of separation between the experiencer and the experienced. But both theistic and nontheistic mystics adopt the cultural language of duality—"presence," "contact," "touching," "piercing," "encountering," "hearing," "apprehending"—since the experiencing *of* something is how all normal cognitive experiencing and all thinking occur. Since we do not have common terms for the distinctiveness of mystical experiences, it is natural for mystics to adopt a culture's common language of "visions" even though they may not be referring to dualistic experiences of seeing or hearing another. Some scholars reject the word "experience" for mysticism because philosophers generally assert that cognitive "experience" is necessarily *intentional*—an experiencer's awareness *of* something in some way distinct from the experiencer—and thus inherently *dualistic*, while mystical experiences do not have a subject/object differentiation of a reality set off from the experiencer. Bernard McGinn prefers "consciousness" (1994: xviii; 2008: 59) or "awareness" (2006: xv–xvi). But "consciousness" and "awareness" are just as intentional in normal parlance as "experience." Longer-lasting mystical *states* of consciousness must also still be distinguished from episodic *experiences*.[4] McGinn also uses "presence of God" (1994: xvii), a phrase common in theistic mystical discourse. It is a natural expression in our culture, but that too suggests the presence *of* something that is distinct from the experiencer (as in a vision)—that is, a dualistic encounter of two things. It also would not apply to experiences of something like Brahman, the Neoplatonist One, the Dao, or a godhead that is always present within us. So too, one can have a "sense of presence" in nonmystical ASCs and in more ordinary states of consciousness. Even calling a mystical experience free of any content but consciousness (which would not be an experience of an object) a *realization* of a reality still involves a duality—the realization *of* something.

All in all, we do not have any experiential terms that do not connote a separation of subject and object, since that is how the terms arose. (Robert Forman prefers the term "event" [1990: 8], but "event" does not capture the felt, experiential nature of the occurrence.) Thus, mystics must use the terminology from ordinary experiences but specify that no separation of subject and object occurs in a mystical experience or state. And since mystical occurrences involve the mind, those of limited duration can legitimately be called "experiences," while those conditions lasting longer can be called enduring "states of consciousness."

Today there is still no agreed-upon scholarly definition of "mysticism" or "mystical experience." Authors in anthologies on the subject often each have his or her own definition. All one can do in such circumstances is stipulate a definition: in this book, what will be considered as central to mysticism are the states of awareness when the sense of self and the distinctions set up by the conceptualizing mind are being overcome or are in total abeyance. Thus, only one segment of the spectrum of ASC experiences and enduring mental states will be deemed "mystical": those states involving the switch to another mode of cognition when the partial or complete emptying of the mind of differentiated content.[5] This definition of "mystical experience" reflects the new scientific interest in such altered states of consciousness connected to meditation and psychedelic drugs, but no definition of "mystical experience" is dictated by science unless all ASCs have the same neurology underlying them, which currently appears not to be the case. Thus, scholars still have to decide what range of ASCs to include in their definition and what range to exclude, and there will probably never be a consensus on the matter. But a designated range is not arbitrary if there is a legitimate reason for it: here the focus is on the states resulting from emptying the mind of its normal content because the different states resulting from this "unknowing" are necessary to the classical mystical quests in all traditions for aligning one's life with "reality as it truly is" (as defined by a given mystic's tradition). The definition employed here is a middle path between including all ASCs as mystical and restricting "mystical experience" only to experiences totally free of all differentiated content—other introvertive and extrovertive experiences and the continuing states of consciousness with no sense of self are included.

"Mysticism"

Thus, the term "mystical experiences" here will denote short-term episodes in an altered state of consciousness involving a direct awareness of a reality free of a sense of a discrete self or conceptualized differentiations, and "mystical states" will refer to more enduring selfless states. "Mysticism" will refer to the doctrines, codes of conduct, practices, rituals, institutions, and other cultural phenomena centered around an inner quest to end the sense of self and to end our conceptualizing mind from controlling our experience in order to bring oneself into a life in harmony with what is deemed ultimately real. Thus, *mysticism* as designated here is more encompassing than simply having *mystical experiences*. Mystical experiences also occur outside of mystical ways of life, but mysticism involves comprehensive ways of life having spiritual practices and a specific goal, with doctrines about the nature of what is deemed real as their philosophical spine. Thus, mysticism cannot be reduced (contra most philosophers) simply to a matter of holding certain *metaphysical beliefs*—it is a *way of life*, or a *way of being*, in which *practices and ASC experiences* are central. This is not to deny that doctrines about the fundamental nature of things (typically adopted from a mystic's religion and culture) also figure prominently in these ways of life—they provide the belief-framework enabling mystics to understand their experiences and to integrate their experiences into their life. Mystical experiences are individual and private, but much of mysticism involves observable social and cultural phenomena. Nor can mystical experiences in classical mysticism be studied apart from the other aspects of mysticism—mystical experiences play an essential role in mystical ways of life, but they are not all that matters in the study of mysticism.

Thus, "mysticism" as the term is used here cannot be reduced to having any "ecstatic" experiences. Nor is religion merely a tool for mystics to have exotic experiences, and so able to be ignored once the experiences occur. Rather, traditional mystics value experiences not as ends in themselves but only for the *knowledge* they give that enables the mystics to transform their lives in line with the fundamental nature of reality as defined by their culture. Classical mystics do not stress mystical experiences for the joy of the experiences—indeed, the quest may be anything but joyful—but for the insight allegedly given and a life aligned with reality.[6] (Enlightening knowledge needs to be realized only once, but maintaining an enlightened selfless ASC is another matter.)

The purpose of following a mystical way of life is to transform one's character and way of being by means of mystical practices, experiences, and states of consciousness. All experiences are internal—our personal experiences of pain or of the color of an object are "subjective" in that sense—but to mystics these experiences are not "subjective" in the negative sense of being merely brain-generated events but cognitive. In the past, mysticism was closely tied to religious ways of life. This connection is natural, since religions present pictures of the ultimate nature and value of various realities (the person, the world, transcendent realities), and mystical experiences seem to most experiencers to involve realizing an ultimate reality and to be connected to the meaning of life. Thus, mystics typically thought of themselves as Christians, Muslims, or members of whatever tradition they belonged to, not as "mystics"—they followed their religion, not practiced "mysticism."

Nevertheless, the role of certain types of ASC experiences and states is what separates mysticism from other forms of religiosity and metaphysical speculation. Today neuroscientists are coming to accept that mystical experiences are based in distinctive neurological events and are not merely products of our imagination (e.g., Newberg, d'Aquili & Rause 2002; Hood 2001). That they are "genuine" experiences does not necessarily mean that transcendent realities are involved in some mystical experiences or that mystical experiences provide knowledge, but only that they are not some more ordinary experiences that have simply been interpreted mystically. Nor are all ASC experiences mystical—some, for example, are dualistic visions. Nor is "mysticism" merely the name for the inner religious life of the intensely pious or scrupulously observant followers of any strand of religiosity or anyone who performs supererogatory practices or who dedicates themselves utterly to God. One can be an ascetic or rigorous in fulfilling the demands of a religion without having the ASC experiences that distinguish mystics. Nor is mysticism the "essence" or "core" of all religion—there are other ways of being religious, other factors that are more central to most religions, and other types of religious experiences. But mystics have been a shaping force in every religion.

Mystics may also have ASC experiences outside of the range of mystical experiences specified here—for example, paranormal powers or experiences such as visions, levitation, telepathy, and out-of-body flights. Not all who have mystical experiences have paranormal experiences or vice versa. Paranormal experiences may occur in mystical practices as the mind is being emptied of a sense of self and differentiated content, but mystical experiences may occur without the experiencer having such experiences. Thus, these experiences are not preliminary or lower-level mystical experiences. But some scholars (e.g., Jeffrey Kripal and Jess Byron Hollenback) consider paranormal experiences to be as much "mystical" as the emptying experiences.[7] And paranormal experiences may well be part of an encompassing mystical way of life—in fact, clairvoyance and other powers may even be intentionally cultivated. But mystics such as John of the Cross and Teresa of Avila (who found her levitations annoying) condemn focusing upon paranormal experiences as a distraction.[8] They also condemn resting content with any transient spiritual experience rather than abiding in an enlightened state of consciousness. So too, John pointed out the dangers of accepting any visions and voices as cognitive—contemplative experiences were deemed more reliable. The *Yoga Sutra* has a place for them, but does not consider them central. Nor do mystical visualization exercises add to the credibility of visions in general. But some theistic mystics who had visions took their visions to be cognitive.

Traditional and Contemporary Mysticism

A contemporary phenomenon presents problems for most definitions of "mysticism" and for the notion that these experiences are cognitive and transform a person's character. Traditionally, mysticism was a dimension of religion, but today people may meditate and take psychedelic drugs in order to have mystical experiences, and the resulting experiences may be mystical in all regards except that the experiencers do not attach any epistemological or ontological significance to them—the experiences are taken to be merely interesting mental states generated by the brain with no existential value. Thus, after mystical experiences secular people may remain secular and naturalistic in their metaphysics and accept that no more than the ordinary brain/mind is involved in these experiences—they can experience altered states of consciousness without afterward transforming their lives. In particular, spontaneous mystical experiences (i.e., ones occurring unexpectedly without any prior cultivation or pursuit of a mystical way of life) or ones stimulated by drugs or other artificial triggers as experiments or recreation are often taken today to have no epistemological or ontological implications but to be only interesting ends in themselves. That is, no matter how intense a mystical experience may be, it will affect how one sees reality and how one lives only if it is taken not to be a purely subjective brain-generated event. In particular, drug-enabled experiences are often seen as overwhelming at the time and as giving some profound insight into the fundamental nature of reality only to be dismissed the next day as merely subjective hallucinations and thus having no existential significance or lasting effects. In sum, mystical experiences need not be given any existential significance but can be given a naturalistic explanation in terms of unusual but perfectly normal brain activity, or of a brain malfunction, and thus have no epistemic significance at all.

— 2 —
Types of Mystical Experiences

People typically refer to mystical experience in the singular—as "*the* mystical experience." That is, the prevailing view is that all mystical experiences are the same in basic nature—only the triggers differ. And mystical experiences do share the common elements that permit them to be classified together. But it is important to realize that these experiences are of various types, and thus not all mystical experiences should be treated as the same or as mere variations of a single type of experience. The difference in neurological states of concentrative and mindful meditators that neuroscientists have detected also suggests that there is not one "mystical state of consciousness." Rather, there are different classes of mystical experiences in the sense specified here, and different types of mystical experiences within each class, even though they involve a "knowledge by participation" (as discussed in chapter 4).

One important distinction is between "extrovertive" and "introvertive" experiences, to use the terminology set by Walter Stace (1960a)—that is, between experiences oriented outwardly and those oriented inwardly. The philosopher William Wainwright offers a typology of four types of extrovertive experiences and three types of introvertive experiences that captures the phenomenological evidence reflected in the recurring low-ramified descriptions of the mystical experiences in different cultures removed from the more highly ramified theological formulations (1981: 33–40).[1] With a modification of his terminology, the types are as follows:

EXTROVERTIVE EXPERIENCES

- experiencing being united to the rest of the natural realm, with a loss of a sense of real boundaries within nature or between people

- experiencing a lack of separate, self-existing entities with no emphasis on a connected whole (mindful states)

- experiencing a vibrant luminous glow to nature ("nature mysticism")

- experiencing the presence of a transcendent reality that exists outside of the world but is also immanent to the world ("cosmic consciousness")

INTROVERTIVE EXPERIENCES

- experiences with differentiated content—e.g., an inner bright white light or being enveloped in a golden light

- experiences of a connection in love or identity with a personal god

- experiences empty of all differentiated content ("depth-mystical")

In traditional mysticism, an awareness of a fundamental component of reality is given in both introvertive and extrovertive experiences that involve an insight into the nature of that reality that people whose awareness is confined to the natural order of phenomenal objects and mental conceptions have not had. In extrovertive experiences, the beingness of the natural universe shines forth in the phenomena of the sensory world. In introvertive ones, a transcendent reality is realized. Postexperiential accounts of that new knowledge are shaped by the cultural categories of each mystic. For introvertive and some extrovertive mystics, a reality *transcending* the natural world is also always *immanent* to the natural realm in the being of a person or as the ground of being of the entire phenomenal realm.[2] Thus, this transcendent reality is open to experience since it is within us, even though it is not experienceable as an object and hence is not a "phenomenon." (If God is treated as "wholly other," then revelations may be possible, but no mystical experience of him by human beings would be possible.)

So too, all mystical experiences of both classes share some phenomenological features in one degree or another: the weakening or total elimination of the sense of being a separate entity (a "self" or "ego") within the natural world, while in introvertive experiences the true transcendent self or consciousness seems deathless; a sense of timelessness; a heightened awareness, including sense-perceptions in extrovertive mysticism; a sense that both the experience and what is experienced cannot be adequately expressed in words or symbols (ineffability); a resultant feeling of bliss or peace (although a mystical experience itself may involve a feeling of ecstasy); and often there are positive emotions toward other people and the rest of the natural world and an absence of negative emotions such as anger or hatred. Traditionally there is also a cognitive quality—that is, a sense that one has directly touched some basic reality and attained an insight into the fundamental nature of oneself or of all reality, with an accompanying sense of absolute certainty and objectivity. One can attain a sense of "pure existence" or "pure being" or "boundless being" either introvertively (as consciousness) or extrovertively by seeing nature free of the overlay created by our conceptualizations. But again, classical mysticism was never about attaining isolated mystical experiences, including any that initiate enlightenment—the objective is living in alignment with realty through the knowledge revealed in mystical experiences.[3]

The mind in both types of experiences is receptive, even when one is actively focusing attention on one item. The experiences feel like they are happening to the experiencers and not initiated by them. Self-will is not involved despite the fact that mystics begin the quest with an active desire and utilize the analytic mind along the way. One may do things on the path to cultivate such experiences, but no act of self-will or any preparatory activity or drugs or other artificial triggers can *force* the change in consciousness that is involved in a mystical experience. (Thus, some traditions speak of "grace," "surrendering one's will to God," and "other-power" as the source of the experiences.) Meditators cannot force or manipulate the mind to become still by following any technique or series of steps, and thus cannot compel a mystical experience. Mystical training techniques and studying doctrines can lessen a sense of self, remove mental obstacles, and calm a distracted mind, but they cannot guarantee the complete end to self-will or the activity of the conceptualizing mind—as long as we are trying to "get enlightened," we are still in an acquisitive state of mind and cannot succeed in becoming selfless. One must surrender, simply let go and not try to control or manipulate reality. But once egocentric striving is ended and the mind becomes receptive by letting go of the attempt to control what is happening and simply letting things be, the mind becomes free of grasping or fear and stills itself. Mystical experiences then occur automatically.

Extrovertive Mystical Experiences

Extrovertive and introvertive experiences differ in the realities experienced. Mystical cultivation may lead to a sense of a connectedness or unity to the flux of the impermanent phenomena of the world once our minds are free of our conceptual, dispositional, and emotional apparatuses. These experiences involve a passive receptivity to what is presented to the senses. Since all extrovertive mystical experiences still have sense-experiences, they are "dualistic" in that sense, but the diffuse phenomena presented to the mind are no longer seen as a collection of multiple ontologically unconnected entities, and most importantly any "subject/object" duality has been transcended in sense-experiences and thus is "nondual" in that sense.

Also note that extrovertive mysticism remains *this-worldly*. Not all mystical experiences are other-worldly or without sense-experience. Even if there is a sense of a transcendent source immanent in the natural realm, the natural world is still the locus of the experience. Thus, not all mystical experiences delve into a changeless transcendent source of being but may involve an experience of the beingness of the phenomena of the world. One sees the external world itself in an ASC. The experiences reveal the fundamental reality behind our everyday world structured by concepts. What is retained from such an experience is a sense of the sheer immutable beingness of the world free of distinct realities—an aspect of the world not revealed in ordinary states of consciousness. Indeed, the difference is so significant that to mystics it is almost as if another sense in addition to our normal five is involved.

If one assumes there is only one type of mystical experience, it is natural to consider extrovertive experiences as low-level, failed, or partial introvertive mystical experiences. But extrovertive mystical experiences are a distinct type of experience grounded in different neurological states. Nor can one type be deemed necessarily superior—Buddhism and Daoism are traditions in which extrovertive experiences are considered more central than introvertive ones for aligning one's life with reality. Unfortunately, many scholars collapse the two categories and make extrovertive experiences of a connection to the world free of conceptual barriers the same as an internal "union with God."

"Nature mysticism" and "cosmic consciousness" both involve experiencing the natural world. These experiences do not often occur in mystical training (or at least they are not emphasized in mystical texts) but occur more spontaneously in the general populace, as with William Wordsworth and Walt Whitman. In nature mysticism, the being of the world is experienced vividly. To William Blake, it is "To see a World in a Grain of Sand / And a Heaven in a Wild Flower, / Hold Infinity in the palm of your hand / And Eternity in an Hour." By a participatory knowledge, one sees past the artificial divisions that we impose on the world, thereby creating phenomena, directly into the noumenal realm (Marshall 2005)—one feels connected to everything or as if one were sharing the common being of everything. Intentionality can also still be involved in such nondual experiences. The natural world may be seen as an interconnected whole or may feel like it is all inside the experiencer. For example, one is so caught up in listening to music that one feels absorbed—being "inside" the music and the instruments (see Richards 2016: 66–67, 155–57). The historian Arnold Toynbee related a brief experience that he had of "history gently flowing through him, in a mighty current, and of his own life welling up like a wave in the flow of this vast tide." Or the entire sensory realm may take on a vivid glow or a radiance, or it may feel alive or made of vibrant light or be translucent and crystal-like. In "cosmic consciousness," a phrase made famous by Richard M. Bucke ([1901] 1969), there is the felt presence in the world of a transcendent god or mind that also exists outside of time—that is, a sense of the living presence of a timeless transcendent reality (often of light or love) that is immanent to the natural world and present in everyday life. Both events may be brief experiences or lasting transformed states of consciousness.

But all of these experiences have in one degree or another a lessening of a sense of self and of any boundaries set up by our analytic mind between the experiencer and the world or within the world, leading to a sense of connectedness or partless unity ("oneness") of oneself with the world—all things share the same beingness, and one participates in that shared beingness in an "eternal now" that exists outside any temporal sequencing. Both nature mystical experiences and cosmic consciousness come in various degrees of intensity, but there is always a profound sense of being connected to the natural world, of knowledge, and of contact with something fundamentally real. Trying to understand the experience or what was experienced abruptly ends the experience by dropping the experiencer out of the ASC into a more "dualistic" state of consciousness.

Mindfulness

Consider the present moment of experience. Living in the moment is not a problem—it is the only thing we can do—but conceptualizing it interferes with the experience: when we think of the "now" of immediate experience, the moment has passed, and the more we focus on conceptualizing it, the more our mind interferes with the immediacy of experience. Mindfulness mystics see this action of our conceptualizing mind as interfering with all our experiences and thereby leading to misperceiving what is really there. But mindfulness, exemplified in Buddhism, involves paying full attention to the present moment and accepting whatever occurs without mental comment—that is, an undirected, open monitoring of our moment-to-moment experiences without conceptualizing what is experienced or thinking about the past or future, and thus being fully in the moment. This focus produces an inner calm and clarity of awareness. The world is then seen as a constant flux without independently existing objects. Mindfulness loosens the grip that the concepts we create have on our sense-experiences and inner life—thereby, the image of the world and ourselves that our mind creates is shattered. The sense of a discrete self vanishes. Mindfulness results in seeing the flow of sensory input and the inner activity of the mind as it is presented to consciousness free of memories, anticipations, judgments, emotional reactions, and the normal process of reifying the input into distinct objects based on our conceptions. It falls into the group of extrovertive mystical experiences when sensory data is involved, but it is not necessarily extrovertive: it may involve monitoring inner mental activity. But with ego-driven consciousness ended, mindfulness is an altered state of consciousness. Such mindfulness may be a transient meditative experience, or it may become an enduring stable state of transformed consciousness.

In mindfulness meditation, one focuses attention on, for example, breathing without trying to control it (as in concentrative meditation) but only observing what is happening. This is not a change in the input of our mental content but a change in our relation to that content—how the content is perceived when our conceptual apparatus is in abeyance. We normally see rugs and hear birds, but with pure mindfulness all structuring would be removed and we would see only unlabeled spots of color and texture free of rugness and hear sourceless noises. There is no mental editing or structuring of sensory input. This is a sustained "bare attention" to what is presented to our senses, without attention to anything in particular and with no accompanying expectations or habitual reactions.

Many people do not consider mindfulness "mystical" at all—only introvertive and nature-mystical experiences and cosmic consciousness are mystical. But mindfulness does involve emptying the mind of conceptual structuring and a sense of self. Through mindfulness there is Gestalt-like switch, not from one figure to another (e.g., from a duck to a rabbit in the Köhler drawing) but from any figure to patches of colors. That is, awareness becomes focused on the *beingness* of the world rather than *the things* that we normally conceptualize out. The greater openness in this receptivity permits more richness to the sensory input that is now freed from being routinely catalogued by our preformed characterizations. The experiences may not have the intensity or vibrance of nature mystical experiences and cosmic consciousness, but perception is refreshed by the removal of conceptual restrictions and thus is more vivid. This type of mystical experience may slide into another type. Even if one is aware that one is meditating or has a sense of the presence of a transcendent reality or ground in the world, mindfulness is still possible.

In stronger cases of mindfulness, any sense of a distinct self within the natural world vanishes completely. The conceptual boundary separating us from the rest of the natural world is broken. But the mindful can be aware that there is content in their mind without dropping out of the experience, unlike in introvertive mystical experiences. However, to mindfulness mystics, as long as we have a dichotomizing mind, we are blocking direct access to reality as it truly is, and only in a mindful state of consciousness do we no longer identify with our thoughts and emotions but simply observe things free of a sense of self, living fully in the moment. The mindful then live fully absorbed in the present and respond spontaneously to what occurs. Actions are not hurried but still deliberate without the deliberation. Introvertive mystics in this state may keep a transcendent reality in mind and believe that it is doing the work, not the individual.

With awareness freed from the dominance of our categorizations and anticipations, our mind becomes tranquil and lucid. The field of perception is no longer fragmented into discrete entities. In the words of the Dalai Lama, "nondual perception" is "the direct perception of an object without the intermediary of a mental image." Note that he does not deny that there is something there to be perceived—only now we see it as it really is, free of our conceptualizing mind setting up dualities. The mind mirrors only what is there, without adding or distorting whatever is presented. Mental categories no longer fix our mind, and our attention shifts to the "that-ness" (*tattva*) of things, as Nagarjuna called it.

But some conceptual structuring remains present in all but a state of pure mindfulness. While on the path to enlightenment, a mindfulness mystic still sees individual "objects," but it is their beingness that is the focus of attention, and once enlightened any self-contained individuality in the experiencer or within the experienced world—including a "self"—is seen as illusory. What the unenlightened conceptually separate out as "entities" are now seen to be only impermanent and conditioned eddies in a constantly flowing and integrated field of events. The enlightened still see the eddies, but not as isolated entities disconnected from the rest of the flow. Mindfulness is thus nothing more (or less) profound than seeing the sensory flow from the mundane world as it is free of the constraints of our conceptualizations and emotions.

Introvertive Mystical Experiences

Mystical experiences in the second class occur spontaneously or in the concentrative track of meditation when there is no sensory input. (Sensory deprivation has been practiced in caves, windowless rooms, or other structures that reduce sensory input.) There is an inner awareness of one's own transcendent being or a transcendent reality underlying the being of all phenomena. The important distinction here is between introvertive experiences with differentiable content and those without. Both theistic and nontheistic experiences occur in the first group. Introvertive experiences are transient, being disrupted by life in the phenomenal world. The state of consciousness enabling these experiences and the analytic "dualistic" state in which language operates are distinct, and so in a sort of mystical uncertainty principle one can either be aware of a transcendent reality or say something about it, but one cannot do both at the same time. To observers, the mystic may appear to be in a trance and unresponsive, but being completely focused on what is being immediately presented to the mind is not a trance-like state of frozen consciousness or a state of unconsciousness: the conceptualizing mind is shut down, but one remains fully awake and focused.[4]

Differentiated introvertive experiences are not merely postexperiential interpretations of the depth-mystical experience: the experiences themselves involve differentiated content. They can be seen as the presence of a reality that is personal in nature, and theists typically take what is sensed as experiences of communing with a benevolent loving god and as instances of being unconditionally loved. The sense of the divine is especially strong when bliss is part of the experience itself. But nontheists dismiss the sense of being loved as merely the product of enculturation in a theistic society or the result of the theists' own mystical training and as arising not from the presence of a transcendent reality in the experience but merely from the experiencer's own subconscious.

Because theistic introvertive experiences are differentiated, it is possible that there may be a unique flavor to these experiences in each tradition due to cultural influences—that is, Christian theistic mystical experiences in general may differ from Hindu Bhakti theistic mystical experiences, and so on.

Depth-Mystical Experiences

The inward focusing of attention begins with objects of concentration, but it can lead to the complete inner stillness of the second category of introvertive experience—the depth-mystical experience. All distinguishable content has been completely eliminated from the mind. Even in the Abrahamic traditions, there are mystics who affirm a "Godhead beyond God" free of all features. Some theistic mystics such as Jan van Ruusbroec report both differentiated introvertive theistic mystical experiences and the undifferentiated depth-mystical experience. According to the Christian Meister Eckhart, by means of a mental faculty that is distinct from reasoning and sense-experience—the intellect (*nous*)—one can breakthrough to the "ground" that is free of self-will, God's will, all creatures and images, and even of God himself. There is a silence since the normal workings of the mind are stilled.

However, without retaining some features after the experience is over, it would be hard to see how the event could be seen as an "experience" or "awareness" at all—these mystics would have to be said to be *unconscious*. But mystics do not black out or suffer amnesia during the period in which they undergo a depth-mystical experience. Rather, a sense of something real and profound is retained. That is, phenomenologically the experience feels free of all content at the time of its occurrence, but looking back at the experience after it is over something is seen as having been present in the silent state. If the experience were truly *contentless*, mystics could label it, but they could not know anything about it, and thus they could not form or deny any beliefs or values about what was experienced based on the experience. Nor could there be any emotional impact on the experiencer. But mystics do claim that something with at least abstract characteristics is experienced: oneness, pure consciousness, immutability, and fundamental reality. Thus, the experience does have content, but content that can be seen as such by experiencers only once they return to a state of consciousness with differentiations.

Thus, the mind in the depth-mystical experience is not actually *empty*. As one's consciousness shifts from this state of consciousness back to ordinary waking consciousness, memory returns and what was experienced becomes an object of reflection. There is no space during the experience itself to make possible labeling the content or interpreting its nature. But what was retained in looking back on the experience in another state of consciousness is now a dualistic image. Plotinus made clear that seeing an image of the One is different from being "one'd" with it (*Enneads* VI.9.10–11) since the analytic mind makes the One into an object, and thus any image cannot reflect the One accurately but necessarily distorts its nature.

In addition, during the states of consciousness transitioning back from a depth-mystical experience to a mindful or ordinary state of consciousness, dualistic phenomena flood back into the mind. Those states are not part of the depth-mystical phase of the event, but once the experience is over, theists may mistake any theistic content from the transitional state for what was experienced in the prior depth-mystical experience, especially if the transition involves subconscious processes and thus does not seem to be coming from the experiencer but rather seems like the experiencer is being infused by another reality.

Thus, elements related to a personal god are not part of the phenomenology of depth-mystical experience proper. The experience is free of all dualities and conceptualizations, including especially a sense of self—if you are thinking, "I am having a depth-mystical experience," you are not having one. The active mind of sensing, thinking, and reflecting has ended, and pure consciousness now prevails. The experience cannot even be called "self-awareness," since the experiencer is not aware that a *subject* is experiencing anything. So too, there is no sense of personal possession of this awareness, since it is devoid of all personal psychological characteristics. In fact, the awareness may not seem to be an *individual's* consciousness at all but something transcending all subjects. Nor is there any self-observation—if one is aware of being aware, a duality is set up. This consciousness is what remains when all intentional content is removed from the mind and yet one remains aware. It is the awareness that exists before our intentional and dualistic awareness of objects arose. It is like a beam of light that illuminates but cannot reflect back upon itself and so is never an object within awareness. Normally, we see only the objects and not the light, but in a depth-mystical experience there are no objects—a light not illuminating any object is all there is. This "light" constitutes the mental content of the depth-mystical experience, even though mystics do not realize that until the experience is over.

Mystical Enlightenment—A New State of Consciousness

The goal of mystical ways of life is not enjoying ecstatic experiences but living one's entire life in alignment with the fundamental nature of reality free of a sense of self—"enlightenment." This is an "everyday mysticism" and not a matter of isolated mystical episodes. It is not simply a matter of adopting certain beliefs but of revamping one's inner life—one must "die" to any sense of self. But no mystical experiences, not even repeated depth-mystical ones, necessarily transform a person's consciousness into a continuing selfless ASC state. No action or event can force it: no self-effort can cause the state of selflessness any more than it can cause mystical experiences.

After a mystical experience, one may recall the experience, but the sense of self may return, and if so, one returns to the ordinary state of consciousness. One once again sees the world dualistically. The experience may radically affect one's beliefs or outlook or attitude toward life, dramatically alter one's way of life, or inspire one to become more religious, all while one's consciousness remains in the ordinary state. Isolated experiences occurring spontaneously or enabled by drugs are less likely to have lasting effects than those occurring to people actively cultivating them within a spiritual quest. In fact, mystical experiences can *reinforce* the ego and lead to self-aggrandizement (since one has "experienced God" and so is special), as seen with some New Age gurus who have had mystical experiences but have not transformed their psyche into a continuing selfless ASC and yet believe themselves to be enlightened.

Thus, simply having a mystical experience does not make one enlightened: one may form a belief that "all is one" or other beliefs after the experience, but the experiences do not necessarily transform a person's *state of consciousness*—they can even transform one's life without producing a lasting altered state of consciousness. Such persons are *mystics*, but not *enlightened* ones: they have tasted the awakening knowledge (as defined by their religion) and may change their beliefs and actions, but they still see the world and themselves in a dualistic state of consciousness. Thus, if one thinks, "I am enlightened," one has fallen back into a dualistic, ego-driven state unless one sees from a selfless state of consciousness and realizes that this is only a conventional claim and there is no self.

However, mystical experiences may also lead to a psychological transformation that ends a sense of self and initiates a new way of being in the world. A mystical insight based on one's religious and philosophical ideas may occur and transform how one sees the world and how one reacts, but only when there is an enduring transformation that completely ends any sense of a phenomenal self is it mystical *enlightenment*. Enlightened insight is not simply adopting the philosophical position that the self is a fiction—it is a change in perception and cognition. And even if a sense of self is our most deeply rooted feeling and has developed for an evolutionary advantage, this does not mean it is impossible to uproot permanently. Meditation works on our consciousness, and in the case of classical mysticism is also part of more encompassing way of life that may achieve this "death of the ego." It may lead to the total loss of one's personality—that is, all that makes a person distinctive. All that may remain is an unimpeded consciousness. In addition, the enlightened state can be *lost* as the effect of the experience or meditation recedes and our normal consciousness returns. There are accounts in Theravada Buddhism of monks who could not maintain enlightenment because of illness. Teresa of Avila stated that one could fall back into an unenlightened natural state for a day or two (*Interior Castle* 7.4.1–2). But falling out of enlightenment involves not simply forgetting some knowledge-claims—if it were, one could regain enlightenment simply by being reminded of the claims. Rather, enlightenment is a change in one's state of consciousness and way of being. Thus, the Buddha continued meditating after his enlightenment as an example for other to maintain their enlightened ASC. (Buddhists claim that the Buddha himself could not lose his enlightened state.)

In sum, enlightenment is not a particular *experience* or even gaining mystical *knowledge* but a new stable *selfless state of consciousness*. It may be a continuing state of mindfulness, a nature-mystical state, or cosmic consciousness. The depth-mystical experience may be the paradigm of "mystical experiences" in the minds of most people, but enlightenment is an enduring extrovertive state of consciousness. Being an enduring state, enlightenment is more difficult to achieve and maintain. Abiding psychological *traits* replace any transient mystical experience. The traits are induced by the experiences and training and involve no sense of self—the self is now seen as just another human construct. One's rest state of mind becomes transformed into a mystical state of consciousness. This severe requirement for mystical enlightenment means that it is rare—when traditional Buddhist meditation masters are asked how many enlightened Buddhists they know, they inevitably say few or none. In Tibet, where ordained monks and nuns constitute about 20 percent of the population, it is said that only about thirty people became enlightened in the twentieth century (Jones 2004: 405n31). Few mystics attain it since the ties to our ordinary mental life and our world in general are very great. Indeed, some Indian traditions deny that enlightenment in this life (*jiva-mukti*) is possible at all.

Enlightenment involves knowing the fundamental nature of reality (as defined by the mystic's tradition) and subsequently living in accordance with reality (normally by following the values and ethics of the mystic's tradition and emulating its exemplars). Both mystics' knowledge and their will are now corrected (since the individual will is based on the error of seeing an independent self within the everyday world). And now free of a sense of self and self-will, mystics effortlessly align themselves with reality. Thus, enlightenment is a way of *being* as much as a way of knowing. Since beliefs and values from a mystic's tradition figure in enlightenment, there is no one abstract "mystical state of enlightenment" but different enlightened states: the beliefs and values that mystics bring to enlightenment will structure differently both their awareness and how they live. Different selfless ASCs may also be involved.

In introvertive mysticism, our everyday sense of a distinct culturally constructed "self" is replaced by the continuous inflowing of what is deemed the ground of either the true self or all of reality. The result is a continuous selfless extrovertive mystical state of awareness, but it is one in contact with a transcendent reality. Thus, there is an immovable inner calm even while the person is engaged in thought and activity—that is, one remains centered in a transcendent reality while remaining fully conscious of thoughts and sensations and acting in the world.[5] The state is also open-ended: more introvertive and extrovertive mystical experiences may occur, and the enlightened state may be further deepened by these experiences or by mystical exercises. That is, the initial cracking of the sense of self does not exhaust the depth of reality open to a mystic. In fact, mystics often attach little significance to any event inaugurating the enlightened state since it is the latter state and its further development that matters. For theists, becoming enlightened may be treated only as a stage in the continuing long-term development of one's relation to God. In Zen Buddhism, after an initial *satori/kensho* one continues to practice meditation as before, without a thought of a goal. But even if the process of development continues, with the last residues of a sense of a separately existing self completely uprooted from one's consciousness and subconsciousness in a stabilized ASC, a new stage of life has begun.

The change that enlightenment entails is a reorganization of the entire inner life of a person—cognition, motivations, desires, emotions, and dispositions. One has gone from thinking "I am walking" to "I am the walking" to "There is walking" or, for theists, "God walks through me." To be a mystic is to internalize beliefs and values (usually of one's religious tradition) in some form—to live them and not merely to accept them intellectually or as only ideals or imagine how reality might be. One *is* emotionally detached from one's actions, not merely *trying to be* or having a dualistic conception of *what it would be like*. Being free of all personal desires, if an enlightened mystic looked into Harry Potter's Mirror of Erised, he or she would only see themselves and the world as they are. Even the desire for enlightenment is overcome—otherwise, it is simply substituting one desire for another. Emotions based on the false sense of a self (such as fear, envy, anger, and anxiety) melt away as one realizes the true state of things and accepts them for what they are.

But even if beliefs and values are fully internalized in the enlightened state by training within a tradition so that they become part of one's cognitive and dispositional framework, the enlightened now know them to be true in a way they did not before: they no longer interpret the metaphysical claims within a dualistic framework but see reality differently: to live properly, we need to see reality as it is, free of hallucinations, and seeing reality through a discrete self is a cognitive hallucination that must be overcome. Thereby one's perception is altered. The knowledge is participatory. In the Buddhist analogy, it is the difference between an *intellectual acceptance of the claim* based on the authority of others that water will quench thirst and actually *drinking* water (*Samyutta Nikaya* 2.115): drinking the water does not reveal any new propositions, and the claim "Water quenches thirst" remains the same, but one now knows that it is true in a way one did not when only relying on the testimony of others or accepting it only theoretically—it is part of one's being. So too, naturalists may accept the propositions that everything is made of one material and that there are no selves in our mental makeup, but only by "drinking the water" do mystics see that these claims are true and integrate them into their being and how they live—they experience the reality and not merely accept a proposition formed and accepted by our dualizing mind. (Sufis make similar distinctions between hearing about fire, seeing fire, and actually being burned.)

Many mystical claims are in fact unexceptional as a matter of metaphysics, but a mystic's understanding of the claims may be very different from those who see the world in dualistic terms and not from an ASC. Mystical insight can change the mystics' understanding of the doctrines of their religion. But mystics usually express new ideas in a tradition's orthodox terms, even if the old terms take on a new significance for them. Mystical experiences may reinforce mystics' basic beliefs, but they also may alter those beliefs, leading to new interpretations of scriptural claims. Mystics typically are conservative about orthodox religious doctrines, but their teachings can also be innovative, renewing a tradition or leading to its evolution—they can even be heretical.

Mystics enjoy the peace resulting from no longer constantly trying to manipulate reality to fit their own artificial images and ego-driven desires.

The serenity accompanying mystical illumination is often described as joy, but any "ecstasy" is not long lasting and may be entirely absent. Rather, there is a sense of peace and contentment at whatever is—thus, the common term "bliss." There is a shifting of one's emotional center toward detachment, harmonious affections, and acceptance. There may or may not be an accompanying sense of awe, beauty, wonder, or amazement at the very existence of the world. Joy may be central to the religious way of life, as with Hasidic Jews and Bhaktas, for both the enlightened and unenlightened. But the inner calm or coolness through detachment of not being troubled by the vicissitudes of life is the principal emotion connected to living a mystical life aligned with "reality as it truly is." This gives mystical bliss an other-worldly air.

However, an enlightened state still involves differentiations—thoughts, sense-experiences, emotions—even if the content is not configured into discrete objects. The enlightened, despite their new awareness and the inner stillness at the core of their being, are still aware of a world of distinctions. They are not in an unconscious trance, as evidenced by the fact that mystics have taught and left writings. Speaking involves words, and any language necessarily makes distinctions. (The only alternative is that the enlightened mindlessly parrot back memorized words still in the mind.) However, unlike the unenlightened, the enlightened do not project the language's distinctions onto reality. Thereby, they avoid the creation of a false worldview of multiple discrete, "real" objects. There is a Zen saying: "Before my training, there were mountains and rivers; in the middle, there were no mountains and rivers; after completion, there were mountains and rivers again." That is, the unenlightened think that a mountain is a discrete entity in our unenlightened way; with extrovertive mystical experiences, it is seen that there are in reality no distinct objects for the terms "mountains" and "rivers" to apply to but only undifferentiated beingness; finally, in the enlightened state the enlightened integrate the analytic mind into their life but still see what is really there without thinking in terms of a set of independent entities corresponding to our concepts. Thus, some phenomena once again can be referred to as "mountains" and "rivers" even if the referents are not disconnected from the rest of reality. Consciousness is "purified," and language is not abandoned but is now seen as referring only to constantly changing eddies in the stream of phenomena rather than to independent parts. Thereby, the enlightened can use language to navigate the world of diverse phenomena and to lead others toward enlightenment. Similarly, Zen Buddhists continue to think in the state of "non-thinking"—they simply do not make the discriminated phenomena into reified objects.

In sum, an enlightened mystic's experience of the world is still mediated by conceptual structuring—it is not a "pure" mindfulness—but that structuring is not taken as representing a pluralistic world of isolated items ontologically cut off from each other.

Much of the enlightened life of one who was on a mystical quest may seem quite ordinary to an observer: the enlightened enjoy all of life and typically follow a tradition's ethics, and so their actions may not look all that different than those of an ordinary believer. The character traits of the enlightened may have only subtle changes if he or she was advanced on a mystical path before enlightenment. But enlightened introvertive mystics remain in touch with the depth-reality that they have experienced, and they now engage the world with a new mental clarity and calmness. They now live in the world in a state of freedom from the attachments and concerns generated by a false sense of an individual self. There is an openness to whatever occurs. The enlightened live with all attention focused on the present, free of the background noise produced by the dichotomizing mind. With no predetermined plans or expectations, indifferent to success or failure, they act spontaneously and effortlessly toward whatever is presented to them as their way of life and values dictate.[6] In Zen, the action is called "nondual" because there is no sense of a duality of an independently real actor and action.

Since the enlightened are no longer imposing their will on things, they often have the reaction common to many dying people who have accepted their impending death: with no self-image to maintain, they are free of any self-preoccupation or attachments or personal desires; their values may change from self-centeredness and materialism toward more concern for interpersonal relationships and a concern for others' welfare; an increase in selfless behavior; death is no longer feared (being is eternal, and they may not care if they continue individually after death); they accept things as they are; they are more flexible and less competitive; they feel that they have nothing to lose and no needs to fulfill; there are no goals to achieve or any future to plan for; life seems meaningful (even if no exact meaning is revealed); all is well with the world as it is and there is no need for social changes; everything is valued in itself; just being alive is appreciated more; things appear more beautiful; they take joy in simple matters; they become less judgmental and more accepting of others; some feel an all-encompassing love and a tremendous sensitivity to other people's feelings and sufferings; greater acceptance of life after death. (Of course, accepting one's impending death may crack the sense of self and initiate a selfless ASC.)

— 3 —

Mystical Paths

Many people today meditate for psychological and physical health benefits, such as alleviating stress, without regard to any possible cognitive insights meditating may generate. But the traditional objective of a mystical way of life is not those effects but to attain the knowledge of what is fundamentally real in order to overcome our basic misalignment with reality. Meditation is only part of a total way of life, and a mystical path is strenuous and may be painful, but participants on a path accept the hardships as necessary to reach their final goal of enlightenment. Both extrovertive and introvertive mystical experiences may occur on this path to enlightenment. While on the path, these experiences would involve only an incomplete elimination of a sense of self. So too, theistic mystics may have progressively deeper experiences of a god. Extrovertive mystical experiences can also transition to introvertive ones, but the neural states of the experiencers then change (Dunn, Hartigan & Mikulas 1999).

Calming our easily distracted mind is not easy—the Buddha said that it was easier to quiet a tree full of monkeys. Our mind normally chatters away and darts between the past, present, and future, shifting from one thing to another and not focusing totally on the present or letting go of desires and expectations. The inner quest for overcoming this fragmentation involves a process characterized differently as "forgetting," "fasting of the mind," or "unknowing"—that is, emptying the mind of all conceptualized content and the sense of self and self-will, and, in the case of the introvertive quest, the elimination of all sensory input and even all inner differentiated inner mental content. So too, one must be unconcerned about the possible effects of one's actions on oneself and become detached from any related emotions. Meister Eckhart spoke of an "inner poverty"—a state free of any created will, of wanting anything, of knowing images, or of having anything; such a state leads to a sense of the identity that has always existed with the being emanating from the Godhead beyond God that is the being of the natural world; anything that can be put into words except "being" encloses God, and we need to strip away everything in this way of knowing and become one with the beingness (2009: 253–55). Through the process of unknowing, all mental content, including all prior knowledge, vanishes and yet throughout the process one remains fully aware. The result is an awareness in which all sensory, emotional, dispositional, and conceptual apparatuses are in abeyance to a degree or completely absent.

Since its early days, the mystical path in Christianity has traditionally been divided into three phases: purgation, illumination, and union. Other traditions divide the inner quest differently. Sufism and Buddhism have many stages or levels of development and attainment. But progress is not steady, nor are all the experiences positive. A mystical quest may be strenuous—it is likened to climbing a mountain. The stress of a mystical way of life can make one physically or psychologically ill. There is the distress and anxiety in periods when one appears not to be making any progress—arid "dark nights of the soul" as John of the Cross called them, in which he felt the pain of God being absent (although God was in fact working on the mind). Theists may have periods of pain even when a sense of God is present. One also may become satisfied with a blissful state on the path—what Zen Buddhists call the "Cave of Mara"—and remain there without attaining enlightenment. The Christian *Theologia Germanica* also warned against leaving images too soon and thereby never being able to understand the truth aright. And after an introvertive mystical experience, the analytic mind usually returns quickly.

Mystics in general do not claim that the transcendent reality that is experienced is to be feared. There is no "trembling in the presence of God," as with many revelations. For Eckhart, God is a source of joy and there is nothing to be feared in God but only loved (2009: 522). Transcendent realities are usually seen as benevolent or neutral. But fear does occur in mystical states if the person does not understand what is happening. In emptying the mind of content, meditation may also open the mind up to "demonic" phenomena, that is, negative states that are usually attributed to demons or to the meditator's own subconscious and are not projected onto a fundamental reality.

Indeed, possible negative effects on a mystical path should not be overlooked. One is working on the mind, and this can be dangerous. Drugs and meditation destabilize the sense of a self and may exacerbate the conditions of people with mental disorders. Introvertive experiences can lead to confusion, fear (in particular, of ego dissolution), panic attacks, and paranoia if meditators cannot handle the experiences. (Whether mystical experiences may be opening the same subconscious territory trod by schizophrenics and psychotics is an issue.) In one drug study, 44 percent of the volunteers reported delusions or paranoid thinking (Griffiths et al. 2011). A quarter of the subjects reported that a significant portion of their session was characterized by anxiety, paranoia, and negative moods; 31 percent experienced "significant" fear. Few reported completely positive experiences without significant psychological struggles such as paranoia or the fear that they were going insane or dying. The researchers suspected that difficult moments were significantly underreported. Walter Pahnke did not mention that most who were given psilocybin in his famous "Good Friday" experiment experienced the fear that they were dying or "going crazy" and that one had to be restrained and given the antipsychotic Thorazine (Doblin 1991: 22). So too with meditation, though to a lesser extent. In one study of intensive Buddhist mindfulness meditation, 63 percent of the meditators reported at least some adverse effects, and 7.4 percent reported negative effects strong enough to stop meditating, and one meditator had to be hospitalized for psychosis (see Lindahl et al. 2017: 5). In one survey, 73 percent of the respondents indicated moderate to severe impairment of one kind or another, with 17 percent reporting thoughts of suicide and 17 percent requiring inpatient hospitalization (21).

Overall, serious work on a mystical path is not fun. Some psychological preparation and a set of beliefs that would prepare meditators or drug subjects to handle what is experienced may be essential before any serious mystical training is undertaken. (Paradoxically, a well-developed sense of *self* may be needed at the beginning of a mystical quest to avoid dangers.) Traditional mystical training provides a person with such preparation as well as a belief framework enabling students to better handle the disruption of the baseline state of consciousness. So too, guidance by an experienced teacher is essential. That the master/student relation is stressed in all mystical traditions attests to this. Without these aids, detachment from normal emotions and a sense of self can lead to depression or much worse.

Asceticism

Mysticism and asceticism are not the same. Most mysticisms embrace simplifying one's life and lessening desires, but not extreme injurious forms of asceticism (self-flagellation, sleep deprivation, starvation, and so on). Many traditions, but not all, prescribe celibacy. So too, some meditative techniques involve working the body, not just the mind. But ascetics see their renunciation of all material things or physical mortification as an end in itself (e.g., to please God or to stop actions) rather than a means to empty the mind of desires and conditioning to induce ASCs.[1]

However, mysticism involves an "inner asceticism" related to the will, knowledge, and desire. Some meditative techniques involve working on the body (or mindfulness of breathing or bodily motions), but the objective when working on the body is to subdue desire and self-will. Thus, the intent is different. One may also become attached to ascetic practices themselves. Nor is asceticism a shortcut to mystical experiences—no mystical experiences may be triggered at all. However, ascetic deprivation practices may enable mystical experience, and some ascetics have mystical experiences. So too, some classical mystics were extreme ascetics (and some of their practices are nauseating to the modern mind). But the Buddha is not alone in ultimately rejecting extreme asceticism as a way to enlightenment—the ascetic practices only weakened his body and mind. Sufism arose out of strong asceticism but soon became less ascetic.

In sum, the focus in asceticism is on the body, while in mysticism the focus is on the mind, but ascetic practices have been utilized to alter consciousness.

Meditation

"Meditation," like "mysticism," is a Western term with no consensus on a general definition and no exact counterpart in most languages. In its broadest scope, it is any attention-based technique for inner transformation (Eifring 2016: 1).[2] It is any practice intended to modify the functioning of the mind or to alter one's state of consciousness. In mystical paths, meditation involves an attempt to calm the mind by eliminating conceptualizations, dispositions, and ego-driven emotions by the sustained focusing of attention on a single item or by opening up awareness. In Livia Kohn's words, meditation is "the inward focus of attention in a state of mind where ego-related concerns and critical evaluations are suspended in favor of perceiving a deeper, subtler, and possibly divine consciousness" (2008: 4). Meditation is a way to try to gain, maintain, and deepen a state of selflessness and a focus on the present moment by controlling mental processes, and in the context of a mystical path it is a way to incorporate that selflessness and focused attention into one's way of life.

But not all meditations are alike. In no tradition is meditation restricted only to breathing exercises while sitting (see Shear 2006).[3] It may involve sitting, standing, lying down, walking, working, or indeed all of one's activities.[4] Visualizations may be utilized. Nor are all techniques passive. Some forms of meditation involve the active analytic mind. For example, in Tibetan Buddhism's "analytic meditation" (*che gom*, Skt. *vichara-bhavana*), one focuses on a point of Buddhist doctrine (e.g., impermanence or compassion), analyzes it, and tries to prove it through textual authorities or reasoning. Koans in Zen Buddhism are another instance of analytic meditation. These "public cases" are mental puzzles that are designed to force the disciple to see how concepts control our mental life and thereby to produce a sudden breakthrough to our true selfless Buddha-nature—using the conceptual mind to break free of the grip of the conceptual mind. An example is Hakuin's famous question "What is the sound of one hand clapping?" Any conceptualization of such a situation must fail, and the disciple is supposed to see that the same applies to all our conceptualizations of reality.[5] One major traditional collection of koans is titled (itself a paradox) the "Gateless Gate" (*Mumokan*).

Overall, meditation has two different tracks. In Buddhism, the distinction is between "concentration" (*shamatha*, "calming") and the more passive, open monitoring of "mindfulness" (*smriti*, *vipassana*). The concentrative approach, as in Transcendental Meditation, focuses attention on an object, for example, breathing, a candle's flame, a visualized deity, a tradition's doctrine, or repeating a *mantra*—any benign object will do. One then progressively withdraws attention from the object, and the mind becomes still. In most Indian concentrative meditation, one sits still (e.g., in the stable cross-legged position) to control the body, in silence to still speech, and with a simple object of concentration to still the mind. Concentration is common in one degree or another in all states of consciousness, but focusing the mind on a single object in concentrative meditation calms and stabilizes consciousness. This culminates in one-pointed attention (complete *samadhi*). Concentration leads to states of feeling absorbed in the object of meditation—for example, only the breathing remains, with no breather. But mindfulness may also do that.

In Buddhism, a certain degree of a concentrated mind is necessary for proper mindfulness and thus for enlightenment. Mindfulness involves a relaxed observation without trying to manipulate anything (e.g., monitoring one's breathing rather than controlling it as in the Yoga school's concentrative approach). Attention is gently brought back to the object when the mind wanders, or in nondirective mindfulness attention is allowed to wander. Jon Kabat-Zinn characterizes mindfulness as "paying attention in a particular way; on purpose, in the present moment, and nonjudgmentally" (2005: 4). One is fully in the present moment, observing whatever floats into the mind without comment or conceptualizing what is occurring. Some framework for understanding is needed in meditation, but mindfulness is a skill that can be developed without commitment to any religious tradition or metaphysical belief. It frees experience by removing any conceptual mediation from perception and thereby "expands" perception ultimately to a "pure awareness." It is an "effortless attention" that mirrors the flow of what is actually real as it is presented to the mind. It can lead to detachment from the sense of self. One becomes receptive to what is occurring in one's mind and in the world. In Buddhist terms, mindfulness is a direct perception (*pratyaksha*) of whatever is presented free of conceptualizations (*kalpanas*). Buddhists characterize this as "emptying the mind" or as switching from a conceptualizing mind to a nonconceptualizing "shining consciousness" that mirrors what is presented to it.

Both meditative tracks can render the conceptualizing mind inactive. Both can empty the mind of the sense of self and all conceptual divisions, leading to a "nondual" awareness that abolishes the distinctions of subject, object, and action. Practitioners can engage in both and shift from one track to the other, since mindfulness requires a degree of concentration and vice versa. And in classical mysticism, meditation is always only one activity of an encompassing way of life.

The Place of Mystical Experiences in Mysticism

Cultivating nonconceptualized awareness is central to mystical ways of life, but classical mystics discuss *mystical experiences* themselves very little, either their own or the nature of mystical experiences more generally—what was experienced is the source of their well-being and the knowledge attained, not the experiences themselves. Few classical mystical texts are like Teresa of Avila's *The Interior Castle*, in which she discusses different types of experiences (and refers to own experiences in the third person). For different reasons, premodern mystics seldom talk about their own experiences even in autobiographies: what is important is what was experienced, not one's own experience of it. There are exceptions, such as the Pali *Theragatha* and *Therigatha* texts. Tibetan Buddhism has a tradition of autobiographies, but even there it is uncommon for someone to claim that he or she achieved the direct realization of ultimate reality. Mystical experiences may not even feel like one's own if they seem to come from a transcendent reality and to wipe out our individuality. So too, most traditions frown upon bragging about one's own spiritual accomplishments. People who have had visions discuss their experiences more.

Thus, that a mystical text does not discuss the author's experiences does not necessarily mean the text or his or her understanding of the tradition's doctrines is not informed by the author's experiences. States of consciousness, including mystical ones, are discussed, and the general nature of experience is sometimes analyzed, but mystical experiences are not a major subject of their discourses. Instead, how one should lead one's life, the path to enlightenment, meditative techniques, knowledge, and the reality that is experienced are more common topics. Since the traditional goal is a continuous new existence aligned with the nature of a fundamental reality, the reality supposedly experienced remains more central than any momentary experience or any inner state of mind. Even when discussing inner mental states, mystics refer more often to a transformation of character or an enduring state of alignment with reality than to mystical experiences, including any transitional enlightenment experiences that end a sense of self. To read all mystical texts as meditation manuals or merely as works about the psychology of different states of consciousness is to misread them in light of modern thought. Nor are works such as Plotinus's *Enneads* performative texts designed solely to induce mystical experiences—they are primarily discussions explaining what is ultimately real and other aspects of mysticism.[6]

But this does not mean that cultivating mystical experiences is not the defining characteristic of mysticism or that the enlightened state is not an altered state of consciousness. It means only that mystics value most the *reality experienced*, the *knowledge attained*, and the long-lasting *transformed state of a person* in the world, not *mystical experiences in themselves*. Again, contrary to the popular idea of mysticism today, such experiences are not the goal of mysticism but only the means to seeing reality correctly in order to inform a new way of living. Even if mystics value the experience of a transcendent reality over all doctrines, still the resulting transformed state of a person into a life aligned with reality is valued more.

— 4 —

The Diversity of Mystical Knowledge-Claims

Mystical experiences may be ego-shattering implosions of reality and typically have a great emotional impact, but for mystics it is the knowledge gained that is important, not the experiences themselves. Mystics assert that they have realized a reality that is present when all the personal content of the mind is removed—a direct awareness either of the bare being-in-itself (the "is-ness" of the natural realm of things apart from the conceptual divisions that we impose) or of a transcendent reality. A transcendent reality is a nontemporal and nonspatial reality existing outside the natural world and thus not open to scientific scrutiny.[1] That is, if we eliminated everything in the natural realm, naturalists claim that nothing would then exist, but those who accept a transcendent reality claim that something would still exist—something in fact "more real" than anything in the natural realm. Appearances in the phenomenal realm become distinguished from a greater hidden reality. Even if a transcendent reality is also immanent to the phenomena of the natural realm, it is not experienceable as an object—thus, it is not a "phenomenon"—and so is not open to third-person scientific scrutiny. Transcendent realities include a self or consciousness existing independently of the body, a creator god, or a nonpersonal source of the natural world.

What is experienced in both introvertive and extrovertive experiences seems "more real" than what is given in ordinary experiences, and experiencers use the language of certainty rather than tentativeness. Such knowledge is not a matter of "knowing that" some proposition is true or even "knowledge by acquaintance" of a reality distinct form the experiencer. Nor is it an intuition in the sense of an intellectual jump from a line of reasoning to a new conclusion or the acceptance of some proposition. Rather, if valid, mystical awareness is another type of experiential knowledge: direct *"knowledge by participation"* or *"knowledge by identity"*—one *becomes* or *is* the reality realized. No distinctions can be made between the subject, the reality, and the act of knowing. No reflection is involved, just being. To emphasize the difference in this knowledge from that attained through sense-experiences and reasoning, mystics often use terms such as "gnosis" or even "nonknowledge" (to distinguish this knowledge from everyday knowledge) or "intellect" (to distinguish the mental function involved in mystical experiences from ordinary cognitive mental modes) or "unconscious" (to denote a state of consciousness utterly unlike normal ones). If one accepts a metaphysics in which God or Brahman is the underlying transcendent source of the being of the natural realm, or in which one has always had a "Buddha-nature," then paradoxically one has not achieved anything in one's quest, no matter how strenuous—one merely realizes what has always been the case.

However, it is also important to note that the alleged *insight* occurs *outside* any introvertive mystical experience: it is an insight into the nature of reality that can occur only when phenomena and thought have returned. (Thus, "insight" has two senses in mystical discussions: it may refer to the immediate mystical *experience* itself or to the *knowledge-claims* adopted after the experience is over. The second is propositional in nature since it reflects the postexperiential understanding that can be stated, but the first is not.) Thus, Advaitins disconnect the depth-mystical experience from the insight that Brahman alone is real. The insight occurs only in our baseline "dualistic" state of consciousness or in an extrovertive mystical state after introvertive mystical experiences are over. In those states of consciousness, the analytic mind makes what was experienced into a mental object of reflection for the mystic.

From the study of the mysticisms of the world, it is apparent that there is no one universal "mystical knowledge." Rather, there is quite a diversity of mystical knowledge-claims. Given this diversity, it is hard to deny that a mystic's values and beliefs, shaped by his or her religion and culture, influence what the insight into reality is taken to be. That is, the actual *knowledge* that is gained in a mystical experience involves elements of the mystic's *beliefs* outside the *experiences* themselves—mystical experiences alone do not determine their own interpretation or knowledge-claims for mystics. If the experiences did directly dictate doctrines in any simple empiricist manner, all mystics with the same experiences would espouse the same beliefs, but they do not. Their doctrines appear to result from a mixture of experiential and nonexperiential elements. (The issue of culture's role in determining mystical claims and experiences will be discussed in the next chapter.)

Mystics and Truth-Claims

A related misunderstanding is that mystics are interested only in having mystical experiences and do not care about doctrines—that doctrines are merely tools to lead to nondual experiences and are otherwise valueless.[2] Those who are interested exclusively in studying the *experiences themselves* can dismiss mystical doctrines not related directly to the content of the experiences as "over-beliefs," to use William James's term ([1902] 1958: 387–88), and focus only on the experiences' phenomenological attributes. But again, mystics themselves are interested in gaining *knowledge* of reality through these experiences in order to align their lives with "reality as it truly is." For this, mystics need to have a sense that they understand what is real and the nature of what they have experienced. Thus, doctrines about the true nature of reality are central to mysticism. (This also makes *reasoning* and the *analytic mind* aspects of any mysticism, contrary to the popular view, even though thought is not a substitute for mystical experiences themselves. Philosophy remains a handmaiden in mystical ways of life, but some analysis is still necessary.) All doctrines may be in abeyance during certain mystical experiences, but mystics need some understanding (usually adopted from their religion and culture) to provide a framework for incorporating mystical experiences into the rest of their lives. Without a religious framework to give them meaning, even extrovertive mystical experiences may seem bewildering and lead to confusion and distress (Byrd, Lear & Schwenka 2000: 267–68). So too, an introvertive experience may cause anxiety or panic if it is not understood as a kundalini experience or given some other explanation by a teacher. Indeed, when dealing with anything unknown, conceptions and beliefs shield us from the full force of the reality by filtering it through a mental framework and thereby making it manageable.

Classical mystics may decry the inadequacy of any doctrinal account, but they do endorse some ontological truth-claims as less inadequate than others. Mystics typically do not claim to be discovering new truths but only to be finding the knowledge already expressed in the basic doctrines of their traditions. In short, classical mystics do endorse truth-claims.[3]

Mystical Metaphysics

This leads to another misunderstanding: there need not be a *single* "ultimate reality," "ground of all being," "Absolute," or consciousness. This idea is implicit, not only in all theisms and also in much Greek and nontheistic Indian thought. But there are mysticisms with multiple irreducible realities, not one—for example, Samkhya-Yoga's pluralism of multiple transcendent centers of consciousness (*purushas*) and a completely unrelated realm of matter (*prakriti*). So too, extrovertive mystics may or may not accept a transcendent foundation to the natural world. Thus, we have to look at the specific metaphysics of each mystical tradition.

Metaphysics involves the basic ontology and structure of reality—our broadest ideas of the nature of a person, the mind, the phenomenal world, and any realities transcending the natural world. A tradition's doctrines present a view of reality that makes sense, not only of the tradition's beliefs and values but also of its practices. Permanence and immutability are appealing criteria for what is irreducibly *real*, but not all mystical traditions adopt them for all basic realities (e.g., Daoism), and even those traditions that do adopt these criteria do not all agree on what are the "ultimate" realities.[4] In addition, we must keep in mind that metaphysics in mystical traditions is advanced in connection to a process of mystical transformation—most mystics are not interested in studying the nature of the world apart from the mystical quest. Rather, the metaphysics set up a way of looking at reality that will work for mystical training. The ontology may reflect experiences in different stages of a mystical quest.

Introvertive and extrovertive mysticisms result in different types of metaphysics with different dimensions of reality. Introvertive mysticisms involve a sense of a reality that transcends the phenomenal self or the entire phenomenal world that also affects the ontological status of the world. They thereby encompass both natural phenomena and transcendent realities. In contrast, extrovertive mystics are concerned with the world of diversity—the realm of "becoming" and not any eternal transcendent "being"—and need not incorporate transcendent realities into their metaphysics as the foundations of the phenomenal world. However, nature mysticism and cosmic consciousness mix both realms. For Richard M. Bucke's cosmic consciousness, the foundation of the world is love: the world is not dead matter but entirely immaterial and alive with a living Presence; death is an absurdity, since everything is eternal; the universe is God and vice versa, and no evil could ever enter it ([1901] 1969: 8, 10, 17–18).

The distinction of dimensions is not always clear, since both extrovertive and introvertive mystics often employ the same language, as do theists and nontheists. They share terms such as "oneness," "being," and "real," but their subjects are not the same: extrovertive mysticism is about the world of diverse phenomena and its beingness, while introvertive mysticism is about the underlying "depth" realities. Introvertive mysticism thus involves a timeless and changeless dimension to a person or to all of reality, while extrovertive metaphysics, such as in early Buddhism, involves only the constantly changing world of becoming. Our "essence" may be a transcendent reality or the lack of any substance at all if we are connected only to other phenomenal realities.

Since both introvertive and extrovertive mystics may use the same language of one religious tradition, we must look at a mystic's work as a whole to determine which type of metaphysics is involved. So too, depth-mystical experiences can be interpreted to fit into radically different metaphysics (as discussed below). Nor is it tied to any particular religious beliefs. Contrary to popular opinion, not all mystics endorse Shankara's nonduality in which a transcendent reality constitutes all of reality. A pantheism that *equates* a transcendent reality with the natural world—for example, God with creation, the One with its emanations, or Brahman with the projected world of "illusion" (*maya*)—does not reflect any classical mystical tradition, although the newer concept of "panentheism" in which a transcendent reality can sustain and perhaps work within the natural realm can accommodate various emanationisms with theism—the universe is in the transcendent god and the god dwells in the universe as its sustainer and perhaps controller.

Moreover, mysticism is not even inherently *religious*, either in the sense of involving transcendent ontologies or of being tied to a meaning of life. Today many people see the significance and value of mystical experiences only in natural terms related to physical or psychological well-being. For them, the experiences remain secular by being understood in terms that are independent of religious ways of life and all transcendent worldviews. If introvertive mystical experiences do in fact involve transcendent realities, an experiencer may nevertheless misinterpret it and give it a naturalistic interpretation; if so, it may not have a transformative effect on the experiencer or be seen as meaning-giving. Nor need extrovertive mystical experiences be interpreted as having religious significance. What seems like a direct experience of God or Jesus Christ to a Christian may seem to the nonreligious to be an unusual but natural occurrence generated by the brain.

Variations in Mystical Metaphysics

None of the different types of mystical experiences have entailed one obvious interpretation or doctrine. Even if the same training, meditative techniques, or drugs generate the same experiences in all human beings regardless of their culture, it does not follow that all mystics' *understanding* of what is involved in the experiences is really the same despite the divergence in terminology that different traditions employ. ("Perennial philosophers" disagree.) Seeing the experiences as cognitive or as only interesting subjective brain-generated events, or seeing what is experienced as a foundation of love for the natural world, or seeing the world as inconsequential all depend on factors outside the experiences themselves. And, it should be noted, disputes over doctrines and rules of conduct are common both between and within mystical traditions.

A sense of "nonduality" is a feature of all mystical experiences, but how the nature of that nondual ASC is understood varies—for example, it may be seen as only unifying one's consciousness. Classical mysticisms reflect two types of nondual metaphysics. In depth-mysticism, it is a nonduality of the transcendent ontological source and of a person or the entire phenomenal world. In extrovertive mysticism, it is the absence of a plurality of independently existing entities within the phenomenal world. Similarly, there are different vertical and horizontal senses of "oneness": realizing the one simple, undivided reality of a transcendent source supplying one beingness versus realizing that everything in the phenomenal realm is connected or of the same nature, sharing the one beingness common to all; or the unity of our transcendent self versus realizing that we are not isolated self-contained entities but impermanent parts of the interconnected natural realm. So too with "nothingness": the introvertive sense is of a transcendent source of phenomena that is the opposite in nature from all phenomenal things and properties (not literally the lack of existence). In extrovertive mysticisms, such as Buddhism, "nothingness" means the lack of discrete objects within the phenomenal world and thus the lack of fixed referents to which words could refer, not the denial of the reality of the phenomenal world.

So too with the idea of "illusion." Contrary to the popular understanding of mysticism, the phenomenal world is not totally dismissed as illusory in any classical mysticism. Nor does the world disappear with enlightenment. In extrovertive mysticism, the idea of distinct, independent, and self-contained entities—in particular, a "self"—within the natural world is rejected, but a reality "beneath" these concept-generated illusions is affirmed. Only the object-ness generated by our conceptualizing mind is the illusion—that is, the illusion results from conceptualizing discrete "real" entities from the continuous and connected flow of things. But extrovertive mysticism involves a *realism* in the broadest metaphysical sense about the experienced realm—something exists independently of our conceptions. Thus, there is something objectively real even if there are no objective "objects." In depth-mysticism, the realism is that something exists independently of our merely individual personal mental state. The illusion here is that the natural universe is independently real rather than having a transcendent foundation. To convey the sense of what is real and what is illusory, *Chandogya Upanishad* 6.1.3–4 gives the analogy of a clay pot: the clay represents what is real (i.e., the permanent substance lasting before and after whatever shape it currently is in), and the potness represents what is illusory (i.e., the temporary and impermanent form that the clay is in at the moment). If we smash the pot, the "thing-ness" of the pot is destroyed, but what is real in the pot (the clay) continues unaffected. Mindfulness mystics focus on the clay and see the entity (the pot) as only temporary, contingent, and incidental. Even for Shankara's depth-mystical Advaita Vedanta the world cannot be dismissed as a complete nonreality: the world is neither the same as Brahman and thus not real (eternal and unchanging) nor distinct from it and thus not totally unreal either (like the son of a barren woman), and so its ontological status is indeterminate and indescribable (*anirvachaniya*).[5]

So too with "ultimate reality." As discussed below, different depth-mysticisms have different metaphysics—the unified state of consciousness is not necessarily expanded to include more than the self. The idea of "ultimate reality" fits a theistic way of looking at things, but it does not fit Advaita (where there is only one reality, not an "ultimate reality" and any dependent realities, or any "degrees" of realities) or Chinese mysticism (where the Dao is not a separate reality from mundane reality). So too, extrovertive mysticisms may ignore the issue of a transcendent source altogether and take the natural realm to be all that is ultimately real. Thus, defining "mystical experience" as the "direct experience of ultimate reality" must be qualified: such a definition would eliminate traditions with multiple irreducible transcendent realities and any extrovertive experiences if the experiencer does not take the phenomenal realm to be "ultimate reality" but the creation of God or an emanation from a transcendent source. Nor do classical mystics argue for an "ultimate reality" in the abstract—something more specific is always given even as mystics assert that what is experienced is more than can be expressed.

Conflicting Metaphysics

In the depth-mystical experience, one's consciousness is unified and the experiencer feels a realness and certainty to the experience. The minimum ontological characterization of the experience is that depth-mystics are inwardly aware of the beingness of the natural realm in experiences as pure consciousness. But mystics may conclude that what was experienced has more ontological significance: when the mind is completely stilled, an awareness bursts forth of a reality greater than consciousness or the being of the natural realm—it is an unmediated experience of a more fundamental reality. But if the experience is in fact empty of differentiable content, theistic and nontheistic mystics have identical depth-mystical experiences and understand its significance differently only after the experience is over.

Theists have incorporated the depth-mystical experience in two different ways that retain the reality of persons and the distinction between creator and creation: an experience of the sheer beingness of God without any of God's personal properties, or an experience of the ontological ground of the self. But it is hard to argue that here theists experience anything *personal* or *being loved* or being in *unison with God's will*, since the experience is devoid of all duality and all content—"cleansed and emptied" of all "distinct ideas and images," to quote John of the Cross.[6] That is, theists do not *experience* personal properties in the moments of the depth-mystical experience, as they do in differentiated theistic introvertive experiences. Rather, after the experience they transfer their previous theistic beliefs to the sense of reality and finality given in the experience.

Thus, in the depth-mystical experience the mind has a positive content: a pure, undiffused consciousness is now fully occupying the mind, even though the experiencer is unaware that this is the content while the experience is occurring. Arguably, this is the experience of the deepest reality within us, but what is its full nature? The full ontological nature of that consciousness is a matter to be decided after the experience. The experience is concrete, but the intellectual content that is retained is so conceptually abstract that the experience is open to very different understandings. In the history of mysticism, there have been four types of ontological interpretation:

- only the natural mind is present; it is either a pure consciousness state of the mind, an inward awareness of the being of the natural world, or a malfunction of the brain

- a transcendent consciousness distinct from the body is present; it may be an individual center (as in the Samkhya-Yoga or Jaina metaphysics) or a universal reality participated in by all sentient beings

- a transcendent nonpersonal ground of beingness underlying all subjective and objective natural phenomena is experienced inwardly

- a transcendent creator/sustainer god that is personal in nature enters the mind (or the mind already participates in the god's being), but only in its nonpersonal aspect (God's being)

Naturalists by definition deny the existence of transcendent realities—only what is open to scientific scrutiny is real. But they can accept that "empty" depth-mystical experiences occur: they simply give it a reductive naturalistic explanation, treating the experience as the product of a brain malfunction or as a useless feedback effect occurring when the mind is empty of differentiated content but still aware—either way, only an illusion of cognition is produced. Thus, "pure consciousness" is not a more fundamental reality: it does not underlie other states of consciousness but is just another state—states with differentiated content are no less real and are in fact more cognitive. Any experienced bliss results only subjectively from the analytic mind being inactive. These experiences may be very intense and seem "realer than real" but are only natural states of mind. They feel significant only because people often have them while looking for God or because they have heard that saints in the past had such experiences.

However, theists can give the depth-mystical experience a theistic reading. After the experience, theists may well see bliss as being fully loved by a god deemed to be limitless and loving. Theists may also have theistic extrovertive experiences that are felt in terms of the presence of God in his creation (cosmic consciousness) and have introvertive theistic mystical experiences with differentiated content. Thus, to theists three types of mystical experiences are theistic.

Overall, these options fall into four types of broader metaphysics:

- nondualisms: only one reality actually exists (Brahman, a godhead, one transcendent consciousness); the phenomenal world is an emanation or appearance of this reality's being or an indetermined "dream"

The Diversity of Mystical Knowledge-Claims / 41

- dualistic theisms: God supplies all being, but the natural world is a distinct creation from God and persons remain distinct realities

- pluralisms: multiple independently existing transcendent selves

- naturalism: mystical experiences are of the self or consciousness or the sheer being of the natural realm, and no transcendent realities are involved

Similar options are open concerning the self. Western theisms stress the reality of the world and individuals apart from God, and thus Western mystics do not typically deny the existence of a soul, although a sense of self may be blocked out during mystical experiences. But for most mysticisms, the sense of a separate self within the natural world is only an illusion generated by our baseline state of waking consciousness. We normally think that we are an independent, self-contained entity, but in fact "self-consciousness" is just another function of the analytic mind: by identifying with our thoughts and feelings and a sense of consciousness, we reify the subject into an object and set it off against the rest of reality in a duality, but this subjective awareness is never experienced as an object.[7] Our sense of a self then runs our life. However, there is in fact no separate self-existing entity within the field of everyday experience but only an ever-changing web of mental and physical processes, and thus we should not identify with any contents of our consciousness, even self-awareness. Once we realize that we are not our thoughts or perceptions, we have four options:

- there is no self—no entity at the center to our mental life—but only natural mental activity (thus, thinking without a thinker, and so on); the sense of "I" is merely an artifice that the ordinary analytical mind generates

- there are individual eternal transcendent selves or souls that retain their individuality after death

- there is one transcendent subjectless consciousness or ground of being that individual selves and other phenomena participate in without being discrete phenomenal realities

- we are identical to the ground of being (like the characters and other content in a dream being identical to the dreamer)

With these options, these experiences can be taken as confirming *that* we exist, but they do not establish *what* we exactly are—even mystics still must determine what we actually are by considerations other than mystical experiences. Today the brain in the transcendent options is usually seen as merely a receiver of a transcendent "Mind at Large," following theories of William James, C. D. Broad, and Henri Bergson: the brain is a "reducing valve" that protects us from the full onslaught of reality by normally allowing into our mind only what we need to survive, but mystical experiences loosen the valve and more of reality pours in.

Different mystical theories do involve some speculation as to what was experienced, but they are not products of detached philosophical speculation: mysticism is a matter of *experiences and practices*, not the intellectual acceptance of some metaphysical ideas. Mystics' beliefs are informed by experiences. Conversely, not all monistic metaphysics is necessarily "mystical philosophy": philosophers such as Spinoza can devise monistic metaphysics for reasons totally unrelated to any mystical experiences or other ASCs. Much of what Kant said about noumenal reality and what Wittgenstein said about language could be adopted by Advaitins. Naturalists can easily accept that all natural phenomena are connected, with no independently existing permanent entities, and that human beings are just outcroppings of nature that developed conscious without this belief affecting their state of consciousness. So too, adopting Whitehead's process philosophy does not make one an extrovertive mystic. Or agnostics may advocate a nonattachment without any resulting ASC. Similarly, one can overcome anger and hate and cultivate love without altering the general state of one's consciousness into a mystical ASC.

Nonmystics may be inspired by mystics, endorse mystics' teachings, and even become "mystical theorists," that is, theologians and their counterparts in nontheistic traditions whose theorizing is influenced by mystics but who have not had mystical ASCs themselves. Simply believing that God is the only reality or is controlling all that happens does not make one a mystic. The logic of God being "wholly other" leads naturally to the inapplicability of language to God and to negative theology even without any mystical experiences. In contrast, mystics may devise their understanding of what is real in conjunction with nonmystics with nonmystical considerations. Thus, one cannot tell if someone is a mystic simply by the metaphysics he or she espouses. In today's antimystical atmosphere, many texts are given nonmystical readings—scholars argue that Eckhart and Shankara were not mystics but only philosophers advancing speculative metaphysics or that Zhuangzi is only an ethical philosopher. And it is rare for premodern mystics to speak of their own experiences, but it is difficult to interpret Eckhart when he wrote "when I stood in the first cause" (2009: 421) or Plotinus when he wrote that he was "many times" lifted out of his body (*Enneads* IV.8.1–10) as not referring to experiences. So too, it is difficult to think of Eckhart's "birth of the Son" in the soul as not connected to experiences. We must study the writings of a given thinker in toto to see if it is reasonable to infer that ASC mystical experiences were an element in devising his or her beliefs.

"Mystical Union"

Most people believe that all mystical experiences are the same and characterize them differently as "union with God," "merging with the Absolute," or "becoming one with the universe." Knowledge by participation can lead to claims of being what one experiences, and this can obviously get theists in trouble if they claim they are God. But these characterizations, even in theistic mysticisms, do not reflect most traditional mysticism. First, "union" can mean different things: from a sense of continuity with the rest of nature to communing with God to identity with a transcendent nonpersonal reality. However, in gaining experiential knowledge of a reality, classical mystics do not speak in terms of a union of two substances into one substance—a *fusion* of the experiencer and another reality into one or an *absorption* into the cosmos or a transcendent reality. Second, the unenlightened are as much "united" to a transcendent source as the enlightened—mystical experiences change nothing in this regard. Through knowledge by participation in an ASC, something new about reality is revealed, and there is a *cognitive and affective change*, but there is no *ontological change* from what we have always been.

In extrovertive experiences, the sense of self and the conceptual barriers by which we differentiate phenomena are broken down, and one perceives "oneness" or a "unity" of phenomena: one realizes that everything *shares* the same substance or being (and so are the same as everything else in that regard) or that we are *connected* to everything else—phenomena become "unified" once our artificial conceptual divisions are removed, but they are still diverse. Thus, one may feel "united" to everything or one with its being.[8] With the loss of the sense of a distinct self-enclosed entity separate from other phenomena and of the conceptual boundaries that we habitually impose within our sense-experiences gone, we *feel* that we are "merging" with the rest of the cosmos. There is a new experiential sense of connectedness, but we already were always ontologically connected through our common being with everything else in the universe. Thus, the experiencer may for the first time feel the connection to the rest of reality, but there is no ontological change from what was already always our true situation.

With the conceptual barriers dissolved, we feel one with any objects observed. But we are not unified or identical with everything on the level of *objects*: the phenomena of the sensory realm remain *diverse*—a transcendent reality may be partless, but the phenomenal world is made of various parts. The spatially diverse phenomena remain intact even if there are now seen to be no fixed boundaries reflecting our cultural concepts. Robert Forman gives a personal instance of "becoming" what he saw: once while driving, he *was* the mile marker he saw (2011: 164–65; see also Newberg &Waldman 2016: 44–45). But he did not physically *become* the mile marker—he was still driving the car without an accident. So too, he still could see distinctions in his field of vision. (Nor did the experience have a debilitating effect on his ability to think or use language.) But there was the loss of a sense of a separate observer witnessing a distinct object. There simply was no boundary dividing the marker and himself—no "something other" set off over against him (2011: 165) as a distinct object, not a new uniting with another reality that had previously been ontologically distinct or any other ontological change.

So too with introvertive experiences. A sense of *oneness* in an altered state of consciousness is characteristic of these mystical experiences, but in the mainstream of the world's major mystical traditions this is not understood as two previously distinct substances becoming *fused* into one reality in a mystical experience. There is a participatory knowledge of a transcendent reality: in an ASC, one's mind is filled with the true transcendent self (a soul, a Samkhya *purusha*, or a Jaina *jiva*), a personal creator god, or nonpersonal Brahman, and so the sense of unity may *feel* like being united in a way that one was not before, but there is in fact no ontological transformation or transmutation of one's nature converting the person into a transcendent reality. Again, it is simply realizing what has always been the case.

The standard position in the Abrahamic mystical traditions is to maintain the idea of creaturehood and insist that we are creatures that cannot be united to God: we temporarily lose awareness of our soul during the blinding mystical experience, but our nature is not changed into God's. One merely becomes aware of the divine being that has already always been within us and in all of creation—the soul is not destroyed. Common images in medieval Christianity include fire heating an iron rod and the air pervaded by the warmth of the sun. But there is no "merging" or "absorption" of one reality into another resulting in only one entity. An example of union is Teresa of Avila saying that "the soul can neither forget nor doubt that is was in God and God was in it" (*Interior Castle* V.1.8), but she never denied the separate existence of a soul. The term *unio mystica* was devised in the thirteenth century, but few Christian mystics used that term before the modern era (McGinn 2001: 132; Harmless 2008: 252–54), and only in the modern study of mysticism has *unio mystica* received a central place (McGinn 2006: 427). The idea was more of "communion" with God than "union," let alone identity. Classical Christian mystics struggled over what "becoming one with God" meant, but they usually meant it in terms of a loving *union of wills* with God's or even a fusion of *the mind* with God's (427–29). This is an alignment of spirit—one has received the Holy Spirit or waves of God's love, but one has not "become God." To Eckhart, there is a loving union of two spirits, one created and one uncreated (McGinn 2001: 46). We are "nothing" without the being of the Godhead, but our individuality is not lost. There is now a "oneness" of will with God's will (522). For Bernard of Clairvaux, it is like a drop of water in wine taking on the taste of wine, but he added that no doubt the *substance* of the person remains distinct, if now in a new form—only the will is melted with God's (McGinn 2006: 436). In often erotic imagery based on the biblical Song of Songs, Christian mystics spoke of a "kiss" and of an enduring mystical state of "marriage," with the personal God or Christ as the bridegroom and the soul as the bride. For John of the Cross, the consummation of the spiritual marriage is the union of two natures in one spirit and love (462), and unlike episodic experiences it remains a permanent state. God's will and the mystic's will are now in "unison"—becoming one in spirit (1 Corinthians 6:17). This is how most Christian mystics understood the biblical passage from Paul that reads, "It is no longer I who live, but Christ who lives in me" (Galatians 2:20). The person is transformed, but his or her identity is not lost.

While some Jewish and Islamic mystics believed the sense of an individual self is an illusion, mainstream mystics in both traditions do not agree. In Kabbalah, "cleaving to God" (*devekut*) never negates the two realities. According to the Hasidic Baal Shem Tov, the devout and God are "glued" together but remain distinct, even though God supplies our being. In Sufism, the annihilation of the self (*fana*) and its replacement by the continuing presence of God or "abiding in God" (*baqa*) is taken to mean that only what is exclusively human passes away—the divine presence remains, but the "gift" of individuality is not destroyed.

For Plotinus, the One supplies the being of the emanated realities, but the One is not identical to those realities. The One supplies our being, and our lower soul may fall away, but our higher soul is never obliterated. Nor does the higher soul ever get past its place in the Nous. Plotinus did use the language of union (*henosis*, "oneness") and of being "one'd" (*henothenai*, "to be brought into unity") (e.g., *Enneads* VI.7.3, VI.8.18) and being filled with the light of the One (VI.7.36, VI.9.4), but for him we remain distinct drops in the ocean of the Nous's Being. We retain nothing of our lower soul, and from our point of view it may look as if we cease to exist, but this is only "as it were" (VI.9.10)—our higher soul's individuality remains. And for the One, nothing changes (VI.9.9). Souls are like multiple circles with one center, the World Soul (VI.5.5); the circles coincide with the One (VI.5.5, VI.9.8, VI.9.10), but their difference becomes clear when the souls move apart.[9]

The situation is the same for South and East Asian traditions: enlightenment is merely coming to realize what one already is. For the Upanishads, realizing that "you are that" (*Chandogya Up.* 6.8.7) is realizing what has always been the case: your ontological essence (*atman*) is exactly the same as that of all other emanated phenomena—Brahman. In Samkhya-Yoga, the sense of unity given in the state of consciousness is understood to be the *separation* of our true individual self (the *purusha*) from matter (*prakriti*), not the union of something with anything. Indian devotional (*bhakti*) traditions do speak of an ultimate state of union of the devotee and God, but when expounding the doctrines Bhaktas typically speak of a communion in which the individual is not totally lost. Tantrism accepts a transcendent monism and sexual union as a way to express and attain this state, but nevertheless it is again a matter of realizing what has always been the case.

Even in Advaita Vedanta, there is no union, although its "nonduality" (*a-dvaita*) is usually mischaracterized as the union of Brahman and the self (*atman*) within a person. Advaitin nonduality means only that there is no second reality after Brahman—Brahman is the one essence (*atman*) of all phenomena. It is not as if multiple individual essences *become* or *unite* with a transcendent reality. There are no real individual selves or essences. Only Brahman is real, and thus there is nothing else to unite with it. For Shankara, there is no absorption or merging of an individual consciousness or essence (*atman*) with a cosmic consciousness. *Atman* is not an entity within us that combines with Brahman—it is simply the name for Brahman when discussing an individual phenomenon. In the depth-mystical experience, one is merely aware of nothing but one's own being. Shankara spoke of "achieving union" with Brahman since the texts he commented on sometimes used the phrase, but he made it clear that in the final analysis this is a faulty dualistic way of looking at the situation: "union" is an inherently dualistic concept—the union of *x* and *y*—but there is only *one reality*. The popular image of a drop of water merging in the ocean does not fit Shankara's metaphysics at all. In fact, Shankara employed an exactly *opposite* image: all of reality (Brahman) is entirely contained in each part of the phenomenal world just as the sun is reflected in its entirety in each ripple on a pond (e.g., *Brahma-sutra-bhashya* 3.2.18–20).[10] It is like our dreams: the entire dreamer's consciousness is present in each portion of the dream, not parceled out in parts into different areas of the dream. Phenomenal objects within the "dream" also remain distinct in this metaphysics: one object is not *in* another—the sun and the moon are not in us or united to us—but the same one *being* is everything.

So too with the Asian mystical traditions that emphasize extrovertive mystical experiences. In Buddhism, *nirvana* is not an entity in any sense, although many Westerners treat it as such: it is the state of the person (before and after death) in which the fires of hatred, greed, and delusion have been exhausted (*Anguttara Nikaya* I.38; *Samyutta Nikaya* III.251)—it is not a reality that could be united with or otherwise attained or a place gone to. Meditative absorptions (*dhyanas*) are a matter of concentrating one's mind, not one reality being absorbed into another. Mindfulness is not a union of anything with anything: there are no selves or "real" entities, and thus no things to become united. So too, any sense of "union" is a misunderstanding of the Buddha-nature that is already inherent in us. For Chinese traditions, the Dao is already flowing in us: we merely have to unblock that flow by ending self-centered desires. Thus, the Dao is not a reality that we have to become connected to—we only have to align our mind with it by stepping out of its way.

In sum, "mystical union" seems natural when we look at mystical experiences from a dualistic point of view, but it misrepresents classical mysticisms. Mystical consciousness does involve a sense of *nonduality*, but the "unitive" *state of consciousness* must be distinguished from the metaphysics of *what is experienced*. Mystics may need to resort to the cultural language of union to contrast these experiences with ordinary experiences, since we have no language specifically designed for mystical experiences, but it is not meant literally. In a mystical experience, we are not "united to God" or another transcendent reality in any ontological way that was not previously always occurring. With enlightenment, a mystic's knowledge, will, and emotions are all that change. These now become aligned with the correct understanding of reality (as defined by a particular tradition). One may feel our true ontological status for the first time, but the experiencer does not "obtain" or "become" anything ontologically new (although one's journey after death may change), let alone two realities becoming unified into one—one merely becomes aware of what was already always the case.

Weighting Mystical Experiences

Also notice that the depth-mystical experience need not be weighted more than introvertive theistic experiences, extrovertive experiences, or nonmystical experiences when it comes to cognitive value. Early Buddhists weighted the insights of extrovertive mindfulness as cognitively more important than those of introvertive mystical experiences, including the depth-mystical experience of "neither perception nor nonperception" in concentrative meditation (*dhyana*): seeing phenomenal realm "as it really is" (*yathabhutam, dharmata*) is the reality/truth of the highest matters (*paramartha-satya*). That is more important for their soteriological concern with suffering (*duhkha*) than any relation of the individual or the natural world to any purported transcendent reality.

Theistic mystics may value introvertive experiences involving a sense of a personal reality over "empty" depth-mystical experiences as conveying the most important ontological insight. For example, Martin Buber valued the mysticisms of the Abrahamic traditions over those of South and East Asia because the former had an "I-Thou" relation with the ultimate reality while, he believed, in the latter one only seeks oneself or attempts to make oneself God. The medieval Christian Richard Rolle valued the "rapture without abstention of the senses" in which the senses and affections are purified over the "rapture involving abstention from the bodily senses," since even sinners can have the latter but the former is a rapture of love coming from God (McGinn 2006: 344–46). Theists may also value a continuing extrovertive mystical sense of God's presence over any introvertive experiences. Theistic mystics may argue that nontheistic mystics experience only a nonpersonal aspect of God empty of all differentiable content (i.e., God's beingness). Or theists may dismiss the depth-experience as a completely noncognitive subjective brain-generated event. Theists may also contend that dualistic revelations offer deeper insights into what is experienced in depth-mystical experiences, and the process of emptying the mind may be valued only for making it possible for theistic differentiated introvertive infusions of love from God or revelations to occur.

Of course, nontheists dispute the theists' metaphysics. Advaitins invert the order and place all differentiated experiences, including visions and theistic mystical introvertive experiences, on a lower plane: all differentiated experiences involve an incomplete emptying of the mind of dualistic content, and only emptying the mind completely leads to the final insight of seeing the nondual nature of reality. They can treat positive and negative differentiated experiences as projections of the unenlightened mind, including subconscious forces. For them, only the nonpersonal Brahman is real, with dualistic theistic experiences being lesser experiences or misreadings of the nature of a depth-mystical experience.

But nothing within mystical experiences themselves can support either a nontheistic or a theistic metaphysics. Theorists in every religious tradition will need to rank the different types of experiences, and ranking either mystical experiences or dualistic numinous experiences as a greater insight into a transcendent reality will depend on factors outside the mystical and numinous experiences themselves. Indeed, that mystical experiences are taken to offer insights at all—rather than being merely powerful exotic but totally natural mental states with interesting psychological or physiological effects—depends on factors outside the experience. In sum, in the end any judgment on what these experiences reveal will depend on factors other than mystical experiences themselves. Such judgments will of necessity be of a philosophical nature.

The Problem of Mystical Knowledge

Thus, mystical experiences involve a sense of having experienced some irreducible and thus ultimate reality. These experiences can transform our understanding of reality. But not all mystical metaphysics is the same. There is no consensus of the world's mystics on any fundamental theory. Indeed, history shows that divergence in understanding of the nature of what is experienced is a prominent feature of mysticism. Of course, one could impose a theological or philosophical understanding that "corrects" the misunderstanding that mystics in other traditions have concerning what is experienced and artificially create a "unanimity of the mystics." But it is clear that there are no abstract doctrines to which any classical mystic of the world has actually adhered (contra perennial philosophy), even if all mystics share the same experiences.

In short, these experiences give a sense of reality and confidence in the meaningfulness of reality, but they do not reveal what that meaning is or dictate specific doctrines. Here the philosophical distinction of the "sense" and "reference" of a word is analogous: even if we assume that all introvertive mystics in fact experience *the same reality*, this does not mean that all mystics really make the same knowledge-claims—mystics' understandings of *the nature of what is experienced* genuinely diverge. There is no one "mystical worldview." Different religions advance competing understandings, and it is the concrete doctrines, ethics, and practices of these traditions that mystics actually follow.

— 5 —

The Interaction of Experience and Culture in Mystical Knowledge

As just discussed, mystical experiences do not determine their own interpretation—how mystics understand their experiences and what significance they attach to them depend on factors outside the experiences themselves. Thus, we have to look at the factors that, in connection with the experiences, generate mystical knowledge-claims. This raises the issues surrounding the interaction of mystical experiences with mystics' own culture and religion.

Mysticism and Religion

The first thing to note is that, while the different mystical traditions can be grouped together under the rubric "mysticism" because of the centrality of similar experiences, there is no abstract mysticism but only concrete mystical ways of life. There are only particular mystics in particular mystical traditions with specific beliefs, values, practices, and soteriological goals. To invert a remark from George Santayana, any attempt to have a religion that is no religion in particular is as hopeless as any attempt to speak without speaking some particular language. And the same applies to classical mysticism: classical mystics were members of different religious traditions, and what they write must be understood in their religious, historical, cultural, linguistic, social, and institutional context. Only in the matrix of a mystic's way of life does mystical experiences give knowledge. (The perennialists' counterposition will be discussed later in chapters 6 and 15.)

All the world religions have mystical traditions, and those traditions and their encompassing religions develop in conjunction with each other. Each mystical tradition has a more concrete sense of specific transcendent realities than an abstract "ultimate reality"—a Hindu Bhakta's idea of Vishnu or Shiva is different than a Sufi's idea of Allah. So too, different enlightened states develop in conjunction with the religion's beliefs and practices. In all the world religions, mystical experiences interact with nonmystical elements. Mystics in turn can alter religious doctrines, including the understanding of a religion's basic scriptures, and may introduce new practices. The influence of mystical experiences on basic doctrines was especially great in Asian religions. But even with a mainstream view of the absolute otherness of God, each Abrahamic religion has had vibrant mystical traditions. Mystical theorizing and nonmystical theorizing have interacted to the point that mystical doctrines and nonmystical doctrines are often hard to distinguish. Indeed, a scholar of Judaism, Brian Lancaster, can say, "There is effectively no such thing as 'non-mystical Judaism' " (2005: 14). So too, a very strong case can be made that many Christian beliefs are merely mystical doctrines formulated dogmatically (Louth 1981: xi).

But while mystical experiences may have influenced the development of each religion, this does not mean that mysticism has always been welcome in theistic religions. The idea of a personal experience of God, let alone any sense of "union" with him, has met resistance. In particular, Protestant Christianity stresses a gulf between creator and creation that cannot be bridged. Mysticism is also often seen as self-centered and not aiding in a church's social work. The idea of actually *experiencing* God may in general seem foreign to the genuine faith of any theistic religion in which God is wholly transcendent. Mysticism is also seen as a form of works rather than reliance upon the grace of God, overemphasizing the nonrational in religion and the inner life over rituals, pantheistic, self-denying, antinomian, too individualistic, quietist, and a divisive elitism that portrays mystics as better than the ordinary faithful.

And religious traditions can control a mystic's understanding of what was experienced. An example of how a religious tradition can alter and control a mystic's understanding of his or her own mystical experience comes from Martin Buber. He had an "unforgettable experience" from which he knew "well that there is a state in which the bonds of the personal nature of life seem to have fallen away from us and we experience an undivided unity" (1947: 24). However, he added,

> But I do not know—what the soul willingly imagines and indeed is bound to imagine (mine too once did it)—that in this I had attained to a union with the primal being or the godhead. That is an exaggeration no longer permitted to the responsible understanding. Responsibly—that is, as a man holding his ground before reality—I can elicit from those experiences only that in them I reached an undifferentiated unity of myself without form or content. . . . In the honest and sober account of the responsible understanding this unity is nothing but the unity of this soul of mine, whose "ground" I have reached. (24–25)

Buber initially interpreted his felt sense of "undivided unity" to be unity with the Godhead, but his "responsible understanding" was that what he actually experienced was the unity of his soul.[1] The latter understanding was dictated by his Jewish background, in which the gulf between God and creature is unbridgeable. But this change in understanding only came later and did not affect his sense of the character of the experience itself, in which he felt an "undivided unity."[2] (Also note that his religious beliefs may have controlled his understanding, but they did not enter his *experience* itself and control its actual *felt content*, contra constructivism.)

Attribution Theory

Today many scholars in religious studies explain away the significance of mystical experiences. Advocates of the newest approach claim that seeing these experiences to be "mystical" is merely an attribution made by the experiencer (Proudfoot 1985; Taves 2009; see also Barnard 1992). That is, "mystical experiences" are merely an attribution that people make to any highly emotional but normal experience. It is this attribution alone that makes an ordinary emotional state "religious." These theorists can point out that today many who have mystical experiences do not attach any religious significance to them but give them a naturalistic explanation. Thus, "mystical experiences" become nothing but a subjective overlay given to our mundane emotional experiences and have no cognitive significance.

However, the attribution of religious significance to experiences does not mean that mystical experiences are no more than ordinary experiences rather than unique ASC events with unique configurations of neural events grounding them in the brain, as neuroscientists are now suggesting. Merely because mystical experiences need not be taken as having religious significance does not mean that there is nothing unique about mystical states or that we can reduce mystical experiences to emotional reactions to mundane experiences—it may be that mystical experiences are still unique mental events. In short, some experiences may be inherently *mystical* even if no experience is inherently *religious*.

Constructivism and Nonconstructivism

Classical mystics themselves probably take their experiences as directly given without any mediation of our conceptualizing mind. But all scholars today agree that the reports by mystics of their experiences or of what they experienced are shaped by their tradition and culture. But do the cultural factors permeate the mystical experiences themselves, or are there only cultural interpretations of the experiences that are applied after the experiences are over? The position of the prevailing school—"constructivism"—is that all human experience is necessarily structured by elements of culture, in particular language (see Katz 1978, 1983, 1992, 2000).[3] The postmodernist Don Cupitt could be speaking for constructivists when he says, "Language goes all the way down; there is no meaningfulness and no cognition prior to language" (1998:11). The basic position is that the mind never transcends language in any cognition: mystical experiences "are inescapably shaped by prior linguistic influences such that the lived experience conforms to a preexistent pattern that has been learned, then intended, and then actualized in the experiential reality of the mystic" (Katz 1992: 5). There is no direct (i.e., unmediated) mystical experience of any reality. As Steven Katz puts it in the most quoted line in the last forty years of the study of mysticism: "*There are NO pure (i.e., unmediated) experiences*" (Katz 1978: 26; emphasis in the original).[4] All "givens" are "the product of the processes of 'choosing,' 'shaping,' and receiving" (59). All mystical experiences, like all other human experiences, are of one nature in this regard. Any experience unconditioned by cultural factors would be "shapeless and undeveloped" (Moore 1978: 116) and thus incomprehensible even to mystics themselves. For Katz, this "epistemological fact" is true because of the sort of beings we are, and thus this mediated aspect of all our experience is "an inescapable feature of any epistemological inquiry, including the inquiry into mysticism, which has to be properly acknowledged if our investigation of experience, including mystical experience, is to get very far" (1978: 26). Mysticism as a category of separate direct and unmediated experiences or "pure consciousness" is an illusion (Penner 1983: 89). In short, there are no culturally independent mystical experiences—the idea that there are is only a modern academic invention.

Constructivists do not focus on Kant's claim of general categories structuring all experiences but on phenomena of specific cultures: all mystical experiences are saturated to their core by cultural ideas. Mystical experiences and their cultural interpretations cannot be separated. Strong constructivists reduce any apparent cognitive content of mystical experiences completely to the experiencer's cultural beliefs. Thereby, the experiences' alleged cognitive content is completely washed away. There is a "clear causal connection" between the cultural structure that one brings to an experience and the nature of one's actual experience (Katz 1978: 51). Cultural phenomena *determine* the content of mystical experiences—indeed, they *overdetermine* it (46). Mystical experiences become, in the words of Robert Gimello, "simply the psychosomatic enhancement of religious beliefs and values" (1983: 85). All alleged mystical knowledge becomes assimilated to prior cultural claims. Yoga properly understood is not an *unconditioning* or *deconditioning* of consciousness but rather a *reconditioning* of consciousness, that is, a substituting of one form of conditioned consciousness for another (Katz 1978: 57).[5] Even if a transcendent reality exists and is experienced (and at least Katz accepts that possibility [1988: 754]), that reality is totally amorphous and ultimately plays no role in determining mystical beliefs: any structure is supplied by conceptions from the mystic's culture, and those cultural conceptions constitute the full cognitive content.[6] Our common neurology accounts for some similar features in the experiences across cultures, but each complete experience always remains unique because each mystic has his or her own unique set of cultural structuring. So too, if a Sufi and an Advaitin both speak of the "ineffability" of God and Brahman, we are not logically justified in concluding that they are speaking of the same transcendent reality.

For strong constructivists, this means that mystical experiences are not independent sources of influence on religious doctrines. Mystical experiences may be accepted as neurologically genuine and unique, but they have no independent cognitive content, and so they cannot make any cognitive contribution to a mystic's belief-framework or play any role in the development of any tradition's doctrines at any point. No valid propositions can be generated on the basis of mystical experiences, and thus mystical experiences "logically cannot be the grounds for *any* final assertions about the nature or truth of any religious or philosophical position," and so mystical experiences are "irrelevant in establishing the truth or falsity of religion in general or any specific religion in particular" (Katz 1978: 22). In sum, nothing cognitively significant would remain if the prior cultural doctrines and other content were removed from these experiences. So too, any changes in a mystic's beliefs must come from nonexperiential cultural sources, not from any new mystical experiences. In the end, there is no such thing as "mystical knowledge."[7]

Moderate constructivists, however, such as John Hick and Bernard McGinn, accept the premise that all mystical experiences are structured to the core by culture—there are no unmediated mystical experiences—but they permit the possibility that mystical experiences may add to our pool of cognitive experiences. For them, culture *influences* the cognitive content of all mystical experiences but does not *determine* it. After all, merely because our sense-experiences are culturally structured does not mean that those experiences do not tell us something about the world. Similarly, what is structured in mystical experiences may also add to our knowledge. The external world constrains our sensory knowledge, and the content of a mystical experience constrains a mystic's knowledge, but the experience is always mediated by cultural construction.

The opposition is led by Robert Forman (1990, 1998, 1999), who argues that some or all mystical experiences are in fact unstructured by cultural influences, and so mystical experiences are independent sources of influence on religions. The role of "forgetting" and "unknowing" in mystical traditions is emphasized. A deep layer or aspect of consciousness unconditioned by culture is involved. Nonconstructivists can hold either that there is an unmediated core to all mystical experiences or that there is at least one unconstructed type of mystical experience. Mystics need a framework for understanding their experiences and for incorporating them into their way of life, and conceptions and beliefs of their culture provide that framework, but those cultural phenomena are not operating during at least some mystical experiences. A mystic's *understanding* of mystical experiences *after the experience* in the baseline state of consciousness or an extrovertive mystical state is necessarily structured by cultural categories and doctrines, but mystical *experiences themselves* are free of such conditioning. Unconstructed experiences are "preconceptual" or "nonconceptual," and mystical practices work to dismantle our habitual culturally conditioned mental restraints.

For nonconstructivists, mystical experiences and their later conceptualizations are, unlike ordinary experiences, two separate events, even if they seem to be one event to the mystics themselves. Mystical experiences may be cognitive of a reality, but only after conceptions return to the mind do cultural conceptions and understandings enter the picture of what is accepted as mystical knowledge. Thus, nonconstructivists can readily agree that we must examine mystics within their cultural context in order to understand their claims, but they reject the idea that such contextualism means that the cultural matrix penetrates into some or all mystical experiences and states of consciousness. *Constructivism* is about the nature of mystical experiences, while *contextualism* is a method for understanding cultural phenomena and does not say anything about what the nature of experiences must be.

Constructivists also must account for the young and the unchurched who have mystical experiences spontaneously without any prior expectations—they had no prior doctrines relevant to shaping the content of their experiences. Even among the religious, the content of mystical experiences often is surprising or even shocking. Constructivism also cannot readily account for the fact that some prominent mystics in the Abrahamic traditions are considered heterodox and even heretical: if the content of experiences is completely dictated by prior religious beliefs, experiences cannot occasion mystics to alter those beliefs, and thus no mystic should become a heretic because of their experiences—rather, their experiences should *reinforce* their orthodoxy. Constructivists also have to explain why some mystics feel the need to introduce wholly new innovations, such as Plotinus's theory of the Nous. They must also contend with the fact that different mystics give different interpretations of their tradition's foundational texts—for example, Shankara's, Ramanuja's, and Madhva's conflicting understandings of the Upanishads. (That the Upanishads contain conflicting doctrines makes it difficult to say that the scripture actually controls the various Vedantists' positions.) Meister Eckhart's shall we say "creative" translations of biblical verses also must be accounted for. It appears that the mystics' own ideas determine their understanding of the scriptures, not vice versa. If so, it is hard to maintain that mystical experiences do not contribute to mystics' understanding, let alone that scripture thoroughly controls the content of their experiences.[8]

If all levels of theory do not penetrate experiences, it may be that many types of introvertive and extrovertive mystical experiences are free of conceptual structuring. But the dispute usually comes down to the depth-mystical experience, or as Forman calls, it the "pure consciousness event"—that is, a wakeful but contentless and nonintentional consciousness (1990: 8).[9] Even if ordinary sense-experiences always involve a subject/object duality and are open to cultural conditioning, it does not follow that experiences that overcome all duality must be similarly conditioned. The depth-mystical experience may be the sole type of introvertive mystical experience that is free of all structuring.[10] Most types of extrovertive and introvertive mystical experiences, like visions, have differentiated content for the mind to organize, and thus there is an opening for cultural structuring to operate. Thereby, constructivism can explain why an experienced "sense of presence" is seen as Mary or Krishna, depending on one's culture. But the depth-mystical experience has no differentiated content, and so it is hard to see how any cultural construction could take place—there is nothing differentiated present in the mind to structure or to do the structuring. Thus, being free of all cultural elements, the experience must be context-free and must be phenomenologically identical in all cultures and eras (assuming the minds of all people are alike in this regard regardless of culture, gender, and so forth). Only the mystic's understanding after the experience is over is dependent upon that mystic's cultural matrix. Thus, if a member of one religion has a depth-mystical experience and converts to another religion and has another depth-mystical experience, the experiences would be identical, only the convert's understanding of what was experienced or of the cognitive significance of depth-mystical experiences might change.

According to nonconstructivists, some content from the depth-mystical experience is retained after the experience and can be recalled immediately after the experience is over, but during the experience nothing is sensed, although the mind is full and alert. Thus, Teresa of Avila knew only after her mystical experience that it was an "orison of union" with God (her understanding of the experience)—during the experience itself the soul sees and understands nothing and there are no words, but "afterward the soul sees the truth clearly, not from a vision, but from the certitude remaining in the soul that only God can place there" (*Interior Castle* V.1.9; see also VI.8.2, VII.1.5).[11] Only after the experience was she aware of anything; during the experience she was conscious but not aware of the nature of the content. Plotinus said something similar: during the mystical awareness of the One, the soul is incapable of thinking that it possesses what it sought because it is not other than what was being known (*Enneads* VI.9.3)—only after this experience one can again reason about the One, and then one knows that one has had a sudden vision of the light from the Supreme (V.3.17).

Can the Dispute Be Resolved?

The dispute between constructivists and nonconstructivists cannot be resolved by the texts: all we have are texts, and both sides agree that the accounts of mystical experiences are conditioned by cultural factors—the question is whether those factors figure only in the postexperiential understandings or in the mystical experiences themselves. Constructivists can argue that even if we have an "innate capacity" to have mystical experiences, as Forman argues, this does not mean that the experiences must be unconstructed—all our experiences may still be culturally conditioned. But Katz admits that his position that there are no unmediated experiences is only an "epistemological *assumption*" (1978: 22). Being unaware of the content at the time does not mean there was no content, but believing after the fact that an experience was an experience of *x* does not logically require that the *concept of x* was active in the experience itself.[12]

Most importantly, because of their central epistemological assumption constructivists cannot claim to derive their position from the examination of mystical texts: their strong prior assumption of the nature of all experience *skews* their understanding of the texts—from the start, they do not permit the texts to speak for themselves and possibly contradict their theory. In the end, to claim that texts support their theory ends up being only a matter of arguing in circles.[13] Katz denies there is any "substantive evidence" for any pure consciousness (1978: 57), but the texts Forman provides and any other apparently conflicting accounts would automatically be construed to fit constructivism—the constructivists' assumption means that it is impossible for them to see any evidence against their theory.

However, it must be said that it is risky for constructivists or other philosophers to rule out the possibility of a type of experience a priori based on a grand theory of what all human experience must be. This is especially so when neuroscientists and empirical psychologists are now suggesting that pure consciousness events are possible (e.g., Newberg, d'Aquili & Rause 2001; Hood 2006). Empirical studies also suggest that constructivism does not apply to all mystical experiences (Chen et al. 2011a; Chen et al. 2011b). Constructivists must show that unconstructed experiences are *impossible*—they cannot merely rely on other experiences such as sense-experience and thought being constructed but must establish that intentionality is inherent in consciousness and thus that the mind is incapable of other ways of experiencing or being conscious. Language depicting experiences is intentional, but we cannot let language dictate or otherwise restrict what is humanly possible. Moreover, nonconstructivists at least can accept mystics at their word based on descriptions from different cultures of experiences in accounts having low cultural-specific content. They can accept that those who have had depth-mystical experiences are in a unique and privileged position on the issue of the phenomenology of these experiences, and so we should rely upon what some of the mystics' depictions suggest. Nevertheless, constructivism has achieved such a dominance in postmodernism religious studies that, in the words of Robert Forman, "it has taken on the status of a self-evident truism" (1990: 4) in mystical studies despite its problems (see Jones 2020).

Essentialism

At the beginning of the twentieth century, one idea guiding William James and others in the study of mysticism was that all mystical experiences were at their core the same in all cultures. The idea of a "common core" can be unpacked in four ways: all mystical experiences are phenomenologically the same; the neurology of all mystical experiences is the same; the same transcendent realities are experienced; or all mystics have the same insight, and so all mystical doctrines are really the same. The first approach involves the issue of whether there are universal mystical experiences or common phenomenological features to all mystical experiences across all cultures and religions—an experiential "essentialism." (Whether there is a common core of mystical of *insights or doctrines* is the issue of "perennial philosophy" and will be discussed in chapters 6 and 15.) Today essentialism's advocates claim a common core to all mystical experiences independent of culture (e.g., Hood 2006, 2017; Chen et al. 2011a; Chen et al. 2011b). That is, there is one mystical experience and it is universal to all cultures, or at least there is a shared unity of phenomenological features in mystical experiences that is invariant from culture to culture and era to era, as evidenced by the common low-ramified accounts of mystical experiences in different cultures—a common mystical consciousness grounds all the different cultural expressions. The common phenomenological core is independent of any religion. It may always be culturally mediated in the expressions of a given mystic's culture, but this does not erase the experiential uniformity, since experience and interpretation can be separated.

For essentialism, one type of mystical experience (the depth-mystical experience) is universal to all cultures and eras; or, if all mystical experiences are constructed and so each mystical experience is flavored differently by a particular culture, there is still a universal state of consciousness producing some common phenomenological features in all types of mystical experiences. (The danger of essentialism is assuming that the various types of mystical experiences may be reduced to one or that all phenomenological features in all types of mystical experiences are to be treated as the same.) Another brand of essentialism concerns the role of mystical experiences in religion: mystical experiences are the core of one or even all religions—for example, William Inge thought mysticism was the "essence" of Christianity. This leads to a dispute over the nature of religion: are personal experiences central, or are practices and other social phenomena?

Essentialists argue that at least the depth-mystical experience is free of all cultural content and thus at least it must be universal to the extent that all human beings are neurologically similar in this regard. But, to constructivists, there are no universal mystical experiences. Nor are there typologies of mystical experiences to help in our understanding, although Katz distinguishes "absorptive" and "non-absorptive" types of mystical experiences (1978: 41). In fact, for constructivists each mystical experience is absolutely unique since each mystic brings a different set of conceptions to each experience. Even if there were such a thing as cross-cultural concepts, the full meaning of concepts in situ is derived from their place within a total matrix of concepts, some of which would be unique to particular cultures, and so the cultural structuring of mystical experience is unique in each culture; and since each mystic has his or her own understanding of the cultural concepts, each mystic's experience is unique.

Moreover, according to extreme constructivists, mystics do not experience the *same reality*. As Hans Penner puts it, the "central point" of a contextualist approach to mysticism (at least in the hands of constructivists and other postmodernists) is that "mystical languages cannot be thought of as referring to the same Reality, because Reality is relative to a language system. Different mystical languages, therefore, represent or express different mystical worlds" (1983: 93). Mystics may even experience the same realities (Katz 1978: 50–52). But essentialists can respond that different cultural languages need not refer to different realities simply because they entail different conceptions. The distinction between "sense" and "reference" is again important: simply because Copernicus and Ptolemy had different concepts when they both used the word "sun," it does not follow that they were referring to different realities—it is not as if each one was referring to a reality in the sky that the other one somehow missed.[14] The same may be true of different mystical concepts of transcendent realities: languages can be thoroughly contextualized and still refer to the same extralinguistic referents. So too, the actual experiences that Copernicus and Ptolemy had when looking up at the night sky may have been the same or at least had a common sensory component. And the same holds for mystical experiences: they may be the same across cultural lines or at least have common elements despite the divergence in conceptualizations and understandings. We cannot simply assume, as constructivists do, that different descriptions in mystical texts must be relating different experiences.

Disputes Remain

Thus today disputes remain over the role of religious ideas in mystical experiences and the role of mystical experiences in mystical knowledge-claims. Even if we accept a diversity of mystical ways of life and knowledge-claims, is there an underlying unity of experiences? Are some types of mystical experiences the same across cultures? Is the depth-mystical experience truly free of any differentiated content that would be subject to the vagaries of cultures and thus necessarily the same throughout history? Can we account for the diversity of mysticisms solely by a diversity of mystical experiences, or is it a matter solely of diverse religious and cultural frameworks applied outside of mystical experiences?

— 6 —

Approaches in the Study of Mysticism

The Western study of mystical experiences and the comparative study of mystical traditions began in the mid-nineteenth century, and for some time was the exclusive domain of Christian theology and its faith-based approach. But since then, the humanities, human sciences, and cognitive sciences have spawned numerous approaches both to mystical experiences and to the other phenomena constituting mysticism. These approaches include:

- history of mystical traditions
- comparative studies of mystical doctrines, experiences, and practices
- analytic philosophical examination of mystical claims and concepts
- perennial philosophy and the reaction of contextualism
- psychology of mystics
- roles for meditation and psychedelic drugs in psychological counseling
- sociology of mysticism and its interaction with society at large
- scientific study of the activity of the brains and other body parts of persons undergoing mystical experiences enabled by meditation or psychedelic drugs
- phenomenology of the felt elements of mystical experiences

- presentations in religious studies of mystical phenomena and their meaning

- cultural and biographical studies

- esotericism

- theological assessments of mystical claims and practices, including those of other traditions

- studies of mystical symbolism, art, music, rituals, and texts as literature

- translations and the philological restoration of texts

Mystical phenomena can be approached in different and with different methods depending on a person's academic, professional, or personal interests. Up until the last quarter of the twentieth century, the modern sense of mysticism led to separating mystics and mystical experiences from the mystics' cultural contexts and allowing them to be studied in isolation. Mystics were treated as essentially disembodied and culture-free. "Mystical experience" was treated in the singular, and all terms referring to any transcendent reality were treated as really referring to the Christian god. Since then, the social nature of mysticism and the cultural context of mystics have gained more attention. Today there are new academic interests in esoteric traditions, eroticism, gender studies, humanistic and transpersonal psychology, New Age spirituality, scientific approaches to mystical experiences, and postmodern approaches to mystical texts. Many approaches are still religious, but secular approaches now offer alternatives.

The Problem of Understanding Mystics

Before turning to the various approaches, a basic methodological question must be addressed: Are those who have not had any mystical experiences or ASCs qualified to study mystics at all? Those in the natural and human sciences who study phenomena adjacent to the mystical experiences may see no need to investigate the inner "subjective" side of mystical experiences themselves or understand mystical doctrines, but do those who want a fuller understanding of mysticism need to have mystical experiences? Do we need to have had a mystical experience or state of consciousness of at least some type to understand any mysticism at all? We obviously cannot get into the mind of another person, but can we understand mystical writings secondhand? Or are we limited to only third-person scientific approaches to mystical experiences? But how can "nondualistic" phenomena be understood, let alone studied, from a dualistic point of view at all?

Frits Staal advocated the need for first-person experiences to study mystical experiences: they can be seriously studied indirectly from the outside through the neuroscientific study of meditators, but such experiences must also be studied directly from the inside—otherwise, it would be like the blind studying vision through physics (1975: 124). Critics may reply that psychologists can understand and treat schizophrenia and psychoses without experiencing those states themselves. But the situation is different with the study of mystical experiences: it is the felt, "subjective" content that is central, not understanding their psychological mechanics merely to be able to explain them. Mystical experiences affect the human mind, and so their fruitful study cannot be confined to approaching them from the outside through mystical literature and scientific studies of the body. Staal envisioned that perhaps one day the study of mysticism will become a branch of an enhanced psychology (116, 194), and for this we need firsthand experiences. Thus, students of mysticism should, among other things, engage in meditation and experiment with psychedelic drugs (xxi). When it comes to studying perception, we do not only analyze reports of those who describe what they had perceived or observe what happens to people and their bodies when they are engaged in perceiving—we start by first perceiving and analyzing our own perceptions (123–24). Similarly, we cannot rely on neuroscience to get the actual felt experiential side of mystical experiences. Ninian Smart also criticized the "armchair approach" toward mysticism and believed that a student of mysticism should, among other things, meditate and experiment with psychedelic drugs (Partridge 2018: 29). Mystics base their mystical sense in the phenomenology of their experiences, not the events grounding them in the brain. But that there are different types of mystical experiences complicates the matter: if mystical experiences are required, do we need each type of mystical experience to conduct any study of all of mysticism? Also, does having mystical experiences as an academic exercise change the character of the experiences?

Outside of studying mystical experiences, students of mysticism also study mystical doctrines and other mystical cultural phenomena. When it comes to doctrines, is a student who has had no mystical experiences in the position of a blind art historian studying Renaissance art? Having a mystical experience may help in a general way to appreciate mystics' beliefs and practices, but it does not mean that we now understand the beliefs and other phenomena of mysticism—an "insider's perspective" also includes having the perspective of a given mystic's cultural point of view. We do not automatically master the doctrines in the Upanishads or Plotinus's *Enneads* by simply having a mystical experience of any kind. Moreover, even if you can construe Plotinus's words to fit your own experience, how do you know that your experience is the same type of mystical experiences underlying his point of view? The problem of determining what types of experiences a given mystic had is exacerbated by the fact that mystics may intentionally hide their own experiences behind the accepted terminology of a tradition's basic texts. In addition, most mystical texts handed down to us today have gone through multiple redactions. We also have to deal with different genres of literature that discuss experiences only opaquely—hagiography, fables, prayers, poetry, letters, meditation manuals, commentaries on basic religious texts, philosophical treatises. And even if after a mystical experience we could claim "Now I know what Meister Eckhart was talking about," we still cannot claim "Now I understand the intricacies of Meister Eckhart's Neoplatonic metaphysics" without actually studying Eckhart's works.

Thus, the study of mystical doctrines of the works of mystics is still required. But nonmystics may be able to understand mystics' works. Understanding the meaning of a text does not require getting into the author's mind: mystics themselves speak and write only while outside of introvertive mystical experiences in mindful or dualistic states of consciousness, and the meaning of their words is objective and independent of the mystic's inner life in the sense that they are expressed in public terms that others can understand. We can at least get at the public meaning of claims even if we cannot see the full significance these claims hold for mystics themselves or have experienced why those claims were made. Any role that mystical experiences played in developing mystical doctrines increases the difficulty in understanding mystical claims, but it does not rule out the possibility of such understanding and thus of the meaningful study of mystical doctrines by nonmystics. Nor is it obvious that it is necessary to practice within a given mystic's tradition to understand his or her claims: outsiders can view mystical claims in terms of the public meaning that a mystic gives a doctrine if we have a sufficient amount of his or her writings and other texts from that culture and era. In short, an outsider can understand to the extent that such meaning is public. Moreover, less than a conversion is needed to understand a tradition, and such initial understanding does seem possible to outsiders—indeed, we would need to understand the tradition's claims before any conversion could occur in order to appreciate what we would be converting to even if our understanding may change afterward. So too with esoteric groups: some teachings may be given only to the initiates (as in Mark 4:11–12), but this does not mean that the uninitiated could not understand them.

Also remember that most mystical writings are intended for the unenlightened, and so the mystics must believe something understandable is being conveyed in their works. Mystics presumably think nonmystics can understand the works despite their general denial of the applicability of language to what is experienced. The Daoist Laozi can say that "those who know do not speak, and those who speak do not know," but he (or assorted masters) did write a book on the Dao. And we can ask whether the threshold for understanding mystical claims may in fact be low. Can students be mystically "unmusical," as Max Weber claimed to be concerning religion, and yet still understand mystical claims? Mystics notoriously have a problem with language and have to resort to similes, metaphors, and analogies. But the unenlightened can follow many of the figures of speech used in a mystical context without much difficulty—for example, Advaitins treating the world as a dream or comparing our misperception of the world to misperceiving a coiled rope as a snake. Our understanding necessarily remains dualistic and thus distorted, but we can understand that the analogies point away from our diverse phenomenal reality, that a transcendent reality is not experienced as a phenomenological object distinct from the experiencer, and that we need a mystical experience to see how the analogies apply and why mystics resort to paradoxes. All attempts to understand or explain mystical experiences will involve intentionality and be from a dualistic stand of consciousness, but this does not mean that we cannot understand that ASCs are involved or force us to reduce those experiences to more commonplace dualistic ones.

Also note that having a mystical experience can actually lead to problems: if there is in fact more than one type of mystical experience, we cannot assume that all mystics must have had the same type that we had: one may have had an extrovertive experience of some type and wrongfully assume that that is the type of experience introvertive mystics have had—we cannot assume that there is only one type of mystical experience. So too, we cannot claim, "It seems to me that anyone who has had a true mystical experience must . . . ," filling in the blank with our own beliefs or values. We cannot approach any phenomena without our own background, but we also cannot impose that background by assuming all mystics must reflect it. The Christian context of a loving life is so important that many today deem a transformation of character and the "fruit" of moral action to be necessary criteria for claiming that a "genuine," "authentic," or "true" mystical experience occurred. But no one can decree that unless a person fulfills our own expectations that he or she did not have a "genuine" mystical experience or is not a "real" mystic. In particular, the relation of mysticism to morality cannot be answered merely by decreeing that mystics must be moral or must exude love to be a "true" mystic because you personally reacted to a mystical experience in that manner. Rather, an examination of the world's major mystical traditions shows that there have a variety of ethical reactions to mystical experiences (see Jones 2004: part 2). There is no objective reason to think others' experiences are inauthentic when the mystics responded differently, only bias.

There is a further danger: does having your own mystical experience inevitably lead to imposing an understanding on all mystical claims based on your own *understanding* of your experience? The sense of certainty and profundity given in your mystical experience may lead you to believe that all mystics must have had that same experience and that you now know what all mystics know. But this can lead to distorting one's understanding of mystics' teachings. Consider the nature-mystical experience that Mark Waldman had while sitting in his office, in which the trees, fence, and weeds outside his window all seemed "perfect" and he felt a "pure bliss." The first thing he remembered saying was "Oh! This is what those Buddhists and Hindus were writing about when they described enlightenment" (Newberg & Waldman 2016: 190). Actually, that is not what the Buddhists and Hindus claim: the Buddhist enlightenment experience is about seeing the impermanence of all phenomena, not their "perfection," and the Hindus' enlightenment involves something that is both interior to our being and transcendent to the natural world, not something seen in the phenomenal realm. In addition, his beliefs suddenly changed at the moment of the experience: he *knew* that there was no heaven or hell or god and that when he died that would be his end. But this is not what Buddhists and Hindus conclude in their mysticisms. After several months, his feeling subsided and feelings of doubt arose. Then one day a small voice whispered to him: "Mark, you don't know a damned thing about religion . . ." (190–91). He then began to study the works of mystics.

In sum, even if we have had a mystical experience, we cannot assume that all mystics must have had that particular type of mystical experience or would endorse our particular understanding of the nature and status of that experience. However, being empathetic in such circumstances may help in initially understanding the point of mystics' claims. But even those without such empathy can follow the arguments and analogies in mystical writings. Thus, being a nonmystic is not an insurmountable barrier to studying mysticism—even a blind art historian can write intelligibly on many aspects of art even without ever having experienced its beauty.

Practical Problems of a Cross-Cultural Study

Another methodological concern is that any cross-cultural study of mysticism necessarily involves studying foreign cultures and different historical eras and mastering alien languages. One must rely on the work of others for all traditions, including one's own. Nevertheless, there is value in a comprehensive view: approaching a general topic from the limited point of view of only one tradition or one subtradition may lead to distorting even that tradition through a provincial understanding of what mysticism is.

The objective of a descriptive account of mystical tradition is to present that tradition's ways of looking at reality—in particular, what is deemed fundamentally real and valuable and their framework of understanding. The approach to doctrines at the descriptive stage is the "methodological agnosticism" in religious studies for the history of religions in which the truth or falsity of a mystical doctrine is not examined—scholars simply accept that believers endorse those beliefs, and thus they do not present any socioscientific or other explanations of causes external to the culture's own religious and philosophical beliefs to show why particular mystics see the world in a particular way, ask the questions they ask, and accept the answers they accept. At this stage, scholars' accounts must be acceptable to informed members of the traditions being described, although they may balk at the use of abstract categories. Imposing a theoretical explanatory scheme can lead to distorting an alien tradition, as occurred with Carl Jung's understanding of Asian mystical traditions (see Jones 1993b). However, one can approach any subject only from one's own background, and a basic problem today for anyone who has been influenced by science is that we see the world through the lens of modern science. This led Joseph Needham to distort the nature of Daoism (see Jones 1993b) and today has led many New Age advocates to distort mysticism in general (see Jones 2010, 2019b).

Despite postmodernists' objections, historians do not doubt our general ability to understand other ages and cultures even if extensive study of those cultures is needed. However, modern science may have made it impossible for us today to see the world the way that premoderns saw it: we simply are not capable of experiencing the "sacred world" of the medieval Christians, let alone experiencing the world as early Hindus or Daoists experienced it. We can *imagine*, say, an animistic world, but we do not truly *believe* it or *see* the world that way. For example, we cannot encounter any reference to the moon without implicitly thinking in terms of modern astronomy and physics—we can *understand* the claim that the moon is a goddess, but we cannot truly *see* it that way or *believe* it. So too, the modern Western emphasis on individualism affects our ability to enter into another culture's world of meaning. Participating in the meditations or rituals of other cultures cannot change that. Sympathetic imagination cannot get us into the inner life of any premodern person from any society. We can follow Plotinus's and Zhuangzi's reasoning and even advance new claims they should accept based on their statements of their beliefs and reasoning, but we cannot claim further to be *thinking* the way they did. Any true conversion from the experiential world of our modern outlook to another worldview would require a suspension of our modern outlook, and this requires a very great effort.

Thus, the possibility that we may inadvertently make other people into mirror images of ourselves cannot be ignored, but this does not mean that in principle we cannot genuinely *understand* the meaning of others' claims or that we must unconsciously always see all claims *in our own terms*. We can grasp the basic outlook of premoderns through study and thus understand what others are saying without experiencing the world as they do. Thus, contrary to what is often claimed in religious studies, scholars cannot convey what it is like to *be* a Christian mystic or a Daoist mystic, but they can make it possible for us to understand their teachings. In sum, with some effort we can understand their claims even if we cannot "walk in their shoes" and see the world as they did.

So too with translating mystical works: translators can never be certain that they are conveying what authors truly meant. The possibility of mystical experiences informing these texts intensifies the issue. When we have only a very limited number of texts from a specific mystic or cultural era, the understanding and translation problems are at their greatest. For example, the *Daodejing* is the second most often translated book in the world (after the Bible), and due to our limited resources for the mysticism of that period the translations must very much be interpretations of what a translator thinks early Daoist thought involved. But this problem can be mitigated if one looks at a large portion of a given mystic's work in the context of his or her tradition and culture. Simply reading brief snippets or isolated statements in translation in William James's *Varieties of Religious Experience* cannot be the sum of one's research since one's general theory of mysticism would then too easily control one's understanding rather than letting the mystic's works build and revise one's understanding. Western theistic beliefs of a personal being external to the natural universe can distort our view of Brahman, the Dao, and Indian theisms. A prime example today involves the popularity of the Buddhist Nagarjuna on "emptiness" (*shunyata*), a term that he seldom used: Westerners who have not actually studied Prajnaparamita and Madhyamaka works routinely go directly against what Nagarjuna actually taught and reify "emptiness" from his usage (as the lack of anything that would give phenomenal things self-existence) into Emptiness with a capital "E" or the "Void" and make it an analogy to God or Brahman as the source of phenomena.

Moreover, making certain personal *mystical experiences* the unique element of mysticism does not privatize all of *mysticism* by making it into an exclusively personal phenomenon or a matter of experiences alone, as many scholars allege: mysticism remains a public phenomenon with multiple dimensions that can be studied as such. The privacy of any experience does not cut off other avenues of approaching mystical cultural phenomena—mysticism remains an observable phenomenon. Each tradition's ways of life are developed collectively through different influences. Nor are there any reasons other than theological ones to treat mystical experiences as privileged phenomena that are immune to examination by the human and natural sciences or to treat mystical doctrines as protected from philosophical analysis. Making ASC experiences central to the phenomenon is not obfuscation, but approaches and methods devised for cultural and social phenomena in general may have to be revised when applied to phenomena in which ASC experiences are central.

Perennial Philosophy and the Contextual Approach

If one approaches the mystical tradition of the world without a theological or philosophical agenda, there does not appear to be one universal "mysticism" but only diverging mystical traditions—diverse ways of life with various beliefs, values, paths, goals, central experiences, and enlightened states that lead to a genuine pluralism of different "mysticisms." We can still speak of "mysticism" in the singular as a class of cross-cultural phenomena, just as linguists speak of "language" in the abstract even though there are only multiple specific languages, and we can discuss mysticism's general features (to the extent that any commonalities among the phenomena are found), just as linguists speak of the nature of language. But we must remember there are only specific evolving traditions, and each mystic must be understood within his or her religious, cultural, linguistic, and historical context.

"Perennial philosophers," however, disagree. They offer a theory about the relation of the alleged reality experienced by introvertive mystics and the doctrines that mystics hold. According to Frithjof Schuon (1975), the same transcendent truth of one absolute and transcendent reality is the origin of all the world's religions and still lies at the heart of every religion and is unanimously affirmed by all mystics. "[T]he goal of mysticism is God, who may also be given such names as the One, the Absolute, the Infinite, the Supreme Self, the Supreme Being" (Stoddart 2005: 59). Some "exoteric" expression is necessary, but all mystical paths lead to the same summit—in effect, there one abstract "mysticism" that all mystics share operating within all religious traditions that is independent of those traditions. Thus, perennialists claim that behind the diverse "exoteric" shells that mystics utilize to make their actual claims there is a timeless "esoteric" core of all mystical claims is really the same. There is no need to understand the cultural settings of mystical claims since the true meaning is provided by the esoteric core. Swami Abhyananda (2012) has written a history of mysticism from this perspective. He often had to disregard what mystics actually wrote and instead told us what the mystics really meant. This badly distorted the different religions of the world by imposing a metaphysics that he thinks all true mystics hold. The metaphysics penetrate down to creating very misleading translations of key terms in order to make all mystical ideas seem the same.

But this distorts the beliefs that inform how mystics have actually lived. Perennialists attempt to show what mystics really believe despite what the mystics actually say. However, mystics see themselves as Christians,

Muslims, Shaivites, or whatever—not as adherents of a common esoteric tradition transcending all "exoteric" shells. To understand how the mystics themselves actually lived and what they believed, we must look at them in their *cultural contexts*. In the hands of strong constructivists, mystical doctrines are reduced to products of cultural sources unrelated to ASCs, but we do not have to go that far to affirm that mystical writings must be understood in their cultural and historical context to be understood as the mystics themselves understood them. That is, the meaning of mystical claims comes from understanding the claims within the setting of a given mystic's culture and era, not from some outsider's philosophical or theological perspective—mystics lived employing the externals of their religions however much their private mystical experiences may have affected their understanding. For actual mystics, the "exoteric" dimension permeates the "esoteric" dimension.

In sum, the perennialists' claim that there is an abstract mysticism that underlies all mystical traditions does not come from actually studying what mystics themselves taught and how they lived. They can make their claim only by imposing an external understanding on the works of mystics that does not show what mystics actually believed and how they lived. Theirs is a theoretical stance that must be defended as such. A contextualist approach, in contrast, focuses as much on the "exoteric shell" of a mystical tradition as the inner dimension of mystical experiences—indeed, strong constructivists focus only on the shell. Contextualists locate mystics, mystical doctrines, and all other mystical phenomena in their cultural and historical context, but, as discussed in the last chapter, contextualists can focus on both the externals of a mystical tradition and the experiential dimension without reducing mystical experiences or claims to the cultural influences. Constructivists muddle the issues by claiming that those who deny constructivism concerning the nature of mystical experiences must also deny contextualism as a method for studying mystical cultural phenomena and endorse perennialism.

Understanding Versus Explaining

Thus, the conclusions here are that nonmystics can understand mystics' works well enough to proceed with descriptive accounts of their teachings and that a contextual approach is needed for the initial understanding of mystics and mystical traditions. Those who offer arguments for the truth or falsity of specific doctrines go beyond such descriptive accounts. So too, those who offer socioscientific, neurological, or theological explanations of mystical experiences may see no need to be concerned with the inner subjective side of mystical experiences.[1] Reductionists in the humanities, human sciences, and cognitive sciences see no need to try to understand the felt mystical experiences at all or to bother with the experiencers' claims, since they explain away all mystical phenomena in terms of nonmystical phenomena.[2] Nonreductionists with respect to mystical experiences can accept that these experiences are unique *human experiences* having an impact on the lives of the experiencers and are not reducible to other human phenomena while remaining neutral on whether any *transcendent reality* is actually experienced or denying the experiences are cognitive. Rejecting reductionism does not mean that mystical experiences must be veridical, must involve transcendent realities, or must transcend cultural conditioning but only that these experiences are merely some nonmystical phenomena and that the mystical aspects must be studied as such.

However, merely *identifying nonmystical bases* within mystical phenomena to help in our total understanding does not necessarily mean that the phenomena must be *nothing more* than those bases. Indeed, one recurring issue for the explanatory approaches is whether they are *reductive* or *nonreductive*.[3] For example, does a neuroscientific explanation of the neurochemical activity occurring in the brain during a mystical experience *exhaust the phenomenon*, or does it merely identify what events are occurring in the brain while that experience is occurring? If the former, there is nothing left of the alleged cognitive content after providing a neuroscientific account: the experience is a brain event produced by natural mechanisms and nothing more—the sense of cognition is merely a mistaken reaction, and all mystical doctrines can be dismissed as Jamesian over-beliefs. If the latter, it is at least possible that the experiencer is in touch with a deeper reality and the experience is cognitive.

Thus, a *natural explanation* of the bases of mystical experiences in the neurology, psychology, or sociology must be distinguished from a *naturalistic reduction* to those bases. A natural explanation specifies the natural conditions for the occurrence of mystical experiences, why a particular person is a mystic, the effect of mystical experiences upon the experiencers, or the role of mysticism in society. Studying the brain events that accompany a mystical experience does not necessarily reduce the experience to those events, nor does studying the functions mystical phenomena play in a mystic's life or culture require reducing those phenomena to nonmystical phenomena. A naturalistic reduction goes further: it is a philosophical judgment that is metaphysical in nature that those conditions exhaust all there is to the experience or mystical cultural phenomena. Reductionists are not denying that the experiences occur but only claiming that they are purely nonmystical phenomena. However, only by confusing a natural explanation with a naturalistic reduction can one conclude that scientific accounts by themselves logically entail the philosophical conclusion. The reductionists' conclusion remains philosophical and must be defended as such—the reduction is not itself a scientific finding (see Jones 2000). Whether a neuroscientific or socioscientific explanation explains away the alleged cognitive content of mystical experiences and thus trumps the mystics' own accounts is a topic about the validity of mystical claims discussed in chapter 11.

A related issue is whether any one approach can exhaust all that we need to know about mysticism or whether each approach accounts for only one dimension of a multidimensional phenomenon and so a complete explanation of mysticism requires multiple approaches to explain all that we want to know about mystical phenomena. Reductionists may argue that a single discipline explains the core of mystical phenomena—for example, sociological phenomena are totally reducible to psychological phenomena, which in turn are reducible to neurological phenomena, with only some incidental aspects of the phenomena remaining to be understood and explained separately. Nonreductionists accept mystical experiences and mystical cultural phenomena as not reducible to other human phenomena—nonmystical explanations do not exhaust mystical phenomena but only illuminate different aspects of them (e.g., the social bases of mysticism within a culture). In a perspectivism, each valid approach (including the one that treats mystical phenomena as an independent variable at work in human phenomena) contributes to the total picture—no one perspective prevails over the others as the sole avenue to the best explanations. However, reductive explanations can kill a phenomenon by explaining it away as *unreal* in some way, as with eliminationists in contemporary philosophy of mind denying there is any consciousness but only brain events.

Thus, those who value mysticism need not reject all explanations from the natural and human sciences but only the reductive *philosophy of explanation*. So too, accepting that multiple disciplines can each provide insights into the different dimensions of mysticism and the life of particular mystics does not mean that treating some human phenomena as "mystical" is not also a source of insights. Treating some phenomena as mystical does not mean that the phenomena can be separated from other human phenomena, as if mysticism were some disembodied transcultural phenomenon (as perennialists argue). We would still have to examine the phenomena within the totality of human phenomena. But dealing with a specifically "mystical" dimension to the phenomena may detect something valuable that the other approaches omit. If so, mysticism cannot be studied exhaustively within other disciplines—unless reductionists are correct, something would be missed without a specifically mystical approach to the phenomena.

— 7 —

Themes in the History of Mysticism

The first priority concerning mysticism in the academic discipline of "history of religions" is to present a mystic's or a mystical tradition's way of looking at reality and way of life expressed in their basic beliefs, values, practices, and goals. Historians try to present mystical beliefs (including those about transcendent realities) as the believers understand and accept them without endorsing or rejecting the beliefs themselves.[1] The history of each tradition can also be presented to show particular mystics' basic beliefs and values without stepping into the next phase of understanding—offering any theological (including any essentialist or perennialist view of mysticism) or secular socioscientific explanations of the data in terms of causes external to the culture's own internal religious and philosophical explanations. Different histories can be produced dependent upon a given historian's interests—focusing, for example, on a tradition's doctrines, art, or meditative techniques.

Presenting the world's mystical traditions individually is not to deny that there have been interactions between the different traditions and cultures. Indeed, the cross-fertilization is sometimes quite significant. Nor does this approach treat the traditions as timeless entities. Nor is any religion's mystical tradition monolithic: each of the world religion's mysticism is made up of multiple evolving subtraditions. There is no one uniform "Christian mysticism" but different Christian forms of mysticism, some within the same era and culture. Nor can all of Hinduism be reduced to Advaita Vedanta or to Vaishnava theism, let alone all Asian mystical traditions to one grand "Oriental mysticism." Even within the same religion, some subtraditions are more "devotional" and some more "wisdom" oriented.² There are variations and exceptions in every tradition. Different mystical groups within the same religion often disagree over basic doctrines and practices. Nor is any mystical tradition "pure": there are always nonmystical influences. But the comparative study of the variety of mysticisms in the world also shows that each religion's mystical traditions have their own cluster of key themes that set them apart from other mystical traditions.

The Prehistory of Mysticism

Shamans in the Stone Age and later tribal societies have engaged in practices to induce altered states of consciousness, and scholars routinely call these shamans the "first mystics" and shamanic practices the "earliest form of mysticism" (e.g., Walsh 1990: 215). However, shamanism does not fit narrow definitions of "mysticism." The important shamanic ASC states and experiences are not the ones central to mysticism, and shamans did not seek the types of experiences free of a sense of self and conceptual differentiations that are central. Shamans' important experiences remain visions and out-of-body flights to the spirit worlds. The central role that shamans play in the communal life of their society (e.g., healing or finding animals to hunt) also is not replicated by mystics as societies evolved, although over the course of time some mystics did become leaders and healers. These societies' worldviews and values typically have no place for the transcendent realities experienced in introvertive mystical experiences or for cultivating an "empty" awareness or mystical enlightened states.

The techniques that shamans utilize to induce their ASCs may open the mind to mystical experiences, but as Roger Walsh notes, shamans traditionally aim for experiences of soul travel in spirit realms and few have explored mystical experiences (1990: 241). Conversely, mystical practices may open mystics' minds to visions and paranormal powers, but these remain peripheral experiences that are not ultimately valued by most traditional mystics. In 1990, Walsh had found no references in any study of shamanism to "mystical union," nor had anyone else (239). He also laid out in detail the differences between shamanic experiences and both Yoga's concentrative mystical experiences and Buddhist mindfulness (223–32).

Ingesting plants and animal parts that produce psychedelic effects does not change this picture. Such plants and animals are common throughout the world, and their mind-altering properties were probably discovered early in our history.[3] They may have played a role in the evolution of the human mind and the development of our imagination and our linguistic and symbolic thinking (McKenna 1992; Weil 1986; Wasson et al. 1986; Winkelman 2017). Use of entheogens may account for some of the divergence between human and chimpanzee neurology (Winkelman 2010). So too may the communal nighttime campfire rituals (e.g., rhythmic drumming) that focused attention (Rossano 2007). But in these societies, these practices more typically induce visions, although they can also enable mystical experiences.

Cultivating ASCs to transcend our baseline state appears to be a cultural universal, and thus mystics are not necessarily drawing on earlier shamanic practices simply because they too alter their waking consciousness. Mysticism as ways of life most likely appeared only after the development of specialized religious professionals (e.g., priests, healers, and mediums) who took over the various functions of the shamans as societies became more complex. It probably arose out of earlier religious practices as a whole, not merely shamanic practices and rituals. So too, it may be more likely that mystical experiences acquired importance as validating changeless realities only at this stage of cultural evolution.

Thus, even if shamans do have some mystical experiences, it is difficult to see shamans as prototypes of mystics, or mysticism as beginning in shamanic rituals and practices. However, some shamanic techniques for altering consciousness have been adopted in early ascetic and yogic meditative practices and survived (e.g., the whirling dervishes of Islam and the Tantric use of drugs in India). So too, mystics may have visions and out-of-body experiences (e.g., the Daoist masters' travels on dragons). However, the centrality of different types of experiences keeps shamanism from being a type of mysticism or a proto-mysticism.

Greek Mysticism

There is some evidence that mystical experiences enabled by mind-altering drugs played a role in the development of Greek philosophy and its culture in general (e.g., Ruck 2006). However, inducing mystical states of consciousness was not a major theme in classical Greek culture. The distinction between appearance and reality became prominent, but the world has reality even if it is not eternal being (*ousia*). The "Greek miracle" that led to science was to search for nonpersonal causes within nature to replace explanations in terms of the wills of the gods and of supernatural beings inhabiting nature. For mysticism, there was one final ontological source and a multiplicity of souls. The soul was not part of the material world, and human beings were essentially spiritual beings. This permits participation in the realm of eternal truth, but only after death can we know the "pure" truth.

Truth and knowledge were central to Greek thought, and knowledge did not end with rational thinking and sense-experience. Distrusting human opinion and valuing divine knowledge was a common theme in both mystical and nonmystical philosophy. Especially for mystical philosophers, reality was eternal and unchanging, knowledge was a matter of certainty, and knowledge of reality was not attained by devising rational truths but was revealed in experiences that were divine in origin. Philosophical reasoning formed only a preliminary step for inducing such experiences—genuine knowledge involved participation in the reality to be known. Mystics believed that at least a taste of the divine knowledge was attainable in this life by turning away from the world and looking inward, leading to mystical experiences. The quest for the divine knowledge was seen as a journey of the soul—an ascent from the darkness of the shadow realm to the light, as with Plato's analogy of the cave (*Republic* 514a–516c). But the objective of philosophy was a transformation of the entire person and living a contemplative life in this world.

As Pierre Hadot has presented well, classical Greek philosophy in general was not simply an intellectual matter but a spiritual exercise that transformed a person's life into a life of well-being (*eudaimonia*). Works were "written not so much to inform the reader of a doctrinal content but to form him" (1995: 264). "Love of wisdom" (*philo-sophia*) was not a matter of accepting some theory but a "radical conversion and transformation of the individual's way of being" (265). Philosophy as inducing a new way of being reveals a continuity with mysticisms as ways of life. Medieval Christianity adopted this view of philosophy as spiritual exercise. And inducing ASC experiences may in fact also have been one objective in many cases of Greek philosophy. Hadot makes a strong case that classical Greek philosophical texts were meant to be delivered orally in order to induce a transformation in the listener's consciousness.

The Greek world produced the most important mystic in the history of the Western world: Plotinus (ca. 204–270 CE). His mysticism was introvertive and nontheistic. His metaphysics centered on a unified, unchanging, nonpersonal transcendent source that for convenience he labeled "the One" (*to hen*). The One's nature is unknown and beyond all dualities. From the One emanates first the Nous that is both Being (*ousia*) and a perpetual divine consciousness (the "intellect") present in everything. The Nous's only activity is contemplation. From the Nous emanates the World Soul (*psyche*). Individual souls and the eternal natural order (*physis*) underlying the material world are in the World Soul. (Matter is not an emanation but a kind of shadow.) Thus, there is multiplicity in the World Soul but not in the Nous or the One. The total otherness of the One makes the *via negativa* central to Neoplatonism.

The purpose of Plotinus's philosophy is to induce an ascent of the soul to the One. The ascent to realizing the One requires turning inward, letting all but the One go, and ending in stillness. In the flight in solitude to the solitary (the flight of "the alone to the Alone"), the higher soul remains in the Nous contemplating the One. The soul is "one'd" with the One in its direct contemplative experience of it, but the individual soul does not *merge* with the One. The soul can be said to emerge from the World Soul and merge into the Nous; thereby, it loses its identity and *becomes* the Nous of all things.[4] But even the Nous never merges with the One but only contemplates it, as does the individual soul. But by becoming the Nous, the soul is "nousified" (*nootheisa*) while in the world. One is no longer subject to the illusion that we are only small embodied selves. This is a stabilized constant state of consciousness within the Nous even while we are aware of the realm of matter. Plotinus's objective was to live with detachment in the Nous in this enlightened mystical state outside the depth-mystical experience of being "one'd." Porphyry states that Plotinus "never relaxed his intense concentration upon the Nous"—even while engaged in conversation, he kept his mind fixed without break on the Nous (*Life of Plotinus*, chapters 8, 9; see Enneads VI.9.9).

Thus, Plotinus refers to three types of mystical experiences: the depth-mystical experience of our awareness being "one'd" with the One in contemplation from within the Nous; other introvertive experiences within the Nous; and an extrovertive enlightened nousified state within the Nous having sensory input and thought. Ecstatic experiences of the One in which nousified awareness is absent may still occur in the enlightened state but only as transient moments within the long-lasting enlightened stage of peaceful repose in the Nous. By the time of the Neoplatonist Christian

Pseudo-Dionysius the Aeropagite in the sixth century, Neoplatonism was more nonmystical and its metaphysics had been significantly altered from Plotinus's, but his doctrine of the One remained important. And Neoplatonism influenced all Abrahamnic mysticism for a thousand years and continues to shape Eastern Orthodox Christianity.

Jewish Mysticism

Mysticism in Judaism is seen as a way to develop one's ability to follow God's will. Humility before God is a central value in Judaism, and in Jewish mysticism this led to experiences in altered states of consciousness—from visions of being in God's presence to direct contact with God.[5]

The framework of Kabbalist and Hasidic mysticism is a panentheistic monotheism with an emanationism from the one hidden transcendent source. This was a way to overcome the inherent tension between a transcendent creator god and introvertive mystical experiences. But the mixture of mystical and nonmystical authorities did not lead to a fully developed negative theology in Judaism (the philosopher Maimonides being the notable exception). This emanationism also removed any further acts of God within the world—God's being permeates the world, but after the biblical period God no longer intervenes in particular events. Overall, Jewish mystics focus on a less personal aspect of God than on a full monotheistic god. However, many Kabbalists and Hasidics claim, as do many Sufis in Islam, that not only is there only one god, but *there is nothing but God*—the idea that an individual person or the phenomenal world exists independently from God is an illusion. Each person is a "part of God from above."

Jewish mystics affirm an unknowable mystery as central to the divine: we can never know one aspect of God—the Infinite (*Ein Sof*) or the Nothingness (*Ayin*). But most Jewish mysticism can be labeled "theosophy." That is, mystics speculated on the inner workings of God himself. The Godhead is separated from the process of creation, but scholars elaborated an emanationist metaphysics of how God created. For many nonmystical Jewish scholars, the system of ten emanated forces (*sherifot*) compromised the unity of the Godhead even more than did the Christian doctrine of a trinity since the emanated forces are not separate from the Infinite.

Kabbalah gave the divine a *female* side in the emanation. This is unique in the history of Western mysticism. Jewish mysticism has another unique emphasis: theurgy—that is, human actions can actually affect the divine by modifying the inner life of the Godhead. Human action was also seen as necessary for restoring harmony in the world and even for completing divine perfection. There is a dynamic ebb and flow of the light of God in the world, and human action is needed to capture the light currently in the evil realm. This role is reserved for Jews and involves Jews obeying the 613 biblical commandments as elaborated in the rabbinical tradition.

Direct individual experiences of God became important. The Middle Platonist Philo Judaeus of Alexandria (ca. 25 BCE–50 CE) was the first person to develop the idea of a personal "union with God" and the first to give a mystical interpretation of the notion of "cleaving to God" (*devekut*) (Deuteronomy 4:4) that became prominent in the Middle Ages. Before then, cleaving had been a communal matter of the Jewish nation as a whole. Philo also introduced the idea of the ineffability of God. The otherness of God from creation is overcome in introvertive mystical experiences. Thus, traditional Jewish doctrines did not stop an experiential sense of unity with God in some experiences, but the orthodox interpretation is in terms of communion with God, not absorption. The existence of the soul and its dependence on God is not denied: during a mystical experience, one has annihilated any sense of it, but the soul is never abolished within the divine reality. For Kabbalists and Hasidics, "cleaving to God" means so total a devotion to God as to renounce the content of the material world and to transcend one's own self to achieve a spiritual communion with God. In their return to a worldly state, the enlightened are transformed, but their true transcendent souls are not ontologically changed in nature from what they originally were. Hasidics emphasize this extrovertive state of consciousness.

Christian Mysticism

At its origin, Christianity appears to have been a mystical religion: the objective was to experience God—to escape the corrupt world and "share in the very being of God" (2 Peter 1:4). But by the first generation after the apostles a division formed between a mystical Christianity bent on the reception of the Holy Spirit and a Christianity based on nonmystical practices and beliefs under institutional authority. After that, mystical practice within Christianity was limited to monastics for most of its history. But Christian mystics have ranged from reformers to heretics, from being canonized to being burned at the stake.

Christian mysticism arose within a combined Jewish and Greek environment, and Platonism came to provide the dominant framework for the Christian world-picture until the establishment in the thirteenth century of the Aristotelianism that rejected emanationism and placed the creator totally outside of creation. But the Christian god is a personal loving reality, not the nonpersonal One of Neoplatonism. Not only are mystics searching for God, but the loving god is also active in drawing them in. Orthodox mystics' belief-claims were solidly theistic: an all-loving god is the source of our reality, and self-emptying love of others reflects ultimate reality. Some mystics in the Abrahamic traditions grounded the loving god in an impersonal godhead, but a loving god remains the creator of the natural realm. The world is not deemed an illusion or unreal, and the Bible is accepted as the only source of knowledge of God available to fallen humanity, and mystics generally accepted the need for the institution of the church. However, as with Jewish mysticism, the words of the Bible are seen as hiding a mystical meaning. Thus, the Bible is accepted as authoritative but is understood and interpreted in light of mystical beliefs.[6]

The roles of the incarnated Christ and the Holy Spirit make Christian mysticism unique: God is not only the ground of being but is active in his creation and creatures through this incarnation and the Holy Spirit. There is less in mystical writings on God's historical incarnation in the world than on God's action in the soul in the present. But that God became incarnate was taken to mean that it is possible for human beings to become united in some sense with God—"God became man so that we might become God." God's grace—a gift that we cannot earn—was required for any experience of God. But by grace, we can gain what Jesus had by nature. Accepting a godhead reconciles the changeless and still being experienced in the depth-mystical experience with the active theistic god. God remains a creator, but the being supplied by the godhead is present in our soul. However, becoming one with God or literal "deification" is generally considered impossible. God is immanent to the natural universe as the sustainer of its being, but classical Christian mysticism is not pantheistic—the transcendent dimension of the creator or Godhead is always maintained.

Human souls have a created nature and are not divine, nor do they participate in the divine nature. Rather, they are dependent on God for their existence (and may share the same being as God's that is supplied by a nonpersonal godhead). There is also a unity of body and soul in Judaism and Christianity that is not derived from Greek thought, where there is a separate divine soul that ascends to the divine. This created nature cannot be overcome in any experience—as Jan van Ruusbroec (1985) put it, never does a creature becomes so holy that it loses its status as a created being and becomes God. The term "mystical union" (*unio mystica*) was rarely used by classical Christian mystics, and when it was used it usually meant *communion* with a personal god, not *identity* in any sense. Awareness of the self may have been reduced to nothing during a mystical experience, but the reality of the soul was not denied, even if it is not totally distinct from its ontological source. Introvertive mystical experiences were seen as a personal relation between the lover and the beloved. The marriage of two persons is a common image.

The mind cannot totally comprehend God. But despite the role of the *via negativa* in mystical training and understanding God, the positive way has always remained more prominent due to the Bible being considered the revealed word of God. There is a divine mystery that is beyond all our understanding, and yet God can be understood as a creator and as love as revealed in the Bible, and thus all negative and paradoxical accounts of the "abyss" are not the final word.

"Love" mystics focus more on Christ, while "knowledge" mystics focus more on the Godhead. Bonaventure can be contrasted with Meister Eckhart here. But Christianity's ethos of self-giving love grounded in God shapes all these mystical ways of life, except for some antinomians. As Eckhart put it: if a person were in such a rapturous state as Paul once entered (2 Corinthians 12:1–6) and he knew of a sick man who wanted a cup of soup, it would be far better to withdraw from the rapture for love's sake and serve him who is in need (2009: 496). Mysticism thus became a way to fulfill fully the commandments to love God and love one's neighbor as oneself (Mark 12: 30–31) by participating in God's love. In the enlightened state, "resting in God's love" becomes the wellspring generating loving action toward others.

Following the Greek philosophers, medieval mystics valued the contemplative life over action toward others, but the Christian ethos of an active life of love for others prevailed: the goal became an "active life" informed by having fully internalized God's love by means of the "contemplative life." John of the Cross warned that those who act without first going through a contemplative stage will accomplish little good or may even do harm. The common position by the late Middle Ages was that, in Ignatius of Loyola's expression, one can be "active in the midst of contemplation." Ruusbroec (1985) argued for the integration of action and contemplation—being simultaneously active and receptive—in the "comprehensive life" and attacked anyone who would devote themselves to the latter while ignoring the former. Thus, the result is the mystics' enlightened state of "contemplation in action."

Thus, medieval mystics placed less value on episodic "mystical experiences" than on an enlightened life of moral action resulting from an inner mystical transformation of character—the goal of the mystical quest was a "God-intoxicated" life aligned with God's will, with all sense of self annihilated, not isolated ecstatic experiences. Traditionally, Christian mystics value mystical experiences only as they help to align one's character and will with God's. A mystical experience is not necessary for salvation but is a way to "perfect" the Christian life of love. Self-will vanishes, and one wills, desires, loves, and intends nothing but the eternal goodness that God wills. For the enlightened "it is no longer I who lives but Christ who lives in me" (Galatians 2:20). Sin is reduced to asserting self-will—to desire other than what one thinks that God desires. As Teresa of Avila said, "Nothing burns in hell but self-will." Prayers are not prayers of petition for any particular benefit for oneself or others but simply that "thy will be done on earth as in heaven" (Matthew 6:10). For Eckhart, the "just" have no will at all: whatever God wills, it is all one to them, however great the hardship (2009: 329).

Islamic Mysticism

Sufis try to "live in God's presence" by following the path laid out in the Quran and exemplified in the life of the "seal of the prophets," Muhammad. The Islamic creed "There is no god but God, and Muhammad is his messenger" remains true for Sufis. Islam exhibits a radical monotheism—the oneness of the divine—but classical Sufis typically go further: God is not only one but is the *only* reality. To most Sufis, "there is nothing real but the Real." That is how they interpret the declaration of faith "There is no god but God" and the Prophet's saying "God was, and nothing was with him." For these Sufis, to affirm the world as a reality other than God was a form of polytheism. (This opened Sufis to the charge that Sufism was not really Islamic.) God supplies the being to all realities, but the creations are not identical to God. There are different views on the relation of God to the world, but no pantheism is affirmed. Rather, the cosmos has only relative existence, and Sufis must distinguish the eternal from the temporal, the Real from the unreal.

Sufis attempt to focus upon God at all times. Meditation is often connected to the constant remembrance (*dhikr*) of God by chanting his names or phrases from the Quran. Over time, such meditation superseded reflective meditation (*fikr*). Saying the basic declaration of faith became a form of meditation, for as one Sufi put it, "No one says 'No god but God' correctly unless he negates everything other than God from his soul and heart." The experiences may be personal, but group ways of meditating—prayers, chanting, dancing—are common in Sufism.

Mainstream Sufism rejects the idea of mystical experiences being the union of two distinct realities. Becoming one with God's oneness (*tawhid*) is a matter of realizing that we already are one with God and have always been so since God is the only reality. All awareness of the individual self is obliterated (*fana*). The oneness of being may be realized in an ecstatic experience (*hal, wajd*), but in differentiated introvertive experiences a loving communion with God is achieved. In the extrovertive enlightened state, one is filled with the presence of God (*baqa*). By such experiences, the submission of one's will to God becomes complete.

Mystical knowledge (*marifa*) is usually given preference over basic revealed knowledge (*ilm*) and becomes the basis for mystical interpretations of Quranic passages. "Sober" claims of a lover and the beloved were preferred over the "intoxicated" claims of union—Sufis may lose sight of the soul when blinded by the light of God during a mystical experience, but after the experience they know that the soul is a separate entity created and sustained by God. That is, the genuineness of the experience of God is not denied, but afterward one sees that although God is the only reality in any phenomenon, God is still the creator, and created phenomena are in some sense distinguishable from him. The personal god won out over the nonpersonal Neoplatonist One for most Sufis, but Sufis typically use the language of both love and mystical knowledge. Different Sufis emphasized one or the other, but both are deemed necessary. However, a state of loving adoration of the essential Reality is the typical depiction of the enlightened state, since God is always the target of limitless attraction.

The role of spiritual masters in conveying the esoteric knowledge was always very important. The masters' spiritual force (*baraka*) also became important, and popular practices bordering on worship developed around it.

Hindu Mysticism

Mysticism is at the foundation of Hinduism (but not the earlier Vedism). Most religious traditional practices in India have been directly or indirectly mystical. Meditation in some form or another is a pan-Indian phenomenon. Mystical traditions in India, both orthodox and heterodox, interacted constantly. Thus, it is hard to isolate "Yogic mysticism" from "Buddhist mysticism," and so on in the history of Indian mysticism. Introvertive mysticisms are central here, each with a metaphysics of a transcendent ground to all of the phenomenal world or to only the individual person. There are nondualisms, pluralisms, and nonpersonal and personal ultimate realities. This variety of depth-mystical metaphysics—perhaps all viable introvertive options—along with the vigorous debates between schools and the quantity of texts refuting other texts, have led to India being called the "laboratory for mysticism."[7]

Sages in the Upanishads turned inward in a search, not to find one creator God, as in the Abrahamic traditions, but to find one unifying reality underlying both the phenomenal realm and ourselves. To be that reality, the "one" must be something that all things constituting the "many" have in common, and thus it cannot have any objective phenomenal features (which would then be limited to only some items), but must also encompass all objective and subjective phenomena. What is real must also remain the same throughout all changes internal and external to a person, and so must be changeless and eternal. This principle must also be experienceable within us, since it constitutes our true reality. In the Upanishads, that principle is called "Brahman." And "you are that" (*tat tvam asi*). It is the essence (*atman*) of all things, including human beings. However, Samkhya-Yoga sets up a duality of matter and a multiplicity of transcendent conscious "persons" (*purushas*). Nothing is gained by a mystical experience except knowledge: our essence (*atman*) is already Brahman or an individual center of consciousness (*purusha*), and we only have to become directly aware of that fact.

Knowledge (*vidya*), not any temporary experience (*anubhava*), is central. It is casting off the basic illusion that the phenomenal world is an independent reality populated by multiple real objects and discovering its (and our) true nature. Our root ignorance (*avidya*) causes a dualistic misperception that veils reality, and thus the enlightening knowledge is not merely a philosophical matter of adopting factual claims but of no longer being deceived by our sense-perceptions and actually *seeing* the world as it truly is. To do this requires yogic practices that alter our state of consciousness. As in the Abrahamic traditions, mystics rely on the basic revealed texts of their tradition as providing the correct knowledge. The standard of knowledge is certainty, and only revealed texts (*shruti*) provide that. But mystics here too interpret the texts to fit their metaphysics. The Vedantins Shankara, Ramanuja, and Madhva are examples of mystics who had to twist the plain meaning of certain Upanishadic passages to make the texts say what they wanted them to say.

Appearance was distinguished from reality, but treating the world as a "magical trick" (*maya*) only means that the phenomenal world is dependent for its existence on a "magician" (and thus lacks independent existence) and that it is outwardly deceptive in character: the world still exists but is dependent upon or is part of something that is permanent, eternal, and transcendent (Brahman or God). Even for Advaita, where only Brahman is real, the world is not totally unreal (*asat*) but has an indefinable (*anirvachaniya*) ontic status like a dream—in between truly "real" and totally "unreal"—since the state of consciousness is real, but the content is not. Seeing the phenomenal realm as independently real is like mistaking a rope as a snake: something real is there but is misperceived.

The common goal of the mystical traditions is liberation (*moksha, mukti*) from the continuing chain of rebirths in the phenomenal realm. In the *Bhagavad-gita*, four paths are set forth: knowledge, devotion, meditation, and work performed regardless of the effect on oneself (*karma-yoga*). The social and religious requirements of Hindu ways of life may be superseded. Stilling all desires through correcting our knowledge is the most common route, but not all Hindu mysticism is dispassionate in nature, as Bhakti devotion and Tantrism show. Enlightenment does not ontologically change anything in our being, but after death the enlightened either do not reemerge from Brahman, become isolated (as with Samkhya-Yoga and Jainism), or remain distinct but in some relation to God (in most nondualistic and pluralistic theistic systems). Detachment and even-mindedness toward all the changes in the world are the central attitudes in enlightened living.

A theistic god does not play a role in all forms of Hindu mysticism. Rather, a nonpersonal reality—Brahman—is deemed more fundamental in Advaita, and there is no creator god in early Samkhya-Yoga. In the later theistic and Tantric schools, a female cosmic power (*shakti*) is deemed equal or even superior to the male.

Buddhist Mysticism

The Buddha's entire teaching has only one flavor: how to end the suffering (*duhkha*) that is inherent in simply being alive (*Majjhima Nikaya* I.22).[8] The goal, as in Hinduism, is to escape suffering permanently by ending rebirths, but Buddhism uses a different class of mystical experiences and a very different metaphysics to achieve this: there is no essence to the person or the universe that we ever experience, nor is there a permanent consciousness in a person. The objective is not to realize that our reality is a transcendent reality but to realize that there is nothing permanent within us to defend or augment, and nothing permanent within the phenomenal world to satisfy our desires.

Buddhism, like other early Indian mysticisms, was world-renouncing, but the focus shifted to the impermanence of the phenomenal world, not to any possible transcendent sources. This world may have the status of a "dream" in Advaita, and so Advaitins focus on the eternal "dreamer," but for Buddhists the focus is only on the impermanence of the content of the "dream"—the question of the ontological status of the world in toto is left unanswered. A root metaphor for the Buddhist analysis of impermanence is a chariot and its parts: only the parts are real, and even the part themselves are impermanent and without any abiding essence that would make a thing a reality existing independently of other things. Early Buddhism emphasized the impermanence of the wholes, while the Prajnaparamita and Madhyamaka texts expanded the lack of an essence in a person (*anatman*) to the lack of anything giving self-existence (*svabhava*) to any phenomenon—all phenomena, the parts as well as the wholes, are empty (*shunyata*).

Thus, Buddhist mysticism at its core is extrovertive, even though its goal remains transcendent (to escape rebirths). Introvertive mystical experiences were first seen as transient ASCs that were only aids on the path to enlightenment for focusing and calming the mind, not cognitions of any transcendent realities or of any ultimate soteriological value. Rather, enlightenment is an insight into the nature of phenomenal reality and oneself. Mindfulness meditations—apparently an innovation of the Buddha—were the practice needed. The resulting mindful state of *nirvana* is an extrovertive mystical state of consciousness in which the enlightened experience the world and themselves as free of any "real" parts (i.e., independently existing, self-contained, eternal, permanent, and unchanging entities). The emotions associated with a sense of self (e.g., desire, greed, and hatred) have ended.

Early Buddhism is unique among the world religions in rejecting any search for a transcendent ground to the phenomenal world or a person. There are deities and demons in Buddhism, but no creator or sustainer of the phenomenal world or loving monotheistic sovereign lord of this world.[9] It is atheistic or agnostic in this regard. But the Indian desire for a transcendent unifying cosmic principle did return in the Mahayana with such doctrines as an innate "Buddha-nature." When transcendent realities entered the picture, introvertive mystical experiences took on greater cognitive and soteriological importance. The Buddha and Bodhisattvas also became deities in some Mahayana traditions. In Tantric traditions, through visualizations one could become a deity, but no mystical union is involved, since Buddhahood is already innate in us. Antinomian Tantrism also arose in one branch of Indian Buddhism (and in Hinduism). This branch of Tantrism uses immoral means to break attachments in order to attain enlightenment.

Helping others in their own quest to end suffering also became a central value in the Mahayana: Bodhisattvas end their own suffering by becoming enlightened, but they aid others and remain in the cycle of rebirths to continue that aid. This shifted the quest from merely ending one's own suffering (as in early Buddhism) to incorporating a moral concern for others. Compassion (*karuna*) became not merely a meditative exercise for self-cultivation, as with the Theravadins—it manifested itself in actual actions helping others.

Chinese Mysticism

The Dao is central to all Chinese mysticisms. The Dao transcends all phenomena as their source, but, unlike the nonpersonal ontological grounds in the traditions mentioned above, it remains an immanent part of the natural universe that guides all of nature and can be followed. Only human beings with our dualizing minds have fallen out of step with it. Pre–Axial Age ideas of ancestors, deities, and spirits were retained, but otherwise there is little interest in realities transcending the natural realm. There is no creator god or principle completely beyond the natural realm. The Dao is not personal in nature and has no will, and yet it can be characterized as benevolent and compassionate to all.

Thus, there is a difference here from both Western and Indian mysticism: we are to attune ourselves to the embedded principle that is actively ordering the natural world from within. Each person is a replica in miniature of the entire cosmos, and thus we can find the Dao within us and thereby resonate with the underlying guiding power of the entire universe. The overall goal was a long life in harmony within a person, between persons, and between humanity and the rest of the cosmos brought about by harmony with the Dao (in Neo-Confucianism the Great Ultimate [*taiji*], the immanent principle guiding the world [*li*], or the ultimate mind [*xin*]). Since this world is the only reality of immediate concern, extrovertive mystical experiences are valued over introvertive ones. But introvertive experience help cleanse the mind and harmonize it with the Dao. However, Chinese Buddhism retained a clearly transcendent goal, and becoming an immortal became the goal in Daoism.

The interlocking positive (*yang*) and negative (*yin*) flows of the world's vital energy (*qi*) needs to be balanced in us. Chinese mystics may speak of uniting the mind to the Dao when a person harmonizes with it, but there is no ontological "union" with the Dao to be attained since the Dao already flows in us—for Daoists, we merely have to clear away the personal and cultural clutter in our mind blocking its natural operation. With an "illuminated" mind, the Dao is manifested in our non-self-assertive actions (*wei wuwei*). This requires mystical "forgetting" and "unlearning," not the cultural learning of Confucianism, although Neo-Confucians did adjust that learning. With the final removal of the mental blocks, our actions automatically follow the natural ordering principle appropriate to human beings. The extrovertive enlightened state of mind, not any experiences inaugurating enlightenment, is emphasized. With the dualizing mind out of the way, the enlightened, in a new state of consciousness, move properly and spontaneously. Language and cultural conceptions are still present in the mind, but the enlightened mind is no longer confined by them.

The term "*wu-wei*" is part of a family of *wu*'s in the *Daodejing*, all indicating the absence of something: *wu-ji* (nonbeing), *wu-yu* (the absence of desire), *wu-xing* (absence of form), and *wu-zhi* (the absence of knowledge). But just as nonbeing (*wu*) is the positive source of being (*Daodejing* 40), so too each absence is filled by something positive: the absence of desire with enjoyment without attachments; the absence of learning with direct, nonconceptual knowledge of the Dao; and the "absence of action" with the power of the Dao. By yielding, we tap into an inexhaustible reserve of power, and all is accomplished: events occur of their own accord (*ziran*, "self-so"). We become empty of all self-assertion through uncultivation and consequently harmonize with the natural course of the Dao. The totality of our inner character is aligned with the Dao, and thus its power (*de*) shines forth. In sum, with our being firmly rooted in the Dao, our actions then express a state of being in which actions flow effortlessly and naturally rather than our struggling to implement some plan or desire. In this way, the enlightened live a long life free from strife.

Eliminating self-assertion and "purifying" or "illuminating" the mind so that it mirrors what is actually real are major themes, but they are not framed within a metaphysics questioning the existence of a self. Thus, the denial of the self is not a theme in Daoism or Neo-Confucianism. Even in Chinese forms of Buddhism, "no mind" is more central than "no self." One must give up self-based thoughts and actions to resonate with the Dao, but there is no denial of the reality of the person. Consciousness became more of a focus of attention after Buddhism arrived.

There is also a political dimension to Neo-Confucianism, and the sage-ruler is central to the *Daodejing*. Thus, mysticism and a political dimension to our social life were fused in much Chinese mysticism in a way not present in the traditions discussed above: this interest was never important in Indian and Western mysticisms—in fact, there it is almost totally absent. Other branches of Daoism are more individualistic, but for Daoists too being in harmony with other people through the Dao is part of being in harmony with all of the natural cosmos.

Buddhism took on a distinctly Chinese character in China, Chan/Zen most of all. Chan was influenced by both Daoist thought and meditation techniques. In turn Buddhism influenced Daoism and Neo-Confucianism. The doctrines of "no self" and *nirvana* played a lesser role. All the schools took on a depth-mystical interest in realities that at least approached transcending the natural realm through the transcendent dimension of the Dao as the "abyss" from which all phenomena flow or through "Buddha-nature," "Buddha-womb," or the immutable "One Mind" that is already always present in all phenomena and persons.

Mysticism Today

By the middle of the twentieth century, Asian religious teachers had began to set up camp in the West. Zen was the most popular tradition, but the most famous was Maharishi Mahesh Yogi's Advaita-influenced "Transcendental Meditation." The second half of the twentieth century also saw innovations in mysticism in the West prompted by natural science. Despite the West's decidedly unmystical culture today, "New Age" thinkers see an "Age of Spirit" dawning that will replace our current materialist and individualistic culture.[10] Some of the budding spirituality, whether separated from institutional churches or not, is mystical in nature. New Agers typically do not advocate a transcendent source of the world. The usual claim is that God is the universe, and so we are part of God. Such doctrines may be pantheistic (unlike traditional mysticisms), espousing a nonpersonal nontranscendent god as a universal force in the world and focusing on the natural realm and one's own well-being in it. When a transcendent source is advanced, it is also immanent to the phenomenal universe and is a cosmic "mind" or "consciousness" energizing the universe with love, and people have a transcendent core. Nature is seen holistically as a divine interconnected whole that is in an eternal process of evolution. Breaking attachments and addictions in a brief mystical experience may lead to a life of mystical detachment, but the experiencer may instead return to an ego-driven life in which these attachments eventually resurface and new ones may be formed. New Age gurus often think that having had a taste of mystical knowledge makes them "enlightened" even if they have not permanently overcome a sense of self and have returned to a dualistic state of consciousness. This has led to abuse of disciples (Feuerstein 1991; Storr 1996).[11]

Our culture's growing naturalistic atmosphere has also produced a new phenomenon: the total separation of mystical experience and meditation from even a superficial spiritual interest—a *secular mysticism*. For many, meditation and yoga are now practiced to relieve stress, anxiety, depression, and substance abuse, to manage pain, or to improve our attention, not the traditional core mystical goal of aligning our very being with a larger reality. The closest to traditional purposes are specific compassion meditations. Science is seen as supporting meditation, but only for its possible physical and psychological benefits. Meditating to enhance one's overall well-being now means well-being only within a secular framework—improved moods, self-esteem, and the overall satisfaction with one's current life. Simple forms of meditation that are geared toward such benefits rather than transforming one's character, such as Herbert Benson's "relaxation response," are growing. Hatha toga and tai chi started out as meditative techniques within mystical ways of life but in the West have now been reduced to stretching and flexibility exercises. Mystical experiences are then merely subjective events produced by the brain and do not involve a transcendent consciousness or other realities, or have any cognitivity. Nor need the experiences relate to the meaning of life.

Thus, mystical experiences and the means to facilitate them—in particular, mindfulness meditation—have become secularized for many people. And mysticism may persist in the West only in this nonreligious form. Religious texts may be useful today for outlining practices and delineating states of consciousness, but eventually they may be discarded as no more helpful here than in astronomy. In fact, while mystical experiences normally have a positive effect on one's religiosity, these experiences can lead to becoming convinced that no god or life after death exists, and to abandoning religion entirely (Newberg & Waldman 2016: 67–81).

Indeed, the emphasis on *experience* in mysticism can lead away from religion as a means to foster mystical experiences or as providing a framework for understanding them. In this way, mystical experiences and their cultivation have been absorbed into modern culture without any interest in understanding what has been experienced. The question of whether mystical experiences provide possible cognitive insights into an aspect of the phenomenal world or into a transcendent reality is not so much denied as simply a totally unseen issue. Neurological theories of the brain will explain all that is of interest—the only "truth" is whether meditation works for better psycho-physiological conditions, not whether one gains an insight into reality or participates in a transcendent reality. Mysticism is reduced from a full way of life to the cultivation of multiple mystical states for limited secular benefits. Psychedelic drugs become means for therapy or mere exotic recreational trips. The drugs may enable an experience in which the sense of self is obliterated during the experience, and after the trip one's perspective or priorities may be altered and thereby stress or anxiety is lessened, but no continuing altered states of consciousness is sought. So too, there is little interest in adopting any traditional mystical way of life. Today a common reaction is one that the clinical psychologist William Richards relates of a successful business leader who had a spontaneous experience that met all of Richards's criteria for a mystical consciousness—his response was "That was nice. What is it good for?" (2016: 124; see also Bharati 1976: 226–27).

— 8 —

Psychological, Sociological, and Cultural Approaches to Mysticism

Are all people equally open to mystical experiences, or are people of certain temperaments or from certain social classes more likely to have such experiences? Why do women appear to be more open to mystical experiences than men? Such questions have led to the examination of the psychological and social conditions underlying having mystical experiences. In the modern era, mysticism has all but been reduced to a psychological matter, and the focus in the study of mysticism has been on the psychology of mystics and their private mystical experiences. In the early twentieth century, scholars in the human sciences moved beyond accounts supplied by mystics and theologians to explanatory accounts of the causes and effects of mystical experiences and the nature of the experiences. The sociocultural setting of particular mystics also gained some attention but still much less than the psychology of mystics. Much of the work before the middle of the twentieth century was faith-based or explicitly atheistic.

Psychological Approaches

Today there are a variety of psychological approaches to mystical experiences (see Wulff 2013; Belzen & Geels 2003). William Parsons (1999) organized psychoanalytic approaches into three groups: regressive (approaches that treat mystical experiences as pathological or delusional), adaptive (approaches that bracket the cognitive issue and treat mystical experiences as a positive therapeutic mechanism to aid the ego), and transformative (approaches that accept mystical experiences as transcending the self and possibly being cognitions of transcendent realities). The latter two may also accept some regressive and pathological elements but treat mystical experiences in toto more positively. All of these approaches are present today, and they also have earlier precursors. (However, they have not affected the empirical psychological study of mystical experiences discussed in the next chapter.)

Early scientific interests included William James's study of first-person reports of conversion experiences and experiments with nitrous oxide. He was interested in the functioning of the mind of the religious, both the "healthy minded" and the "sick soul." He believed that mystical experiences had cognitive value ([1902] 1958: 292–94). However, since James Leuba in the 1920s, others have argued that these experiences are nothing but subjective brain events. Leuba saw mystical experiences as merely a matter of emotion and the need for self-esteem, with no cognitive import.[1] He also advanced the reduction of mystical experiences as involving "some activity of the sexual organs" ([1929] 2000: 138). That reduction is not endorsed much today, but treating mystical experiences as merely matters of emotion, and mystics' use of erotic symbolism as sublimating sexual urges remains common.

Sigmund Freud wrote little on mystical experiences, but he believed that they involve an "oceanic feeling"—a phrase he borrowed from his friend the Nobel Prize–winning novelist Romain Rolland.[2] Mystical experiences are a matter of emotion—a feeling of something "limitless, unbounded, something 'oceanic'" ([1930] 2010: 8–9). It is more a continuous state than a distinct experience—"a feeling of indissoluble connection, of belonging inseparably to the external world as a whole" (65). It is the vestige of an infantile condition in which the libido is not yet oriented toward objects in the outer world but directed inwardly (65). The state is something like limitless narcissism of the bond in breast feeding in which the ego is not differentiated. It is not the source of any ultimate truths and not the true source of religion (65). Freud wrote to Rolland that he had as little appreciation for mysticism as he had for music, but he saw it as a consciousness of the material world. Thus, Freud treated mystical experiences as more than religion (which he dismissed in *The Future of an Illusion* as a universal neurosis), but mysticism is still treated as pathological—seeking the "restoration of a limitless narcissism" before the ego was differentiated. Mystical experience is a regression to a childlike and prelinguistic state (Parsons 1999). Freud's last pronouncement on the subject was that a mystical experience "is the obscure self-perception of the realm outside of the ego, of the id" (quoted in Vergote 2003: 91) that is grounded in the libido. The ego has turned inward and obscurely perceives something beyond the constituted ego (93). Freudians today see mystical experiences as pathological and deviant—a regressive form of unconscious merging in which the experiencer reunites with the primal parent (Jacobs 1992: 262, 275).

Carl Jung accepted mysticism as one healthy path to growth and individuation (the integration of the personality). He believed that all experiences had content—"pure consciousness" is not possible. So too, consciousness is tied to the ego: "consciousness is inconceivable without an ego," for "if there is no ego there is nobody to be conscious of anything" (quoted in Kelly & Grosso 2007: 557). Mystical experiences are direct experiences of the universal archetypes in the collective unconscious. Jung's understanding of Asian religions was deeply flawed (Coward 1985), and he imposed his own psychological system onto them (Jones 1993b), but he influenced many theorists in mystical studies (e.g., R. C. Zaehner and Mircea Eliade), and his theory influences many in psychology and in the New Age movement today. His student Erich Neumann (1968) believed that human beings are *homo mysticus*: mystical experiences are a fundamental category of human experience and occur whenever consciousness is not centered around the ego—they are encounters with the non-ego and a part of the process of individuation involving the liberation of repressed psychological elements from the subconscious that leads to the ego's encounter with the "numinous transpersonal."

Both Freud and Jung, however, reduced mystical experiences to something natural, not encounters with something transcending the natural realm through negating and transcending the ego. Any alleged cognitive content is explained away. So too, for Abraham Maslow's (1964) transformative "humanistic psychology": mystical and nonmystical "peak experiences" are purely natural events that need not be interpreted religiously. These experiences are a type of knowledge and perception beyond that motivated by ordinary needs. They are not a matter of pathology but are part of the development of a psychologically healthy individual—indeed, they are the apex of "self-actualization." This theory also sees mystical experiences in terms of the separation and autonomy of the ego. Erich Fromm and Herbert Fingarette also retained a natural ego in their understanding of Zen. But for the more recent "transpersonal" movement, one does go beyond the sense of self to integrate with transcendent realities. This approach also incorporates mystical interests and embraces a spectrum of ASCs (Grof 1998; Washburn 2003; Ferrer & Sherman 2009). The theory in the humanistic and transpersonal schools relies upon perennial philosophy for doctrines or at least an essentialism of common phenomenological features in all mystical experiences and a universal inner mystical faculty in all people. But these schools have been marginalized in recent decades (McDaniel 2018: 310).[3]

Meditation and psychedelic drugs are now being used in psychotherapy (especially cognitive therapy) to deal with addiction, depression, and anxiety about death. This "applied mysticism" is used in conjunction with traditional talk therapy. Therapists are not interested in whether the experiences are veridical but only whether the experiences or the chemical changes help their patients. But the purpose is not that of classical mysticism. Rather, mystical experiences are being used in *the service of the ego*, as with Jung's individuation process. There may be a loss of the self-narrative, but the sense of a phenomenal self ends up being strengthened, not eliminated as in classical mysticism. Mystical techniques are utilized to integrate the ego, not expose that what makes up our individual personality is part of an illusion. In therapy, the "death of the ego" leads to the birth of a transformed and stronger ego and thus a more entrenched sense of a self. This leads some advocates of classical mysticism to see psychotherapists, including those who try to adapt Buddhism, as "pimps for *samsara* (the cycle of rebirths)," in the words of one Buddhist advocate. Like mysticism, psychotherapy is about altering our inner life and reducing anxiety, depression, and so forth, and it can alter one's former way of being, but mysticism's aim is transpersonal and incorporates ASC knowing by participation, while psychotherapy accentuates the ego—mystical knowledge of the nature of the self is not psychological self-knowledge. Indeed, mysticism may eliminate much of what makes each of us distinctive individuals in uprooting all self-centeredness and self-will in the inner quest to align ourselves with reality. Only aspects of one's individuality that are compatible with "reality as it truly is" as defined by one's traditions would remain.

Developing a sense of "self" involves neurological, psychological, and social factors, and most psychologists would no doubt see any loss of a sense of self or the surrender of all self-will as a sign of madness and would not recommend any way of life advocating abolishing that sense: the sense of self as a reality distinct from its own experiences, thoughts, emotions, and so forth that it has may vanish during a mystical experience, just as one loses a sense of time, but psychologists tend to see the later denial of the reality of the self as insane—such a reality is necessary to what it means to be human and is not an illusion. The happiest person on earth may be a mystic blissfully meditating alone in a cave for years without a sense of self, but that person would not be a complete human being.

But ego-dissolution is not necessarily a pathological experience: the mystical loss of a sense of self is not *self-destruction*—the reality that is truly there still remains intact. Only a loss of a sense of a distinct entity separated from the rest of the phenomenal world vanishes. Experiencers having mystical ASCs have a positive mental "set" of beliefs and expectations producing a more ordered, unified, and positive experience, not a fragmented state. The experience is independent of social reality, but mystics have a framework to stabilize the state. Even the hallucinations emerging from the subconscious can be positive. In Joseph Campbell's image, mystics and schizophrenics are thrown into the same water, but mystics have the training and framework to swim while schizophrenics are scared and panic. To some, this proves that mystical experiences are nothing but natural mental states; to others, the fact that schizophrenics cannot handle the state does not mean that the state may not open people to more of reality, and mystics may be able to handle it and have insights. In addition, while mystical experiences share some phenomenological features with schizophrenia in the disruption of a sense of self, the overall phenomenology of the two states is not the same, and despite superficial similarities the position that the two are the same is "absurd" (Parnas & Henriksen 2016: 76), even if schizophrenic episodes have often been seen in religious terms. Those who have mystical experiences appear to be as well-adjusted and physically healthy as their peers (Kelly & Grosso 2007: 555). In fact, apparently no other variables correlate as strongly with psychological well-being as having frequent mystical experiences (Sosteric 2017: 8; also see Hood & Byrom 2010).

Some psychologists see mystical experiences as a regression to the womb, the chaos of birth, infancy, or the connection of nursing—at least one psychologist saw mystical experiences as the regression all the way back to the union of sperm and egg at conception (Maven 1972).[4] The mystical and early infant states of consciousness do share a lack of linguistic ability and a sense of connection, but beyond that there is not anything except a psychoanalytic theory to suggest treating them as identical or that the insights resulting from the mystical experiences are related to the early experiences or are necessarily delusional. Ken Wilber emphasizes the "pre/trans fallacy": transcending the ego after the sense of self has emerged cannot be automatically equated with a return to a condition prior to that. Fewer psychologists adhere to this reduction today than in the past, but Jeffrey M. Masson and Sudhir Kakar used this theory in the 1980s and 1990s to analyze early Indian religiosity in terms of pathologies and traumas.

So too with the reduction of mystical experiences to repressed sexual impulses. Even if a diverted sexual drive is one natural condition within a celibate mysticism, it does not follow that mystical experiences can be reduced to that. The married mystics of Judaism, Islam, and other traditions would also have to be accounted for. Mystics have resorted to the intense language of a kiss, embrace, and sexual intercourse as analogies for the sense of merging, since we do not have a unique vocabulary for the felt sense of unity in mystical experiences alone, but this does not mean that the two experiences are identical or even have anything substantive in common. Why nontheists such as Advaitins and Theravada Buddhists are not prone to use such symbolism would need explaining if all mysticism could be reduced to misdirect repressed sexual urges. Tantrics who utilize sexual desire as a means to overcome attachments should be the norm—and since these mystics are not repressing or sublimating sex, why they still have any mystical drive at all is not obvious. Studying the role of the body in mystical practices, eroticism, and homoeroticism in mysticism has increased recently, but, as with Jeffrey Kripal's analysis of Ramakrishna (1995), this has understandably proven controversial.

Psychology can also contribute to the broader question of whether mystics express all that there is to being human. Being detached and passionless may reveal more to reality than we normally see and also expose the true reality behind a phenomenal "self," but aren't emotions and attachments also equally real and part of what it is to be truly human? Integrating mystical insights into our lives may expand what we are, but can the goal of life be to contemplate a nondual reality in an "eternal now"? Does a life aligned with reality involve more than what is revealed in mystical experiences?

Sociological Approaches

Mystical experiences involve inner personal experiences, but mysticism is a public social phenomenon. However, there was a tendency in the past to dismiss any social dimension to mysticism, or at least to downplay it as insignificant—the modern psychologization of mysticism limited its study to individuals' inner mystical experiences. So too, mystics were treated atomistically. In addition, mysticism was seen as inherently opposed to social interests and free of social influences. Scholars noted that mystics' actions mainly involve only individual one-to-one encounters, not social or political reform. Liberals within Christianity criticize mysticism for not being prophetic. Overall, the authority and restrictions of religious institutions make mysticism and institutionalism, in the words of William Inge, "strange bedfellows" (1947: 21).

However, that certain personal experiences are the unique element of mysticism does not privatize mysticism in the sense of making it solely an individual person's internal phenomenon. Mysticism is not a matter of psychology alone and cannot be reduced to episodic experiences or continuing states of consciousness. The goal of classical mysticism is an inner transformation of a new enlightened way of life, but the institutional and other social aspects of mystics' total ways of life remain important parts of the process. Thus, while the goal of mysticism is individualistic and private, this does not mean that mysticism is not an observable *sociocultural phenomenon*. So too, each tradition's beliefs and ways of life develop collectively over time. Mystical experiences are embedded in these ways of life, and so understanding a mystic's social context is needed to understand his or her claims. Trying to understand their claims and actions outside of their sociocultural context would be like trying to understand an animal outside of its physical environment—aspects of the animals can be so studied, but not all of them.

Thus, mysticism can be seen as a personal matter of cultivating certain states of mind without concluding that all traditional mystics are completely distinct from their communities. Most known mystics lived communally or otherwise within a society.[5] Mystics generally do not play the central cultural role that shamans play in tribal societies, but they have a role as teachers, preachers, and models of religious ideals. Even the wandering ascetics of Hinduism played a role in their society as a whole (being a source of karmic merit by receiving donations). Within religious institutions, some mystics have been known to be leading administrators and reformers. Cultivation of mystical experiences may be private, but there are social activities involved—the teacher/disciple training that is essential in all classical mysticism, rituals, group forms of meditation and prayer, social leaders (e.g., charismatic Sufi *shaykhs*), and monastic institutions. Mystics often join renewal protests, emergent groups, and messianic and millennian movements whose dynamics can be studied. The social dimensions in the construction of some mystical experiences can be studied (Spickard 1993: 114–17). Mystics may provide religious legitimation to their culture's ideology, social order, and status quo, or challenge them.

In sum, mystical social and cultural phenomena are not "expressions" of mysticism that can be expunged but *aspects* of all mystical ways of life. Thus, the study of the sociocultural dimension of mysticism is not tangential but the study of something mystical. In the past, some attention was paid to mysticism in general sociological studies of religion, but there was comparatively little attention paid to anything explicitly mystical. However, mysticism in established religions, new religions, and New Age groups can be investigated. There can be studies of, for example, the interaction of mystics and their societies, the social structure of mystical traditions, the role of a charismatic leader within a mystical community, mystics in religious institutions, the impact of modernization on mysticism, and the social and economic impact of monasteries and traditions of accepting many individual mystics in a society.

Throughout history, mystics have tended to be conservative on social matters except when coupled with a radical movement arising for nonmystical reasons (Ellwood 1999: 190). It also appears that most mystics in the past supported their religious institutions, but some mystics have been in tension with the established religious order of their time. Some reacted against the apparent worldliness of the clergy and the laity. Some (including women) have presented challenges to the power and authority of those in charge or to the accepted roles in society and have been seen as subversive. Is mysticism a means to empowerment? The anthropologist I. M. Lewis (1989) theorized that religious ecstasy is a means of access to political and social power for the politically and economically disenfranchised and marginalized groups. But Andrew Greeley (1975: 59) did not find this in his sociological research on mystical experiences in our modern industrial society. Today the postmodernist interest in power, oppression, class, race, ethnicity, and gender guides much research in this area.

But it is true that mystics in general want to transform the inner life of individuals, not outward worldly institutions. Early in the twentieth century, Jiddu Krishnamurti voiced the mystical point of view: social reform only scratches the surface; what is needed is an inner change of the person. But there have been exceptions. In the political branch of Daoism, Laozi saw transforming society as an effect of individuals aligning with the Dao. Mohandas Gandhi's life of "grasping the truth" (*satya-graha*) involved social and political dimensions—in particular, liberating India from British control and improving the social position of the "untouchables" within Indian society. Mystics' practice can also clash with the established order even when that is not the intent. For example, the Buddha's egalitarianism—accepting all people as followers regardless of class, caste, wealth, or sex—and telling his disciples to teach in the languages of their listeners rather than Sanskrit had repercussions for the Hindu Brahmanic order.

Thus, there are social actions to study in mysticism, as well as its social impact and its social structures such as gender, class, race, or ethnicity. So too, social historians may offer explanations for why, for example, societies in some eras and not others embraced mysticism as a way to holiness; or why so many of the high points in European mysticism occurred in periods of social disruption caused by plagues, a divided church, and technological innovations; or why "love" mysticism became dominant over "knowledge" mysticism when it did. The social organization of Zen has been studied (Preston [1988] 2012), and there have also been several anthropological studies of Buddhism (e.g., Spiro 1982; Gombrich 2006; Samuel 1995). But sociologists have generally ignored mysticism, even when studying religion (Spickard 1993: 124; Wexler 2013; Sosteric 2017). Andrew Greeley, Peter Berger, and a few others showed some interest in it, but the last theoretical model to be advanced was in 1912 when Ernst Troeltsch ([1912] 1981), using both broad and narrow definitions of "mysticism," divided religion into church, sect, and mysticism; mystics are a separate type within the social institution of the Christian church, with the church controlling the content of mystical experiences (Hood & Zhuo 2017: 582–84).

James Spickard noted in 1993 that up to then there had been little sociological work on mysticism (1993: 124), and things have not changed since then. Part of the sociologists' neglect is due to the fact that most sociologists simply have a hard time believing there is anything in mystical experiences worth studying (Sosteric 2017: 4). So too, they have tended to see mysticism as only a matter of personal experiences, and thus its study lies outside the scope of their interest in institutions and class. (But sociologists tend to accept a social construction of the self—a "self" exists only in relation to a community—and not treat persons atomistically.) Nor has the subject been a way to get ahead in an academic career but only a way to risk ridicule (4, 6). However, the observable social aspects and the social impact of mystical ways of life can be studied. Even the social dimensions of how different groups of scholars understand "mystical experiences" can be studied.

Gender Studies

The first women writers in the West, with a few exceptions, were Christian mystics (nuns had access to education); and they were also leaders and innovators within the Christian community (Hollywood 2002: 6). So too, there are women mystics who have been made saints. The four women "doctors" of the Roman Catholic Church (Teresa of Avila, Therese of Lisieux, Catherine of Siena, and Hildegard of Bingen) are all mystics. Even though many women were visionaries rather than mystics, the significance of women in Western Christian spirituality grew in the thirteenth and fourteenth centuries, when "love" mysticism came into prominence and when withdrawal from the world into monasteries and convents was no longer deemed necessary to cultivate mystical experiences. The lay Beguines influenced Meister Eckhart.

In the last quarter of the twentieth century, more attention began to be paid to mysticism as a cultural phenomenon and to mystics as embedded in cultural contexts. One approach is constructivism. Gender studies is another. Feminist scholars have been important in bringing out the cultural setting and social impact of mystics in Christianity. They have pointed out the male-dominated language and symbolism of Christianity in general (starting with "God the Father" and Eve being created from Adam) as well as Christianity's patriarchal organization. Suppressing women's visionary and mystical experiences was an effect of the general subordination of women by the church.[6] Medieval Christian ecclesiastical and cultural authorities also thought women were more susceptible to being possessed by the devil. Such beliefs led to marginalizing women and their experiences. The belief expressed by Julian of Norwich in the fourteenth century that "as truly as God is our Father, so truly is God our Mother" was ignored—indeed, in the Middle Ages the church prohibited women from interpreting the Bible and from engaging in formal philosophical discussions.

These medieval attitudes carried over into modern mystical studies (which was also male-dominated). Many medieval women mystics were often neglected. Grace Jantzen (1995) attacks the modern valuation of individuals' private experiences over the social and political effects of mysticism, and the treatment of such experiences as distinct from cultural settings that resulted from the early modern construction of the autonomous individual.[7] As she notes, any definition of "mysticism" is a social construct (12), and the modern definition seems male-oriented: the preoccupation with experience to the detriment of other aspects of mysticism (such as service to others), favoring "knowledge" mysticism over "love" mysticism (i.e., the intellectual and disembodied "ecstasy" over the emotional and "embodied" experiences integrating body and spirit and valuing relationships), valuing an overpowering "wholly other" transcendent reality over an embodied lover or marriage, discounting visions, and in general deemphasizing the role of the body and eroticism in the spectrum of mystical experiences (Hollywood 2002: 6). Women are presented at the high end of the emotional scale, and men at the high end of the intellectual scale; Teresa of Avila is presented as "hyperemotional," and Meister Eckhart as "serenely calm" (Wawrytko 1995: 200). Women are seen as more given to hysteria and also to using imagery of a suffering Christ more than are men. Marguerite Porete in 1308 was accused of heresy when she advocated a more "masculine" form of mysticism, and critics claimed she was not a "real woman."

But this situation is changing. Feminists focusing on medieval Christian mystics are building on the work of Caroline Walker Bynum in the 1980s on a distinctive female form of Western Christian mysticism emerging in the thirteenth century. Dorothee Soelle (2001) advocated a "democratized" mysticism that emphasizes it as a possible source of social and political change. She found in mystical literature "a refreshing liberation from categories of thought that belittle and denigrate women's spiritual lives," since mysticism is based on personal experiences of God and not on authority (Lanzetta 2005: 40–41). Beverly Lanzetta also believes that mystics search for the true nature of reality outside of social conditioning or established religion (41) and that social transformation would be part of any feminist mysticism and would erase the distinction between internal experiences and external political phenomena. But, she noted, contemplation as lived experience is not free of the gender bias, clerical exclusion, and theological subordination of women in patriarchal cultures (42).[8] However, a direct experience of a transcendent reality may be one place that frees women from male dominance. The fading of a sense of self in a mystical experience is seen as natural, since the self, along with gender identity, is taken to be socially constructed.

To read these women as merely engaging in social protest would be to miss the fact that they were genuinely expressing their inner experiences. Women predominate in the area of religious experience in general (Jacobs 1992: 277), and there is at least some evidence that women have a proclivity for certain types of mystical experiences—the connecting or uniting of the mode body-oriented "love" and "bridal" mysticism rather than the oneness and emptiness of the depth-mystical and "knowledge" experiences (277). But not all men's mystical experiences are of the "disembodied" type (i.e., a depth-mystical experience), nor are all women's of the "embodied" type (other introvertive and extrovertive mystical experiences). But are there some mystical experiences that are unique to women? Are there general differences in neurology in men and women grounding different experiences? Janet Jacobs (1992) suggests that men and women may have different mystical experiences. But further research is still needed to establish whether women contemplatives experience God differently than do their male counterparts, and thus whether there exists an experience that is uniquely women's (Lanzetta 2005: 42). Feminists agree that in the West women have a disproportionally greater percentage of mystical experiences than men—perhaps because women are brought up to be more receptive and to value relationships with others (masculinity is identified with autonomy and separateness and thus is a barrier to these experiences)—and that after mystical experiences women construe them differently than men (Jacobs 1992; Mercer & Durham 1999). According to Sandra Wawrytko, "more masculine" mystics tend to espouse an active, even aggressive role for the soul in its relationship to the divine—they possess God rather than vice versa (1995: 209). Among "more feminine" mystics, God transforms the soul into God's being (211). Eros is the most distinctive and pervasive element of feminine mysticism, manifested both as passionate outpourings and as erotic overtones in imagery (Wawrytko 1995: 203).[9]

There is a difference of emphasis (in particular, joy over knowledge) and in stylistic expression in Christian women mystics' writings that often reflects the individual mystic's social and educational background (Wawrytko 1995: 199–200). But does this mean that the actual *experiences* are different? Do women's introvertive differentiated experiences have a different content from men's? Or do women simply more typically take the path of love rather than that of knowledge? Or is there only a preference for the model of interpersonal relationships ("God the lover/spouse") over a relationship to "God the father" to explain the experience after the experience is over (1995: 219)? How does gender figure outside of experiences in total mystical ways of life? Further study of the role of women in Sufism, Tantrism, and other mystical traditions, and the nature of the cosmic female principle (*shakti*) in Bhakti Hinduism and Tantrism, may change our picture of women mystics further.

Different Dimensions of Mysticism

Currently there is no consensus of which approach is best for understanding the mystical element in persons and cultures, nor which theory within each approach is best. Does the choice itself depend on power dynamics? Sociologists make class or some other social structure primary for explanation. Sociologists use their particular tools, including surveys. Anthropologists have employed participant observation while trying to maintain objectivity and have attempted to provide "thick" descriptions of mystical phenomena. Anthropologists may also advance theories of how mystical experiences may have affected our physiological evolution and how mysticism affected our social and cultural evolution. Scholars in religious studies may employ meditation and psychedelic drugs to study mystical experiences, and participant observation to study other aspects of mysticism. Feminist theorists make gender one essential structure. Are race, class, and gender part of the total proper social context for understanding mystical experiences and other phenomena? Psychologists make the development of the person and the mind the proper context for understanding. But in the past the psychology of mysticism was "mostly impressionistic" (Staal 1975:116). Today there is more empirical testing of theories in clinical studies.

Social explanations also have not often been very satisfactory. Not only do they not explain how social forces could generate mystical experiences, their explanations of mysticism in general usually reflect broad theoretical perspectives rather than tightly tested hypotheses. Opposite causes have been proposed to explain the same mystical phenomenon. For example, the rise of Buddhism has been explained both as the result of the new wealth in northeastern India at the time and as a response to the overall poverty in India at the time. So too, the role of the changeless transcendent Brahman in the Upanishads has been explained as an idea of permanence and stability that countered the turbulent political, social, and economic changes occurring in society at the time, while the Buddhist emphasis on impermanence has been explained as reflecting those same changes. But if the same social conditions could produce very different mystical reactions, they offer no explanations at all.

Social explanations in the past, like psychological explanations, have often been reductive. Even if some theorists see mysticism as fulfilling a positive role in society, they still often dismiss mystical claims as nothing but reflections of social structures, and thus they conclude that mystics are mistaken about the true causes of their experiences. For example, the anthropologist Edmund Leach believed that the spirits of highland Burmese Buddhists are nothing more than projections of social relationships upon the cosmos—ways of describing the formal relationships that exist between the real people and groups of ordinary society (1954: 182). However, such reductive approaches are not as popular today as in the mid-twentieth century. Today reducing all aspects of mysticism to either personal experiences or observable sociocultural phenomena seems problematic. Nevertheless, most social scientists today do not seem interested enough in the issue of the possible cognitivity of mystical experiences to bother taking a stand on the matter.

However, none of the different approaches appear to be exhaustive or *the* explanation of mystical experiences and other mystical phenomena. No human phenomenon is one-dimensional—purely psychological or sociological or cultural. Mysticism clearly has psychological, social, and cultural dimensions (including religious meanings). As noted in chapter 6, mystical experiences and other mystical phenomena are not sui generis realities that are shielded from study as human phenomena, but for nonreductive scholars in mystical studies that does not mean that they must be reduced to something nonmystical. Many accept that only when all the different approaches are taken collectively, with each approach illuminating one dimension of mysticism, can we arrive at our best picture of mysticism. This would include the origin and functioning of mystical experiences and mysticism for a person and within society. More awareness today of mysticism in non-Western settings is also challenging parochial approaches and theories. But currently psychologists and sociologists and members of other disciplines studying mysticism generally do not appear to be communicating with each other to devise a more encompassing theory.

— 9 —

The Scientific Study of Mystical Experiences

The scientific study of people undergoing mystical experience goes back to the 1930s and picked up in the 1960s and 1970s—for example, studies of respiration, skin conductance, EEG examinations of meditators' brain activity, and John Lilly's sensory-deprevation tanks. Herbert Benson explored the "relaxation response" detached from any religious context (Benson & Klipper 2000). In the 1980s, Michael Persinger made news with his claim to be able to generate religious visions with his "God helmet" (1987). There were also studies of the powers of yogins to, for example, change the temperature of parts of their bodies and to affect systems in the body thought to be automatic. So too, research showed that meditation produced effects different from simply sitting quietly and resting with one's eyes closed. And since the 1990s—the "Decade of the Brain"—neuroscientists have become interested in consciousness, and advancements in noninvasive brain imaging technology have led to a marked increase in studies of the effects in real time of meditation and psychedelic drugs on the brain's activity. Indeed, scanning subjects' brains during meditation and controlled psychedelic drug sessions has become an important part of the budding field of cognitive neuroscience. In particular, the neural mechanisms supporting mindfulness meditation have become a hot topic.[1] Neuroscientists are both collecting empirical data on brain activity and advancing new explanations and theories of how the brain works.

Neurological Effects of Meditation

It is hard to doubt that there must be a biological basis enabling mystical experiences to occur. These experiences are firmly embodied: even if theistic mystical experiences involve a unique input from God, there still must be some basis in the human anatomy that permits God to enter our mind. The Dalai Lama suggests that there may be no neural basis for a transcendent "pure consciousness" (Gyatso & Goleman 2003: 42), but even if such consciousness exists independently of human beings, there still must be some basis in the brain that enables us to become aware of it. So too with Brahman, a godhead, or the ground of being making itself manifest in our awareness. That is, mystical states of consciousness must somehow be mediated by the neurological processes in the brain, and that activity can be detected. Mystical experiences do not differ from any other experiences in this regard. Thus, pointing out neurological bases in no way begs the question about mystical cognitivity: even if these experiences produce an insight, they need a biological basis to do so.

The neuroscientific approach depersonalizes mystical experiences in that it focuses only on brain activity, not the "subjective" experiences themselves, and for this the personal history of an experiencer is deemed irrelevant. Neuroimaging technology is beginning to identify the areas of the brain that become more active or less active during mystical experiences enabled by meditation or psychedelic drugs. Establishing one-to-one correlations of conscious states with physical states of the brain would permit the stimulation of the areas in the brain that are more active during mystical experiences, thereby enabling an experience. But neuroscientists have established that meditation has reproducible and measurable effects on the body.[2] Different techniques and stages of practices (beginners versus advanced yogins) produce different effects. The effect of meditation on various physiological functions have been studied (e.g., changes in heart rate, respiration, or a general reduction of metabolic activity), as have changes in neural activity in the brain. Meditation's effect on such mental activity as attention, working memory, responses to stimuli, perceptual processing, a sense of self, and the regulation of emotional states have been studied.

The brain is not a collection of isolated parts but an interconnected web. Thus, all areas of the brain are active to one degree or another during these experiences, but specific areas and structures are drawing attention. The left and right parietal lobes ground both a sense of a self that is separate from the rest of the universe and a sense of one's body in space. Decreased activity in the lobes is associated with the loss of a sense of self and an increased sense of unity or connectedness with the rest of the universe. The thalamus processes sensory input and the communication between different parts of the brain; it is important for alertness and consciousness in general. The limbic regions are related to processing emotions, including a sense of peacefulness. Nondirective mindfulness meditation decreases activity in these regions, while guided meditation (such as compassion meditations) increases it. The hippocampus in the limbic system relates to long-term memory and spatial orientation. The right insula and caudate nucleus are related to empathy and compassion. The frontal cortex relates to higher cognitive activity such as reasoning, analysis, and imagination; initial meditative reflection may lead to an increase in activity leading to a sense of clarity, but further meditation leads to decreasing activity there that permits deeper parts of the brain to become more active, and this may be connected to the sense of certainty in mystical experiences. The temporal lobe appears to be the locus of language, conceptualizing, and abstract thought, and this area appears to have some decease in activity during mystical experiences (Newberg, d'Aquili & Rause 2001: 24–25). The decrease in this activity may permit integrating thought processes in different areas of our brain and permit in more information from parts of our brain that had evolved before the frontal lobes (Winkelman 2014, 2016).

Neuroplasticity also comes up in the study of meditators. Meditation appears to be a case of mind affecting matter: apparently it rewires the brain by expanding the connections between parts of the brain not normally connected, and increasing the size of areas of the brain that are normally underused.[3] It seems to effect functional and structural changes and may increase the density of gray matter in the prefrontal cortex and insula (Newberg & Waldman 2016: 41–63).[4] In advanced meditators, brain alternations are present even in deep sleep (Goleman & Davidson 2018: 234). Meditation may affect the molecular level—for example, stress-reducing practices may quiet genes that cause inflammation. In short, it may be the case that not only can we modify our mode of awareness but we can also shape our brain and thus affect our mind to the extent it is dependent on the brain. (If consciousness is a causal reality affecting the brain or other parts of the body, then neuroscience as practiced today is not merely incomplete but fundamentally misguided.)

Whether mystical experiences involve real insights into the nature of reality or are delusional, today it is increasingly becoming apparent that they are real and can be observed and measured (e.g., Newberg, d'Aquili

& Rause 2001: 7, 143; Yaden et al. 2017a: 60). There may be no one area of the brain devoted to mystical experiences, but there is evidence of distinctive configurations of brain activity uniquely associated with mystical experiences—certain areas light up more during scans, indicating that a mystical experience is occurring even if it is not enabled by only those areas. However, by "real" neuroscientists mean only that mystical experiences involve *distinct neurological events*—that is, they are not merely ordinary experiences interpreted as mystical or products of the imagination. Many scientists are remaining neutral on whether these experiences are authentic encounters with a transcendent reality or are delusions. That is, "People may or may not actually be connecting to God or the supernatural, but ultimately there is something very powerful going on *inside* the brain" (Newberg & Waldman 2016: 25). That many experiencers today understand their mystical experiences in nonreligious and sometimes explicitly atheistic ways should again be noted (e.g., 69–75). So too with mindfulness: scientists may confirm that, say, Buddhist meditative techniques calm the mind, but this does not confirm Buddhism's theories of rebirth and liberation. Learning more about the necessary neural or physiological bases to these experiences may help in reproducing them, but that does not relate to the doctrines that mystics espouse.

Can Mystical Experiences Be Studied Scientifically?

The results of these studies have garnered enthusiasm both from the religious who believe the results prove that mystical experiences are genuine and thus cognitive, and from materialists who believe that the results prove that mystical experiences are only brain events and thus refute religious claims. But we still must ask whether *mystical experiences* themselves can be studied scientifically.

In 1993, Eugene d'Aquili and Andrew Newberg conducted experiments on experienced meditators—three Christian Franciscan nuns and eight Tibetan Buddhist monks—using SPECT neuroimaging technology to measure blood flow in different areas of the brain during meditation. By observing the limbic system of the right temporal lobe, the thalamus, the prefrontal cortex, and the parietal lobes they found that certain concentrative meditative techniques (which focus attention upon one object) led to the hyperactivation of the limbic system through the overload of sensory and kinesthetic stimulation, while certain "emptying" meditative techniques also led to the hyperactivation of the limbic system through sensory deprivation (d'Aquili & Newberg 1999: 110–16).[5] The decrease of activity in the temporal lobe leads from a sense of being in control to a sense of surrender. D'Aquili and Newberg hypothesize that both the overload of sensory and kinesthetic stimulation and the deprivation of such stimulation lead to the partial or total elimination of neural signals to the orientation and association areas of the parietal lobes that are responsible for maintaining both a sense of a "self" separate from the rest of the universe and a sense of one's body in space, thereby leading to mystical experiences—that is, a loss of any sense of an individual self.[6] The decrease of activity in the parietal lobes was accompanied by an increase of activity in the prefrontal cortex in the right hemisphere related to attention, focusing, and concentration. When combined, these lead to a sense of selflessness and being absorbed into an infinite spaceless and timeless void.[7] (Brain lesions in the same areas may have the same effect.)

D'Aquili and Newberg got *similar neurological readings* for both groups, and yet the Christians and Buddhists claimed to have had *radically different experiences*—the Christians experienced a closeness and mingling with God ("union with God") while the Buddhists experienced a lack of boundaries (being "endless and intimately interwoven with everyone and everything the mind senses") (Newberg, d'Aquili & Rause 2001: 6–7). The two groups had different meditative techniques, but the resulting experiences affected the same areas of everyone's brains (Newberg & Waldman 2016: 91). This raises an important issue for the question of whether neuroscience provides any understanding of mystical experiences: did the nuns and monks have *different experiences*, or did they merely *interpret* (or misinterpret) the *same experiences* differently when they looked back on the experiences after they were over? If these nuns and monks had genuinely different experiences, this means that exactly the same set of neurological bases were present for different mental events. Earlier Herbert Benson found a great variety of "subjective" (i.e., experiential) responses—including no change of consciousness at all—accompanying the same physiological changes produced by his concentrative relaxation technique (Benson & Klipper 2000: 130).

But if different types of mystical experiences occur with the same neurochemical state of the brain (the inverse of the "multiple realization" problem in philosophy of mind) or in the same ASC, that would need an explanation. If different states of the mind can have the same biological base, scientists may be capturing the brain activity during a meditative state that may be the same whether a mystical experience is occurring or not. So too the brain conditions may be the same and yet different mystical experiences or other ASC experiences are occurring. Thus, the explanation of the experiential level would still be missing from any neuroscientific account. The experiencers' entire ASCs might have been quite different, not merely different experiences within the same state of consciousness. Perhaps in the future differences in the neurological bases during these experiences may be found with new technologies that do establish one-to-one correlations of different experiences and brain states. But without such precise correlations a neuroscientific explanation of mystical experiences is not possible: all mystical experiences would be grounded in some brain state, but simply identifying the brain state would not explain why a given experience was realized in that brain state. Nor would an explanation rule out that that experience might be realized with another brain state. This would have major implications: How could we be certain that similar third-person data about brain activity for different meditators indicates similar experiences? Are these experiences (or experiences more generally) not products of the brain at all?

Moreover, it is hard to argue that neuroscience actually studies *experiences* at all. It is not as if mystical experiences are observed by examining certain activity in the brain. Consider the well-known problem of a gap between brain conditions and consciousness (Jones 2013: 109–110): how do we get from the action of matter to something completely different—the felt experiences and the other subjectivity of the mind? Consciousness is something that we can be aware of only subjectively—we can speak about it as an "object," but that is not how we know it.[8] No analysis of matter suggests the presence of phenomena of a radically different nature or why it should appear—we cannot get from the physics of a broken leg why there is the felt experience of pain, and so with all of the inner experiences of consciousness. Eliminationists in cognitive science simply deny subjectivity altogether. Reductionists reduce all mental phenomena to brain activity or bodily behavior, and so studying the brain *is* studying conscious experiences (98–102). But for the rest of us, the gap problem presents a very real issue of whether the *subjectivity* inherent in any experience can be studied *scientifically* at all. No third-person scientific account or second-person interview can capture first-person experiences.[9] Any third-person observation of brain activity cannot give us knowledge of anything but an object, and the felt experience cannot be made into an object: even if the mind and the brain are materially identical, there is a lived "inside" to experiences and perspectives that cannot be studied from the "outside" by examining the brain. Even the emerging technology that "reads minds" reads only brain states, not experiences or subjectivity. Neurological scanning can show only what the brain is doing or not doing during an experience but not the experience itself.

The inability of one person to witness what another one experiences applies equally to meditative and other mystical experiences: identifying what is going on in the brain when a mystical experience occurs is one thing; what meditators are actually *experiencing* is quite another—the felt sense of selflessness, unity, timelessness, and so on simply cannot be studied at all by examining the electrochemical activity of the brain. Mystical "knowledge by participation" does not bridge the gap between the felt experience and the observable objective brain events underlying the experiences. This means that scientists do not study *mystical experiences* at all when they study the neurological basis of an experience. In the end, neuroscientific findings are simply irrelevant to questions of the *nature* of mystical experiences. At best, neuroscience may tell us something of the general human experiential and cognitive ability by showing what our brain does but not anything more specific regarding the experienced content.[10]

Are There "Pure Consciousness Events"?

Most naturalists believe that there can be no consciousness without an object being present to the subject. Following the nineteenth century philosopher/psychologist Franz Brentano, most philosophers accept that consciousness is inherently intentional: when there is no object, there is no consciousness. As John Searle puts it, "Conscious states always have a content. One can never just be conscious, rather when one is conscious, there must be an answer to the question, 'What is one conscious of?' " (1992: 84).

However, some neuroscientists and psychologists today are quite comfortable accepting a pre-reflective, "pure" experience free of all intentional objects (e.g, Hood 2001). If so, some experiences are not experiences *of* anything: if the depth-mystical experience is in fact empty of all content but consciousness itself, the experience would not have an object distinct from the experiencer or any differentiated content in the mind. D'Aquili and Newberg suggest that scientific research supports the possibility that awareness can exist without a self (Newberg, d'Aquili & Rause 2001: 126). Personal reports also are also relevant (see Forman 1990, 1999, for examples). The psychiatrist Philip Sullivan (1995) reported his own experience of an empty awareness of "something that was not nothing." It was an experience that was devoid of content, and yet he was not unconscious but aware—an awareness without any subject of awareness or sense of personal ownership and without any object of experience. Only the transitional states back to the ordinary baseline state of consciousness that were separate from the pure consciousness event had any informational content (53, 57). So too, mystical states themselves become objects of consciousness only after the they are over and the experiencer has returned to a dualistic state of consciousness.

Psychedelic Drugs and Mystical Experiences

Scientific interest in psychedelic drugs waned after the 1960s. But Rick Strassman (2001) experimented with DMT in the 1990s. And interest in psychedelics has been renewed today in the study of the brain. These drugs apparently deactivate regions of the brain that integrate our senses and our sense of a self, thereby permitting other areas of the brain to become more active. That is, psychedelics expand the mind by (paradoxically) inhibiting certain brain activities. In addition to more intense visual and auditory sensations, this can lead to an extrovertive mystical sense of being connected to the rest of reality without any memory loss. Psychedelics have been found reliably to disrupt self-consciousness and occasionally ego-dissolution in an orderly dose-dependent manner (Nour & Carhart-Harris 2017: 178).[11] The sense of self that is dissolved in a number of ASCs, including mystical ones, is the coherent ego-identity (the "narrative self") built up by different neural networks, but when that is dissolved, the "minimal self" of first-person experiences, including a sense of unity, ownership of experience, and agency, remains (177; Lebedev et al. 2015). (Mindfulness meditation can also dampen the activity in the brain that generates a self-narrative.[12])

It is important to note that, as with meditation, ingesting a psychedelic does not assure *any* ASC experience. William Richards reports that a substantial number of people have ingested psychedelics on many occasions without experiencing any profound ASCs (2016: 15)—indeed, people can take psychoactive drugs hundreds of times without encountering the sacred (2016: 657). J. Harold Ellens agrees: many persons also have taken psychedelics repeatedly and never come close to experiencing profound states of consciousness, spiritual or otherwise (2014: 2:22–23). Thus, calling drugs "*triggers*" is something of a misnomer since nothing can *force* a mystical experience in a mechanical fashion to occur 100 percent of the time—even with a supportive set and setting, having a mystical experience is not guaranteed.[13]

In addition, different drugs appear to act differently—LSD and psilocybin have different effects on serotonin receptors that regulate neurotransmitters, and LSD mystical experiences seem less intense than psilocybin-enabled ones (Winkelman 2017: 3). So too "cosmic consciousness" and LSD visionary experiences may be qualitatively different states of consciousness (Smith & Tart 1998). As Huston Smith said, "There is no such thing as *the* drug experience per se—no experience that the drugs, as it were, secrete" (2000a: 20). Drugs break the hold of the ordinary self-driven dualistic subject/object mode of mind by altering the chemistry of the brain in relevant areas, but what occurs in the mind after this "default mode network" of our baseline consciousness is disrupted depends on other factors than the brain chemistry. For this reason, it is not correct to refer to drugs as the *cause* of a mystical experience: it is part of a package of causes and conditions that can enable a mystical experience by disrupting a sense of self, but it is not a simple mechanical causal trigger of any experience. In sum, ingesting drugs is one way to arrange the necessary conditions in the brain for a mystical experience, but it is not sufficient to create any particular experience.

In one psilocybin double-blind study, one-third of the participants considered their experience the most significant spiritual experience of their lives, and for another quarter it was one of the top five, and this significance was still persisting when the participants were questioned fourteen months later (Griffiths et al. 2006, 2008, 2011; also see Barrett & Griffiths 2018). The researchers found that the experiences enabled by psilocybin were meaningful and life-altering, producing persisting positive changes in attitude, mood, life satisfaction, behavior, altruism/social effects, and social relationships with family and others. A long-term study of Walter Pahnke's 1962 "Good Friday" psilocybin experiment also showed that for many participants the drug-enabled mystical experiences had lasting positive effects on their attitude and behavior, and persisting negative effects for a few; how they saw their experiences also changed slightly over time (Doblin 1991). (No participants became enlightened but returned a dualistic state of mind.) The effects included recognizing the arbitrariness of "self" boundaries, a deepening of faith, and a heightened sense of joy and beauty. Most of the psilocybin recipients had subsequent mystical experiences in dreams, prayer, out in nature, or with other psychedelics. Significant differences between their non-drug- and drug-enabled mystical experiences were reported: the drug-enabled experiences were reported as both more intense and composed of a wider emotional range; the non-drug-enabled experiences were composed primarily of peaceful, beautiful moments, while the drug-enabled experiences had moments of great fear, agony, and self-doubt. Feelings of unity led many of the subjects to identify with and feel compassion for minorities, women, and the environment; it also reduced their fear of death.

The negative side of psychedelics mentioned in chapter 3 should be noted again: these drugs can enable disturbing and terrifying experiences—visions of hells, not only heavens. "Bad trips" can deeply disturb a person's emotional balance. (Meditation may also enable very negative experiences, but it appears to do so less often.) The dissolution of a sense of a self is an "experience of death," and destabilizing a sense of a self can be terrifying and dangerous for someone not prepared for it, even if one is psychologically healthy, and can exacerbate mental disorders and lead to psychotic episodes. (Researchers suggest that more screening of participants for psychological difficulties would lessen the number of negative experiences.) It seems that the disruption of consciousness occasioned by drugs may lead to too much too fast for some people. But if one is prepared psychologically and has a framework of meaning, one can better handle experiences associated with the changes in brain activity. Moreover, the negative effects, unlike the positive ones, do not appear to last past the drug session as often (Griffiths et al. 2006, 2008).

However, such experiences have also led some drug users to adopt a mystical way of life. But when a drug-facilitated experience occurs to someone not already seeking a religious way of life, they may dismiss any sense of oneness or interconnectedness the next day as nothing more than a delusion produced by the chemical reaction in the brain, just as LSD's effects on perception are usually dismissed. Thus, drugs have not proven to be efficient in producing mystical lives. Hence, the mystical objection to drugs: mysticism is about aligning one's life with reality, not any brief experience, not even if it is a taste of a selfless consciousness. Psychedelic drugs lead some people to Buddhism or Hinduism, but those who seriously pursue a tradition usually give up the drugs since they do not initiate a continuous state of mystical consciousness but enable only transient experiences. Most drug users and meditators return to our ordinary baseline state of consciousness after their experiences, not to a state altered by the loss of the sense of a self. Enlightenment establishes a new default state of consciousness for the mystic, but becoming enlightened requires hard work, not a brief experience. Meditation and other practices within a tradition help internalize the tradition's worldview and values—without that preparation an isolated experience, no matter how profound, does not. These experiences can show us that we are not identical to a phenomenal self, but the self can return quickly. The experiences may break attachments and addictions and lead to a life of mystical detachment, or one may return to a life in which these attachments resurface and new ones formed. In sum, drugs can occasion glimpses of alleged transcendent realities in introvertive mystical experiences and can break the cycle of attachments at least momentarily, but they are not as effective in integrating these insights into a person's life. Thus, a psychedelic experience is not an easy substitute for a mystical way of life.

As noted above, drugs alone do not touch off a mystical experience but open the mind to having possible visions or mystical experiences depending on other factors in the experiencer's mental makeup. Thus, "set and setting" are important in producing mystical experiences. That is, differences in a user's background beliefs, preparation, expectations, disposition, propensity for ASCs, personality traits, mood, and past experiences with drugs (one's mental "set") and the physical and social environment in which a drug is ingested (the "setting") at least partially account for the great variation in the experiences enabled by the drug.[14] Genetics may be a factor, even if there is no specific "God gene." Thus, every experience involves a mixture of at least three ingredients: the drug, one's mental set, and the social and physical setting (Smith 2000a: 20). A frame of mind prepared for or expecting some religious experience to arise or the possibility of a mystical experience occurring and a religiously inspiring physical and social environment increase the likelihood of such an experience, even if the resulting visionary or mystical experience is not what the experiencer expected. A laboratory setting may negatively affect both the possibility of having a mystical experience and its phenomenological content. Even a researcher calling the drug an "entheogen" rather than a "hallucinogen" affects the experiencer's mental set through an "expectancy bias."[15]

This eliminates any simplistic reduction of mystical experiences to a mechanical effect of drugs: drugs disrupt the neural events underlying our normal state of consciousness and bring other natural brain processes into prominence, but what experience occurs depends on other factors.[16] For example, people who are highly open to new experiences are more likely to have positive experiences, while people who are emotionally unstable or rigidly conventional in their views are likely to experience greater anxiety and confusion and have disturbing experiences. Psilocybin users who are relatively unchurched are more likely to have mystical experiences than those who are deeply entrenched in traditional beliefs and practices (Newberg & Waldman 2016: 240, 247). When drugs are used recreationally, fewer mystical experiences occur (235–36). Ralph Hood (2013: 301) found that persons rate prayer-occasioned mystical experiences as more legitimate or "real" than drug-enabled ones, more so to the extent that persons are religiously dogmatic, and that the more "spiritual" persons report drugs as a trigger, whereas the more "religious" do not. Nevertheless, even with a naturalist set and setting, about a quarter or a third of the general population will have a religious experience; when subjects have a religious proclivity in a supportive environment, the figure jumps to three-quarters (Smith 2000a: 20).

The role of our mindset in mystical experiences raises the issue of whether members of different religions and nonbelievers all have the same mystical experiences. Each person has a unique subconscious mindset making each experience unique, with the only possible exceptions being a depth-mystical experience that is completely empty of any differentiated content (and thus having no content to be affected by individual differences) and a concept-free "pure" mindfulness experience.

Are Drug-Enabled Theistic Mystical Experiences the Same as Natural Ones?

According to the scientific reports, psychedelics enable visions of realities distinct from the experiencer more often than mystical experiences. In addition, psychedelics do not enable introvertive mystical experiences as readily as extrovertive ones, and the introvertive ones are typically those with differentiated content rather than the depth-mystical experiences without differentiated content. Any sense of a transcendent reality is typically non-personal, and theists sometimes later reinterpret their conception of "God" as nonpersonal (e.g., the ground of being or consciousness) in order to fit the experience.[17]

But one recurring issue is whether mystical experiences occasioned by drugs are the *same in nature* as those occurring either spontaneously or through mystical practices. Are drug-enabled experiences in fact not duplicating the full phenomenology of a mystical experience occurring "naturally" even with a positive religious set and setting? Or are some experiences that are facilitated by drugs not merely *similar* to what are deemed "genuine" mystical experiences but in fact *genuine* mystical experiences? The prevailing view in scientific discussions of psychedelics is that drug-enabled mystical experiences are the same in nature as those facilitated by other means such as yoga or fasting—the drugs produce the same effects in the brain as those activities do, and thus the resulting mystical experiences are of the same type. The evidence for this is that the phenomenology of the experiences enabled either way appears to be the same, as revealed in the firsthand depictions of mystical experiences in descriptive accounts from both traditional mystics around the world and today's drug subjects. As the philosopher Walter Stace said of chemically facilitated experiences, "It is not a matter of its being *similar* to mystical experience; it *is* mystical experience" (quoted in Smith 2000a: 24). Huston Smith concurred: given the right set and setting, "drugs can induce religious experiences that are [phenomenologically] indistinguishable from such experiences that occur spontaneously" (20). The triggers are a matter of "causal indifference" (Stace 1960b: 29–30).

However, many theists object on theological grounds that drug-enabled theistic experiences are not "genuine" mystical experiences but only pale copies—true theistic mystical experiences are different in nature and content and come only from God. Drug experiences are delusions to be dismissed, like their cousin the LSD distortion of perception, not the mystical "intoxication with God" through a direct encounter with a transcendent personal reality that is given by God's grace. The Roman Catholic R. C. Zaehner was an early advocate of this view (for a similar claim, see Katz 2013: 3–4; Horgan 2003: 44–45). Zaehner believed that the drug taker's consciousness bears only "a superficial resemblance to that of the religious mystic" (1957: xii).[18] He did accept that "nature" and "monistic" mystical experiences may be enabled by drugs, but he insisted that "theistic" introvertive mystical experiences can be produced only by acts of grace from God (14–29). That is, no set of natural conditions or "artificial" stimulation, such as ingesting a drug, can *compel* God to act in any way or force himself to be known against his will. So too, if genuine mystical experiences could occur to people without Christian faith, then grace would not be restricted to Christians. That comparatively few *theistic* mystical experiences occur through drugs also upsets theists—most drug-enabled introvertive mystical experiences do not involve any sense of connecting with a reality that is personal in nature. Some theists have found their own drug-enabled mystical experiences to be more intense than "natural" ones (Doblin 1991: 14), but drug-enabled experiences, especially those occurring outside of mystical training, apparently are not as full in content as cultivated mystical experiences.

The identity of natural and drug-enabled experiences is so only if the phenomenological content of the experiences is indeed the same, but the variety of mystical and visionary experiences, both natural and drug-enabled, complicates the issue. Nevertheless, the experimental reports indicate that at least some of the experiences enabled by drugs share the full phenomenology of spontaneous and cultivated theistic mystical experiences and cannot be dismissed as mere "drug experiences." Indeed, there is empirical evidence that drug-enabled experiences are *more intensely mystical* (perhaps because of the degree of visceral subjective and sensory changes), more positive in their impact, and more related to spiritual and existential outcomes than those enabled by other means (Yaden et al. 2017b).[19] Members of different religions, seekers with no religious affiliation, and atheists may have different experiences due to their mental set, but differences in the set and setting or dosages account for any differences in the phenomenology of drug-facilitated experiences. (That drugs cannot *force or guarantee* a mystical experience weakens the objectors' case—more than the drug's neurological effect is always involved.)

Thus, despite theological objections, based on the empirical evidence, there is no reason to believe that mystical experiences that occur under the influence of drugs are different in nature from all those resulting from meditation—the former are as genuine as the latter, and the neurochemical condition of the brain is the same in both cases. In short, there is no evidence in these experiments for the theists' claim that God intervenes only in non-drug-enabled experiences.

Mystical Experiences and Pathology

Another area of scientific research was touched upon in the last chapter: the relation of mystical experiences to experiences resulting from pathology—for example, brains damaged by trauma, psychosis, or schizophrenia. A reduction based on pathology was common in the mid-twentieth century and to a lesser extent continues today.

Epileptic microseizures in the left temporal lobe were also a common explanation. Early in the twentieth century, William James derided the "medical materialism" that explained away Paul as an epileptic whose vision on the road to Damascus was merely a discharging lesion of the occipital cortex; Teresa of Avila as a hysteric; and Francis of Assisi as a hereditary degenerate ([1902] 1958: 29). It remains common to conclude that there is "little doubt" that the experiences of at least some mystics from history, such as Teresa of Avila and Catherine of Siena were the result of temporal lobe epilepsy even though scientists admit that their biological details are "too meager to allow an accurate assessment" (Dewhurst & Beard 1970: 504). But a more recent study of medieval Christian mystics and ascetics did not turn up evidence of any major forms of mental illness such as schizophrenia or manic-depressive disorder (Kroll & Bachrach 2005: 208).

Moreover, positive ecstatic experiences of well-being, self-transcendence, and certainty from temporal lobe epileptic seizures are very rare (1 percent to 2 percent of patients) (Devinsky & Lai 2008)—that may be significantly less common than in the general population. Nor are all mystical experiences "ecstatic" in the emotional sense—serenity and calm characterize many such experiences. The epileptic experiences usually last only a few seconds out of a larger episode and usually are a matter not of joy but of fear and anxiety (Kelly & Grosso 2007: 531–34). If seizures were the cause, then the reason the vast majority of patients do not have mystical experiences would have to be provided. So too, pathology does not explain why people with healthy brains also have mystical experiences.

But stimulation of the temporal lobe is still advanced as a way to explain away all features of all religious and mystical experiences. Michael Persinger found that brain-injured patients sometimes had a "sense of presence": if the damage is to the left hemisphere, the presence may be a voice and be positive; if the damage is to the right hemisphere, the presence is more likely to be frightening and seen as an evil ghost or demon. From his work with his "God helmet" that stimulates a temporal lobe (with which he claims 40 percent of participants experience a sense a presence), Persinger sees the experience of God as nothing but "a biological artifact of the human brain" (1987: 17). Isolated mystical experiences are explained by short electrical bursts in the relevant locus in the brain, and longer-lasting states are explained by chronic lower-charged disturbances. (Note that these experiences are *visions and voices* rather than mystical experiences.)

However, as the scientific study of the brain has expanded more recently, these relatively simple explanatory models have declined in influence; current explanations of religious experiences are relatively complex, integrating structures and systems outside the area of the brain affected by epileptic seizures (Bradford 2013: 103). While pathological conditions may trigger mystical experiences in a small percentage of patients, mystical experiences have a different phenomenological content, and, as David Bradford says (113), studies aligned with the temporo-limbic model truncate and misrepresent the experiential features of mystical experiences. These models also make emotion, rather than cognition, the central feature of mystical experiences—the cognitive and perceptual content are the same as in ordinary experiences but are simply tagged by our limbic system as profound (Saver & Rubin 1997). This jibes with attribution theory but not with the historical record (Bradford 2013): emotion typically does not precede and initiate perceptual and cognitive changes. The emotional and the cognitive are different aspects of one unified mental process, and the emotions connected to mystical experiences are varied and nuanced (Bradford 2013). So too, mystical experiences more often have a positive impact on the life of an experiencer than do pathological experiences. The loss of a sense of self outside of the latter experiences is associated with maladaptive outcomes such as a sense of disconnection from other people and a loss of empathy, but mystical experiences are more often correlated with positive changes in family life, reduced fear of death, better health, and a greater sense of purpose, although some patients do require therapeutic care (Yaden et al. 2017a: 59) and with healthy indices of personality and adjustment (Hood & Byrom 2010).

Limitations on the Neuroscientific Study of Mystical Experiences

Research in the neuroscience of mystical experiences is still relatively new, and scientists may develop new models and hypotheses in the near future. Meta-analyses of the models to date show that current models conflict—even the collected data is not totally consistent (Ospina et al. 2007)—but there is no reason at present to doubt that neuroscientists, perhaps with the help of entirely new technologies, will eventually identify the exact changes in brain activity in these experiences as indicated by electrical activity or blood flow and reach a consensus on theories. And neuroscientists appear to have already established that mystical experiences are not simply interpretations of ordinary experiences in the baseline state of consciousness or necessarily the product of a damaged brain but involve unique configurations of neural activity of healthy brains functionally properly, that psychedelic drugs in proper dosages can duplicate these configurations, and that these configurations ground ASCs. So too, scientists have found different neurophysiological effects from extrovertive and introvertive meditation (Hood 2001: 32–47; Dunn, Hartigan & Mikulas 1999) and can distinguish the neurological effects of concentrative and mindfulness meditation (Valentine & Sweet 1999). Science may also lead to a new typology of mystical experiences, improved meditative techniques, or the direct noninvasive stimulation of areas of the brain that enable the different types of mystical experiences.

However, the above discussion also leads to the conclusion that there are major limitations on the significance that current neuroscience can have for understanding the nature of mystical experiences: neuroscience remains a matter of studying the states of the brain, not the accompanying states of mind or the experiences—scientists are not studying the lived *mystical experiences* but only the brain states associated with them. The general problem of the subjectivity of experiences and the possibility that the same neural base may ground different ASCs removes the possibility of neuroscience as currently practiced being a true science of mystical experiences and consciousness—it would not even be able to establish one-to-one correlations of experiences and brain states for predictions. Mystical experiences are distinguishable from other types of experiences by the bases involved, but beyond this science cannot inform us about the nature of mystical experiences. Studying the neural substrate accompanying mystical experiences will help to explain why an experience is *present*, but the *phenomenal content* of the experience will remain separate.

The most important conclusion for mysticism is that the limitations on the third-person neuroscientific approach limits the ability of these studies to tell us anything substantive about the nature of these experiences. At present there is no "neuroscience of mystical experiences": identifying the basis in the brain for particular conscious events is not getting into the conscious events themselves. Even a complete neural account of what is happening in the brain during a mystical experience does not tell us about the experience itself. But merely identifying the neural activity of any conscious state tells us nothing about what consciousness is or its nature or explains why it exists.[20] Neural correlates are not consciousness but only something consciousness adjacent. Mystical experiences, like all conscious events, are "attached" in some way to the brain, but we still do not know what the significance of a change in the brain's activity in a given area is or what causes it.

The inability of others to see what is going on in a person's mind during a mystical experience will always limit any science of meditation—a "science of meditative experiences" is not achieved by a science of meditators' brains. Moreover, current neuroscience cannot answer the basic etiological question: does the brain merely *enable or permit* these experiences to appear, or does it substantively *create* them? Normal waking consciousness evolved for our adaptive needs, but some "higher" states of consciousness may also have evolved (or are by-products of something useful for our survival) that may enable insights into a larger universe—that question cannot be answered by science alone.

— 10 —

The Relation of Mysticism and Science

The last chapter leads to the field of "religion and science." Does mysticism have implications for the relation of religion and science? In particular, how does mystical knowledge relate to scientific knowledge? Mysticism has become attractive to many in the modern West who question the ultimate scope of science. And since natural science is the paradigm of knowledge in the West, New Age advocates also want the imprimatur of science to make their mystical claims more generally acceptable today. Western apologists for Buddhism in the latter half of the nineteenth century first portrayed it as scientific. Soon Western-influenced Neo-Vedantists were doing the same for Hinduism. But with a few exceptions, the issue of the relation of mysticism and science languished until being revived in the 1960s and took off in the mid-1970s when Fritjof Capra and Gary Zukav published books on physics and mysticism that are still popular today. Books on how mystical thought may have influenced twentieth-century physics have also appeared (e.g., Kaiser 2011). However, the question of the relation of mysticism and science has remained confined mostly to New Age "parallelists" who see mysticism in terms of science and vice versa. Many preeminent physicists in the first half of the twentieth century showed interest in mysticism (see Wilber 1984), but probably more scientists today would agree with Stephen Hawking, who, in responding to his colleague Brian Josephson's interest in Asian mysticism, said that the idea of any mystical influence on science is "pure rubbish," adding: "The universe of Eastern mysticism is an illusion. A physicist who attempts to link it with his own work has abandoned physics" (quoted in Boslough 1985: 127).[1]

The New Age approach would remove one popular reason to reject mysticism: that mysticism necessarily conflicts with science. But a staple of New Age thought goes further: today science and Asian mystical claims are *merging*. That is, after hundreds of years of strenuous work modern scientists are finally discovering what mystics from around the world have known for thousands of years. It is as if scientists, after struggling up the mountain of empirical research, found mystics meditating at the top. The old "dualistic" science arising from Newtonian physics is being replaced, and today theories in particle physics and relativity are becoming one with claims in Buddhism or with an abstract "Eastern mystical worldview." New Agers tell us that that Buddhists had already uncovered the basic principles of quantum physics through meditation that are only now finally being confirmed by scientists. In the end, mystics and scientists are saying the same thing, only in "different languages" (Capra [1975] 2000: 8; Mansfield 2008: 88, 141, 16).

But the New Age ideas for the convergence of science and mysticism collapse upon examination—mysticism and science do not "parallel," "converge with," or "confirm" each other on any substantive points (see Jones 2015, 2019b). Looking at the nature of the two enterprises shows why this is so.

Mysticism and Science as Ways of Knowing

Parallelists typically go no further into the nature of science than noting that science involves empirical observations and claiming that Newtonian science is dualistic and reductionistic.[2] But only one point needs to be emphasized here: basic science is about *how things in nature work*—that is, identifying the structures in nature responsible for the lawful actions of the phenomena that we observe and offering both tentative explanations of phenomena in terms of these underlying causes and also encompassing theories of those structures' nature that ultimately depend on observations checkable by others to counter biases or errors. Realists and antirealist empiricists disagree over whether we can gain any genuine knowledge of those alleged causal structures that cannot be observed. But empiricists accept that there is some unknown reality and do not reduce reality to an idealism of only what is experienced.

Mysticism could converge with science in two ways: specific mystical claims about the nature of the world could converge with scientific theories, or mystical cultivation could converge with the "scientific method" as a way of knowing reality. However, mystics focus on the sheer "beingness" of the natural world or a transcendent reality in ASCs. Extrovertive mindfulness mystics make claims about the impermanence and connectedness of the macro-objects that we directly observe in the everyday world. Neither introvertive nor extrovertive mystics make any claims about unexperienced structures of the world, unlike theoretical scientists. Scientists may expand the impermanence and conditionality of the everyday world into the subatomic level, but extrovertive mystics remain on the everyday level, and introvertive mystics' experiences transcend the natural realm altogether.

However, scientists work in our baseline state of consciousness through the mediation of concepts to find structures underlying the changes that we experience in the everyday world. To determine how things work, scientists must distinguish objects and see how they interact with each other, and differentiations among phenomena are necessary for that. Thus, they focus precisely on the differentiations among phenomena that extrovertive mystics claim prevent us from seeing reality as it truly is. This includes fields and the smaller and smaller bits of matter being theorized. Even the *mass* of an object is measured only by the interaction of objects. And since beingness is common to all particulars, it cannot be studied scientifically: beingness is uniform for all phenomena, and thus it cannot be poked and prodded. Nor is there anything for it to interact with. Hence, no hypotheses about the nature of beingness can be scientifically tested in any way. Beingness is not simply a different scientific level of structuring but is an aspect of reality that is not open to scientific investigation.

In such circumstances, it is hard to argue that mystics are making claims about the underlying causal features of nature that scientists are only now revealing, or that scientists are approaching the same aspect of reality as mystics are. Rather, mystics realize a dimension of reality that is missed in scientific knowledge and vice versa. Scientists and mystics each see something different about reality, and their subject matters are irrelevant to each other. Thus, their claims do not cross, let alone converge. Both endeavors are interested in what is "fundamentally real" but in different aspects of it. In short, they are not merely reaching the same claims through different routes. Mystical experiences do not give us any scientific knowledge of reality, and no science gives us any mystical knowledge. There are two fundamentally different aspects of what is real that are approached through different functions of the mind, and this forecloses any substantive convergence of scientific and mystical knowledge-claims.

Buddhism is not a "science of the mind" in any sense connected to natural science. Buddhism's central objective is not to acquire disinterested knowledge about how the mind works—the Buddha's teaching has only one flavor: to end suffering (*dukkha*) permanently (*Majjhima Nikaya* I.22) by ending the desires that drive rebirth. To substitute a disinterested focus on how the parts of nature work—including even the mental states involved in ending suffering—merely in order to learn more about the universe distorts the fundamental soteriological nature of Buddhism entirely. The identification and explanation of the structures of reality can only increase attention to the differentiations in the world and will never lead to the calming of the mind by emptying it of differentiated content. The Buddha condemned astronomy/astrology (*joti*) as a wrong means of livelihood because it was unrelated to the religious concern (*Digha Nikaya* I.12). To use the Buddhist analogy: when we are shot with a poisonous arrow, we do not ask about who made the arrow or what the arrow is made of (or any other scientific question related to the arrow)—we just want a cure for the poison (*Majjhima Nikaya* I.63). The Buddha would no doubt leave all scientific questions unanswered (including those involving the brain) since they are irrelevant to the soteriological problem of suffering, just as he did with questions of the age and size of the universe (*Digha Nikaya* I.13, III.137; *Majjhima Nikaya* I.427; *Anguttara Nikaya* II.80). This explains why throughout its history Buddhism has been hostile to science (Lopez 2008: 216).

Daoism in classical China is a good example of the explicit rejection of the discursive type of knowledge of which science is the paradigm: the Daoists' interest in nature remained contemplative and did not lead to a scientific interest in how things in nature work (Jones 1993a). We cannot simply equate any interest in nature with a scientific interest in understanding the hidden causal order behind things that explains how things work. Daoists were interested in flowing with patterns inherent in nature—the Dao—through nonassertive action (*wei wuwei*), not in any scientific findings or explanations of the efficient causes at work in those patterns. In the Daoist "forgetting" state of mind (*xu*), our mind is no longer guided by our own mentally conceived divisions of nature but responds spontaneously to what is presented without any preconceptions. Anything free of conceptions cannot guide scientific observations or theorizing, since scientific observations and experiments involve predictions, and theorizing is based in our conceptions.

Thus, science and mysticism pull in opposite directions. Scientific experiences remain ordinary, everyday-type observations, even when scientists are studying extraordinary parts of nature through experimentation or technology-enhanced observation, while mystics' experiences are extraordinary even when they are looking at the ordinary. As discussed below, the picture is complicated by the fact that mysticism involves more than just cultivating mystical experiences. However, the divergence of interests and subject matters in science and mysticism means that it is impossible to say that science and mysticism "converge" or that science "confirms" the specifically mystical claims of any tradition or vice versa: scientists approach reality through an analytical point of view that divides and isolates, even if reality in their resulting theories lacks distinct entities, while mystics reject that approach for a "knowledge by participation," even if analysis and reasoning is necessary for devising mystical metaphysics and ways of life.

Dimensions of Reality

Parallelists, however, miss the fact that mystics and scientists are discussing different dimensions of reality. For example, they misconstrue the "search for unity" by not distinguishing the mystical quest to experience the unity of being from the scientific quest to unify the structures of nature. Any scientific unity unifies apparently different structures (e.g., unifying magnetism and electricity), while the oneness of being has no parts to unite. Thus, the searches for unity differ in content and converge only in the abstract. Nothing on the possible unity or disunity of structures is disclosed in mystical experiences. Nor is there anything in any classical mystical tradition suggesting any interest by mystics in attempting to unify the structures at work in the world—a "theory of everything" still remains a matter of structures alone, not of being. Nor do mystics reach new structures of reality that scientists fail to reach.[3] Nor are mystics aiming at a more comprehensive unification than scientists that combines structures and beingness. Nor do mystical claims offer "theoretical support," since they are about beingness or transcendent realities, not the structures of nature. Mysticism is simply neutral to the question of whether physicists can reduce the apparent levels of structures to only one level of physical structure, or whether, as antireductionists contend, non-physicists are discovering equally fundamental levels of structuring. Perhaps if scholars used "*identity* of being" when discussing mysticism and not "*unity*" (which suggests a unification of parts), fewer people would be misled concerning mystical "oneness."

As noted above, extrovertive mysticism remains exclusively on the level that can be *directly experienced*. And nothing in the writings of the great

Asian spiritual masters suggests that mystics become aware of the quantum realm or experience subatomic structures or experience anything other than the mind and the everyday level of phenomena in the external world. Contrary to what Fritjof Capra says, mystics in higher states of consciousness do not have "a strong intuition for the 'space-time' character of reality" ([1975] 2000: 171–72) or for any other scientific explanatory structure. Indeed, the connection of space and time would be news to Buddhists—nothing in the Buddhist teachings would predict that time is connected to space. In fact, Theravada Buddhists would be quite surprised: they exempt space, but not time, from being "conditioned" (*samskrita*) (*Anguttara Nikaya* I.286)—this makes space as independent and absolute as is possible within their metaphysics and precludes any encompassing holism. So too, in classical Indian culture space (*akasha*) is a substance pervading the world, but it is not the source of anything else or in any sense *the* fundamental reality—it is not any type of "field" connecting everything with everything else nor out of which entities appear. Rather, space is one of the five elements of the world (along with earth, water, fire, and air)—it is not the ground or source of the other elements or of anything else. It is independent of all other elements, not influencing them and not influenced by them. Nor is there any reason to believe that depth-mystical experiences are of "the four-dimensional space-time continuum" of relativity theory or the "ground manifold state" out of which quantum phenomena emerge and are reabsorbed—such constructs remain structured aspects of reality, not pure beingness, while depth-mystical experiences are free of structured or otherwise differentiated content.

Like mysticism in general, Buddhism has no interest in the analysis of underlying structural layers of organization or in identifying the lowest structural level of physical realities. Buddhism has never given a *physical* analysis of matter. Buddhist metaphysics involves the analysis of what we experience into its components as a way to help us escape our suffering. This soteriological focus is on the world "as it really is" *in our experiences* rather than the world in itself independent of our experience.[4] The closest concept in Buddhism for "matter" is the factor of experience (*dharma*) "form" (*rupa*).[5] It is one of dozens and dozens of factors of experience in the Abhidharma analyses of our experiences. And even then *rupa* relates only to our experience and not to "matter in itself"—it is the form of things as we directly *experience* them and not about any possible *substance* behind the appearance. In short, it is how things *appear* to us. Identifying a new subatomic level in a scientific analysis of matter will not lead to discerning any of the *dharmas*. If anything, the scientific analysis of matter only increases the danger of discrimination for the unenlightened by introducing a new layer of possible objects and creating new distinctions.

Nor did the Buddha twenty-five hundred years ago in any way set out the hypothesis that elementary particles are not solid or independent. In fact, the early Abhidharma Buddhists went beyond the soteriological *dharma* analysis and posited minute discrete *indestructible particles of matter* (*paramanus*) that are unopen to sense-experience, and yet they affirmed the impermanence of the objects of the experienced realm—such permanent atoms simply do not affect the impermanence that Buddhists are interested in. Buddhist ideas of impermanence are about the world of *everyday phenomena* that we experience and thus are compatible with anything physicists find about the underlying *structures* responsible for the phenomena—that is, even if the structures are permanent, the structured phenomena are still impermanent.[6] Thus, science could not falsify or confirm the Buddhist claims or converge with them because its findings would not affect the impermanence of the "constructed" things of the everyday world that we actually experience.

Nor is the Buddhist claim of "emptiness" (*shunyata*) about the lack of matter. It is the emptiness of all phenomena of any inherent "self-existence" (*svabhava*) that would separate things from each other as distinct and self-existing realities, not the emptiness of space on astronomical scales or the lack of solid particles in a sea of energy on a quantum scale. Rather, it is the absence of any ability to self-exist. Nevertheless, many people agree with the physicist Victor Mansfield when he said that particle physics and Madhyamaka Buddhism have "many deep links" and "remarkable and detailed connections" (2008: 6). But the Buddhist claim stands or falls on the thorough impermanence, conditionality, and connectedness of what we experience in the everyday world.

Nor did the Buddhist Nagarjuna have any concept of a featureless "Void" that is the source out of which anything arises. His concept of "emptiness" is not the "quantum vacuum" out of which things arise. Emptiness is not the *source* of anything. The term simply denotes the true state of everything in the phenomenal world—that is, the absence of anything that would make a phenomenon permanent, independent, and self-existent. But parallelists routinely reify emptiness into a cosmic "Absolute Reality" that is the underlying source of phenomena or a counterpart to Advaita's Brahman or the Daoists' Dao. However, according to Nagarjuna, anyone who reifies the mere *absence* of anything that could give self-existence into a *reality* of any kind is simply *incurable* (*Mulamadhyamakakarikas* 13.8).

So too Advaita's Brahman has been pressed into the service of "quantum mysticism." For example, the physicist Amit Goswami (1997) gives consciousness a causal role in physics and also treats consciousness as the ground of being. However, there is nothing in Advaita's Brahman doctrines about consciousness affecting, or interacting with, any phenomenal object. In fact, all that is real is only the partless Brahman, and thus there is nothing for Brahman to interact with. All phenomena have the status of objects in dreams, and Brahman is never portrayed as any type of causal agent within the dream world. Thus, to make Brahman the cause of the collapse of the wave-function in particle physics is to change its nature. Brahman is the same undifferentiated reality for all phenomena and thus cannot explain why one phenomenal state of affairs is the case rather than another, and thus it cannot function as a scientific explanation. It is not that mystics go further than physicists on observation (contra Capra [1975] 2000: 331)—what mystics are claiming about what is experienced in depth-mystical experiences is fundamentally different from any alleged interaction of the observer and observed in particle physics.

In mindfulness mysticism too, there is nothing about a subject's consciousness affecting objects: we "create" objects by imposing artificial *conceptual boundaries* onto what is really there in the world, not by somehow *physically affecting* what is there. That is, we create illusory "entities" in the phenomenal world by erroneously separating off parts of the flux of phenomenal reality with our analytical mind—it is a matter of the conceptualizations of our everyday perceptions and beliefs and has nothing to do with the idea that consciousness is a possible *causal factor* in events.

In sum, mystics do not directly experience "the same truth" that scientists arrive at tentatively or approximately through the route of theory and experiment. Each endeavor, if each is in fact cognitive, pursues the depth of a dimension of reality but not the same dimension. The *content* of science and mysticism will always remain distinct, and thus their theories and ideas can never converge into one new set of theories replacing theories in either science or mysticism. Nor can either endeavor confirm or discredit the other. Mystics' claims about the impermanence and interconnectedness of the experienced everyday realm in no way "validate" or "verify" any scientific theories of underlying structures, nor can any scientific theories or empirical data about structure verify mystical claims about beingness or its source. The change from Newtonian physics to relativity and quantum physics did not alter that.

Mysticism and the Scientific Method

Mystics and scientists value different types of experiences (conception-free participatory experiences versus concept-driven dualistic observations) and value conceptualizations differently (becoming free of conceptualizations versus coming up with better conceptualizations of how nature works), and this precludes any deeper convergence in method. Overall, science utilizes the analytical function of the mind and increases the number of conceptual differentiations in our mind by its analyzing, selecting, measuring, and theorizing. As noted above, it increases attention to the differentiations within the phenomenal world and thus diverts attention from what mystics consider the only approach for aligning our lives with reality. For mystical experiences to occur, one needs to empty the mind of the very conceptual stuff that is central to science. The aim is to achieve a knowledge inaccessible to the analytical mind.

But the emphasis in mysticism on *experience* as the source of knowledge becomes through the New Age lens *a scientific method*. All meditative exercises become scientific experiments on the mind. Buddhist claims become tentatively advanced, empirically tested hypotheses. The basic point that the Buddha exhorted his followers to rely on their own experiences and to examine phenomena dispassionately (*Majjhima Nikaya* I.265) means that the Buddha must have been a scientist—not that he was merely trying to get them to follow the path that the Buddha had laid out in order to end their own suffering.

Consider the *Kalama Sutta*. Here villagers expressed to the Buddha their confusion about the conflicting religious doctrines they had heard. He urged them not to rely upon reports, hearsay, the authority of religious texts, mere logic, influence, appearances, seeming possibilities, speculative opinions, or teachers' ideas, but to know for themselves what is efficacious and what is not (*Anguttara Nikaya* I.189). But he was not exhorting them to conduct mental experiments over a range of inner states and see what happens: the villagers had been told in advance what would work—the Buddhist prescribed path to ending suffering—and the Buddha already knew what the villagers would find. That is, what they will find is set before any mental exercises are undertaken, unlike in science, where scientists do not know beforehand what their experiments will disclose when testing predictions. The villagers' subsequent experiences cannot even be seen as attempts to duplicate an experiment in order to confirm or disconfirm an earlier finding, since any lack of ending suffering on the part of the villagers would not be seen as disconfirmation. As the Indologist Wilhelm Halbfass summed the matter up, "Following the experiential path of the Buddha does not mean to continue a process of open-ended experimentation and inquiry. There is no 'empiricist' openness for future additions or corrections; there is nothing to be added to the discoveries of the Buddha and other 'omniscient' founders of soteriological traditions. . . . There is no programmatic and systematic accumulation of 'psychological' data or observations, no pursuit of fact-finding in the realm of consciousness. . . . There is no more 'inner experimentation' in these traditions, than there is experimentation related to the 'outer' sphere of nature" (1988: 393–94). (He made a similar remark concerning Shankara's Advaita [390–91].) Buddhist meditation is less an open-ended inquiry into the mind or consciousness than a method of perceiving for oneself the same insight that the Buddha had already realized. The efficacy of the practice for ending suffering had already been established. In the *Kalama Sutta*, the Buddha is merely saying that by following the path the villagers will then know the truth for themselves because they will have *experienced the end of suffering themselves*. We have to distort Buddhism badly to see this as anticipating the skeptical empiricism of the modern scientific method. Finding something out for yourself through experience does not necessarily make you a *scientist*—sometimes it is only a matter of correctly following a path that others laid out for you.

So too, advancing a taxonomy of mental states relevant to ending suffering (as Buddhist Abhidharmists did) was not the result of a scientific method or intent. Nor does it make meditation scientific. The Buddha did not use the "scientific method" to test various hypotheses to create a general scientific picture of the inner world. His method does involve experiential realization of inner mental states, but the objective is not to learn more about the inner world—once he found what worked to end suffering, he prescribed it for others. The Buddhist analogy of the man struck by a poisonous arrow mentioned above obviously applies here. Buddhists following the prescribed path to end suffering have not developed, as Alan Wallace thinks, a "science of consciousness" by "collecting data by observing mental processes and experimenting" (1989: 29–101). Of course, scientists may utilize the data from meditators or examine classical mystical typologies of states of consciousness to help develop their theories of the brain, but this does not make mystics scientists. The attempt to calm and clarify their minds does not mean that Buddhists are "experimenting" in the scientific sense at all. Merely because unenlightened Buddhists have not yet experientially realized their prescribed goal of enlightenment themselves does not mean they are "testing hypotheses scientifically" through their meditative practices and behavior.

Buddhists have developed rigorous methods for refining attention, but not to explore the nature of consciousness scientifically or to disinterestedly catalog various states of consciousness. In fact, the impartiality of mindfulness actually *interferes* with scientific observation by disabling concept-guided observation: in a mindful state, there are no predictions, preset categories of objects, or other conceptual guidance as is needed to conduct a scientific observation. There is a "bare attention" to what is presented to our senses, without attention to anything in particular. However, scientific observations that test hypotheses require responses to predictions created by questions and thus are necessarily driven by concepts—such directed observations are not the free-floating, open-monitoring observations of whatever occurs as in a mindful state.

In short, not everything *experiential* is *scientific*. The need for the direct experience of mystical truths is not science. While meditation is certainly experiential, this does not make it the *concept-guided observation* of the empirical method of scientific knowing. Nor can we speak of Buddhist metaphysics as "a verifiable system of knowledge" when other traditions with knowledge-claims that conflict with Buddhist claims about the nature of the mind are "verified" by the same experiences. Moreover, the Buddha's exhortation to experience for oneself did not prevent Buddhist schools over time from accepting the Buddha's testimony (*shabda*) as a means of valid knowledge. Faith or trust (*shraddha*) in the authority of the Buddha is a theme of the widely accepted *Lotus Sutra*. So too, Zen masters such as Dogen say that you must believe what a Zen master tells you. The Dalai Lama realizes that accepting such authority as settling matters separates Buddhism from science (Gyatso 2005: 28–29).

The Relation of Mystical Claims and Scientific Theories

As discussed, mysticism encompasses more than simply having mystical experiences: mystical experiences are only part of broader ways of life concerned with aligning oneself with a fundamental reality (as defined by a mystic's tradition). Mystical ways of life have frameworks that include beliefs about the nature of the phenomenal world and human beings—and here mysticism and science may converge or conflict. Mystics and mystical theorists can adapt mystical beliefs to the science of their day. For example, in the mid-twentieth century Teilhard de Chardin and Sri Aurobindo both attempted to incorporate evolution into their frameworks of beliefs. Mystics may also utilize ideas from science as a source of analogies for expressing mystical knowledge.[7]

But comparisons to science are also always tied to the theories of the day, and there is the danger that the convergences that parallelists now see will disappear in the next generation. That is, if a mystical claim is the same as a particular scientific theory, then if the science changes and that theory is rejected, the mystical claim must be rejected too. As Victor Mansfield saw, since physical theories are intrinsically impermanent, it is a guarantee of obsolescence to bind Buddhism or any philosophical view too tightly to a physical theory (2008: 6–7). It is also well to remember that there were books written in the late nineteenth and early twentieth century in America and Europe that portrayed the Buddha as a good Newtonian. In the 1960s, when interest in Buddhism and science revived, the Buddha had become an Einsteinian.

Today, the inconsistency between quantum theory and relativity theory leads many physicists to believe that their current theories are not final but only approximations. So too, the element of randomness and the general statistical nature of quantum physics suggests to many particle physicists that their science has not yet captured the true structures at work on that level. Overall, there is no agreement on the interpretation of the empirical data of quantum physics—the options around since the 1930s remain. A whole new conceptualization may be needed in fundamental physics. If so, the current alleged parallels to mystical claims may prove to be only temporary. Moreover, that we may never have a final scientific picture of fundamental reality must also be considered—for example, the energies needed to explore deeper and deeper levels of the quantum realm may not be attainable on earth. Yet, if claims from assorted mystical traditions can be attached to whatever theories may eventually come to be accepted in particle physics, then there must be very little substance to the alleged convergence, and any alleged convergences would not be very illuminating.

Fritjof Capra illustrates a related problem. In the 1970s, Capra championed his teacher Geoffrey Chew's S-matrix theory in particle physics, in which there are no fundamental entities or laws of nature. However, the S-matrix's competitor—the particle approach of quarks, leptons, and bosons—won out. Nevertheless, Capra still adheres to the S-matrix theory even while physicists keep making advances under the particle approach.

But Capra sees nothing that has developed in physics in the intervening decades as invalidating anything he wrote ([1975] 2000: 9).[8]

Today "Neo-Buddhists," including the Dalai Lama, illustrate another problem. The Dalai Lama finds scientific discoveries in physics, cosmology, and biology fascinating, and he wants Buddhist monks to study them. He starts out his book *The Universe in a Single Atom: The Convergence of Science and Spirituality* apparently approaching science with openness and humility, giving science a free hand and asserting that Buddhism must conform to its findings (Gyatso 2005: 3). He does not want "to unite science and spirituality" but considers them "two complementary investigative approaches," and he wants "to explore two important human disciplines for the purpose of developing a more holistic and integrated way of understanding the world around us" (4). However, the Dalai Lama will go only so far to accommodate science. He can readily abandon the Indian folk cosmology of a flat earth and so forth (80), since that does not affect any core Buddhist doctrines, but he is not ready to give up anything that would cause a radical reformulation of core Buddhist ideas. So too, he is ready to assert that the Buddhist philosophical analysis of the experienced phenomena of the everyday world rules out finding any bits of permanence in the subatomic realm or any other type of permanence within the space-time realm, despite the fact, as he admits, that one of the early Buddhist schools had a theory of indivisible, partless constituents of the phenomenal world (52–55). In cosmology, the big bang does show the impermanence of the content of the entire phenomenal universe, but the Dalai Lama denies that the big bang is the origin of the universe rather than just the beginning of a new cycle within an infinite universe (82–84). Thus, he favors any of the multiverse models on religious and philosophical grounds, not from any empirical study of the cosmological data. He also asserts that past beings' karmic residues survive into the new universes and that the law of *karma* is one of the strictly causal factors shaping the material universe (90–92).

Most importantly, the Dalai Lama refuses to treat *consciousness* as a product of nature that expires with the death of the body. That some neuroscientists deny the existence of a single unified control center in the mind—a "self"—dovetails with the Buddhist "no self" doctrine, but the Dalai Lama's belief that consciousness has existed since the beginning of time requires him also to deny that the neo-Darwinian evolutionary theory in biology is even potentially a complete explanation of the history of life on earth. The human body may be the result of evolution (Gyatso 2005: 97), but natural selection and the random mutation of genes is not the way consciousness came to exist in the phenomenal universe. Consciousness is not the product of matter but is co-temporal with it. In fact, consciousness *causes matter*: the world of sentience arises from the mind, and the diverse habitats of beings in it also arise from mind (109). Treating the mind as a cause would radically affect the basically materialist research program in neuroscience. At a minimum, it would set the limits of what neuroscientists could prove about consciousness.

So too, neo-Darwinism gives us a "fairly coherent account of the evolution of human life on earth," but *karma* must be given a central role in understanding the origin of human sentience (Gyatso 2005: 111, 115). We are the product of "karmic genes" from past lives as well as biological genes. In addition, there must be a "hidden causality" behind the apparent randomness of mutations that assures the appearance of life and conscious beings: that mutations are purely random is "unsatisfying" (104, 112). Furthermore, under traditional Buddhism, human beings devolved from celestial beings through a karmic process (107–8) rather than evolving from less complex life-forms. Thus, the Dali Lama is rejecting any theory that denies rebirth and reduces human beings in toto to nothing more than biological machines or the product of pure chance in natural events.

These Buddhist beliefs are not a case of mysticism helping science by being ideas that can be reworked into scientific hypotheses and empirically tested. They are demands on what would make science acceptable to Neo-Buddhists. The Dalai Lama's position is an instance of wanting beliefs that are accepted solely on grounds unrelated to scientific findings to control the outcome of science. The problem is not simply the philosophical framework underlying current science, or that empirical data does not constitute legitimate grounds for developing a comprehensive worldview (Gyatso 2005: 13). Rather, Neo-Buddhists must reject parts of science as it is currently practiced—for example, the role of randomness in evolution. This limits the Dalai Lama's stated aim of incorporating "key insights" from evolution, relativity, and quantum physics within a Buddhist worldview—the insights must be modified and controlled by religious considerations to be made compatible with Buddhist philosophical beliefs. It is true that the claim that all mental processes are necessarily physical is a metaphysical assumption, not a scientific fact, and that in the spirit of scientific inquiry we should leave this question open (128). But Buddhist ideas cannot force experimental results to conform to a particular belief any more than any ideas can, but those ideas may affect theory construction. And while it is true that he is "not subject to the professional or ideological constraints of a radically materialistic worldview" (93), the Dalai Lama fails to see that his Buddhist beliefs can be just as restrictive.[9] He also fails to see that these restrictions on science violate the complementarity of the "investigative approaches" of science and Buddhism that he wants to espouse (4).

One other issue should be noted: mysticism cannot be reduced to a matter of belief or philosophy by following Alfred North Whitehead's method of "rationalizing mysticism" through translating mystical claims into scientific ones. If we separate mystical claims from their context as ASC experiences, they are no longer mystical. The metaphysical claims remain the same, but they change character when seen through a dualistic prism. Mystical claims voice mystical practices and another way of seeing the world. Mystical metaphysics have helped science in the past by giving scientists ideas to rework into scientific theories (see Jones 2015: 63–76), but that takes the ideas out of their mystical context and does not make mysticism into science.[10] So too, one might adapt the metaphysics of some mystical tradition for a framework that absorbs the current body of scientific theories and findings into an encompassing mystical worldview, but this does not make science into mysticism or vice versa—it would be a matter of analytical metaphysics alone, not mysticism or science.

Are Mysticism and Science Complementary?

At the end of the epilogue to *The Tao of Physics*, Fritjof Capra states something correct about the relation between science and mysticism: mysticism and science are entirely different approaches involving different functions of the mind: "Neither is comprehended in the other, nor can either be reduced to the other, but both of them are necessary, supplementing one another for a fuller understanding of the world" ([1975] 2000: 306–7). Nevertheless, in the body of his work he still advances unsupportable claims of "convergence" and "confirmation" (114, 161, 223)—and he does so even in the epilogue just quoted (305).

However, difficulties arise for the idea of complementarity too. Mysticism and science do not separate neatly into different compartments. It is not as if mysticism is about the inner world of consciousness while science is about the outer world of material objects—mystics work on consciousness, but they are interested in the beingness of all of reality, including the beingness of the "outer world," and scientists are interested in the mind. There are also limitations on any compartmentalization of all elements of mystical ways of life from science due to the fact that mysticism encompasses full ways of life and not only mystical experiences (Jones 2015: 156–77).

But the idea of complementarity at least affirms that science and mysticism involve irreducible differences and different approaches to reality. However, the most popular way to reconcile mysticism and science as complements is to claim that mystics are dealing with the "depth" of reality and scientists with the "surface" of *the same aspect of reality*. That is, mystics and scientists are using different approaches to reality, but they apprehend the same aspect of reality, not fundamentally different aspects of reality: introvertive mystics simply turn observation inward and arrive at a deeper level of the same truth that scientists reach observing external phenomena. Science and mysticism thus both lead to the same basic knowledge.

But again, scientists and mystics are studying different aspects of reality that result in completely different types of knowledge-claims, and if both endeavors do in fact produce knowledge, then both endeavors are needed for a fuller knowledge of reality—that is, both the analytic and contemplative functions of the mind lead to knowledge and both are needed to see reality as fully as humanly possible. The revolutions in physics in the early twentieth century did not change this. It is not as if all we have to do is push further in science and we will end up mystically enlightened, or push further in mysticism and we will end up with a theory of everything incorporating all science. Of course, science and mysticism can be said to have a "common pursuit of truth," or be "united in the one endeavor of discovering knowledge and truth about reality," or "seek the reality behind appearances," but this only places both endeavors into a more abstract category of being knowledge-seeking endeavors since they are not pursing the *same truths*.[11]

Reconciling Mysticism and Science

This discussion highlights the differences between mysticism and science. It shows that New Age claims to convergence do not pan out. But mysticism and science can be reconciled on basic claims and approaches to reality by accepting that the two endeavors are dealing with fundamentally different aspects of reality, and hence they do not intersect at all and thus cannot converge or conflict or support each other even in principle. This would make reconciling mystical insights and science relatively simple as long as mystics' knowledge-claims are confined to claims about a transcendent self or ground of reality or about the beingness of the phenomenal world. (The distinction between *mystical experiences* and *mystical knowledge-claims* about what is experienced is important: scientific findings and theories do not affect the experiential insight as long as the insight is confined to knowledge-claims about transcendent realities or the beingness of the phenomena realm.)

Thus, mysticism is not necessarily in conflict with science. For classical introvertive mystics, the metaphysics of naturalism would have to be abandoned, and some transcendent dimension to both the natural world and a human being that is open to experience would have to be accepted. But science is not the philosophy of naturalism, and thus giving up naturalism is not giving up science: science can be placed in a wider metaphysical framework and still focus only on the natural mechanisms at work in the phenomenal world. (But whether cognitive scientists will give up *materialism* and treat *consciousness* as a causal force is a crucial issue.)

Merely because mystics bracket the structures of nature during their experiences does not mean that the structures are unreal, any more than does the fact that scientists are not focusing on beingness mean beingness is unreal—waves are as much a part of reality as the water constituting them and need to be understood and explained as waves. Seeing reality without a sense of self or its accompanying desires may well reveal something fundamental, but it does not necessarily exhaust all we can know about reality. Thus, it is not a matter of mysticism replacing science but supplementing it with a different type of knowledge of reality. We can interpret mystical experiences as a cognitive insight into the depth of the beingness of reality and still affirm the full reality of the phenomena of the natural world and the value of instrumental states of consciousness for studying natural structures—not all mystics need despise the world or treat it as unreal or as a dream. Thus, there would be a role for different states of consciousness enabling different ways of knowing. Mystical claims would be limited to the issue of beingness, and even depth-mystical experiences would not be taken as overwhelming all other types of cognitive experiences.

If so, we need not deny science as cognitive to accept mysticism as cognitive or vice versa. Classical mystics can give science its due. Even Shankara, who dismissed the entire phenomenal world as having an undetermined status that deceives us about its nature, still could say that sense-experience and reason hold sway over matters not covered by scripture (such as creation)—for him, a hundred scriptural verses saying that fire was cold would not make it so (*Bhagavad-gita-bhashya* 18.66). In Indian philosophy in general, nature is seen as operating by rational principles. So too, a scientific explanation of the biological bases of mystical experiences could still be affirmed (as discussed in the last chapter). Mystical doctrines of transcendent realities would not need to be revised in light of any scientific findings or theories, but other doctrines of mystical ways of life may have to be revised to incorporate the then-current scientific insights. Thus, there is not a dialogue of equals between science and mysticism, but neither is science a threat to mysticism. So too, it is not necessary to naturalize introvertive mystical experiences for a reconciliation: one can accept the classical mystical position that these experiences involve transcendent realities while still fully affirming science. The conceptualizing analytic mind and concept-guided perceptions are still needed to conduct science and to live in the world. The enlightened with their continuing ASCs may be able to live calmly focused totally on only the present moment while still handling concepts—they are free of a sense of self but otherwise engaged with what is sensed and the thinking mind. But for the rest of us integrating a mystical sense of selflessness and of the beingness of things into our analytical mind is difficult.

However, this reconciliation reflects a nonmystical point of view, since it gives equal weight to a nonmystical approach to the world, and it would lead to what from a classical mystical point of view is a truncated mysticism. Nevertheless, the possibility of such a conciliation removes one objection to the cognitive validity of introvertive mystical experiences by showing that their claims to be an awareness of a transcendent reality are consistent with science's cognitive claims. Thus, we are not forced to choose either "the path of spirituality" or "the path of reason," as the biologist Edward O. Wilson and many other naturalists assert, at least when it comes to the core of mystical knowledge-claims.[12] Indeed, perhaps Bertrand Russell, despite rejecting the cognitivity of mystical experiences, was correct when he remarked, "The greatest men who have been philosophers have felt the need both of science and of mysticism: the attempt to harmonise the two was what made their life, and what always must, for all its arduous uncertainty, make philosophy, to some minds, a greater thing than either science or religion" (1917: 1).

— 11 —

Are Mystical Experiences Cognitive?

Today many people see mysticism only in terms of experiences and dismiss differences in metaphysics and ways of life as irrelevant. Others see mystical experiences only in terms of its powerful emotional impact. But classical mystics also claim that they realize something previously unnoticed about reality when all of the personal and conceptual content of the mind is removed—they gain a knowledge that can be realized only by these experiences. This raises the most basic philosophical questions concerning introvertive mysticism: Do mystical experiences reveal something about the universe that experiences in our ordinary, baseline state of consciousness cannot? Are these experiences reliable sources of knowledge generating valid claims about reality? Do they support the doctrines of one religious tradition over others? If so, how can we tell which understanding is correct or at least best? Or are these experiences all "subjective" in the pejorative sense of being merely generated by the brain and not cognitive at all? Does the sense of their profundity only reinforce what a mystic already believes? Do the neural, psychological, and social mechanisms at work when a mystical experience is occurring or in devising mystical claims trump a mystic's own understanding and determine the truth or falsity of the alleged insight? How can we determine which case is correct? Should all mystical doctrines be dismissed as merely speculative "over-beliefs"? In sum, how do mystics know they are right?

Can Nonmystics Judge the Cognitivity of Mystical Experiences?

An important preliminary question is whether nonmystics are in a position to make any judgments about whether mystical experiences are cognitive.

Mystics certainly are privileged with regard to the phenomenology of their experience—anyone is privileged with regard to felt aspects of their own experiences. But even mystics themselves can evaluate the significance and cognitive import of their experiences only *outside* of introvertive experiences in a state of consciousness, whether enlightened or not, when the mind is aware of differentiations and can consider different factors. In those states, what is experienced becomes a mental object even for mystics, not what was experienced "as it really is." Mystics such as Meister Eckhart say that transcendent realities cannot be "grasped by the mind"—or as the Pseudo-Dionysius said, God is unknown even to those who have experienced him except in the moment of experience. So too, alleged mystical insights into the true nature of what was experienced arise only as postexperiential events occurring outside of introvertive states: mystics may have experienced a transcendent reality, but it is only after the introvertive experiences that mystics see how things in the phenomena world "really are." And all such formulations involve more factors than mystical experiences alone. Even if (contra Kant) mystics have direct and unmediated access to a noumenal reality free of any categories that make phenomena and free of our cultural structuring, what cognitive significance they see in their experience arises only after the experience is over.[1] Indeed, that a mystical experience is taken to be *an insight* at all rather than a delusion depends on factors outside the experience. But this means that mystics in the end are in the same epistemic situation as nonmystics when it comes to the nature of what was experienced, even though they have a larger experiential base from which to make their decisions about what is real.

In such circumstances, there is no reason that the mystics should be privileged in the state in which such decisions are made to determine the cognitive value of their experiences. Nor does being a mystic necessarily qualify a person to see the various issues involved in making claims to knowledge. Thus, in the end nonmystics are not compelled to accept the mystics' own assessment of their experiences. Mystics routinely merely accept the understanding of their own tradition. That the understandings of these experiences conflict among mystics from different traditions brings out the problem: mystics cannot simply say, "Sorry, we've had the experiences, and you haven't" when it comes to the cognitive status of their claims—we cannot doubt that they had an experience or its phenomenology, but we can question their understanding of what was experienced when mystics equally well-positioned in experiences and reasoning disagree. In fact, the strong emotional impact that mystics usually feel from these experiences may well make it harder for them to examine their own experiences and claims critically and to avoid an unwarranted sense of certainty in their own particular understanding of their experiences. Thus, a philosophical examination is especially important in this field.

The Analogy to Sense-Perception

It also should be noted before proceeding that philosophers can distort mysticism by how they analyze it. One example is the argument for the cognitivity of mystical experiences based on treating the experiences as analogous to ordinary sense-perception (e.g., Alston 1991). Some philosophers argue that it is just as reasonable to accept mystical claims as it is to accept claims based on sense-perceptions: under a general principle of "reliabilism" or "credulity" we accept sense-experiences as reliable until they are shown to be otherwise, and so too we should also equally accept mystical experience as reliable until its mechanisms have been shown to be unreliable, which neuroscience has not done to date.

But for the analogy to apply, transcendent realities must be like ordinary intentional objects, and mystical experiences must have a dualistic subject/object structure—otherwise the reliability of sense-perceptions is irrelevant to whether mystical experiences are reliable sources of knowledge. But the fundamental problem is that mystical experiences involve a knowledge by "participation" or "identity," not anything like a "nonsensory sense-perception" since it has no object-like content separate from the experiencer to perceive. It is entirely contrary to being "confronted with an object or reality that appears to or is present to [mystics] in a nonsensory way" (contra Gellman 2001: 11). To think of mystics as "perceiving God" as an object distinct from themselves that is "presented" to them is to go off in the wrong direction—it sets up a duality of experiencer and what is experienced that mystics explicitly deny. The states of consciousness permitting participatory knowledge make these experiences unique, and thus we have no reason to believe that this analogy is applicable (see Jones 2016: 85–88).

Do Scientific Studies Validate or Invalidate Mystical Claims?

One major issue is whether neuroscientific or socioscientific explanations can validate or refute mystical claims. Can neuroscience show that mystical experiences reveal something about the nature of reality, or show that these experiences are in fact nothing more than brain-generated events and thus to think that they elicit an insight is a delusion?

Many contemporary New Age advocates enthusiastically conclude that the neuroscientific studies of meditators have validated age-old mystical claims by showing mystical experiences are not the result of a damaged brain. But to naturalists, the significance of the experiences is exhaustively explained by scientific accounts: only the natural mind and body are involved in these experiences, not a transcendent consciousness or other reality—the perfectly ordinary effects of meditation or drugs dampening activity in the areas of the brain associated with a sense of a self that is separate from the rest of the universe explain the loss of a sense of self and the blurring of the lines between oneself and the rest of the world. Similarly, the sense of profundity and bliss are produced only by meditation or drugs increasing the activity in the areas of the brain responsible for feelings. So too, any potential psychological or physical benefits of meditation could occur just as well if the cognitive claims are false and the experiences are the product only of the brain. The commonality of mystical experiences across cultures does not necessarily mean they are veridical but only that we are all constituted the same way with regard to these experiences. Theists erroneously attach more significance to any experiences of light or warmth as "experiences of God" only because of the strangeness of the states of consciousness and because of their prior belief in a supreme transcendent deity. They think that earlier famous mystics had experienced God, and so these experiences must be the same too. But even if a transcendent reality does exist, an introvertive mystical experience is still not an experience of anything but natural phenomena. For naturalists, the most positive understanding that can be given to mystical experiences is that they disclose something about the nature of the natural mind or consciousness, but these experiences are merely brain-generated internal events.

Or consider triggers such as psychedelic drugs. Does the fact that mystical experiences can be induced fairly regularly by such means mean that they are merely products of brain states and no other reality? Do bad drug-enabled experiences reveal the nature of all ASC experiences? Or do the drugs merely set up the base neural conditions permitting a genuine infusion of a transcendent reality to occur sometimes? Does the role of "set and setting" affect the issue one way or the other? Even if scientists do discover a drug that triggers a depth-mystical experience 100 percent of the time, the core issue remains: is an introvertive mystical experience a purely natural phenomenon, or have the scientists merely created the conditions in the brain making a person receptive to the infusion of a transcendent reality?

In sum, do the drugs in proper dosages *enable* a transcendent reality to enter the mind (or in the case of extrovertive mystical experiences an ASC perception), or is that mystical sense a delusion *caused* only by the brain? To many of those not already committed to naturalism on this point (including most scientists who are aware of the philosophical issue), that scientists can in principle identify all the neural correlates no more explains away the insights than a neurological explanation of sense-perception explains away claims based on scientific observations. That is, merely identifying what is occurring in the brain during a mystical experience no more undercuts mystical claims to cognition than identifying the mechanics at work in valid sense-perception renders those perceptions cognitively empty. There appears no way for science today to tell us if brain activity causes mystical experiences or if meditation only sets up the necessary base conditions in the brain for receiving contact with a transcendent reality in some cases (see Jones 2016: 151–59). Perhaps something like disrupting the normal activity in some part of the brain is necessary to have any mystical experience, but this does not mean that therefore the experience is only a product of the disrupted mechanisms and could not possibly be cognitive. Whether the experiences are cognitive or not, the scientific findings would be the same. The issue is philosophical in nature and may remain so in the future.

In short, science per se cannot establish whether mystical experiences are cognitive or not. That drugs are a natural substance does not rule out a possible experience of a transcendent reality: all the drugs may do is merely disrupt the brain conditions underlying normal consciousness, allowing in a transcendent reality in some cases. All the science shows is what is occurring in our neural circuitry during mystical experiences and cannot go further in determining whether brain events cause the experiences or whether something more to reality causes the brain events. (That beingness is not subject to scientific tests was noted in the last chapter, and transcendent realities are by definition not subject to scientific testing.) Socioscientific explanations are even looser: if it is shown that persons with a certain psychological disposition or coming from a certain social class are more likely to become scientists, this does not in any way invalidate their scientific observations, and the same holds for mystics and whether their experiences are cognitive. Naturalists will take the fact that scientific claims can be checked by others as separating mysticism from science, but that again goes beyond the science itself.[2]

Thus, the experiences may or may not be experiences of a transcendent reality, but we can never be confident one way or the other. The depth-mystical state may simply be an awareness of our own consciousness, and other introvertive mystical experiences may only involve subconscious material welling up into our consciousness once our baseline consciousness is broken. Extrovertive experiences may distort only our sensory apparatus, as with LSD experiences—the brain produces a very interesting effect on our sense-experiences and our sense of time, but the resulting experiences are irrelevant as insights into reality because they are only the products of a scrambled sensory-apparatus.

However, that drugs impair our ordinary cognitive and perceptual apparatus does not rule out the possibility that by doing so they also open the doors to other types of cognitive consciousness. Not all ASCs can be automatically grouped with getting drunk when it comes to cognitivity. Not all changes to the nervous system or consciousness need to be negative—for example, meditation may improve our health and enhance our perceptions. Of course, if people who have mystical experiences *all* have *damaged brains* or suffer from other *pathologies*, then the naturalists' approach becomes a compelling argument that no insight is involved: it is hard to argue that a physically damaged brain can gain a new insight into reality that a healthy brain misses—that God, as it were, reveals himself only to people with defective brains. If, however, these experiences are common among healthy people, this argument fails. And there is empirical evidence that spiritual experiences are widespread among normal persons (Hood 2006).

Moreover, even if it turns out that mystical experiences are associated with parts of the brain that more commonly produce hallucinations, advocates of mysticism can turn this situation around and argue that the hallucinations are the products of the malfunctioning of brain mechanisms that when functioning properly enable veridical mystical experiences, even if the former are more common. As discussed in chapter 8, dissociative states of schizophrenia and some psychoses may result from the same implosions of a transcendent reality that occur in mystical experiences, but the patients are simply not equipped to handle them, and so the disconnect from a self or everyday reality produces confusion and panic; mystics, however, have a belief-framework and the training or psychological preparation needed to handle the disintegration of the mundane worldview positively and to later reintegrate into the normal world successfully.

The Epistemic Effect of Scientific Studies

The point here is that the scientific findings on the brain activity during a mystical experience will not themselves answer the philosophical question of whether the experience is cognitive or not. But even if scientific accounts cannot directly refute mystical claims, they can *neutralize* mystical claims as uncontested evidence of a transcendent realism. That is, the science may aid mystics' claims by showing that mystical experiences have unique neural bases and that they are not merely the result of a damaged brain, but they now offer *a plausible alternative* to mystical understandings of these experiences, and thus these experiences lose any epistemic presumption of being evidence of a transcendent reality that they might have enjoyed in the absence of a natural explanation. Thus, we cannot automatically assume that if mystical experiences come from a healthy brain that they must involve the cognition of a reality. The depth-mystical experience may result from nothing more than the brain spinning its gears when it has no mental content to work with: the brain evolved to help us survive in the natural world, and if we succeed in removing all sensory and other content from the mind while remaining awake, the brain may well malfunction badly and not be cognitively reliable. In sum, we cannot simply assume that mystical experiences are *reliable cognitive processes* even if the brains of all the experiencers are healthy.

Thus, the damage of a natural explanation is not to the possibility of a genuine mystical experience but to the experience's philosophical value as *evidence* in an argument in favor of transcendent realities. We are left not with proof that transcendent explanations are wrong but in a more uncertain situation. To oversimplify: if our brain is not malfunctioning, we may be hardwired for self-transcending mystical experiences, but did God wire us to experience transcendent realities, or did evolution wire us just to think so because it somehow aids in our survival, or are these experiences merely the cognitively empty by-products of some useful evolutionary development? So too, mystical experiences may in fact be common, as sociological research suggests, but this does not mean that a transcendent reality is involved. A demonstrated commonality may bear on the question of whether mystical consciousness is a more normal mental state of healthy people than naturalists typically accept but not on the question of the experiences' proper explanation. That we all may experience the same optical illusion of a mirage does not make the water in it objectively real. The frequency of such experiences is simply irrelevant to the philosophical question of what scientific explanations accomplish.

Advocates of mystical cognitivity believe that mystical experiences "feel so vividly real" after mystics return to their baseline state of consciousness—indeed, they feel even *more* in touch with what is fundamentally real than during experiences in ordinary consciousness—that they must be rooted in a direct contact with a reality and thus are not merely the subjective product of our brains. In general, most people consider ASCs as less real (Yaden et al. 2017a: 55), but people who have had both mystical experiences and demonstrable hallucinations typically do not believe they are the same. After they are over, they do not have the feel of hallucinations or dreams, which are seen to be illusions once the experiencer returns to a normal state of consciousness; rather, the memory of these experiences has at least the same sense of reality as memories of ordinary "real" events (Newberg, d'Aquili & Rause 2002: 112). In one study, 69 percent of those who had intense spiritual experiences felt the experiences were "more real than the usual sense of reality" and used words referring to connection, a greater whole, and certainty rather than personal pronouns and words suggesting tentativeness (Yaden et al. 2017a). Naturalists would dismiss a "vivid" subjective sense that what is experienced is "more real" or "realer than real" as only the result of some internal activity of the brain. The impact of the experience does not mean that a "pure consciousness" is our "true self," leading to dismissing the ordinary state of mind with desires and a sense of self as our true state, but only another state of consciousness.

On pragmatic grounds, proponents will also point out that many experiencers enjoy a general enhancement of our sense of well-being (i.e., a sense of satisfaction with life or of a purpose or meaning to life). Critics reply that mystical experiences are not uniformly beneficial—some people experience very negative effects. Nor do the experiences always have a lasting effect once the initial glow has subsided. Meditation also can end up aggravating negative mental conditions and personality traits—some meditative experiences lead to a mental breakdown. Thus, not all experiencers turn out to be healthier or to live more effectively in the natural world. Nor is the sense of joy, calmness, or bliss in itself indicative of a cognition or insight: one can be "blissed out" regardless of whether transcendent realities or delusions are involved in the introvertive experiences—the feeling may come from freedom from a sense of self, or simply from the mind being undisturbed when it is empty of all differentiable content but is still active. So too, mystical experiences may have positive effects on our happiness even if no transcendent realities are involved, just as LSD therapy helps to break the hold of depression and addiction and helps to comfort the dying by lessening their fear of death.

And secular mysticism must again be noted: today not all mystical experiences are seen by the experiencers as cognitive or as having any religious significance. We do not appear to be in a position to see if mystical experiences are delusions or veridical or what is their proper interpretation since transcendent realities are not open to third-person examination. The preferability or even plausibility of the various naturalist and transcendent options must be answered on grounds other than the mystical experiences themselves. Ultimately, one's decision on such matters may depend on one's intuitions of what in the final analysis is real. The scientific and sociocultural explanations themselves will not determine our choice.

The Conflict of Mystical Claims

Since the early twentieth century, the position that mystical experiences and mystical knowledge-claims are really the same in all cultures has been used to validate mysticism. But today the emphasis on the diversity of mystical claims has led to a second challenge to their truth. Classical mystics do not tentatively set forth what they believe they have experienced—*certainty* is a general characteristic of classical mystics, but the certainty is in the specific claims of a given mystic's tradition, not in abstract realities or in mystical experiences being cognitive in the abstract. Mystical experiences give knowledge only in the context of wider systems of thought, and thus the mystics' confidence in what they *know* about reality is in terms of their system, not in the phenomenological accounts of their experiences. But as Richard M. Bucke had pointed out, a sense of *certitude* does not in fact entail *certainty* ([1901] 1969: 70–71).

The basic problem is that the understandings of what is experienced not only diverge but *conflict*. There are theistic and nontheistic monisms, dualisms, and pluralisms, each supported by mystics. Consider some basic matters for introvertive mysticisms: Is what is experienced in the depth-mystical experience the source of something phenomenal? If so, is it the source of all natural phenomena or just the ground of the self? Is it nonpersonal, or do depth-mystics experience only the nonpersonal beingness of a personal god? Is depth-mystical experience an experience of God's being or the experience of only the root of the self? Does an experienced consciousness underlie matter? Must there be one source to everything, or are matter and consciousness separate as in Samkhya? Does a depth-mystical experience confirm Advaita's view of a fundamental consciousness that is the only reality, or does it confirm Samkhya's view of multiple transcendent conscious "persons" (*purushas*)?[3] Or does it confirm no more than a natural consciousness experienced in a pure state? Is it just an intense awareness of the natural ground of the beingness of the world with no further ontological significance? Do these positions conflict with the extrovertive Buddhist view that consciousness is a series of temporary impermanent conditioned events? How do we decide between accepting a Buddhist discovery based on experiences that there is no soul or a theistic mystic's claim equally based on experience that there is an eternal soul underlying our being in the "dream" realm? If all theistic introvertive experiences are of the same god, are they of the trinitarian god of Christianity, or of the simpler divine unity of the one-person god of Islam and Judaism, or of an immanent god, or of just a nonpersonal deistic source? Having any mystical experience while praying fervently to Jesus would naturally be taken by the person to be confirmation that Jesus still exists and is the Lord, but is it? Is the transcendent source moral or morally indifferent?

Of course, religious theorists within any tradition will be able to advance reasons to prefer one understanding over others, but equally obviously members of other traditions with other basic beliefs will most likely remain unconvinced and will offer their own reasons for their positions. If mystical experiences are cognitive, how do we account for the conflicting diversity of mystical claims that mystics have held? Are all understandings merely postexperiential speculative Jamesian "over-beliefs" that are not justified by any of these experiences? When it comes to conflicting sense-experience claims, sense-experiences cannot be presented for examination, but others can test the credibility of the evidence for a claim by their own sense-experiences. But no such intersubjective procedure is possible for mystics' claims. Unlike scientific predictions, there is no new fresh mystical experiential input to check claims but only more experiences of the same nature. This removes one social dimension to mystical knowledge, even if mystical knowledge claims are formed socially. That prior beliefs may affect the phenomenological content of at least some mystical experiences devalues the evidential value of predictions: any new mystical experiences would be taken only as confirmation of the experiencer's own previous beliefs.[4] In sum, mystical experiences themselves cannot adjudicate the competing claims or between naturalism and the possibility of a transcendent realism. Masters in meditative traditions may have tests to determine if a practitioner is enlightened, but from the scientific point of view those tests are still indirect and subjective—at best, they may be able to confirm that an experience or enlightenment occurred (as defined by that tradition), but they cannot confirm that the tradition's doctrinal interpretation is correct or better than that of others. Mystical experiences simply radically underdetermine any theory.

That mystical experiences are open to being seen as supporting conflicting claims has one major consequence: even the *mystics themselves* are not justified by their experiences alone in accepting their own experiences as strong confirmation of their tradition's doctrines. Even if all mystics do experience the same transcendent reality or the depth of the self, the fact remains that each mystic typically thinks that his or her doctrine (and thus doctrines in other traditions that concur with it) is the "best" or "least inadequate" understanding of the nature of what is experienced and that any conflicting doctrine is less adequate. No matter how powerful the experience may be for an experiencer, this does not exempt the experiencer from the possibility of error concerning the existence and nature of what was experienced. Moreover, mystics cannot even confirm or be certain that some transcendent reality in the abstract was experienced—some experiencers today think that their experiences result only from natural states of the mind. Naturalists can see why the experiences may well overwhelm mystics, but they still claim that the experiences are only natural events resulting from the brain being emptied of all differentiable content.

Thus, since the naturalist option is a viable alternative, even if introvertive mystics in fact have direct, unmediated access to a noumenon, how can they be certain that that is so? How can theistic mystics be sure, in the words of the medieval English "Letter of Private Counsel," that they have "seen and felt . . . God as he is in himself"? That claim is about something real apart from the state of mind itself. When you have a headache, you can be certain that you have a headache, but that is not a claim about reality apart from your state of mind, or about the headache's causes. So too, a mystical experience is self-validating as a state of consciousness but not about any given interpretation of its nature. In such circumstances, how can mystics be certain about the state of affairs apart from their state of consciousness and its causes?

In addition, mystical knowledge may be grounded in experience and thus not purely speculative, but, as noted in chapter 4, the variety of understandings in the world's mystical traditions shows that mystical knowledge cannot be deduced in a simple empiricist fashion from phenomenological descriptions of the experiences themselves. There is no direct way to deduce any highly ramified concepts from low-ramified accounts of the phenomenology of the experiences. All knowledge-claims, even here, are always more than what can be justified by experiences alone. For example, how could Advaitins know by any experience that a transcendent consciousness is common to all persons and all worldly phenomena? They would have to offer more than their inner experiences to identify our essence (*atman*) with the ground of reality (Brahman) or to argue that Brahman is conscious and is the only reality.[5] Shankara rightly separated enlightening knowledge from mystical experiences.

Also note that classical mystics did not take their own experiences as an *empirical verification or proof* of their tradition's doctrines or as authority for those doctrines. Rather, *the reverse is true*: they appeal to their tradition's *authorities, doctrines, and texts* to establish the *correct understanding* of their experiences. For them, their tradition's doctrines do not need any empirical proof, and classical mystics never advanced mystical experiences as proof—indeed, they might have been quite surprised at such a maneuver. In short, unlike a modern approach, a tradition's basic scripture validated the experiences, not vice versa. Shankara appealed to the Vedas, not experience (*anubhava*), for justification of his doctrines. Shankara said that this appeal to revealed authority (*shruti*) is necessary since philosophers constantly contradict each other.[6] Even if such mystics as Eckhart and Shankara interpreted their scriptures to fit their ideas, nevertheless they saw their scriptures properly interpreted as the source of knowledge. And even Buddhist schools over time came to accept the Buddha's testimony (*shabda*) as a means of valid knowledge, along with perception and inference. If mystics have to check their beliefs against one revealed source or another to understand the experiences properly or even to be sure that their experiences are veridical, they ultimately are in no better position than the rest of us for determining the actual nature of what was experienced, since mystical experiences cannot tell us which authority we should accept, if any.

Since introvertive experiences are open to numerous competing understandings, they obviously are not self-interpreting even if mystics typically think their own experiences are. The sense that one has experienced a fundamental reality may be incorrigible, but no doctrinal account of what is experienced is impervious to error. Again, many who undergo mystical experiences today see no cognitive significance in them—to them, they are merely exotic experiences generated by the brain. Naturalists also point to the conflicting understandings of mystical realities from around the world and throughout history as an indication that no reality at all is actually experienced and that these experiences are not cognitive. But that does not follow: it only shows that postexperience understandings conflict—competing understandings do not rule out the possibility that introvertive mystics in fact experience some transcendent reality or that one account may be the best possible (as discussed below). At most, all that follows is that even mystics themselves cannot know the nature of any transcendent reality that they experience.

But that does mean that the mystics' certainty in the highly ramified accounts that they advance to close off some mystery is misplaced: it may be that many—perhaps most or even all—mystics *misinterpret* their introvertive experiences and thus are wrong. There may be a common phenomenological element to all introvertive mystical accounts—for example, a profound sense of a direct, unmediated experience of a nondual and fundamental reality—that transcends cultures, but there is no simple, neutral account of the full nature of that reality. Thus, the competing understandings of either category of introvertive experience raise a serious problem: if mystics disagree among themselves about what is experienced, how can we treat these experiences as *reliable sources of knowledge*? If one understanding is correct, then ipso facto all mystics who dispute that understanding are wrong. This means that many mystics, perhaps the majority or all, *misunderstand their own experiences*. This radically undercuts the alleged reliability of mystical experiences and thus the credibility of any mystical particular knowledge-claim. It also damages privileging mystical experiences in general over other experiences for understanding reality, no matter how powerful the experiences are or the experiencer's resulting certitude.

Creating Mystical Agreement

A related argument is that, despite appearances, there is in fact a cross-cultural agreement among mystics on what is experienced, and that this "argument from unanimity" justifies belief in a transcendent reality—that is, mystics from around the world converge on the same substantive claims, once we discount the differences in expressions due to cultural differences.[7] In William James's words, there is an "eternal unanimity" among mystics ([1902] 1958: 321). Theists take mystical experiences as positive evidence, or even conclusive proof, that a creator god exists and has certain features. But the plausibility of naturalist interpretations today harms the strength of the argument: any common experience may be produced simply by our common brain structure and not a common transcendent reality. And even if that issue can be circumvented, theistic premises can never be shown to be definitively better grounded in experience than nontheistic counter premises. Most people may be theists and see what is experienced anthropomorphically, but nontheistic mystics appear to be in the same epistemic position as theistic ones. Thus, even if advocates of this argument can counter natural reductions and establish that there is some transcendent reality, the problem remains that beliefs of the nature of that reality genuinely conflict.

Of course, one can artificially create such a consensus by distorting the beliefs of some mystics, as with perennial philosophers imposing their metaphysics. Theists may interpret nontheists' accounts along their own theological lines and thereby create a consensus for theism, but nontheists can just as easily do the same to make a consensus for their nondualistic or dualistic beliefs. Seeing mystical experience as supporting the specific doctrines of any particular tradition requires dismissing at least some accounts by mystics in other traditions and arguing that those mystics really are experiencing something other than what they think. An example of the problem is Nelson Pike's (1992) argument that the depth-mystical experience is really *phenomenologically theistic* since it occurs at the culmination of a sequence of theistic states in which the subject/object duality is gradually overcome and so the "climax moment" has a theistic "ancestry" that colors the depth-mystical experience itself. That is, the prior beliefs and practices somehow color the experience of consciousness, and so no consciousness is truly "pure." But, for example, Advaitins would see the same series of experiences with differentiated content on the path as gradually overcoming all dualities and leading to the obliteration of any sense of a personal god—no theistic residue would be involved in the culminating event. That theists immediately after the experience take it to have been an experience of God only points to their prior beliefs and training—Advaitins would similarly react and conclude that it is an experience of the nonpersonal Brahman.

Religious theorists are just as willing as naturalists to tell mystics that they are mistaken about the content of their experiences. For example, Caroline Franks Davis has to twist the Advaitins' and Buddhists' accounts to show that mystical experiences really support a "broad theism"—that is, Shankara was really experiencing God although he explicitly argued that the nonpersonal and nonloving Brahman alone is real, and the Buddha was totally unaware that he was experiencing a god. She claims that all mystics, despite what they say, really experience "a loving presence . . . with whom individuals can have a personal relationship" (1989: 191). That is just what one would expect someone raised a Christian to see as the true "common core" of all mystical experiences. But the same process, mutatis mutandis, would occur for people raised in other traditions for their claims. We cannot simply translate one tradition's highly ramified concepts depicting a transcendent reality into another tradition's equally highly ramified but different concepts, nor can we simply assume that all low-ramified concepts about the phenomenology of a mystical experience support one's chosen set of highly ramified theological concepts over other interpretations and then conclude that all mystical traditions really support one's own tradition's doctrines although outsiders do not know it. Certainly, if the depth-mystical experience is indeed empty of anything but consciousness, it cannot support a "broad theism."

In sum, this argument runs aground on the hard fact of genuine religious diversity: religious theorists must twist other religion's conceptions and doctrines in order to fabricate an "agreement." Such arguments rest squarely in religious reasoning and are not based on mystical experiences. In such circumstances, mystical experiences themselves remain neutral on the matter of which understanding, if any, is valid. As William James came to realize, when religious history is examined "the supposed unanimity disappears" ([1902] 1958: 324).

Can One Mystical System Be Established as Best?

Mystical knowledge-claims appear genuinely to conflict, not merely diverge, but conflicting claims do not rule out one mystical system being better than others if there is an agreed-upon neutral procedure for adjudicating between competing understandings or for justifying one set of mystical doctrines as epistemically superior. However, there does not appear to be any criteria. And even if there were, the application of the criteria would no doubt turn on the competing underlying metaphysics from different traditions—that is, theological and metaphysical beliefs would determine how any neutral criteria are applied. For example, for Christians who take the incarnation of Christ as the central event of history, any view that ignores that in characterizing our situation is not being *objective*.

A pragmatic criterion for true mystical experiences was mentioned above, and William James proposed a pragmatic test for determining true mystical doctrines ([1902] 1958: 368): if a mystical experience produces positive results in how one leads one's life, then the experience is authentic and the way of life one follows is vindicated, and so the teachings leading to the positive life are correct. In short, the "truth" of one's beliefs are shown by one's life as a whole. Christian mystics have often used a pragmatic criterion—for example, Teresa of Avila said that one can tell if an experience comes from God or from the Devil by its fruits in actions and personality (along with the vividness of the memory of the experience, conformity to Christian scripture, and confirmation by church superiors) (*Interior Castle* 7.4.6–7, 5.3.11). For her, humility and charity result from an authentic God-given experience.

However, the "moral fruits" test has problems. First, all traditions have produced mystics with such effects in their lives, and so these effects do not show that one tradition's doctrines are superior to others. Second, as will be discussed in chapter 13, mystical experiences need not make a person moral or more socially active: while all enlightened mystics shift toward selflessness, not all enlightened mystics fill their newly found selflessness with a moral concern for others—the enlightened cannot be self-centered, but they can exhibit a "holy indifference" to the welfare of others. Whether one becomes moral appears to depend on factors outside of mystical experiences. In Jainism, the ideal for the enlightened is to stop harming any creature, and so they take no actions at all, leading to their death by starvation. But how is this proof that these people had no mystical experiences or are not enlightened? Certainly not merely because the ideal conflicts with Christian values for an active enlightened way of life. Third, there are antinomian mystics in every tradition. Fourth, the nonreligious who unexpectedly have spontaneous mystical experiences may also reflect only the values of their cultures in their understanding or not change at all—this cannot establish the doctrines of one tradition. Thus, the "fruit" seems more a matter of one's background beliefs than the product of the disruption of a sense of self given in a mystical experience.

In the end, it is difficult to imagine a set of criteria or procedures to determine one set of mystical doctrines as supreme that is truly neutral and does not reflect the values of one tradition or another. What is accepted as a true doctrine turns on religious or naturalist criteria rather than the impact of the experiences themselves or any neutral criterion internal to the practice of mysticism generally.

The Limitation of Any Mystical Claim to Knowledge

Classical mystics are certain that they have *experienced* some fundamental reality—in "knowledge by participation," transcendent realities are directly known. Nevertheless, while introvertive experiences of a transcendent reality may be direct and not inferred, the *understanding* of what is experienced remains a matter of interpretation, and we are not in a position to know which understanding is best. So too, other knowledge-claims of mystical ways of life are only indirectly inferred. For example, Buddhists claim that enlightenment is the end of the cycle of rebirths by ending a sense of self and its accompanying desires, but do they *experience* only the end of desires and *infer* the end of rebirths based on the theory that the cycle of rebirths is driven by desires grounded in a mistaken sense of a self? Why do mystics in the West speak of ending desires and a sense of self but say nothing about this event ending a cycle of rebirths? It is easy to understand that mystics would not normally see a difference between the experience and the interpretation imposed onto it, but the difference is exposed by the comparative study of mysticism. Mystics may know *that* something fundamental exists, but *what* it is, beyond being "real," "one," "immutable," or "beingness," is not given but instead is open to different understandings outside the introvertive mystical states of consciousness. In the end, one studying mysticism too is left with mystery.

This greatly limits the extent of any specific "mystical knowledge" that the experiences actually justify. At a minimum, this means that even if mystics are cognitive of some reality, this is not a good reason by itself to assume the specific beliefs of any particular tradition. Rather, theists, nontheists, and naturalists are all in the same boat in claiming they understand these experiences correctly and others do not. But the role of external beliefs and practices in determining one's own understanding of the nature and status of one's mystical experiences cannot be ignored. Thus, the experiences have less cognitive content than mystics realize: knowledge-claims are not determined or validated by these experiences alone.

This leads to another issue: even if we assume that some transcendent reality is experienced, do *any* mystical knowledge-claims actually capture the reality experienced, since there will always be a human-generated, nonexperiential element to any knowledge-claim? And even if one of the possible understandings is in fact the best that is humanly possible, in the absence of neutral criteria for adjudication the presence of conflicting interpretations that have stood the test of time will remain a barrier to our determining which one it is. Even if a consensus develops over time for one existing understanding concerning what exactly is experienced in each type of introvertive experience or a new religious option arises in the future, how can we be sure it reflects what is real? Consensus does not mandate truth—after all, before Copernicus there was a consensus in Europe concerning a Ptolemaic cosmology for over a thousand years. So too, a consensus may arise for political or other nonmystical reasons and not from a discussion of the experiences.

Mystics may insist that only they know reality's true nature or that the proof of their claims lies within their own hearts and that their experiences confirm their beliefs. Nevertheless, the problem again is the competing answers to all the basic questions noted above: mystics cannot get around the fact that other mystics who apparently have had experiences of the same nature support conflicting views and have the same personal conviction of their claims being "self-evident" or "self-establishing." Thus, a mystic cannot say "Just meditate—you'll see that ours is the true knowledge" when making claims about the nature of what is experienced since equally qualified mystics are advancing conflicting understandings. As noted, even if a mystic could claim certainty in having experienced something transcendent, this certainty cannot be transferred to his or her *theory of the nature of what was experienced*. There are no "self-confirming," "self-authenticating," "self-validating," or "self-verifying" doctrines about the nature of what is experienced, no matter how powerful the experiences are, even if one doctrine is in fact correct or the best.

In sum, there is an epistemic gap between experience and doctrine—between any phenomenal claim and any ontological claim about the reality experienced. That gap cannot be bridged even by the participatory knowledge of mystical experiences. The claims need a justification that goes beyond the experiences themselves.

Is It Rational to Accept Mystical Knowledge-Claims?

If we accept that no set of mystical knowledge-claims can be established to be the best in any neutral way, we must accept that no mystical knowledge-claims can be *proven* in the sense that it would be irrational for anyone familiar with the issues of natural explanations and competing sets of mystical knowledge-claims to reject the set of such claims. But can we at least determine if it is rational for mystics themselves or for nonmystics to hold their own doctrines based on mystical experiences? That is, can we lower the bar from trying to establish the *truth* of particular mystical doctrines to merely establishing that it is *rational* to hold some mystical doctrines?[8]

First, can mystics themselves rationally commit to their own doctrines and traditions once they are aware of competing understanding from other mystics? Is it rational for mystics themselves to count their experiences as evidence for the doctrines they hold? William Alston (1991) held that it is rational for Christians to regard the Christian mystical practice as sufficiently reliable to be the source of prima facie justification for the Christian beliefs that it engenders, and so Christian mystical perception should be accepted as a reliable cognitive access to God and the foundation for other beliefs. But he admits that Hindus and Buddhists are *just as rational* in engaging in their own socially established doxastic practices, even though many of the claims in these three traditions are incompatible (274–75). The doxastic justification makes the assertion of the equal rationality of mystics who have been trained in established traditions fairly easy to establish—in fact, it is hard *not* to be rational by Alston's criterion of any established social practice that we do not have sufficient reason for regarding as unreliable (6), since each tradition has responded extensively to the scrutiny and criticism of opponents over a long period of time, and natural explanations do not at this time refute all mysticism. All established practices would be equally rational and well-informed epistemic peers: each has the same or relevantly similar experiences; each is aware of criticism and other positions; each produces impressive supporting arguments; and each ends up with well-reasoned positions, with only the *hope* that interreligious contradictions will be sorted out over time (7).[9] The result for now is an apparently irresolvable relativism—all are rational and none are irrational for rejecting others' claims.[10]

But this presents a problem. As Alston admitted, the diversity of outputs from religions that are not consistent *lessens the rationality of all mystical practices* (1991: 275). Indeed, the substantive inconsistencies between traditions undermine the idea that mystical experiences are at all *reliable as a basis of belief-forming* in general—the beliefs of different traditions still conflict, and if one set is correct then most multiple doctrines on each given point must be *false*. How then can we treat any of the doctrines as claims warranted by expert testimony? This even undercuts the rationality of accepting that mystical experiences justify the abstract claim that there is at least some transcendent reality even if we do not know its nature (especially in light of naturalist alternative explanations). In addition, there is divergence even within Christian mystical practices themselves—as Alston realized (192–94)—and this is a major problem: if the practices cannot converge even within one tradition, the rationality of mysticism is even more severely challenged. Once the religious know of the variety of socially established but conflicting mystical practices there is the issue of the *arbitrariness* in their choice.

Nevertheless, the threshold for rationality is low enough that we can conclude that mystics can rationally accept the knowledge-claims of their tradition based on their experiences even without the hope that the contradictions will be resolved someday. For similar reasons naturalists too are rational in rejecting all transcendent mystical knowledge-claims. As long as you have examined the alternatives and possible objections to your position and can still hold your position without incoherence, you are being rational in your commitments. Since science alone cannot refute mystical claims (as discussed), introvertive mystics can rationally accept their own experiences as cognitive of a transcendent reality as understood in their tradition until their knowledge-claims are shown to be incoherent. (Advaita is a favorite target for the claim of incoherence.) However, the diversity of competing and equally well-established mystical ways of life and understandings of what is experienced does lessen the degree of confidence any mystic can have in his or her own doctrines, but this loss is not enough to make it irrational to hold them if their claims have been rationally examined and found defendable.

However, is it rational today for those who have *not* had mystical experiences to accept mystics' experiences as evidence for holding the doctrines of their own tradition? William James believed that mystical states are "absolutely authoritative" for those who have had them but not for those who have not ([1902] 1958: 324, 382, 414): the experiences are so vivid for the experiencer that the problem of religious diversity is an issue only for nonmystics. But the presence of competing doctrines brings into question the epistemic right of *all believers*, whether they have had a mystical experience or not, to say that their tradition's understanding must be better than others'. That lowers the degree of rationality for mystics and nonmystical believers alike. Indeed, the rationality of both groups is on the same footing: since mystical claims are made in a web of beliefs—not dictated by experience—it should be as *rational* for those who have not had the experiences but have reason to accept that others have had them to affirm the tradition's claims that are ultimately agreed upon. (That the nonmystics make any transcendent realities into objects reflecting their traditions' conceptions will be discussed in the next chapter.) The experiences may be *psychologically compelling* for the experiencer, but the conviction they produce in the doctrines of the mystic's tradition does not change the experiences' epistemic status or the overall rationality of their beliefs. It is not so much that nonmystics are in a worse position than mystics as that mystics are not in a better epistemic one, despite the impact of their experiences on them personally.

Our Epistemic Situation

To summarize: mystical experiences cannot guarantee their own cognitivity, and we are not in a position to determine with any certainty whether introvertive mystics experience transcendent realities, let alone know their nature. Mystics may be rational in believing their tradition's claims, but they do not have an epistemic right to assert that they know either that those claims are true or even that at least some transcendent reality exists. The ground of being may illuminate a person's consciousness during a mystical experience, or these experiences may simply be powerful delusions. These experiences may be cognitive, and some particular concrete depiction true or at least the best, but we cannot tell. Mystical experiences awaken a person to there being more to reality than the normal phenomenal world, or more to the mind than ordinary states of consciousness, but the experiences do not validate specific metaphysical claims. Classical mystics may be naive realists about their own claims, but the conflicting accounts of what is allegedly experienced expose the limitations of our understanding in this area. In the end, mystical experiences do not favor one tradition's set of doctrines over another or even a transcendent realism over naturalism, and there are no theory-neutral ways of determining which set is best, if any.

— 12 —
Mysticism and Language

Mystical literature is quite varied—hagiography, parables, poetry, prayers, some meditative exercises, and instruction manuals for practices (see Keller 1978). But what interests most people is why mystics have trouble describing what they have experienced when we do not have that problem in describing something phenomenal that we have experienced. This comes up in mystics' declarative use of language in their cognitive claims, especially in such texts as commentaries on basic religious texts and philosophical treatises. Mystics often consider what is experienced to be inexpressible and even unnameable—yet they proceed to describe it. Some have advanced elaborate metaphysics centered around it. Thus, mystics can be very confusing when it comes to language: they can write copiously and impressively about what they have experienced and then immediately turn around and assert that nothing can be said on that topic or that language cannot convey the truth. Can one know a reality but not be able to express it? Laozi again comes to mind: how can he say that "those who know do not speak, and those who speak do not know" while writing a book on the Dao (*Daodejing* 56)? Are we to conclude that he doesn't know the Dao since he is speaking about it? All in all, how are we to make sense of anything mystics say?

Mystics want to speak, since something real and profound is allegedly experienced, but how can they do that without making that reality into something like a phenomenal object? Consciousness or transcendent realities may not be objects, but language treats them as such. How can an Advaitin speak of the eternal *subject* Brahman without making it into a grammatical object and thereby making it like every other *object*? So too, how can the *unity* that introvertive and extrovertive mystics experience be expressed in any language since all languages must make distinctions and hence are inherently *dualistic*? Doesn't grammar make all realities objects? How can a *transcendent* reality that is utterly unlike any phenomenal object be described in a language that references *phenomenal properties*? On the extrovertive level, how can any language (which necessarily consists of *static terms* setting up *divisions*) express phenomenal reality when reality is actually *dynamic and without discrete parts*? Giving new meanings to old terms or inventing new words that have no prior phenomenal reference (e.g., being "one'd") will not help—it is the nature of language itself that is the problem. Shouldn't all mystics be reduced to silence?

The Denial of Positive Characterizations

Both what is allegedly experienced and also the experiences themselves seem totally other than our normal experiences and reality. Thus, mystics are concerned that speaking about them transforms them into something ordinary. Language seems necessarily to distort the nature of both the ASC experiences and what is experienced. Language by its very nature labels things and thereby sets up a duality for everything, including the self and any transcendent realities experienced inwardly in ASCs—language encodes the "dualistic" consciousness that externalizes what is in one's consciousness, thereby creating a pluralistic world with a subject and multiple objects distinct from each other. We reify labels into discrete entities, and reality is reduced to a collection of discrete objects. Thus, language blocks us from seeing reality as it really is. To extrovertive mystics, our linguistic inventions that we impose on reality generate an illusion—a false world of multiple independent "real" entities. So too, to give expression to what is experienced in introvertive mystical experiences seems to change its ontological nature and give it the same nature as phenomenal objects. Moreover, attempting to express what is experienced drops a mystic out of the altered states of consciousness of introvertive mystical experiences, and therefore language cannot accurately express those ASCs—there is always an element of human conceptualization and hence interpretation in any expression. Hence, every assertion must be denied.

Yet, don't mystics at least need to *identify* the reality with a word in order to specify what they talking about, or even to say that the reality is "ineffable"? But names separate one object from other things as much as any nouns do by classifying things. Plotinus tells us that it is precisely because the One is not an entity that "strictly speaking, no name suits it" (*Enneads* IV.9.5). Meister Eckhart said that God is nameless and that to give God a name (as he appears to have just done) would make God part of thought and thus an "image" (2009: 139). How can he say "God is above all names" (139, 153) when he just identified the reality by name? Something is dubbed "God." Indeed, he even said that by *not* being named, we *name* God (219). Shankara claimed that Brahman is unspeakable (*avachya*) and inexpressible (*anirukta*) (*Taittiriya-upanishad-bhashya* 2.7.1) while creating a metaphysical system about it. For him, even the words "*atman*" and "Brahman" are only superimposed onto what is real (*Brihadaranyaka-upanishad-bhashya* 2.3.6). The idea of Brahman as an entity is superimposed on the name "Brahman" (*Brahma-sutra-bhashya* 3.3.9). Indeed, for Shankara the whole phenomenal realm of the root-ignorance (*avidya*) arises entirely from speech (2.1.27). Even though only Brahman exists, the word "is" is not applicable to it since we use that word in reference to phenomenal objects. In Buddhism, only phenomenal reality as it truly is (*yathabhutam, dharmata, tattva*) is real, and so the differentiated objects that we conceptualize cannot be said to "exist"—there are no real (i.e., self-existent) entities for "is" to apply to.

All positive characterizations are qualified. Plotinus noted that we need to add "so to speak" (*hoion*) when speaking of the One (*Enneads* VI.8.13). He said that he spoke of "the One" only to give direction—to point out the road to others who desire to experience it (VI.9.4). "Whoever has seen knows what I am saying" (VI.9.9). Shankara said that the positive characterization "truth/reality" (*satya*) cannot denote Brahman but can only *indirectly* indicate it (*Taittiriya-upanishad-bhashya* 2.1.1). Words do not properly "describe" or "signify" Brahman but only "imply" it or "direct our attention" toward it (2.4.1, *Brahma-sutra-bhashya* 3.2.21). So too, the word "self" (*atman*) is qualified by "as it were" (*iti*) to indicate that the word does not actually apply (*Brihadaranyaka-upanishad-bhashya* 1.4.7). Shankara's disciple Sureshvara said that Brahman is indirectly signified just as the statement "the beds are crying" indirectly indicates the children who are lying upon them. But he conceded that this type of suggestiveness based on literal meaning only inadequately implies the *atman* since whatever is used to refer to Brahman becomes confused with it.

The primary way that introvertive mystics counter any possible misunderstanding is to deny any phenomenal characteristic to transcendent realities since such realities are totally unlike anything phenomenal. Thus, mystics are major advocates of the *via negativa*—the denial of any positive description of the transcendent. ("Love" mystics use it less than do "knowledge" mystics.) Hence images of darkness, emptiness, a desert, an abyss, and nakedness are common. In the *Brihadaranyaka Upanishad*, Brahman is famously described as "not this, not that" (*neti neti*) (2.3.6, 3.9.26, 4.2.4, 4.4.22, 4.5.15), thereby denying the applicability to it of all features based on anything we experience in the phenomenal world. For Shankara, words like "Brahman" and "*atman*" have to be superimposed onto the real (*satya*) since describing the real without recourse to limiting adjuncts (*upadhis*) is an "utter impossibility" (*Brahma-sutra-bhashya* introduction). But he asserted that all positive characterizations of Brahman—reality, knowledge, and infinity—are meant only to *remove other attributes*: Brahman cannot be the agent of knowing, for that requires change and denies the unchangeable reality and its lack of finitude; knowledge merely negates materiality; and the other two negate knowledge (*Taittiriya-upanishad-bhashya* 2.1.1). Thus, characterization is merely a process of negation (*apavada*). And since the real is in fact free of all differentiations, we are left with describing it as "not this, not that" in order to remove all forms.

So too, the Buddha denied that any concepts concerning existence apply to or "fit" (*upeti*) the state of the enlightened after death (*Majjhima Nikaya* 1.431, 2.166) since these terms apply to *dharmas* (the factors of the experienced world) and to constructed entities, but after death the enlightened have no *dharmas,* nor are they constructed entities. Thus, affirming any option for the enlightened after death—that they "exist," "do not exist," "both exist and not exist," or "neither exist nor not exist"—would show a misunderstanding of the nature of reality and would only create a mental prop to become attached to (*Samyutta Nikaya* 4.373–402).

The *via negativa* was introduced into the Abrahamic traditions through Neoplatonism. Plotinus said no words apply to the One (*Enneads* VI.8.13). For example, the One cannot be a "cause" since that term applies to phenomenal actions (III.8.11, V.5.6). Any property is a characteristic of being, not the One (which is beyond being), and so all properties must be denied (VI.9.3). In a remark echoed by Augustine and Thomas Aquinas about God, Plotinus said that we can only state what the One is not, not what it is (V.3.14). All predicates must be denied: even "the One" does not apply to what is transcendent, since "one" is a number among numbers (rather than only indicating the absence of plurality in it), and thus it may suggest some duality; silence is ultimately the only proper response (V.3.12–14, V.5.6, VI.7.38, VI.9.5). Only the "sheer dread of holding to nothingness" forces mystics back to the everyday realm of language (IV.7.38). Eckhart said that God is "neither this nor that"—God is a non-god, a non-spirit, a non-person, a non-image detached from all duality; he is not goodness, being, truth, or one (2009: 465, 287). So too, the Godhead is beyond all depiction. Indeed, the logic of transcendence dictates negation: if a transcendent reality is *wholly other* than anything phenomenal, no language can apply.

But the *via negativa* in mysticism is motivated by experiences, not speculative theology.[1] And for mystics there is always a fundamental *positive affirmation* beyond the negations—a reality that is experienced. Thus, although the *via negativa* is a movement beyond any linguistic affirmations, it never leads to a complete denial—there is always a "negation of negation." For example, according to Shankara, one can deny the existence of an alleged reality only by appeal to another reality (*Brahma-sutra-bhashya* 3.2.22). Thus, the negative approach does not deny that there is some *positive reality*, but in the case of introvertive mysticism negation only emphasizes otherness and the lack of phenomenal properties or phenomenal existence. Thereby, negation directs our attention away from the phenomenal realm. And the basic danger will remain that the unenlightened will transform anything mystics say into a statement about a phenomenal object: any concepts or statements about a transcendent reality will be misinterpreted by the unenlightened as referring to an object among objects in the phenomenal universe. The complete denial of anything phenomenal to a transcendent reality can also lead the unenlightened to think it is *nothing at all*—that is, that it does not exist.

Thus, something must be affirmed about transcendent realities to avoid nihilism, but all that the unenlightened will have are the mental objects produced by the analytical mind. Thus, in an important sense the unenlightened do not know what they are talking about when they use mystical concepts—any description changes what was experienced into something objective in the sense of being a phenomenal object and so changes its nature. To say "Brahman is not open to conceptualization" does not conceptualize Brahman, but it does make "Brahman" a noun, and our conceptualizing mind will treat it as any other noun—the subject of the sentence must be an object. Thus, even if some words are better than others in depicting God or another transcendent reality, or for directing attention away from the phenomenal realm, negating them is even better. But the danger in the very process of negation is of merely separating one object from other objects. Or with negation we affirm the opposite, thereby still creating an object of thought. Indeed, negations are as much human conceptualizations as affirmations, and both affirmation and negation operate in the realm of duality—thus, neither approach can work for a transcendent reality. So too, if phenomenal attributes cannot be attributed to God, we need not even bother to negate them. And if something transcendent is the only reality, then there are no phenomenal realities to negate. Thus, for Pseudo-Dionysius the Areopagite and others, in the end neither affirmation nor negation applies to God (*Mystical Theology*, chap. 5).

Thus, the "negation of negation" does not affirm any phenomenal characteristics to a transcendent reality, but its reality is not negated. However, the Pseudo-Dionysius did not connect the *via negativa* with *experience*. The negative approach has never been the predominant trend in the Abrahamic religions for more than brief periods except in Eastern Orthodox Christianity, where it has remained dominant. Even Muslims, who stress the unknowability of God to all but prophets and mystics, do not emphasize this approach. The silence filled with a positive transcendent reality during empty introvertive mystical experiences did not translate into silence as the preferred linguistic move. Theists always attribute positive features to God from their scriptures, thus making some terms (e.g., love) more appropriate than others even if God is ontologically utterly unlike anything in the phenomenal world. In Christianity, in the beginning was the word (*logos*) (John 1:1), not silence. The same holds for the Quran among Sufis.

The Problem of Paradox

Thus, it is quite understandable why mystics reject the applicability of language to what they experienced. Language is our main way of encoding and utilizing the distinctions that we see, and so any way of viewing reality free of distinctions will have a problem with utilizing language. Mystics often end up using paradoxical statements. From the *Kena Upanishad* 2.3–4: "Brahman is conceived by him who does not conceive it. He who conceives it does not know it. It is not perceived by those who perceive it. It is perceived by those who do not perceive it. When one awakens to knowing it, it is conceived."

Overall, the mystics' problem arises for three reasons. First, conceptualizations must be advanced for even mystics themselves to understand what is experienced, but all conceptualizations are inherently dualistic (since they distinguish subject from object and one thing from others as distinct entities), and this changes the character of what was experienced into an object. Second, the experiences themselves and what is experienced both seem "wholly other" than anything worldly, and so any language applicable to worldly phenomena is deemed inapplicable to what is experienced. Third, the states of consciousness in which the introvertive and some extrovertive mystical experiences occur differ from the states of consciousness in which language can operate, and so language must be jettisoned from the mind for a mystical experience to occur.[2]

In short, conceptions must both be advanced and also abandoned and also denied, thus leading to the contractions embodied in paradoxical statements that violate the logical principle of noncontradiction; for example, "God is *x* (by analogy to something phenomenological) and not *x* (since God is wholly other)."[3] In extrovertive mysticism, the problem arises from the fact that phenomena exist but are not discrete and self-existent, and hence they exist but are not "real" in that limited sense. Consider the Buddhist *Diamond-Cutter Sutra* (3): "However many sentient beings there are in the world of beings, . . . all sentient beings will eventually be led by me to the final *nirvana*. . . . And yet when this unfathomable number of living beings have all been led to *nirvana*, in reality not even a single being actually will have been led to *nirvana*." Bodhisattvas see that sentient beings "do not exist" as self-contained realities, and yet they paradoxically do not abandon them but lead them to an equally nonexistent *nirvana*. The Prajnaparamita texts are replete with such confusing claims: "*Dharmas* are not *dharmas*"; "The teaching is a non-teaching"; "The practice is a non-practice"; "The nature of all factors is a non-nature"; "Bodhisattvas strive for enlightenment, but there is nothing to strive for"; and "I am enlightened and yet it does not occur to me that I am enlightened." The Sanskrit in each case makes it clear that contradictions are intended, even when consistent forms could have been stated in Sanskrit. And the sheer length of the texts testifies to the fact that these writers did not reject language in general.

Thus, paradoxes seem to be at the very heart of the Bodhisattva way of life (see Jones 2012b: 220–23). However, these contradictions can be rendered intelligible by paraphrasing and explanation. The central point is that the factors of the experienced world (*dharmas*) do exist as parts of the phenomenal world but are not "real" only in one particular metaphysical sense: they do not exist by their own power or have some unchangeable intrinsic nature (*svabhava*) that separates each from other things. Thus, there *are dharmas* in the world, but they all are conditioned by other phenomena and thus do not *exist separately and permanently*. There is nothing paradoxical about the factual content of the claim even if the form—"there are *dharmas*, but there are no *dharmas*"—is contradictory: there are *dharmas* in one sense (as dependently arisen parts of the world) but not in another (as self-contained entities). So too with the Bodhisattva paradox: there are no self-existent beings, but there is something there (the impermanent, changing configurations of *dharmas* that we label "persons" for convenience) to point toward *nirvana* (which also is not self-existent)—something real underlies the "illusion." The same is true for the apparent paradoxes resulting from the Buddhist "two truths" strategy in which the conventional point of view is combined with the point of view of highest purposes (*parama-artha*): conventionally there are impermanent configurations that can be labeled "houses" and "trees," but from the ultimately correct ontic point of view there are no self-existent units and thus such entities are not real.[4] So too Zen Buddhists speak of "no-mind" and "no-thought," but they can discuss matters formulated by the mind without a "dualizing" mind that sets up divisions between "real" entities. Thus, the Buddhist claims that are stated in paradoxical forms can be resolved consistently and intelligibly: "There is no real, self-existent 'I' (or *dharma*, beings, and so on), but the conventional term is still useful for denoting fairly coherent but constantly changing parts in the flow of phenomena." In short, things do exist but not in the way the unenlightened mind imagines. The "paradoxes" result from juxtaposing the enlightened and the unenlightened senses of the same word.[5]

Those examples of paradoxes were from Buddhism, but paradoxes in general in mysticism appear to be restatable or explainable consistently once the different contexts of the claim of each branch of the contradiction are set forth—in the fuller claims, the "paradox" disappears.[6] For example, Plotinus's One is both everything (since it supplies being to everything) and not anything (since it is not a phenomenal reality) (*Enneads* V.2.1–2, V.2.24, V.7.32)—the two ways of looking at the world (as one and as many) are not affirmed at the same time in the same way. The One is everywhere and nowhere (VI.8.16), both the seeker and the sought (VI.8.15), the seer and the seen (VI.7.35, VI.9.5). Or consider Sufism: Allah is deemed the only reality and is "veiled" from us by the material world, but *the veils are also Allah* (since he is the only reality there is). So too, Allah is both the Reality sought *and* the seeker seeking it—"No one loves Allah but Allah himself." But these are explained in terms of an emanationism: there is both the transcendent Allah-in-himself and the emanated realities that are distinct in one sense from Allah-in-himself but are also nothing in themselves since their existence is supplied exclusively by Allah—thus, from the unenlightened point of view, it looks like different parts of a whole (Allah) are involved.

More generally, many religious participants seem to delight in feeling that they do not have to be consistent—they believe that a need for consistency is merely the "hobgoblin of small minds." But probably all the mystical paradoxes in both extrovertive and introvertive traditions have some resolution or explanation supplied by the mystics themselves or their tradition, although mystics must sometimes deny the prong of the paradox reflecting the unenlightened point of view as ultimately true in any sense.[7]

Understanding Mystical Claims

Mystical paradoxes also bring up a broader issue: no one is warranted in believing a proposition that he or she does not *understand*. An "ineffable insight" is a contradiction in terms: mystics must retain something of their experiences outside of an introvertive state and be able to state something of their understanding of it. A transcendent reality may be *more than* we can express, but an experiencer must retain *something* about it and be able to express that—if a reality were literally unknown, the experiencer would not know that it even exists and there would be nothing to say about it. So too, the awareness of a transcendent reality may be free of conceptions, but part of any postexperiential insight must be statable to claim that something was *experienced*. A rational mystic cannot say "I have no idea what I experienced, but based on my experience I now believe it is *x*." The insight that is gained occurs outside the introvertive experiences when enlightened mystics see the significance of what they experienced, and so is also statable in that state.

For the unenlightened believers to be rational, they too must be able to understand mystical claims, and such understanding appears possible. Consider an analogy. Imagine living in a two-dimensional flatland world. Now imagine claiming to your fellow beings that you have experienced a three-dimensional object. Your fellow beings cannot form mental images of three-dimensional objects any more than we can form images of four-dimensional objects. Now consider drawing the two-dimensional Necker stick cube for your fellow beings and trying to explain it to them:

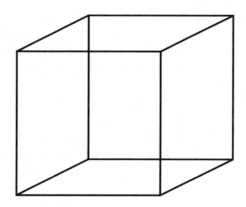

(Of course, being able to draw and see a two-dimensional figure would itself require a third dimension—again, the problem of making analogies from the phenomenal world is exposed.) This is a mixture of correct and misleading information—the straight lines and number of vertices reflect the cube, but the angles are not all ninety degrees, and some edges intersect.

More importantly, the drawing distorts the cube's basic nature by omitting the third dimension. Being forced to draw in two dimensions introduces this omission and these inconsistencies, but there is nothing we can do about it. You might add more detail by shading some sides, but this will not help since your fellow beings still cannot imagine a third dimension. But some things can be said correctly about the cube, and wrong statements can be rejected. Nevertheless, any verbal description will sound paradoxical to someone who has never seen a real cube: "All the angles are really the same, and it is not 'flat' (a term that may have no meaning for these beings), and the six sides are all the same shape and touch only on the outside." The beings cannot help but reduce the cube to a two-dimensional object—that is all their experiences enable them to imagine. In exasperation, you might even exclaim that the cube is ineffable since the drawing distorts what it really is like and changes its nature from three dimensions to two. But the drawing is in fact an accurate representation as far as it goes—we simply need to realize that it is only a drawing and that there is a dimension not conceptualizable in "two-dimensional language."

Most importantly, we need *the experience* of actually seeing and handling a cube to see why this drawing and not others is appropriate and in what sense it is accurate. Nor does the expression affect the prior experience of what is drawn—the inner experience and the outer expression used to understand what is experienced remain fundamentally different. (After concepts such as "vertex" and "sides" are introduced, they may structure later experiences.) But only with such an experience will the odd and contradictory features be understood in a nondistortive manner. In particular, the drawing cannot convey its own flatness: the missing third dimension cannot be captured by a drawing. Thus, studying the drawing is no substitute for experiencing a real cube. Those beings who are sympathetic may come to understand that the drawing is not the cube and thus they would try not to assimilate the drawing to their normal reactions. But the cube analogy shows that we can apprehend a reality even if the result of trying to translate the experience into an expression leads to the paradox of having both to affirm and to deny some features of the drawing.

This predicament parallels that of introvertive mystics in one way: since the unenlightened do not have the requisite experiences, they reduce any talk of transcendent realities to a kind of unusual phenomenal object. Because of mystics' linguistic "drawings," transcendent realities are relegated to the status of a familiar phenomenal object. And because the expressions seem contradictory, many philosophers reject the possibility that transcendent realities can be real, and treat the expressions as meaningless. But just as some of the features of the cube are captured by the drawing (the straight edges, eight vertices, and some angles), and the drawing overall is accurate if understood properly, so too linguistic descriptions of a transcendent reality can be accurate if we reject idea that transcendent realities are phenomenal entities: mystical statements do not falsify, but we need a mystical experience to properly see how they apply and even to understand the claims correctly. The enlightened will be able to see both why the particular language is used for what was experienced and why it is deceptive if it is all applied literally (i.e., in their phenomenal sense)—only they will see what is right and what is wrong about a mystical utterance. Some features of transcendent realities (nonduality, realness, immutability, transcendence of the phenomenal realm) are accurately conveyed if the unenlightened are not able to overcome transforming them into a phenomenal entity. More detailed highly ramified terminology of any particular tradition only increases the possibility of distortion.

The mixture of correct depictions with distortive possibilities accounts for the mystics' hesitancy to affirm the adequacy of any conceptualizations and to assert paradox. But the cube analogy shows that we can coherently *know* a reality through experience even if the results of trying to translate it into language are paradoxical. So too, mystics have reasons based in experience for their claims—it is no longer a question of believing a contradictory verbal construction as totally accurate. Having a mystical experience reorients how mystics understand mystical cognitive utterances, just as seeing a cube reorients how we see the drawing. The language remains the same and is the only way mystics can convey anything about what was experienced, but it is no longer as confusing. However, our unenlightened dualistic consciousness will distort what is heard by making what is not a phenomenal reality into a distinct phenomenal entity. The mode of existence of transcendent realities would be altered by the unenlightened, but the enlightened can use language free of that metaphysical mistake in order to convey some knowledge, just as we can draw the cube without being misled by the distortive aspects of the resulting drawing. And those without mystical experiences can come to understand something of what mystics are saying (and even to distinguish accurate descriptions from inaccurate ones) by at least getting a sense of the direction of mystical analogies and seeing what is negated. But without having the experiences, the unenlightened person's understanding will always remain tainted.

Rationality

This discussion shows that alleged mystical paradoxes are not evidence that mystics are inherently irrational. In fact, mystics in general are rational in their statements and arguments. Mystics may also be philosophers—Plotinus, Shankara, and al-Ghazali being prominent examples. After all, mystics themselves have to try to understand what they have experienced and need to incorporate what was experienced into their way of life, and so some philosophically minded mystics advance theories.[8] Much of the writings of some mystics—for example, Shankara—is a response to critics alleging contradictions in their own beliefs and an advancement of rational arguments against other schools. Logic, the study of valid deductions and laws of thought, became a topic in India and China once debates between different schools became formalized. More generally, investigation and analysis are part of the encompassing mystical ways of life even though analysis and logic represent a dualizing point of view. Indeed, reasoning is part of every mystical tradition even though thought is not a substitute for mystical experiences. Mystical experiences expand mystics' sense of what is fundamentally real and thus may well alter their judgments about the nature of reality and human beings, but their reasoning exhibits the same logic as nonmystics (see Jones 2016: 233–60).

It should also be noted that *mystical experiences* are not inherently irrational. No experience in itself is rational or irrational—experiences just are (and thus are "nonrational"). Logic applies only to our claims, not to our experiences. Experiences do not conform to the canons of reason or conflict with them. Nor do they conflict with each other—only our *understanding* of them can conflict with our understanding of other experiences. Thus, paradox is not a product of any experience in itself but of our search to understand an experience and to create a coherent picture for understanding all of our experiences. Because of this, mystical paradoxes occur more often in matters of doctrine than in lower order descriptions of the experiences themselves: contradictions occur more often when mystics are describing the reality allegedly experienced or trying to explain the experiences in light of everyday experiences or defending claims in terms of the philosophical beliefs of a given tradition. We deem an experience "irrational" or a "delusion" when what is allegedly experienced does not cohere with what the experiences that we consider cognitive tell us about the world. But it is an epistemic judgment that everyday experiences are more cognitive than mystical ones.

Ineffability

The above discussion leads to the issue of mystical "ineffability." Ineffability actually is not that unusual: *all* experiences are "ineffable" in one sense—it applies to any experience others have not had. Try to describe the taste of licorice to someone who has never tasted it. We *know* the taste through experience, but how do we *describe* it? Something deemed "inexpressible" does not imply that it is not knowable by experience. Thus, a distinction should be made between *knowing* something and being able to *communicate* it adequately—the inability to adequately communicate what was experienced does not contradict the experience's cognitive quality. Ludwig Wittgenstein gave the example of trying to communicate the sound of a clarinet. Only once one has had the experience will any description be fully understood. So too, any object of experience is ineffable in another way: any attempt to describe what is *unique* about anything—what differentiates something from everything else—will necessarily fail since descriptive terms all involve perceived commonalities and general categories. Using any terms to describe something will automatically group it with other things. But any phenomenal object is also not ineffable: it is accurate to call a pen "a pen," even if it is only crudely "captured" by language. Thus, we do not consider phenomenal objects to be "utterly beyond words."[9]

Mystical experiences share these senses of ineffability with other experiences, but what is unique to mystical ineffability is the sense of *otherness* from the conventional of both the reality that is experienced and the experiences themselves. *Maitri Upanishad* 6.7 sums it up: "Where knowledge is of a dual nature [of a knower and a known object], there indeed one hears, sees, smells, tastes, and also touches. One knows everything. But where knowledge is not of a dual nature—being without action, cause, or effect—it is inexpressible, incomparable, and indescribable. What is that? It is impossible to say." No attributes of any phenomenon apply even analogously to what is transcendent—God or Brahman does not even "exist." So too, there can be no analogies of proportionality since the transcendent has no phenomenal properties and is not an object.

"Ineffability" in the sense of complete inexpressibility is a modern philosophical obsession—classical mystics usually state that what is experienced is *more than can be expressed*, not that it is *utterly inexpressible*.[10] That is, mystical realities are "ineffable" not because nothing can be said about them but because the realities are deeper and fuller than can be captured by language—the realities overflow any attempt to enclose them by our conceptualizations. Those who view mystical experiences in terms only of emotion rather than cognition explain ineffability in terms of the inexpressibility of the *degree* of one's love or joy. Mystics also often affirm that mystical experiences do not exhaust the reality that was experienced, and thus mystery still remains even for those who have experienced that reality. So too, the experience may be "bright and dazzling," not obscure—even if it described as a "dazzling darkness brighter than light"—but it still baffles the conceptualizing mind. Nevertheless, theistic mystics accept that their scriptures tell us something of the nature of what they experience.[11] They believe that they have experienced a reality that is personal in nature and claim some definite things about God. God is indescribable only in that he is *so much greater* than they can express, not because mystics know nothing of him—that is, as William Johnston put it, human formulations are not wrong but hopelessly inadequate (1978: 58). If the experiences or what is experienced were empty and had nothing to express, there would no basis for any claims and no reason to adopt (or reject) any particular description. But mystical experiences do have content, and mystics routinely do affirm something of what they see as the nature of what was experienced even if they then dismiss their accounts as inadequate or meant only figuratively.

Thus, the claim of mystical ineffability does not contradict mystics' claim that the experiences are cognitive. But calling what is experienced "ineffable" does accentuate its otherness and also its value. We do not call the taste of licorice "ineffable" because the matter is so routine, not something profoundly significant, as mystics claim of mystical experiences. Mystics may wish to describe what was experienced to those who have not had the experiences, but they cannot—it is a matter of describing colors to the blind. The blind would not be able to experience color and so cannot adequately envisage it or understand color terminology. Also remember that most mystics may not be especially interested in defending conceptual formulations or philosophical arguments and may be as clumsy as anyone in trying to express something extraordinary by means of their tradition's language.

However, the mystics' problems with language can be mitigated if we give up the idea that language can function only by mirroring the structure of language (see Jones 2016: 208–13). If so, the nature of the realities can be discussed outside introvertive mystical states of consciousness, but the language, symbols, and analogies still must all be qualified as not discussing the objects of our ordinary dualistic consciousness and may still be negated in the end.

Art

The mystical condemnation of language can be seen as an expansion to include all mental images of the Jewish and Christian prohibitions against creating physical images of God (Exodus 20:4–6) and the Islamic prohibition against connecting Allah with anything phenomenal (*shirk*).[12] But the incarnation of God in Christ gave Christians an image of the invisible God. More generally, art is another form of mystical expression, and one way to explore mysticism is through studying its art and its influence on art outside of mysticism. Indeed, most classical art in all cultures has a religious theme—it is often hard to distinguish the religious from the nonreligious—and mysticism may have been a fount of inspiration for much of it.

Mystical views of the world and of transcendent realities have been expressed in paintings, sculpture, music, dance, movements, gestures, theater, poetry, architecture, and crafts. In illiterate society these have been a major way to convey ideas. Mystical art has been a vehicle for contemplation, as with Eastern Orthodox icons, Buddhist *mandalas*, and depictions of deities in Tantric traditions such as the Tibetan *thangka* paintings. The fragility and emptiness of passing things is expressed in Daoist and Zen landscape paintings. The architecture of a Muslim mosque, with its stark design incorporating calligraphy and geometric designs, contrasts with the elaborate architecture of medieval Christian cathedrals and the decorations of Hindu temples, but all are attempts to render the invisible visible. Buddhist reliquaries (*stupas*) reproduce basic Buddhist doctrines (e.g., four doors representing the four noble truths). William James suggested that music rather than conceptual speech is the element through which mystical truth speaks to us ([1902] 1958: 420–21). Chanting and singing are ways to induce ASCSs. Much of the music in Hinduism has roots in mystical practices. Hymns are a way to express Brahman as sound (*shabda-brahman*). According to experts, some of the most beautiful Persian poetry is by Sufis. John of the Cross considered his poetry to be closer to his mystical experiences than his commentaries—it represented an overflow in figures and similes from the abundance of God's communication (Kavanaugh 1987: 27). Mystical themes can also penetrate secular literature, as with Aldous Huxley's last novel, *Island*.

Symbolism, whether meant as a representation of doctrine or not, is also widely utilized in all traditions—for example, in Buddhism a white lotus floating in muddy water represents the purity of enlightenment arising from the filthy world of rebirth. Art works can be used as analogies to illustrate a point. For example, to help some monks in Germany understand his "coincidence of opposites," Nicholas of Cusa sent them an icon of Jesus that was painted in such a way that its eyes appear to be looking right at the monk no matter where he stood or moved. This was symbolic in two ways: when we look at God, he is also looking right at us, no matter where we are; and no matter how many viewers there are, God is always looking at each person individually.

Thus, the presentation of beauty is another way to express diverse mystical points of view and help lead people toward a mystical insight. Art in this context is always connected to the ultimate meaning of the universe, unlike secular art, and can evoke a mystical experience. (But modern secular art is being reexamined by some scholars who see a spiritual dimension to some of it [see Nelstrop and Appleton 2018].) However, the problem that mystics have with language recurs even when poetry, music, or nonrepresentational visual art is used: it may open us to transcendent realities, or our unenlightened mind may inevitably lead us back to phenomenal realities.

The Enlightened and the Use of Language

Even though the enlightened state of consciousness is free of any sense of a discrete subject and discrete objects, it is not an undifferentiated awareness—diffuse phenomena are still presented to the senses in the selfless extrovertive altered state of consciousness. And the enlightened can use the differentiations of language, as their writings on how language fails show. But they now use language without reifying the terms into distinct entities. Thus, the Buddha taught without "clinging" to the words or being led astray by them (*Majjhima Nikaya* 1.500; *Digha Nikaya* 1.195). Nor does anyone claim that the Buddha fell out of an enlightened state of mind when he spoke. He could use "I" (*aham*) and first-person verbs without believing in a real and separate self—"I" is merely a useful shorthand for the current state of one constantly changing bundle of aggregates in the flux of phenomena.

As discussed, for mindfulness mystics the analytic mind alienates us from what is real, and language is its most effective tool: conceptualizations embedded in language distort our perception of the continuous and impermanent nature of what is actually there—language is as much a *cause* of seeing differentiations as a repository of the differentiations we make. But the enlightened in their altered state of consciousness and with conceptualizations not fixing perceptions can utilize language without the falling into an unenlightened state. How the enlightened view language has changed. For the enlightened, there are no self-contained, "real" things for terms to denote—there is thus no match of categories and reality. In short, language cannot map what is actually real. Language cannot "capture" the ever-active flow of phenomenal reality, and we distort reality if we start thinking in terms of distinct permanent "entities." Nevertheless, language is not useless: it still works as a tool for directing our attention to impermanent configurations within the phenomenal world and for pointing others toward enlightenment. Mystics can employ the language of their own culture; the only change may be to use the passive voice more than the active one (since there is no self to act or because one feels acted upon). But the enlightened now use language to indicate the constantly changing and interconnected eddies in the flow of the phenomenal world without projecting their linguistic distinctions onto that reality, and thereby avoid creating a false ontology of a set of distinct entities. The same problem occurs for introvertive mystics—for example, to speak of a "mystical union" leads the unenlightened to think of God as a distinct phenomenal object and a mystical experience as a fusion of two entities, or the "eternal now" of the depth-mystical experience becomes the infinite duration of time rather than something transcending the temporal orders of phenomenal events.

The Zen analogy of language as merely "a finger pointing at the reflection of the moon in a pool of water" accepts that there is in fact a moon and that we can direct attention to it by pointing. We simply should not get caught up in words by becoming attached to the pointing finger, nor mistake the words for what is real, nor substitute understanding for experience, but instead should follow the direction indicated. Some terms work better than others because of what actually exists in the world. Saying that words are mere "names" or "designations," as Buddhists do, does not change the fact that something impermanent but stable in the world can be "designated." The word "moon" works in the analogy and not "truck" only because there is in reality a moon (albeit not an independently existing or permanent entity) being reflected in the pool that we can refer to, if only indirectly.

Accommodating Language

When mystics write for nonmystics, the different strategies with regard to language are meant to direct the unenlightened mind away from the worldly entities and toward phenomenal beingness or transcendent realities. But the unenlightened, like those mistaking the drawing for the cube, may mistake the pointing finger (the words) for the moon. All analogies and metaphors (e.g., the dream/dreamer or rope/snake in Advaita) are of necessity drawn from our dualistic experience within the phenomenal realm and so are limited and problematic: all analogies and metaphors come from a certain context, and the danger is that the unenlightened may reduce transcendent realities to entities within that context.

However, while no statement can be a substitute for *experience*, one outside of an introvertive ASC can state such "ultimate truths" as "Brahman is nondual" or "There are no self-existent entities." To use a Buddhist analogy mentioned in chapter 2: to know that the statement "Drinking water quenches thirst" is true, we need to drink water, but while the act of drinking "surpasses" that statement, it does not render the statement false in any way or only "conventionally true." Nor does it make the act of drinking an "unstatable higher truth" or "beyond language" in any sense other than the obvious and uncontroversial one that the act of drinking is not itself a statement—the statement itself remains true and not in need of revision or qualification.

The problem is moving from beliefs and concepts fabricated by the dualizing mind to what is intended by these beliefs and concepts in the mystical context. Because of the concern for possible misunderstanding by the unenlightened, it may seem that introvertive mystics want things both ways—that statements and symbols both apply to transcendent realities and do not apply. But the claims to ineffability are meant only to emphasize the wholly other nature of transcendent realities to the unenlightened who may misconstrue the nature of the intended realities. So too, with the rejection of any metaphoric statements, analogies, and symbols based on worldly phenomena: none can apply positively or negatively to transcendent realities without the unenlightened misconstruing their nature—by definition, all will remain inherently dualistic in nature for the unenlightened. But if we can resist reifying terms into distinct phenomenal objects, everyday language can be utilized to reveal at least something true of alleged transcendent realities or the true nature of the phenomenal world even if there must be metaphorical extensions to a new referent and even if we need the requisite experiences to see why these are accurate or appropriate. But even the word "experience" is problematic for mystical consciousness: it arose in connection to ordinary phenomena—"experience *of*" something distinct from the experiencer. Thus, mystics are more aware of the inadequacy of language in capturing all of reality because of their ASC experiences, but they can still utilize it to direct others toward enlightenment.

— 13 —

Mysticism and Morality

Helping others can change our perspective in a way that lessens self-centeredness and the desire for self-assertion, and thus can lead toward selflessness. It can also lead to a strict impartiality that eliminates giving priority to oneself—one sees no difference between love of oneself and love of another. Seeing that we are all fundamentally the same, with the same needs and desires, can lead to a more universal point of view even more than a sense of compassion for the suffering of others. In sum, helping others can aid in the inward turn of mysticism.

But are mystics truly treating other people morally or only using them for their own mystical development, with any benefit to them only a fortuitous side-effect? Must moral and mystical values converge? Morality concerns, not all of our actions and values, but only with those that concern how we deal with other people. Being moral is not a matter of merely conforming to a tradition's code of conduct but of *why* we act as we do: to be moral, our actions must be *"other-regarding"*—that is, we must take into consideration the welfare of the people upon whom our actions impinge and not only our own interests (see Jones 2004: 21–47). We need not be exclusively other-regarding to be moral. We can also advance our own interests and still be moral as long as a genuine concern for others' welfare is part of our motives for acting. But if we act only out of self-interest, our actions are not deemed *moral*, no matter how beneficial their effects might be for others.

Thus, motivation and intentions, and not actions alone, matter in a moral assessment.[1] Even when mystics' acts have positive social effects, does a mystical focus change their moral status? What are we to make of Mahatma

Gandhi's answer when asked why he was helping some poor villagers: "I am here to serve no one else but myself, to find my own self-realization through the service of these village-folks," adding "My national service is part of my training for freeing my soul from the bondage of the flesh. Thus considered, my service may be regarded as purely selfish" (see Jones 2004: 71). Or consider the curious case of lay Burmese Buddhists donating huts (a means for the donors to gain much karmic merit) for an auspicious monk because he was so austere that he refused to live in any hut (Spiro 1982: 411): since no one used the huts, only the donors themselves benefitted from their gifts by gaining merit for themselves. The huts were built in the knowledge that they would sit empty—indeed, the huts were built precisely because the monk would not live in any of them. Thus, what seem like acts of moral giving turn out to be only self-serving.

It is obviously easier to deal only with the codes recorded in a tradition's texts than to look at the "inside" mystical actions (a mystic's intentions and motives for following a code), but it is only by examining the latter that we can determine whether a person is moral or not. Since motive and intention matter, we need a "thick" description of explicit and implicit mystical beliefs and values. However, scholars routinely present only "thin" accounts of ethical codes or lists of virtues of religious ways of life. Few discuss the issue of *why* these norms are observed—in particular, whether codes are followed out of a genuine concern for the welfare of the people with whom mystics interact (and thus the mystics are being moral) or for mystical cultivation alone (and thus the mystics are being selfish and not being moral). The usual level of analysis among scholars is that if mystics follow a code of conduct it is assumed that they must be moral, since anything connected to religion is by definition moral.

Notice that morality involves worldly relationships between people, while mysticism involves an ontological orientation toward attaining experiences of the beingness of phenomenal reality or of transcendent realities. But are all mystical ways of life totally unrelated to any moral concern for others? If the realities experienced in introvertive mystical experiences are in fact beyond all attributes from the phenomenal world, this would include *moral values*, and so how can any moral action guides be grounded in those realities? So too, desiring the welfare of others and abhorring their suffering are attachments, but introvertive and extrovertive enlightened mystics are free of all attachments—so aren't such mystics necessarily "beyond good and evil" and indifferent to all worldly concerns and values? The only change that matters is the inner remaking of oneself—doesn't that mean that the rest of the world must be ignored? Thus, must mystics remain "other-worldly" and "world-denying"? How can mystics possibly value anything in the phenomenal realm at all? How can mystics see other people as fully real in their own right or the object of moral concern? And don't mystical experiences reveal everything in the world to be "perfect" simply as it is, and so no changes are warranted?

Some scholars argue that those who devote their lives to their own mystical cultivation cannot be considered anything but totally self-indulgent and hence selfish—thus, they must be immoral, and so mysticism and morality cannot be compatible. Indeed, the factual belief that only Brahman, God, or the One is real means that there is no other reality (other real persons) toward which one can show a moral concern: mystics cannot but treat people within the world as unreal phenomena of no consequence, and thus they cannot be moral—one cannot rationally be concerned about the welfare of characters in a "dream." But other scholars argue the opposite: that mysticism is in fact the source of our sense of connectedness with others and of a concern for others, or even that only mystics are truly moral or compassionate since only they have truly escaped all self-centeredness.

Are Mystics Necessarily Moral?

Walter Stace presented the mystical theory of morality: mystical experiences are the empirical justification of our moral values, since they are the human experiences out of which moral feelings flow (1960a: 323; 1960b: 27). The sense of separate individual selves produces the egoism that is the source of conflict, grasping, aggressiveness, selfishness, hatred, cruelty, malice, and other forms of evil; and this sense is abolished in the mystical consciousness in which all distinctions are annulled (1960a: 324). Love and sympathy result from the incipient and partial breaking down of the barriers that the sense of separate selves has erected; when this breakdown is complete, it leads to the sense of the identity of "I" and "you"—thus, love is a dim groping toward the disappearance of individuality in the Universal Self that is part of the essence of mysticism (329). Feelings of love and compassion are components, or necessary and immediate accompaniments, of mystical experiences. In fact, this is the *only* source from which love flows into the world (327). Without this sense, there could be no such thing as love or even kindly feeling in human life, and life would be a wholly unmitigated Hobbesian war of all against all, for there is no rival nonmystical source of morality (324–25).

However, not all enlightened mystics become moral, and thus Stace's theory is hard to defend—there would be nothing in an enlightened mystic's mind emptied by a mystical experience to impede a reversion to an innate moral state if morality were a necessary part of mystical states. But as Agehananda Bharati stated, isolated mystical experiences will not change an immoral, self-indulgent, or antisocial person into a moral one—if one was a stinker before the depth-mystical "zero-experience," one may remain so after it (Bharati 1976: 53). The zero-experience is a mode of consciousness that has no moral value or implication (74–75). That experience does not entail any beliefs or any actions, although mystics typically believe the experience validates their tradition's teachings (69). The zero-experience will change one's perspective, but "it does nothing to the person in his interactional patterns with other people and with human society at large" (100). A momentary experience of nature-mysticism or cosmic consciousness will not necessarily make someone a moral saint. Nor does mastering breathing techniques or other meditative exercises have any bearing on one's values. An isolated depth-mystical or extrovertive experience may shatter one's old views and one may elect to become moral, but an experience of selflessness may in fact *increase* one's sense of self-importance and pride if one feels graced by God. Charles Manson cracked a sense of self in LSD experiences and concluded that "All is God" and asked what actions could then be bad. Or consider the morally questionable recent "perfect masters" in the West—for example, the Buddhist Chogyam Trungpa Rinpoche, with his open drunkenness and sexual exploitation of followers. History is full of narcissistic gurus who declared themselves to be enlightened and to be "beyond good and evil" (Feuerstein 1991; Storr 1996).

The moral mystics whom Stace cited are all instances of mystics who cultivated a moral way of life on the path to the enlightened state or otherwise practiced within moral religious traditions. But mystical traditions may not be moral. "Left-handed" Tantrikas reverse orthodox Hindu and Buddhist codes of conduct and utilize their personal desires that attach us to the cycle of rebirths. Indulging the desires is seen as a "quick path" to enlightenment, even though this may mean an immoral use of others for a Tantrika's own end. So too, there are antinomians in all the Abrahamic religions who deny the authority of both civil laws and religious commands and so believe that the religion's virtues are no longer needed—love of God did not translate into love of others. Among antinomian Sufis, the love of God sometimes was considered so absolute that nothing else could be loved, and divine commands had to be disobeyed because they distracted from loving God. Enlightened medieval Christian Free Spirits considered themselves free from virtues and from church or secular authorities—they were free of self-will, and so they could let their bodies do whatever nature demanded and attributed everything that happened to God. (Some antinomians in Christianity were charged with crimes, but how much immoral conduct they actually indulged in despite their rhetoric is a matter of debate.) Even asceticism and unworldliness can lead to the extreme of indulgence.

G. William Barnard argues that becoming loving and compassionate is the normal result of a mystical experience and that those who are not moral have distorted the basic insight of love (Barnard & Kripal 2002: 78–90). He cites the general lack of antinomian "anything goes" indulgence as evidence that the "true" mystical experience is moral, since being moral would be the only alternative to being immoral. However, even if mystics are rarely truly immoral, the possibility of the enlightened being simply indifferent to the suffering of others cannot be ruled out. That is, there is a third possibility: *nonmorality*—that is, aligning one's life with reality and merely being indifferent to the welfare of others. Immorality requires knowingly harming others, but nonmorality involves adopting values for one's life other than immoral ones but being indifferent to the welfare of others. (Barnard, like most scholars, does not distinguish "nonmoral" from "immoral," grouping them together under the heading of "amoral.") One can be nonmoral in valuing one's own quest for enlightenment above all else and ignoring others but still not intentionally or knowingly harming others with one's other-impinging actions. The enlightened cannot intentionally harm others for personal gain (since all sense of self is ended), but they may still be unconcerned with the suffering of others and thus nonmoral.

Some major mystics have adopted clearly nonmoral values or factual beliefs that conflict with morality, and these justify only indifference. The beliefs and values advocated in Shankara's writings are a prime instance (Jones 2004: 95–114). If mystical experiences compelled one to radiant compassion or love, why didn't the Upanishads or Shankara emphasize it? Shankara mentioned only nonpersonal properties for Brahman—in particular, omniscience, omnipotence, and omnipresense (e.g., *Brahma-sutra-bhashya* 1.1.1)—not compassion, love, or concern for people. Nor did he say that the enlightened must be compassionate or morally concerned. Shankara's nonmorality is especially telling since he was indirectly influenced by moral Mahayana Buddhism through his line of teachers. So too, mystical training also need not be moral: the self-restraints of Theravada Buddhist cultivation result in not intentionally harming others, but the motive for following them is not other-regardingness but only one's own spiritual self-development (149–79). One may not advance on any mystical path by acting selfishly, but one may simply be indifferent to the suffering of others, as with the Theravada monks who ignored the suffering of their fellow monks—they literally stepped over the sick monks to get to the Buddha until the Buddha made a special Vinaya rule against that practice. The Buddha's traditional first address to his disciples (*Samyutta Nikaya* V.420–25) is a later construction, but if compassion or helping others had been a central concern of Theravada Buddhism, as with the Mahayana, it certainly would have been incorporated into it, but it was not.

One cannot argue that these experiences are pregnant with moral significance in such circumstances. Indifference is perfectly consistent with a sense of selflessness, and it is hard to argue based on comparative mysticism (rather than from theological conviction) that indifference must be an aberration or distortion or that any of the three options is the norm. Obviously, Stace risks arguing in a circle—making morality the criterion for what counts as the "highest" or "best" or "genuine" mystical experience, and then concluding that in its essence mysticism contains love (1960a: 340).

But morality may be part of a mystic's values. Remember again that the aim of mysticism is not having mystical experiences but a life aligned with the way reality truly is, and if the fundamental reality that a mystic accepts is deemed a compassionate self-emptying reality, then that mystic's enlightened life aligned with that reality will reflect that. For Christian mystics, morality is built into the ground of reality: emulating the way of God (*imitatio dei*) means an "active" life of moral action integrated into a "contemplative" one. So too with Jewish and Muslim mystics walking in the ways of God. In Daoism, impartiality and compassion or great humaneness are part of the Way. For Mahayana Bodhisattvas, morality is not a matter of the reflecting a transcendent reality, but morality was adopted and built into their path and the life of supreme enlightenment (*bodhi*). Bodhisattvas gain a greater goal than mere enlightenment (*nirvana*) by being other-regarding, but they are no less moral because of that—doing good for others may have the effect of also helping oneself, but this does not make the actions selfish. For classical mystics, the values are grounded in reality, not human judgments, and thus the mystics are value realists. Even the Daoist Zhuangzi, who today is usually portrayed as a moral relativist, ascribed an objective moral value to the Dao—an impartial "great humaneness" that exists prior to our conceptualized humaneness (*ren*) and thus is not a human product (*Zhuangzi* 2, 12).

Thus, merely because mystics try to align their lives with reality does not mean that morality may not be of supreme value. But the explanations for why some mystics are moral, some nonmoral, and some immoral must lie outside these experiences. For example, if a Christian sets out on a long strenuous life of training to become more loving, a depth-mystical or theistic experience will no doubt be seen in those terms and make him or her more loving, but any change of character will come from previous training, not mystical experiences alone. And, it must be noted, love has not always been manifested by Christians in ways we would deem moral today. Some great Christian mystics supported activities of dubious morality, such as the Crusades and the Inquisition. The Flemish mystic Jan van Ruusbroec advocated burning heretics at the stake.

In sum, in light of the teachings and actions of mystics from around the world, it is hard to argue that love is necessarily given in mystical experiences or that moral action is compelled. The enlightened are now acting out of the deepest level of their being, but an implosion of the ground of reality does not necessarily lead to an explosion of moral action. Religious values from a mystic's tradition, not mystical experiences themselves, play a determining role in one's value-commitments.

Mystical Selflessness and the Presuppositions of Morality

Arthur Danto presented a version of the opposite claim from Stace's—that the *factual beliefs* of the Asian mystical ways of life are in fact logically incompatible with being moral (1987). In particular, two such presuppositions of morality are a problem: the need for a moral agent and the need for a reality toward which one can act morally.[2] Danto is arguing that morality is no longer a possible concern because according to classical Asian factual beliefs there are no real moral agents to be concerned with others or real persons to be morally concerned about. In short, once enlightened, one sees that there are no real "persons" to help or be helped, and so moral concerns end. (It is important to distinguish the *unenlightened* and *enlightened* here: the unenlightened will be operating with a faulty belief in the distinction of beings and so are open to acting morally based on their erroneous ontological beliefs—it is the enlightened, with their correct view of reality, that is the issue.)

Advaita Vedanta does exemplify Danto's position. Its factual belief that Brahman is the only reality closes the space necessary for the moral concern of one real person for another real person to operate. On the path, moral actions may well lessen a sense of self, but as long as one thinks that there are independent individuals who warrant our moral concern one is unenlightened. Once enlightened, one realizes that all that is real is the one unaffectable Brahman. There are no real individuals (*jivas*) to be compassionate toward, or whose suffering could concern us, or who could otherwise make a moral demand upon us. Even though actions are still possible for the enlightened, the realm of differentiations is reduced to something not fully real (*maya*), and along with it any possible moral concern for other parts of the illusion dissolves: we could have no more concern for parts of this world than we could for the fate of characters in our dreams. However, the other major Asian mystical traditions do not adopt a nondualistic metaphysics and also illusionism with regard to the phenomenal world.[3] These traditions grant sufficient reality to the parts of the realm of differentiations to provide for the possibility of morality. Outside an introvertive mystical experience and some forms of meditation, the factual beliefs permitting moral choice and action can be adopted.[4]

The metaphysics of selflessness also presents an issue for an actor: if we have no independent center of reflection and agency—no real "self" or "soul"—how is morality possible? Doesn't moral reflection, decision making, and agency need a sense of identity and agency? But our phenomenal ego (the *jiva* of Indian mysticism) is seen as an illusory creation that does not correspond to anything real, while our real transcendent self (the *atman* in Advaita, or *purusha* in Samkhya) is changeless and does not act. The true reality of our mental life is seen as activity without a controlling center. Buddhists accept the thinking, perceptions, motives, and feelings associated with agency but reject an "I" in addition to the temporary bundle of impermanent mental and physical elements—no *thinker* but still the *thinking*, and so on. But it is not clear why an independent entity is needed in this mix to be the controlling agent for moral responsibility.[5] What would it do that the other elements do not already do? Reductive materialists in the West today, such as Daniel Dennett, can accept agency without an agent (a "self") that controls the mix. All that morality requires for agency is a mental capability to think, to choose, to will, and to act accordingly—an additional separate actor is not required—and of the major Asian mystical traditions only Advaita is committed to a belief-claim that conflicts with that.[6]

This also bears on the second problem: whether there is a reality toward which moral concern is possible. Buddhists believe there are changing collections of phenomena that involve suffering and can be directed toward the end of a chain of rebirths even though there is no substance or center to the collection we label a "person"—no "I" that suffers. How can we be compassionate toward impersonal objects (Wainwright 1981: 211–12)? But for Buddhists, a "person" is "unreal" only in the sense that there is nothing permanent to us—no enduring ontologically distinct independent center to our mental and physical configuration. But there is the chain of suffering parts we designate a "person" that can be ended. In no way does this reduce people to impersonal "things" in any morally negative sense: there is something real there that "has" all the interests and capacity to suffer that we can take into moral consideration—there is still the suffering that can be ended even if there is no real sufferer.

"You Are That"

Some scholars see the Advaita's interpretation of the Upanishads' phrase "*tat tvam asi*"—that is, "You are that (Brahman)"—as grounding morality. Franklin Edgerton believed noninjury (*ahimsa*) is logically deducible from the nondualistic doctrine of the Brahman/*atman* identity: "We injure ourselves when we injure others since the Self in each of us is identical" (1942: 155). Paul Deussen saw this identity as grounding the Golden Rule: you should love your neighbor as yourself because you *are* your neighbor ([1907] 1966: 49).

However, this position misconstrues the Brahman/*atman* identity in two ways. First, that "Brahman is *atman*" does not mean that persons (*jivas*) in the phenomenal world are identical to each other. There is no identity between the various surface phenomena within the realm of multiplicity like the morning star being the evening star. The differences within the "dream" remain intact—if you have a broken leg, it does not mean that I am affected in any way. Different people and objects are not one in that sense: I am not you, but we emerge from, or in our beingness are identical to, one unchanging underlying beingness. Thus, harming you (one *jiva* in the "dream") does not mean that I (another *jiva*) am necessarily harming myself—that we have a common source or a common being does not alter this. Second, what is in fact real (Brahman) is unharmable no matter what we do (*Katha Upanishad* II.18–19), and so the real "you" under this interpretation (Brahman) cannot be harmed. In no way do you harm the real you (Brahman) by harming another phenomenal person (*jiva*). Conversely, noninjury or compassion is equally groundless: helping another person (one *jiva*) does not necessarily help yourself (another *jiva*), and what is real about each of us (Brahman) cannot be helped or affected in any way. In sum, the metaphysics simply does not permit the existence of another real person to love. Nor was "*tat tvam asi*" ever used to ground ethics in classical Indian traditions. As Deussen had to conclude, once the knowledge of Brahman has been gained, "every action and therefore every moral action has been deprived of meaning" ([1907] 1966: 362).

Indeed, under this metaphysics it is impossible to *kill* people in this realm, since there are no real people to kill, nor can we even affect what is truly real. *Bhagavad-gita* 2.19–21 adopts this view: Krishna tells Arjuna that no one really slays and no one is really slain—the true self is unaffectable. He then uses this as one reason why Arjuna should participate in the war. The enlightened Arjuna then carried out his duties as a warrior spontaneously, "with a semblance of a smile." This doctrine did not lead to immoral behavior or antinomianism in Advaita, but only the possibility of a nonmoral indifference was justified. (But one can act "selflessly" even with a metaphysics of ultimately real selves: if one accepts that the other selves are real and also affectable, then one can act morally and even selflessly by valuing others over oneself.)

Morality and a Metaphysics of Wholeness

An extrovertive metaphysics of an interconnected wholeness fares better. One may be moral with such a view: the parts are real, not isolated monads that cannot be affected by our actions, and the reality of the parts permits concern by one part for the welfare of other parts. But being connected does not *require* moral concern. It is not inconsistent to try to manipulate other parts of a connected whole for the advantage of our part: even if all parts are impermanent and without substance, we can still try to manipulate the configuration of parts to help our little node in the web of the universe at the expense of other nodes. A value-choice still must be made. So too, one part may have to be harmed to maintain the whole, just as we would amputate a cancerous limb to save the body—indeed, it is precisely because the parts are connected that there is a problem. Conversely, if the belief in not harming any other part of the whole did follow from the metaphysical belief, then it is hard to justify even eating anything or otherwise using any part for one's own benefit.

Similarly, if we believe that the lack of an independently existing self means that we could not rationally act *selfishly*, then it would be equally true that there are no other selves to help, and so we could not act *morally*. It is the other side of the same coin. If hate and greed are impossible because these presuppose a self and there is none, then it is just as true that love and compassion are impossible because these presuppose the same type of reality in others to help and there is none. Conversely, if there is in fact something real in others to help, then there also is the same type of reality in ourselves that we could be selfish about—again moral concern does not necessarily follow from the metaphysics. Consider Buddhist Bodhisattvas: if there is no self or any other reality in *themselves* to be concerned with, then it is equally true that there is no comparable reality in *others* to be concerned with either. So too, preferring another's welfare over one's own is as much an attachment as being selfish and thus is just as unenlightened. Moreover, being concerned exclusively with others rather than yourself also does not reflect reality since you are as real as they are—to devalue oneself does not reflect reality as it truly is and would be as dualistic as concern only for one's own suffering.

Mystics who adopt holism may believe that the ground of being breathes a love of everything. In the extrovertive cosmic consciousness of Richard M. Bucke, this world is not composed of dead matter governed by unconscious laws but is a living presence whose foundation is love ([1901] 1969: 17–18). But morality is not deducible from the belief in the interaction of the parts of the world and is in fact far from obvious from the violence among animals exhibited in nature. Holists would have to explain the millions upon millions of years of evolution that produced animals eating other animals and such effects as disease-causing viruses that are harmful to us. Our ecological environment is one whole that reveals not just cooperation and beneficial symbiotic interrelations but also competition and violence. Overall, it is hard to reconcile the suffering of animals and human beings through eons of evolution with a sense in a mystical experience of an all-encompassing love that makes all life precious, no matter how powerful that sense of love may be. (That not all who have differentiated introvertive mystical experiences come away believing the source of the phenomenal world is loving also should again be noted.)

But even though morality is not deducible from wholeness, it is still compatible with this metaphysics: as discussed, in the Buddhist metaphysics the conventional "self" is unreal and our components (*dharmas*) are impermanent and dependent upon other parts, but there is still a configuration of components that suffers and can be led to the end of suffering—there are no real "persons," but there are still "streams of impermanent entities" that can be directed toward enlightenment. There are no enlightened "beings," but the streams of rebirth can be ended (see Jones 2004: 189–92; 2012b: 192–98). But again, this metaphysics does not require morality: Theravada followers have a "selfish" nonmoral ethos even without espousing a metaphysical "self" (Jones 2004: 149–79). Bodhisattvas must make a choice (192–93), and they in fact choose the moral option over selfishness or moral indifference.[7]

In short, metaphysics of selflessness does not dictate an ethics—we cannot deduce an enlightened "ought" from the enlightened "is." A value choice remains.

Mysticism and Social Action

Moral mystics' aid to others may be this-worldly, as epitomized by the Christian Meister Eckhart valuing giving a cup of soup to the sick over remaining in a mystical experience (2009: 496). Or it can be other-worldly aid in helping others to escape this realm entirely, as with the enlightened Bodhisattvas. Most typically, the focus in mysticism is on only one individual at a time or on teaching small groups. Some have a more social and political focus (e.g., Gandhi, political Daoism, and Thomas Merton).[8] But mystics do not uniformly condemn wars. Wars are accepted as part of culture in the *Bhagavad-gita*, and Arjuna learned how to combine mystical knowledge and detachment with being a warrior. Christian love (*agape*) did not prevent Bernard of Clairvaux from advocating the Crusades. Even

Buddhists have a "just war" doctrine: a greater good may be achieved by killing non-Buddhists if the Buddhist teaching is thereby preserved (Jones 2004: 156–57). But the Vietnamese Zen monks, including Thich Nhat Hanh, who protested the war in the 1960s were the latest example of those who opposed wars. Today a newly envisioned "socially engaged Buddhism" has appeared in the West. But overall, there is little incentive to reshape society or band together for social action.

Mystical ways of life are not necessarily or always counterculture or subversive—inner cultivation and mystical ways of life appear adaptable to any political structure, and mystics seem able to fulfill any social role. Any social role that one adopts can be filled effortlessly. The hippie antinomian counterculture of the 1960s is not representative of classical mysticism. Classical mystics typically left political and economic matters to those already in charge, whether they withdrew from society at large or not. Mystics' general lack of interest in broad social structures had the effect of making mysticism typically socially and politically conservative. For all their iconoclasm, Zen Buddhists rarely attack political structures, and Zen temples in Japan trained soldiers for World War II (Victoria 2006).

The classical mystical stance on "social reform" is to reform the inner life of individuals. Only by the inner reform of all individuals will society change for the better. So too for advocates of meditation today (e.g., Goleman & Davidson 2018: 290–91). Inwardly transforming the attitudes of individuals through meditation or mystical training will make persons calmer and help them feel connected to the rest of society and the world, and this will result in changes in their actions. For example, it will lessen material desires and may well generate more compassionate actions toward others. These inner changes in individual persons, advocates believe, will have a cumulative effect on a society-wide scale.

Mystical Detachment

Danto also raised an issue related to the *emotions* associated with morality: how can mystical even-mindedness be compatible with compassion or any other concern with others? The enlightened live, in Eckhart's phrase, "without a why" (*sunder Warumbe*), that is, without a personal purpose or benefit or even a command from God—"I live because I live" (2009: 129, 239). In this state, the chief emotion is "detachment": freedom from personal desires or motives or anger and stress, indifference to what comes next to oneself or to what direction one's life goes, and freedom from any personal attachment to any outcome. For theists, one is steadfastly attached to God, remaining the same through the good and the bad. The "inner" person remains unmoved while the "outer" person acts (571). Unmoving detachment is the unmoving hinge on which the door of actions moves (571). For Eckhart, detached love has no reason to act, not goodness or even God—one desires nothing and is not inclined toward oneself or the person one is helping (99–100, 110). To use a common image (e.g., Shankara's *Brahma-sutra-bhashya* 2.3.42; Matthew 5:45–46; see *Daodejing* 5, 23), the source of this world is like sunlight or rain in that it uniformly gives to all, the just and the unjust, without discrimination, and thus the mystic's actions mirror this, giving to each person what that person needs without judgment. One does not prefer oneself or one's parents over others (Eckhart 2009: 135). With no attachments and no love or hate, detached actions come across as cold. The coldness of detachment is demonstrated in Eckhart's remark that if the "son of God" is born in him, then "the sight of my father and all my friends slain before my eyes would leave my heart untouched" (75). One is dispassionate to success or failure, pleasure or pain. One has no fear of death, nor any desire for it. There is nothing to do or fear. The enlightened live focused totally on the present moment—calm, free of expectations or hope for the future or remorse for past decisions or actions, and free of doubts and anxieties.

But Danto's objection has problems. First, detachment relates only to the mystic's reaction to the possible effects of an action on him- or herself, not to its impact on others. Mystics are detached from their *own* pain and pleasure—not necessarily indifferent to the effect of their actions on *others*. A lack of any personal desires or attachments to outcomes for oneself need not lead to moral indifference—being *disinterested* in the personal repercussions of your actions does not mean you must be *uninterested* in their consequences for others. Nor does such detachment need to lead to a withdrawal from the world. So too, selflessness leads to being receptive, but this does not mean that only inactivity can result. Thus, outside periods of quiet meditation, one can be detached (concerning an action's effect on oneself) and compassionate (toward others) at the same time. Indeed, it can be argued that detachment is valuable for cultivating other-regardingness. Second, detachment and even-mindedness may lead to a radically impartial other-regardingness toward all without preferences. Third, being personally detached in circumstances in which others are emotional may in fact aid moral actions, even if mystic's actions then come across as cold and almost machine-like.

Thus, it is better to call this disposition "*personal nonattachment*" rather than "*detachment*," since the latter suggests being detached from the consequences of their actions for others or detachment from the world in general. However, mystical enlightenment in itself gives no new values. Mystical selflessness does not determine whether one is moral or not and what actions are to be carried out, but it affects *how* one acts—being unattached to any results, expecting nothing, unconcerned with the opinions of others, and focused only on the present, one's behavior becomes more spontaneous, effortless, and efficient (see Jones 2004: 310–14). Only this may make mystics recognizable by their behavior and distinguish them from the unenlightened in their tradition. Eckhart's detachment (*Abegeschiedenheit*) from both images and emotional attachments and letting God be God in oneself (*Gelazenheit*), the *Bhagavad-gita's karma-yoga*, and the Daoist's freedom from personal striving (*wei wuwei*) to let the Dao act all involve acting in accord with values and beliefs about reality (as defined by a mystical tradition) and without a personal will interfering with the will of God or the course of natural events. It is more a *way of being* than a matter of *doing*, since one is no longer following any rules.

Mystical detachment must be seen in light of mystical selflessness. In mysticism, self-will, or its cognitive base (a sense of self-containment and separateness), comes to be seen as the cause of all dissonance with reality. Realizing that there is no self to enhance becomes the cognitive ground out of which one operates. Emotional states connected to self-will and self-love—pride, hatred, envy, anger, and so on—become targets. Each thought, word, and deed is seen as having an effect on the inner life. Virtues that lessen a sense of self are valued—for example, kindness, compassion, honesty, patience, generosity, gentleness, forgiveness, tolerance, and humility in the sense of seeing one's true place in the scheme of things. Rules that restrict actions that might harm others are valuable in lessening a sense of one's individual importance, but rule following is only the first step on the path for a practitioner and is later transcended. According to Teresa of Avila, withdrawal from desiring "earthly delights" and viewing them as "filth" leads to improvement in all virtues (rather than the other way around) (*Interior Castle* 4.3.9).

All personal desires must be ended, including any desire for a reward for one's actions toward others or remorse over the results. Ironically, one's own spiritual well-being is promoted by forgetting oneself and (for those mystics who adopt morality) giving oneself over fully to the welfare of others. For moral mystics, compassionate action becomes the expression of what they are. By becoming selfless, moral mystics go beyond even complete impartiality (i.e., attaching no more importance to oneself than to any others) to denying any value to themselves.

"Beyond Good and Evil"

Sengcan, the third Zen Patriarch, extolled his listeners, "Be not concerned with right and wrong—the conflict between right and wrong is the sickness of the mind." The dichotomies of "good and evil" and "right and wrong" are set up only by the conceptualizing mind and must be gotten past. That the enlightened mind is free of conceptual distinctions of "good" from "evil" leads to the claim that they are "beyond good and evil" and thus cannot be moral but must be value nihilists. The enlightened pass no judgments because there are no judgments to be made—all other-related values are rendered utterly groundless. "Good" and "evil" are merely products of the unenlightened mind, reflecting unenlightened interests (especially those of self-interest). At best, morality is consigned to the path to enlightenment—since thinking about the welfare of others helps lessen a sense of one's own self-centeredness—but it is jettisoned along with all other unenlightened baggage upon enlightenment. The enlightened are free of all such restrictions and may do whatever they want. They are beyond all sanctions and all authorities, and no course of action is binding. They are truly autonomous. Antinomian behavior is only to be expected.[9] Mystics focus simply on the task they are doing without any goal and with a callous disregard of the consequences to others.

However, this position does not follow from the enlightened's freedom from conceptual categories. The mystics' dispositions have been transformed, and so rule following to adjust their behavior or to keep negative emotions in check is no longer needed. In their enlightened state, mystics are no longer consciously applying values, but moral mystics will have *internalized moral values* that they had practiced on the path. They simply are no longer reacting to a label they themselves had previously utilized for a situation. There is no longer a question of "ought" or "duty," but moral mystics are now incapable of committing a selfish act, and their selflessness is structured by a moral concern, and so they can act only with other-regardingness. Having fully internalized their tradition's beliefs and values, the enlightened typically do not need to ponder or calculate.[10] Experts in chess do not calculate their next move—they *see* what to do—and enlightened mystics see what to do (according to their beliefs and values) without deliberating in dualistic terms of "good" and "evil." But even if they are not thinking dualistically that "This is good," thereby allowing their responses to be more spontaneous, the enlightened moral mystics are still operating implicitly with moral values.

This means that enlightened moral mystics are "beyond good and evil" only in the morally innocuous sense that they are beyond all rule following, as any expert in virtues would be. Consciously following a rule would mean that one is not yet enlightened—it would indicate making decisions using the analytical mind to dichotomize the situation into unreal entities, and so one is not acting perfectly. But in the enlightened state, a mystic has removed the training wheels of the rules and now acts spontaneously and effortlessly. The internalized values now become literally a second nature. So too, the enlightened's actions need not be aimless: they can have an implicit intentionality based on internalized factual beliefs. What has changed is what moral mystics are: they now *are* moral to their core; they do not simply decide to *do* some moral acts. In Augustine's phrase, moral enlightened mystics can "love God, and do what you will"—all resulting acts will always be moral (even if one's factual beliefs are erroneous). The enlightened have reached the spirit behind the letter of the rules and no longer need the letter. An image applied to both the Christian Francis of Assisi and the Japanese Buddhist Basho contrasts the ease and steadiness with which they unconsciously walked in the exact footsteps of the founder of their respective religions—precisely because of their lack of effort to do so—with the faulty and clumsy efforts of the learned who try to put their feet in the footsteps but with thought and hesitation.

Mystics' beliefs can lead to inaction (as with the enlightened ideal in Jainism and one option under Advaita), but not all mystics embrace "holy indifference" and the passivity and lack of action of moral quietism. Stilling the mind and the personal will leads to an inner emotional passivity and to becoming "resigned" to whatever God does, but this does not necessarily lead to moral indifference—the mystical and moral senses of "quietism" should not be conflated.[11] A mystic can see his or her moral activity as reflecting the "will of God." In fact, many Christian mystics were very active in society or in administering their religious institutions. However, mystics' actions need not be nonviolent but may in fact appear to the unenlightened to be very harmful, as with Arjuna's actions in the *Bhagavad-gita's* war. In medieval Japan, Zen was adopted by Samurai into the way of the warrior (*bushido*).

A transcendent source can be called "good" in the nonmoral sense in which Plotinus called the One "good" in that it supplies our reality—that is, it is *good for us* that it exists or else we would not. But *moral* goodness does not necessarily follow. No mystical tradition has considered a transcendent source evil. Indeed, both introvertive and extrovertive mystics often have a sense that there is a fundamental rightness to things at the deepest level. (As noted above, *natural suffering* is hard to reconcile with the idea that the ground of reality is loving and compassionate.) This may also lead theistic mystics who have an overwhelming sense of a loving source to deny that evil is real: everything is benign or even perfect as is. Suffering and death do not matter, if they are deemed real at all, since they do not affect what is eternal and transcendent. So too, nontheistic mystics may experience an "intrinsic rightness" or "ultimate perfection" to everything as is, leaving nothing more to do and nothing to fear. Ram Dass tells of walking in Bangladesh with his guru among scenes of horrific suffering, and his guru kept saying "Can you see how perfect it is?"

But seeing God in everything can lead to moral indifference or antinomian actions: everything shares the same being of God, and so everything is innately good and free of evil as is; or everything is the creation of a perfect, compassionate god, and so everything is perfect the way things are, and so there is not any need to change anything, or indeed any *right* to change anything. Either no actions matter or all actions matter equally, whether moral or not. No actions are prohibited. Thus, free of a sense of self-will, the enlightened can do whatever their body desires, since our body too is just part of a perfect creation. Eckhart stressed overcoming *self-will* in one's actions, not the acts themselves: he said that if the pope were slain by his hand but not by his will, he would go to the altar and say mass as usual (2009: 94). This can also lead to fatalism: whatever happens is God's will, and so whatever we do is by definition God's will (240)—there is no point in praying "Thy will be done on earth as in heaven" because no matter what occurs *is* God's will. So too, some Hasidic Jews proclaim that we cannot *not* do God's will—even the wicked obey him.

Mystical Selflessness and Morality

To summarize: mystics are necessarily less *self*-oriented, but they need not be *other*-oriented. There are three options for both the path and for the selflessness of an enlightened state: being moral, being immoral, or being nonmoral. Thus, the generalizations "Mystics are necessarily moral" and "Mysticism and morality are incompatible" are both wrong. Mystical enlightenment does not entail one set of values or one ethical system: the enlightened may express their sense of selflessness and freedom in different courses of conduct grounded in their different sets of factual beliefs. The same basic worldview can ground both a nonmoral ethos, a moral one, or even an immoral one (as in Buddhism). A conflict with morality may be a matter of values (as with Advaita and Theravada Buddhism for the monks and nuns) or of the factual presupposition of morality (as with Advaita) that requires that there is a reality to be morally concerned about (another real person) and a reality to act morally.[12]

Moral values and mystical values are not identical, and one set does not entail the other: mystical values are *reality-centered*, not necessarily *other-regarding*. For the enlightened, there is a radical shift in their point of view away from all self-centeredness, but how the enlightened fill their new sense of selflessness and freedom, and thus how they act, depends on factors *outside* mystical experiences themselves. Thus, mystical experiences are themselves morally neutral, and mystical paths and enlightened states are filled with values and action guides, typically from a mystic's own religious tradition. Mystical experiences only get mystics to a state of selflessness—another step is required for that space to be filled with other-regardingness. Thus, mystical experiences have less logical relevance for morality, either positively or negatively, than is usually supposed—they are tied to not morality but to a selflessness, however expressed. Mystical values are oriented around enlightenment, not necessarily around moral concern, and while the two sets of values are not incompatible, they do remain logically independent.

But again, this shows that it is important to distinguish here between *mystical experiences* and the encompassing *mysticism*: values filling a mystical way of life come from outside of the mystical sense of selflessness. Morality can inform a way of life, and mystics practicing in a moral religious tradition may well see mystical experiences as the source of their moral concern, but the moral concern for others must come from a source outside of any mystical experience, as would the specifics on how to help. So too, mystics can be "selfish" even without the belief in a permanent entity called a "self": one can still be immoral by trying to enhance the well-being of one's impermanent node in the interconnected web of the universe by exploiting other nodes.

Overall, the terrain of mysticism and morality is a more complex than is indicated by the stereotype of the peace-loving, celibate, mystic sitting serenely in self-absorbed meditation. We have to actually investigate specific mystics and specific mystical ways of life to see if a given mystic is moral or not or if a moral concern underlies a given tradition's ideal values (see Jones 2004: 79–298). Mystical selflessness may lead moral mystics to devote more time and energy toward helping others, and it may enable them to go beyond an ordinary moral concern to a broader even-minded concern. Today the scope of this concern may be expanded to include animal and ecological concerns.

— 14 —

Comparative Approaches to Mysticism

Broadly construed, the comparative study of mysticism has been present in the West since the nineteenth century, when scholars starting with the German Indologist Friedrich Max Müller and intellectuals such as Ralph Waldo Emerson and the New England transcendentalists began to study Hindu and Buddhist mystical writings. Mysticism was also part of the study of esotericism and the occult that arose in such groups as the Theosophical Society. This comparative study led to differentiating types of mystical experiences (Otto 1932; Zaehner 1957).

Comparison as a general matter actually permeates all of our understanding: in trying to understand something new or simply to place something into a category, we see how it is similar to and different from something that we think we already understand. All concepts involve a degree of generality and are applied through comparisons. But the process of comparison does not mean that we will only see what is common between two phenomena: holding two things up for study reveals what is not unique and what is unique about each, and more contrasting elements than common ones may be exposed. Nevertheless, the danger in comparisons is that we may see other phenomena only through the prism of the familiar and thereby distort the nature of the new phenomena or make members of other cultures into mere reflections of ourselves. In cross-cultural mystical studies, the question is whether such dangers can be checked or preclude altogether the legitimacy of comparing mystical phenomena from different cultures and eras.

Religious Studies

A comparative approach is important in the academic discipline of religious studies. Religious studies is multidisciplinary—incorporating historical, phenomenological, socioscientific, and other approaches to religious phenomena—and does not assume the truth of a particular religious faith (as theology does). The functions that religious phenomena play within a person and within a culture are also studied. Originally religious studies scholars attempted to convey, in Huston Smith's words, the *meaning* that religions carry for the lives of their adherents: to get into the heart of living faiths to see and even to feel how and why they guide and motivate the lives of those who live them—in short, to present the lived experience of a faith. Religion was seen as constituting a unique dimension to cultural phenomena—religious phenomena were not treated as independent of other cultural phenomena, but they cannot be reduced to anything nonreligious and thus require their own study. Religious studies scholars examined such things as the basic metaphors mystics use to communicate the ineffable mystery that they affirm; the most significant procedures used by spiritual masters for becoming aware of the nature of life at its most profound level; the basic notions of the self; what is religiously problematic about the human condition; the nature of ultimate reality; the spiritual qualities (e.g., purity, love, or illumination) that are emphasized; how the nature of true knowledge, insight, or understanding is described; and the conditions that aid in the transformation of desire, motivation, and will (Streng 1991: 130–31). Mystics' beliefs, symbolic expressions, social authority, monastic communities, and the daily activities of monastics and laity are examined, as are mystics as spiritual models, sources of power, and teachers (136). This places mysticism in specific historical moments and focuses on cultural and biographical contexts (136). The presuppositions, procedures, and purposes enshrined in authoritative texts can lead to exploring the meaning of mystical awareness for a religion (137). With the introduction of a comparative perspective, the diverse mystical cosmological, psychological, and ontological notions are clarified (137). A general analysis of the nature of mysticism may also be included.

Descriptive accounts of the beliefs, values, and practices of any mystical tradition are to be presented without any theological or philosophical judgments about the insiders' beliefs. Such accounts are primarily by outsiders and involve some cross-cultural terminology, but they must be acceptable to insiders knowledgeable of the issues. After the descriptive phase, comparisons follow—for example, what about being a Sufi or a Vaishnavite Bhakti is unique and what they have in common. Cross-cultural themes are utilized, and variations are revealed. But no mystical phenomena are exclusively mystical, and thus religious studies also examines other dimensions: with anthropology, it shares the attempt to understand other cultures in their own terms; with philology, the study of texts; with philosophy, the analysis of concepts; and with the social sciences, the attempts to explain religious phenomena either reductively or nonreductively. But showing what is common and what is unique to each religious tradition carves out a niche for the focus of religious studies alone. Friedrich Max Müller famously said that "to know one religion is to know none"—one can understand what makes one's religion *a religion* only by studying other religions. Only by comparisons can one see what is unique about one's religion and what is common or even universal in it. This also helps members of a particular religion to understand their own religion better. The same applies to mysticism: a Christian mystic who knows no other mysticisms does not know what make Christian mysticism mysticism and what is unique about it and what is not.

Religious experiences became the subject of study around 1800 with the Christian theologian Friedrich Schleiermacher's theory that all religions grew out of a prerational "feeling of absolute dependence" and that the "true nature of religion" is "immediate consciousness of the Deity as he is found in ourselves and in the world." Only then did religious experiences become seen as the primary element of religion. The theologian and comparativist Rudolph Otto's idea of dualistic "numinous experiences" followed in the twentieth century. In *The Varieties of Religious Experience*, William James focused on conversion and other religious experiences. But comparative religion for the first half of the twentieth century remained largely theological—scholars argued from within a circle of faith that Christianity is superior to other religions and that all religious experiences are experiences of God. There was also a universalist outlook ignoring differences in mysticisms and mystical experiences. But "history of religions" also began to develop as an academic discipline. The phenomenology of religious phenomena such as rituals became a focus. It bracketed questions of the truth or falsity of religious claims in favor of describing observed religious phenomena and classifying them into systematic cross-cultural typologies.[1] Mircea Eliade's *Patterns in Comparative Religion* is the paradigm of work in this area. Explanations were made in terms of generalizations and ideal types.

The Disparagement of Experiences in Religious Studies Today

The study of mysticism was important in religious studies throughout most of its history, with the focus almost exclusively on Christian mysticism. Any Western study of non-Christian mysticism fell into the category of "comparative mysticism." Rudolph Otto (1932) produced a comparative study of Meister Eckhart and Shankara. Comparisons were made of two or more entire traditions or of themes cutting across multiple traditions. Many scholars took mystical experiences to be the very origin and essence of all religions.

But by the late twentieth century the focus in religious studies became only the observable externals of religions and their relation to the rest of a culture—not individuals' private inner states or experiences. The inner meaning of phenomena, faith, and how religion makes a difference in someone's life were no longer central. Anything like Frits Staal's approach to understanding mystical experiences was out. Religious experiences and other phenomena became more open to being reduced to nonreligious phenomena. In effect, the role of religious study scholars now is to explain away its subject matter by denying anything unique to it and reducing it to other phenomena—and by reducing claims of religious experiences to material claims, "the field has, in effect, denied its own subject matter" (Kripal 2010: 26).[2] In postmodernist circles, talk of "religious experiences" became seen as having a legacy of normative cultural baggage tied to European colonialism and assumptions of Christian superiority, and talk of an independent private realm of experience became seen as only part of the modernist form of governmentality that pacifies individuals by obscuring the extent to which the so-called internal experiences are in fact constituted merely by external social structures (see Martin 2016). Comparative religion and the phenomenology of religion came under attack for being methodologically naive in claiming to be neutral and objective and for importing Western theological values into the enterprise. In particular, Eliade's work has been attacked—even at his old university, his work is considered dead, and graduate students are told to focus on "area studies" rather than comparative studies, to focus on languages, and to forget about that "consciousness nonsense" (McDaniel 2018: 1, 8).

Robert Sharf (1995) points out that today meditation does not play as central a role in the lives of Buddhists as it is usually portrayed, but he goes further and claims that meditative experiences never played a significant role in the development of Buddhist doctrines or practices. For him, all talk of "experience" is like talk of alien abduction—there were in fact no originating events behind the memories (1998: 109; but see Bush 2012).[3] In effect, mystical experiences are like unicorns: there are no unicorns, but scholars can still discuss people's use of the word "unicorn" and its history. Indeed, the entire "experientialist" approach to mysticism is becoming obsolete in religious studies. There has been a recent uptick in academic interest in mysticism and the growing field of "contemplative studies," but interest in religious experiences in religious studies in general is ebbing. A "new materialism" has taken over (see Taylor 1998) in which "attention to discourse, social practices, power, and material culture displaces attention to subjective, phenomenological consciousness" (Bush 2012: 199–200). According to June McDaniel (2018: 1), in the meeting of the American Academy of Religion in 2017, a "visceral hatred of religious experience" was shown. Interest in the mystical and ecstatic experiences of other cultures is considered "so old-fashioned" (McDaniel 2018: 1; also see Wasserstrom 1999). There is hardly a more "beleaguered category than 'mysticism' in the current academic study of religion" (Schmidt 2003: 273). Knee-jerk negative reactions to altered states of consciousness are common among academics and others who are committed to social and psychological reductions of religion (Bronkhorst 2017: 7). Religious faith becomes a matter of observable social and political actions. Studies of power and conflict within a religion are currently hot. Harold Roth (2006), an advocate of contemplative studies in higher education, proposes to reinject studying "subjective" religious experiences into religious studies, rather than maintaining only its current reliance on observable historical and sociological phenomena of the public life of the religious, but he remains very pessimistic about the prospects for change. There is now a "hostility" toward the very idea of mystical and ecstatic experiences "that used to be found in theologians talking about heresies" (McDaniel 2018: 3).

In sum, the lived internal side of religious experiences and faith has been replaced with the study of the externals of religious traditions alone. The field of religious studies has largely given up the study of religious consciousness and experiences (McDaniel 2018: 10). Polls show that about half of Americans have had religious or mystical experiences (4), and these may be the most intensive experiences in a person's life, but postmodernists in religious studies tend to deny that there are any genuine mystical experiences and to ignore neuroscientific studies suggesting that mystical experiences are neurologically unique. Ann Taves, who does consider neuroscientific studies, still believes that the study of religious experiences is passé "in an era that has abandoned experience for discourse *about* experience" (2009: xiii–iv). The "paradigm of language" has replaced the "paradigm of experience" (Bush 2012: 200).

The dominant approaches in religious studies of constructivism and attribution theory (discussed in chapter 5) also downplay the significance of mystical experiences. Under the latter, mystical experiences become nothing but a mystical reading given to our mundane emotional experiences and thus have no cognitive significance. Under the former, mystical experiences are accepted as possibly genuine and unique events, but they have no independent cognitive content—cultural beliefs totally determine their alleged cognitive import—and so they play no role in the development of any tradition's doctrines and practices. Only the observable cultural phenomena need to be studied. There can be no truth to any possible religious claims about ecstatic and mystical states since there is nothing to be found beyond history, culture, language, and the material body (McDaniel 2018: 3). Each mystical experience is unique: at best, even if there were a noncultural experiential element in each experience, it is literally ineffable and so there is no way to compare or contrast experiences and no way to identify cross-cultural commonalities to study. Any talk of "mysticism" is only an attempt to smuggle in essentialism or perennialism.

Thus, scholars focus solely on nonexperiential cultural phenomena. This postmodern stance enables scholars to ignore mystical experiences altogether and to focus only on what mystics *say about* their experiences. As the philosopher Jacques Derrida says, for all matters there is nothing outside the text.[4] Indeed, under postmodernism mysticism is reduced to merely a form of writing (Cupitt 1998: 137; see Harmless 2008: 235). Mysticism becomes exclusively a matter of the everyday world of the public symbol systems of different cultures and is not based in private ASC experiences. Thus, there is nothing to study of mysticism outside of mystical texts, and the study of mysticism becomes the study of merely what mystics say about the things of the cultural world.[5] Texts speak only to other texts. In Sharf's words, "It is a mistake to approach literary, artistic, or ritual representations as if they referred back to something other than themselves, to some numinous inner realm" (2000: 286). The trouble mystics have with language (e.g., paradox and the claim of ineffability) are not indications of puzzling experiences and experienced realities but merely a creative way of writing that speaks only to other texts—"comparative mysticism" becomes "comparative mystical literature."

Even scholars who accept "special" experiences outside everyday consciousness do not focus on the experiences but on the social phenomena accomplished by appeals to experiences and on the discourse that scholars employ to talk of "experience" (Martin 2016: 537–38). And even those who accept that there are mystical experiences dismiss out of hand any claim that they are cognitive: truth and reference are no longer involved—texts tell us only about other texts or about the social power situation of the authors. More generally, any mention today of mysticism in the study of specific religious traditions is becoming rare—at best, it is mentioned only to be dismissed. Indeed, in the humanities mysticism has become "unfashionable" and now has a "bad name" (Cupitt 1998: 56, 45). Instead, naturalist cognitive science and cultural evolutionary theory that give causal reductive explanations of the origins and phenomena of religion are becoming increasingly fashionable for theories in religious studies. (A cognitive scientific approach has not yet been applied to mysticism except in neuroscience. Johannes Bronkhorst [2017] makes a plea to consider religious experience as more substantive in cognitive scientific studies.) These approaches tend to explain away any cognitive significance of religious experiences and in general downplay any inner experiences. This only makes the prospects bleak for the study of mystical experiences to become important again.

In sum, in postmodern religious studies mystical experiences have gone from once being seen as the origin or essence of religion to being dismissed entirely.

Postmodern Objections and Their Problems

Postmodernists in the humanities and social sciences also raise objections to the Enlightenment project of attaining universal, culture-free "objective" knowledge, and this leads to rejecting any comparative studies. All grand narratives covering all cultures and all claims to culturally neutral foundations or principles leading to absolute knowledge or universal rationality are rejected in favor of a radical relativism. Meaning comes exclusively from our historical setting. Knowledge-claims are only cultural products limited to their local cultural setting. There is no transcultural human nature—the "self" and our consciousness are created differently in each culture. There is no cultural universal except the quest for power (McDaniel 2018: 8). Concepts from different cultures and eras are incommensurable, with no commonalities: similar-sounding descriptions of mystical experiences from different cultures may suggest that the experiences are the same, but in fact the descriptions only seem similar because we impose an essentialism on the descriptions—the actual meaning of a description is totally contextualized by the different theories in each culture. Reasons become internal to the conceptual framework of a "form of life," with no common ground to all such forms, and thus each form is immune to criticism from outside and there is no ultimate justification by a universal foundation. The culturally limited meaning of each mystical tradition precludes any cross-cultural elements or any generalizations or broad theories—mystics in different cultures inhabit "different worlds." Thus, each mystical phenomenon is unique, foreclosing any meaningful comparisons. There can be no full-scale comparisons of two or more traditions—even a point from one mystical tradition cannot be compared to a point in another tradition.[6]

For postmodernists, the very process of comparison is seen as only creating artificialities. All comparisons are based on undefendable modernist assumptions about a universal nature of human beings and cultural universals, and on the projection of Western ideas and values. Moreover, the term "mysticism" is a modern invention, and its application to other cultures is merely an unjustifiable academic move. Our concepts of "mysticism" even shape how we see earlier Western phenomena. So too, we begin to see phenomena from other cultures through the lens of Western "mysticism." Even to label some phenomena within Western culture with a category that is applied cross-culturally implicitly assumes that there are comparable phenomena in other cultures. Our modern Western perspective indelibly shapes our perception of other cultures—Martin Buber may have written a dissertation on the early Chinese Daoist Zhuangzi, but his Jewish background irreparably warped his understanding of Daoism. Historians of religions cannot display what is like to be a mystic in the abstract but at best only what it is like to be an eleventh-century Tibetan Buddhist mystic or an eighteenth-century Moroccan Sufi and so forth (if they are able to escape the vise of their own culture and era). Only the uniqueness and "otherness" of each culture, not commonalities, remain. Comparativists see commonalities arising only from their own point of view when in fact there are none, and see only superficial features of any culture—only the particularities of each culture give meaning, and thus only differences matter. All alleged commonalities have the stamp of only one's own culture.

Thus, postmodernists reject any comparative project. Most basically, they deny that any cross-cultural categories such as "mysticism" are legitimate. Although the term "mystical" has roots going back two thousand years, the nouns "mysticism" and "mystic" are inventions only of the modern West and do not have exact counterparts in the other cultures or even earlier Western cultures. This has led postmodernists to question whether the term "mysticism" can be used to classify phenomena from any other culture or era: it is inherently Eurocentric and anachronistic in any nonmodern and non-Western contexts. In fact, they argue that the term "mysticism" should be thrown out (see Schmidt 2003).[7] According to Grace Jantzen (1995: 326), the social construction of "mysticism" is closely connected with issues of power relations. She points out that mysticism in Christianity has been tied to male authority and that reducing mysticism today to individual mystical experiences only reflects modern Western individualism. Much of the study of non-Western mysticism also has an "orientalist" bias: Westerners see non-Western cultures through a prism of Western categories, grand narratives, and stereotypes—the "mystical Orient" was seen as irrational, backward, immoral, feminine, and so on, while the West was seen as rational, progressive, moral, male, and so on (see Clarke 1997). All non-Western mysticism is treated as the same and static, and it is viewed in terms set by Westerners. Westerners invented the terms "Islam," "Hinduism," and "Buddhism," and view the designated phenomena in terms of Western ideas of religion. So too, when historians in religious studies talk about "mysticism" they are really only talking about Christian mysticism—all "true" or "genuine" mystics must reflect Christian mysticism and are seen in terms of Christian mysticism. Any generalizations end up reflecting only Western theological biases and cannot capture the individuality of each culture's mysticism. Different "area studies" focusing on only specific cultures replaced "comparative religion," but even those are subject to distortion by Western values and interests. All understanding of other cultures involves only Western intellectual imperialism and colonialism (see King 1999). Ethnology becomes, in the words of the anthropologist James Clifford, only "a fantasy reality of a reality fantasy" (quoted in Patton & Ray 2000: 2–3). In the end, there is no difference between the academic study of other cultures and playing a game of Dungeons & Dragons.

However, there are problems with this approach. Although the terms "mysticism" and "mystical experience" (and "religious experience") are modern Western inventions, it does not follow that no phenomena that existed earlier in the West or in other cultures can be labeled "mystical" in the modern sense. Nor must the term's use be inherently linked to modern Christian theological concerns or otherwise distort other cultures' phenomena.[8] This is true for any term: the invention of a *concept* does not invent the *phenomena* in the world that the concept covers. The natural historian Richard Owen invented the term "dinosaur" in the 1830s to classify certain fossils that he was studying, but to make the startling claim "Dinosaurs did not exist before 1830" would at best be only a confusing way of stating the obvious fact that classifying something with a concept is not possible before that concept is devised—if dinosaurs existed, they existed many millions of years earlier, and their existence did not depend in any way on our concepts, whenever and wherever they were devised. Jonathan Z. Smith made the surprising claim that *"there is no data for religion.* Religion is solely the creation of the scholar's study" (1982: xi), but his discussion shows that he meant only the constructivists' position that there are no "bare" unconstructed religious experiences or other phenomena, not that there is nothing for religious scholars to study (and two sentences after those just quoted Smith referred to "the student of religion"). Scholars "create" the data only in the sense of filtering out certain phenomena to study through their concepts and theories in the way Owen "created" dinosaurs. Terms limit what phenomena are included and what is excluded in a study, but they do not create the phenomena in any meaningful sense. To modify a postmodern image, a map does not create the territory that is mapped. Different types of map projections will reflect different interests, but all can be useful for particular purposes, and none need distort once the projection is understood. So too, all maps involve such theorizing, but they cannot properly be made without first carefully studying the phenomena. And the maps may well illuminate the phenomena in a new way by giving them a new context. So it is with the use of cross-cultural umbrella terms.

    Modern scholars may invent new terms in their interaction with what is being studied. Even if there are no equivalents of "mysticism," "mystics," and "mystical experiences" (or a comprehensive term for all types of "meditation") in Arabic, Hebrew, Sanskrit, Chinese, or any other language, this does not rule out that scholars may find phenomena in other cultures to which the modern Western terms apply and that the concepts may help to reveal something important about such phenomena—the absence of similar umbrella terms in other cultures is irrelevant. It would be an anachronism to say that classical Hindus had the term "mystical," but it is not an anachronism to say that they had phenomena to which the modern term "mystical" can apply.[9] Mystical phenomena may not have been understood as "mystical" in a particular culture, but the phenomena are nonetheless mystical, and using the term "mystical" does not change their cultural character. Using Western terms as umbrella terms does require making explicit what is meant, but classifying something from India or China as "mystical" in the modern sense does not make it Western or modern any more than classifying Sanskrit or Chinese as a "language" makes them into English phenomena or mashes all languages into one. Few scholars would advocate expunging the word "language" from English or deny that linguists can legitimately study the history of language without distorting languages or deny that the cross-cultural study of languages may reveal something of the nature of all languages. But scholars do question whether "mysticism" exists (e.g., Keller 1978; Penner 1983). Nevertheless, only extreme historicists rule out the possibility of the meaningful study of other cultures and eras and the possibility of finding common elements. So too, once scholars expose and examine the implicit biases of the past that reflected European imperialism and colonialism, the use of all Western terms today is not necessarily still biased or carrying past ideological assumptions and overtones. And the fact that Westerners have produced accounts of other cultures, including their mystical traditions, and translations of texts that are accepted by qualified members of those cultures severely damages the postmodernists' position.[10]

Thus, introducing modern umbrella categories such as "mysticism," "ultimate reality," "meditation," or "enlightenment" for cross-cultural purposes need not change the character of phenomena in any particular culture. The umbrella terms are in fact often derived from studying phenomena from different cultures. Cross-cultural categories are filters that select certain aspects of human phenomena for attention and need not reduce them to copies of modern Western phenomena. Rather, they may lead to insights about the phenomena. Merely because scholars of mysticism focus on mystical aspects of cultural phenomena does not mean that they believe that mystical phenomena are sui generis and autonomous from other human phenomena. Nor does it mean that there are no nonmystical dimensions to cultural phenomena that have a mystical dimension or that only scholars of mysticism can study such cultural phenomena—any human phenomenon has multiple dimensions that can be explored by different approaches. Nor does the use of transcultural categories mean that particular mystical phenomena need not be studied in their cultural contexts—with the possible exception of neuroscientific studies of mystics, mystical phenomena cannot be isolated from culture. Historians must focus on the cultural context of a mystic to understand his or her writings, but they still may see common elements for generalizations. Indeed, as noted above, studying mysticism in other cultures may reveal something about mysticism in one's own culture and also reveal what is distinctive about it in one's own culture and era, and the cross-cultural study of mysticisms may lead to learning something of the nature of all mystical phenomena. So too, only with a cross-cultural perspective can one come up with genuinely useful general theories of mysticism. Caution of course must be used to avoid overgeneralizing or otherwise distorting phenomena, but using modern Western categories is not per se objectionable.

A related postmodern attack is that the use of the term "mysticism" suggests some necessary unchanging, transhistorical "essence" common to all mystical phenomena when in fact there is none or that all mystical phenomena in different cultures and eras are in their "essence" actually the same despite appearances (as with the perennialist approach). No one is confused by the term "language" into thinking all languages are the same or unchanging, but this is not so with "mysticism." So too, the fact that "mystical experience" is usually referred to in the singular—"*the* mystical experience"—leads people to believe without reflecting on the matter that all mystical experiences are of the same nature and type and that all mysticism is really the same. However, if one actually examines the works of mystics, it is hard to maintain that there is one common "mysticism" rather than differing mystical doctrines, traditions (with subtraditions), cultural phenomena, and different types of mystical experiences.

We can use an abstract concept to highlight aspects of phenomena for study without assuming that those aspects are the unchanging "essence" of the phenomena but are only parts of the phenomena that are the focus of attention. In fact, by the postmodernists' reasoning no classificatory terms of any kind could ever be used. To deny any general categories leads in the end to a nominalism in which only proper names unique to each referent are left standing. There would be, to continue the same example, no such thing as a "language": no one speaks "language" in the abstract but only a concrete language—English, French, Japanese, or whatever—and according to postmodernists they cannot have anything in common. So too, there can be no history of "language" or anything to say about the nature of all phenomena classified as "linguistic." But an umbrella term can indicate general defining characteristics for phenomena to qualify being covered by that term, and yet the phenomena can still be constantly changing.

The same applies to the abstract classificatory terms of mysticism: there is no unchanging "Christian mysticism" or "Buddhist mysticism" but only individual mystics and evolving subtraditions. Labeling someone today a "Christian mystic" does not mean that he or she believes the same doctrines or practices the same way of life as early Christian desert hermits but only that they belong to the same historical tradition. Even if the "essence" of Christianity is to accept that there is a creator god and that Jesus of Nazareth had a unique relation to him, particular conceptions of God and the role of Jesus have changed over time, and the total web of beliefs of a given Christian mystic incorporates that abstract "essence" differently. In short, there are different expressions of key themes but no timeless unchanging "essence" to any tradition that different mystics are trying to express. Abstract categories may in fact only work in terms of what Ludwig Wittgenstein called "family resemblances," but this does not mean that the classification may not lead to seeing something significant about the nature of such phenomena.

In sum, all claims are made from particular perspectives that are set up by culturally dependent conceptualizations and beliefs, but this does not mean that they cannot capture something significant about reality, any more than the fact that scientific claims are made from points of views dictated by particular scientific interests and specific concepts and theories means that scientific claims must be groundless. All understanding involves a framework and some degree of theory. Classifications and categories are embedded in even basic descriptions. There is no neutral "view from nowhere"—all theories filter and organize phenomena, reflecting our interests and values, and descriptions are dependent on those theories—but theories can still be useful tools for understanding the phenomena of the world.

The New Comparativism

Moreover, postmodernists are subject to the same sort of ideological shaping of which they accuse modern thinkers to falling prey—even if there are mystical experiences free of cultural construction, the study of mysticism remains thoroughly contextualized. As Michael Stoeber says, in the case of some recent studies of mysticism, "one gets the sense the definitions, readings, and prescriptions of mysticism are being somewhat 'over-determined' by the contextual preferences of scholars—be they feminist, liberationist, social transformational, ecological, or erotic—rather than simply focusing on the actual context of the mystics in question" (2017: 26). These contemporary interests are certainly legitimate, but this does not mean that earlier interests in mystical experiences and ASCs are not valuable or that the study of such phenomena today must be determined by matters of social power. However, in the hands of the postmodernists the new approaches have led to eliminating the study of the experiential side of mysticism. So too, after

Steven Katz's introduction of constructivism into mystical studies in 1978, postmodernism almost killed off comparative studies for a generation. But today there are comparativists in religious studies who take the criticisms of postmodernism seriously and yet still believe a comparativist approach survives (see Patton & Ray 2000; Paden 2016).

In particular, the demand to study mystical phenomena within their cultural context and era is seen as necessary to any comparative study. "Thick" accounts of mystical phenomena in their particular culture, not "thin" accounts in terms of abstract categories or superficial accounts of doctrines, are needed. So too, scholars can refer to experiences without assuming that they are unmediated, absolutely private, or universal (Bush 2012: 223). A mystic, like any other human being, is situated in a cultural environment and cannot be studied as just "a mystic" in the abstract or by cross-cultural themes or types alone. Comparisons in the past tended to focus only on common or universal elements through the application of abstract categories and to ignore the details and differences, thereby creating false or superficial presentations of religious traditions. Instead, the meanings exposed by cross-cultural comparisons involve the complex cultures themselves, not some abstract structures postulated by academics. But identifying themes and making generalizations need not distort what is studied if they are built from the ground up (i.e., starting by examining mystical phenomena in their cultural and historical context) rather than imposed from the top down by a theological or a universalist perspective. Everything is unique if we restrict categories enough, but everything also has common features. Historicism can be as distortive as a universalism that washes out all individuality: comparativists can affirm unique cultural configurations of common elements, while postmodernists must deny the existence of common elements altogether and must see everything as unique. So too, comparativists need to make judgments, but they need not privilege our present phenomena to understand phenomena from the past or from another culture. Nor need they adopt an ahistorical approach that merely groups mystical phenomena into timeless ideal types—instead, they can be sensitive to the evolution of mystical doctrines and practices.

In sum, older comparativists saw only similarities while postmodernists see only differences, but the new comparativists are freed from the "myopia of single-culture analysis" and able to acknowledge the naturalness and structural variety of the world's religious life (Paden 2016: 103). Holding two or more mystics or traditions up together will illuminate both differences and similarities—what they have in common and what sets them apart—but this approach does not dictate in advance what is to be found or declare that either differences or similarities are more important. Because of the role of culture in any human phenomenon, there may be no cross-cultural identities to be revealed except as phenomena falling into abstract categories. Similarities and differences will appear in any comparison, but what counts as a "similarity" or a "difference" in a cultural context is a matter of judgment. The significance of any cultural phenomenon is not confined exclusively to the elements unique to that culture: comparativists can find the presence of general or universal commonalities without reducing the cultural phenomenon to only those features or reducing people to some transcultural "human essence."

The danger of overly facile identification of similarities or of distorting phenomena by taking them out of their cultural setting still remains. Nevertheless, comparativists attempt to identify underlying cross-cultural commonalities that improve the understanding of different cultural items and try to understand why they exist. Cross-cultural commonalities also expose what is unique to each tradition. But neither common elements nor the culturally specific is privileged; resemblances are neither ignored nor simplistically collapsed into a superficial sameness (Paden 2016: 103). Commonalities or cultural differences may be more significant depending on each situation. Studying comparisons may bring out differences or similarities that were not apparent at first, reveal superficial or deep similarities or differences, and bring out what is unique about each culture and teaching. So too, the revised comparativist approach need not undermine the "old Enlightenment purpose of enlarging our understanding and commitment to a wider embrace of humanity" (Patton & Ray 2000: 13). Comparativists will always have a perspective, and like theories, descriptions, evaluations, and interpretations, perspectives are never neutral. So too, comparativists must critically examine their own presuppositions to limit any imposition of their values onto different mystical traditions and make their interpretive perspective explicit. (Uncovering one's own biases and examining them is harder than it sounds.)

All thought, including that of comparativists, is embedded in a specific cultural context. But this does not mean that the scope of thought must be circumscribed by one's culture.[11] Indeed, new thoughts can occur only if we can transcend our prior thoughts by utilizing our old concepts in new ways or devising new concepts. The comparativists' terminology will arise in one cultural context, but comparativists must devise terminology that is intended to transcend any one culture in its application—culturally specific terminology would be confined to its culture of origin. And again, employing a Western umbrella term for cross-cultural purposes does not mean that comparativists do not need to understand phenomena from other cultures in their own terms or to study other traditions in detail. Phenomena from different cultures would be subsumed under general comparativist terms such as "mysticism," "mystical experience," and "enlightenment," but this does not mean that all mystical experiences must be seen as the same or that some transcultural essence underlies all mystical doctrines or that all enlightened ways of life are the same. That "God" and "Brahman" are grouped under the category "transcendent realities" does not make them the same reality or mean that all the terms mean the same thing and can be translated as "God." Nor does it mean that comparativists employing the category cannot see any differences among them any more than when we label people from different cultures and eras "human beings." So too, the initial comparativist categories may be reevaluated and revised in light of other cultures' phenomena, or more appropriate ones may be devised.

The meaning found by studying phenomena in context need not be lost by seeing where those phenomena fall within abstract cross-cultural categories. Translations of texts can be guided by understanding the culture in which a text is composed, not by grand theories. Any attempt to see one tradition in terms of another can lead to distortions, as early Chinese Buddhists quickly found out when they initially translated Buddhist terms with Daoist ones (the *geyi* method). The phenomena may even be redescribed in transcultural terms without losing their original cultural meaning if sufficient details are included.

Comparativists, however, remain in the minority. Studying common themes is considered "boring," "dated," "pointless," and "in general a waste of time" (McDaniel 2018: 1). Area studies prevail over broader comparative studies (8). As of yet, few new culturally sensitive studies in comparative mysticism have been forthcoming (starting with Toshihiko 1983). Few scholars could master even two cultures and their languages well enough to do a meaningful in-depth comparison of them. Most comparisons in mystical studies remain examples of the older comparative approach. Nor has a methodology yet been agreed upon (see Stausberg 2011). But the new comparativists show that the prospect is not dead. (However, the new comparativism may stick to the current interest in religious studies in observable social phenomena and not revive interest in *experiences*.)

Seeing Something New

William James once remarked, "Probably a crab would be filled with a sense of personal outrage if it could hear us class it without ado or apology as a crustacean, and thus dispose of it. 'I am no such thing,' it would say; 'I am myself, myself alone.'" Many Christians do not like Christianity being classified as a "religion" and grouped with other "religions" or labeled an "Abrahamic religion." They believe that they have the unique word of God and the incarnation of God as their foundation and that this separates Christianity from these human creations. Of course, most of the faithful of other religions believe something similar about their own religion. But viewing comparatively each mystical tradition within the world religions may reveal aspects of it that the believers themselves did not notice—what is unique to a tradition and what is common to many or all mystical traditions. And this may lead believers to modify their beliefs in light of others' beliefs and values. So too, for scholars of specific traditions, the comparative study of mystical systems replaces the tunnel vision of specialization and thus can help them to see what is distinctive about each system and about mysticism in general.

— 15 —

Theological Approaches to Comparative Mysticism

Outside of religious studies, other scholars have grander frameworks within which mystical phenomena are placed. Theologians and their counterparts in nontheistic traditions create religious theories and make judgments from within a circle of faith. But first another normative approach should be examined.

Perennial Philosophy

A modern universalist approach to mysticism that contrasts with the contextualism of the new comparativism was introduced in chapter 6: perennial philosophy. To be more precise, there are two types of perennial philosophy: the contemporary "traditionalist" or "primordialist" school arising in the 1930s and 1940s out of modern Western esotericism and more directly from the ideas of René Guénon in reaction to modern science and relativism (see Schuon 1975; Smith 1976, 1987; Nasr 1981), and the syncretic approach of Aldous Huxley (1945). The latter involves a search for one universal path, while the former treats each traditional religion across the globe as a separate path up the same mountain, and so there is no need for a convergence of all exoteric mystical traditions into one "world faith." The same unchanging, timeless Truth underlies all mystical expressions. Perennialists thus believe that the apparent conflict between mystical claims from different traditions is only superficial: there is a common "esoteric" core of principles that are of divine origin underlying the diverse "exoteric" expressions of authentic traditional religions. These principles are revealed to those with a developed "intellect" (Lat. *intellectus*, Gk. *nous*)—a mental faculty distinct from both sense-experiences and reasoning that is directly connected to the divine. Thus, all mystical knowledge is actually the same despite different cultural expressions of it. Most perennialists may accept that there are unconstructed mystical experiences that are independent of all the vagaries of culture and history that informs all religions, but perennialism is about doctrines in all religions and a full metaphysics of alleged realities. That is, perennialism is not about *mystical experiences* but about *doctrines* and *knowledge* of the transcendent source of the universe and the structure of the universe and a human being. Thus, perennialism should be distinguished from the essentialism discussed in chapter 5.

Perennialists place the doctrines of all mystical traditions into a philosophical framework. The perennialist position rests on three premises: there is a single referent for all mysticisms; this referent corresponds to the ultimate nature of reality; and mystics can directly access this ultimate reality (Ferrer 2000: 13). The transcendent Truth can be known because our souls participate in that principle. The Truth is the origin of all the world's religious traditions and still lies at the heart of every traditional religion and underlies all religious knowledge. All mystical doctrines have the same referent, just as "*water*" and the French "*eau*" have the same referent (Smith 1987: 561). That is, different religions are like so many different languages speaking the same Truth (Nasr 1981: 293). Huston Smith likened the universal perennial philosophy underlying all religions to Noam Chomsky's theory of an innate universal grammar underlying all natural languages despite their very different surface grammars: the common underlying metaphysical structure articulated by perennialists enables us to understand all the apparent differences in mystical systems (Smith & Rosemont 2008). Any conflict of mystical claims can be dismissed since the claims can be reinterpreted through the prism of perennialism to fit the esoteric core. All mystics are really members of one underlying unified tradition regardless of the religion that they practice, and they experience the same transcendent reality and share the same beliefs. Thus, there is a "transcendent unity of religions," not on the exoteric level but on the level of a common esoteric core of principles. Those principles are revealed to those with a developed *intellectus* that has been inspired by the divine.

In sum, mystical doctrines in the different traditions form different exoteric shells affected by cultural teachings, but they cover the one esoteric identity of all mystical claims. In this way, perennialism is one stance for a transcultural understanding of the various mystical teachings of the world. Traditionalists retain the different exoteric shells as paths, but they see no need to study the cultural exoteric claims themselves to understand mystical doctrines: the true meaning of all mystical doctrines is supplied by the common transcultural esoteric wisdom, and thus perennialists can see the true meaning in all mystical claims without studying anything of the cultural contexts at all. Thus, perennialists deny contextualism. (Theologians in particular theistic traditions may also deny contextualism for understanding mysticism in other traditions since their own tradition supplies the true understanding of all mystical experiences. But, contrary to what constructivists claim, this does not make such theologians "perennialists," since they typically will endorse some theology from their own tradition and not perennial philosophy.)

Despite its names, "primordialism" or "traditionalism" is only a modern creation—classical mystics did not espouse it—and rests on a faulty distinction of exoteric and esoteric elements in mystical doctrines (see Jones 2021). The perennialist approach is the paradigm of a top-down perspective of understanding and of imposing ideas from outside a culture to understand cultural phenomena. It involves translating all local terms in generic terminology (e.g., "God" or "consciousness") without any sensitivity to local meanings. To maintain that there is only one set of metaphysical beliefs underlying all religions requires a theoretical overlay and is not derived from studying the actual doctrines of mystical traditions. The history of mysticism that results is seeing all mysticisms as simply different cultural expressions of the same alleged underlying perennial wisdom (see Abhyananda 2012). Thus, it is the inverse of postmodernism: here, an alleged common knowledge is all important and differences in expressions can be ignored.

Perennialism is almost extinct in academia today. It still survives in "contemplative studies" (Komjathy 2018: 6) and transpersonal psychology (Ferrer 2000). But it survives more not to label a set of doctrines underlying all mysticism but as a name for a transcultural essentialism of mystical experiences (either mystical experiences being present in all religions or there being common phenomenal features in all mystical experiences).

Recent Theological Approaches

When modern Christian theologians first began to write about other religions, they showed little understanding of the other religions but asserted the superiority of their own tradition and "corrected" the understanding of mystics in other traditions.[1] The usual approach involved theological judgments of religious phenomena and the status of other religions. Theologians argued that Christianity was the one "true religion" or the "fulfillment" of other religions. They also saw other religions in Christian terms (e.g., *nirvana* as heaven and *karma* as sin) and saw all mystical experiences as experiences of a trinitarian personal god. Well into the twentieth century, books on "world mysticism" were 90 percent about Christian traditions, with a short chapter at the end on Judaism and "Oriental mysticism" or "pagan mysticism." In the second half of the twentieth century, however, Christian theologians began to take other religious traditions more seriously. As theology, the starting point of any such approach is a commitment to one's own faith, but three new theological approaches have arisen that involve genuinely trying to understand the faith of non-Christian mystical traditions better and to come to terms with those in other religions who claim to experience "ultimate reality" in either theistic or nontheistic terms.[2]

The first new approach was to enter into dialogues with members of other religions, not to convert them but to get to understand their points of view and to explain a Christian point of view to them. This may also lead to revising one's own religious beliefs. Mysticism is a prominent focus in some discussions, at least in Catholic circles. The Trappist monk Thomas Merton was enthusiastic about intermonastic dialogues. He studied Sufi, Hindu, and Buddhist mystical traditions, found some commonality, and became interested in a dialogue with other religions as a way of deepening one's own faith.[3] He was especially interested in Buddhist mindfulness practices. But through all this, he never gave up his Catholicism, and in private criticized Asian religions for embracing nonpersonal transcendent realities. A Benedictine, Aelred Graham, wrote on Christianity and Zen. The Catholic priest and scholar Raimon Panikkar (2014) advocated a participatory approach toward other religions and saw human beings as a "mystic animal" and mysticism as "the human characteristic par excellence," with the pure consciousness experience being open to everyone.

A second approach does not engage other religions but revolves around the religious issue of whether Christianity alone is salvific or whether other religions also lead to the same salvation after death—the question of "exclusivism," "inclusivism," and "pluralism" (see Hedges & Race 2008). Liberals favor an overarching religious pluralism in which more than one religion can lead to salvation (see Hick 1989). When mysticism becomes involved in this approach today, the mystery of transcendent realities becomes emphasized. But this theology of religions requires believers to revise their own religious doctrines—believers must accept other religions as also ways to the same salvation, and cannot hold their beliefs as the one absolute truth or uniquely the best. Conservatives respond that pluralism at least dampens one's commitment to one's own religion when it is reinvisioned as no longer an exclusive vehicle of salvation but merely one vehicle of salvation among many that is no better in any absolute sense than the others, and when all religious doctrines become provisional. However, exclusivism—that is, that one must belong to a certain religion to be saved—would mean that the vast majority of humanity is not saved for no reason other than being born in the wrong part of the world, and most theists do not want to believe that a merciful god would set up the world that way. (It should be noted that when classical Christian mystics addressed the matter of non-Christians, they, like most traditional Christians, were exclusivists, with a few exceptions.) In inclusivism, members of other religions can be saved because of the Christ's saving sacrifice for all people—the Catholic theologian Karl Rahner spoke of "anonymous Christians"—but this appears to many as merely an epicycle to preserve one's own religion as privileged.[4]

The newest approach is a reaction against pluralistic theologies of religion: the "comparative theology" championed by another Catholic, the Jesuit Francis X. Clooney (2010). The intent is not to be neutral or objective: this is an explicit stance of religious "faith seeking understanding" of the divine rooted in one faith by exploring aspects of other faiths in depth (in Clooney's case, Hinduism) to disclose truths about one's own religion and to gain insights from other religions to reform one's own faith. It is the first approach that stresses the possibility that other religions may offer something of value for understanding and developing one's own religion. The objective is not to harmonize religions or to make a theological judgment about other religions but to understand one's own religion better, both its beliefs and practices. For example, John Keenan (1989) believes that Buddhist Yogachara's analysis of consciousness is a better way to express Christian mystical insights than Neoplatonism.[5] This goes beyond dialogue, but it still requires understanding other religions in their own terms. In the mid-twentieth century, the Benedictine Henri Le Saux set up a Christian ashram in India, and he and his student Bede Griffiths attempted to integrate Hindu practices and beliefs into a Christian framework. He took mysticism to be the origin and goal of all religions. Le Saux became a *sannyasin*, taking the name Abhishiktananda. A theological understanding of the differences in beliefs does not appear to be part of this project, but comparative theology does open up the scholar to the possibility of a personal transformation.[6]

Some theologians adopt an essentialist approach toward mysticism. For example, Paul Knitter writes, "There is a core mystical experience [of the 'same Divine Mystery or Reality'] pulsating within the religious traditions that have endured through the ages" that is sometimes only discernible on the esoteric level (2002: 125). However, mysticism overall is not a major topic within the theology of religions today, and comparative theology remains primarily a Christian endeavor. Nor is mysticism a major field in modern theological training in the Abrahamic traditions. A generation ago, the Jesuit William Johnston lamented "From the time of Thomas à Kempis better men than I have been attempting to convert the theologians [to the need for theologians who are also mystics]—and they have been conspicuously unsuccessful. The theologians remain unregenerate" (1978: 58). Today there is a small shift: some American seminaries now offer courses and programs in "ascetical theology." But the Benedictine monk Willigis Jäger could not find mystical guides within the Catholic Church and had to ask his superiors for permission to study Zen in Japan. According to him, there has been no place for mysticism in Christian theology for two hundred years (2006: xix).

Indeed, as in religious studies, liberal theologians today have largely shifted their attention to the social and political world (McDaniel 2018: 2). With a few exceptions, Christian philosophers, theological historians, and comparative theologians have not contributed to the discussion of mystical experiences today (Spencer 2021: 3). In comparative theology and theology in general today, any "experientialist" approach to mysticism that would affirm any genuine mystical experiences is, as in religious studies, "thoroughly dated" (Nicholson 2011: 194). Within Protestant theology, the experience of God is deemed impossible on logical grounds (since God is by definition wholly transcendent)—to view God through the lens of "experience" is "hopelessly naive" (see Hart & Wall 2005: 2). The *via negativa* is discussed without mention of mystical experiences. So too, mystical experiences appear to play no role in contemporary Continental "mystical theology" (see Lewin et al. 2017). Instead, the term "mystical" has reverted to its original Christian use as denoting a type of interpretation of texts but without any ASCs informing the interpretations. Mysticism is about church matters and not psychological states or experiences. The questions that Christian mystics raise for theology visibly embarrass many academic theologians (McIntosh 1998: 14)—"experiences of God" cannot be taken seriously in today's naturalist atmosphere in universities and by the secular general media, and so theologians and religion professors do not want to mention them in front of their secular colleagues. One "highly distinguished Christian theologian" once suggested to Daniel Spencer that "the proper response to such [mystical] claims [as Aldous Huxley's] is to shrug the shoulders, say 'Some people believe crazy things,' and move on" (Spencer 2021: 4).

Seekers are left, with the exception of relatively few churches, to New Age groups to find the meaning of their experiences. But even some scholars who speak of "spirituality" rather than "religion" and who focus on an individual's personal development (rather than religious institutions or the traditional doctrines of a particular religion) now believe that the past focus on interiority in any spirituality was a mistake (e.g., Thomas 2000).

— 16 —

The Importance of Studying Mysticism Today

The definition of "mystical experience" that has been employed here centers around altered states of consciousness in which both the conceptual apparatus of the mind and the sense of separate phenomenal self are weakened or are in total abeyance, along with the accompanying emotions and dispositions. The diverse types of experiences in these ASCs are the central experiential component of classical mystical ways of life. The ASCs—including a possible state of unified consciousness in which all differentiated content is eliminated—are important in our understanding of the nature of our consciousness and thus of what a human being is. This should interest even those who have not had a mystical experience themselves and also those who meditate only for the practice's pragmatic effects on their overall psychological and physiological well-being. It also takes us beyond the current interest of professionals in religious studies who focus only on the observable phenomena of mysticism.

Mystical experiences raise questions that go beyond intellectual philosophical and theological arguments. The most basic issue is whether such experiences are cognitive. Do mystical experiences tell us something about reality apart from how our brain works? Are introvertive mystical experiences in touch with a fundamental reality? Does the ground of all reality illuminate the mind in these experiences, or are they merely brain-generated events that mislead experiencers into delusions? How do we determine what is knowledge? Are these experiences the supreme achievement of being human, fulfilling our greatest potential, or are they only hallucinations, or something in between? Are mystics calming the mind and discerning the real (to cite the title of a Buddhist work), or are they misguided in cultivating these experiences? Is the "naked desert" of the depth-mystical unified ASC a profound cognitive state of what is ultimately real, or is the brain just misfiring? And if the experience is cognitive, what is the nature of what is experienced? Are mystics aligning their lives with reality, or only wasting their lives regardless of any positive worldly side-effects? Even if mystics disagree over what is experienced, do the experiences at least tell us that there is more to reality than meets the naturalist eye? Do the experiences show that life is purposeful even if no specific "meaning of life" is given? Do mystical experiences present an obstacle for naturalism and scientism? How should we respond to the dark side of possible negative effects on the mind from meditation and drugs? Does the abuse of certain "enlightened" gurus show that these experiences need not be positive? Is it safe to permit the internal bomb of a mystical experience to have a life-changing impact? In such circumstances, how can we be certain that the experiences induce "wisdom"? This issue of cognitivity should cause us to reexamine our beliefs about what is real and about what we are as human beings. Thus, even if one has little aptitude for mysticism, these experiences raise philosophical and existential matters that warrant attention.

Or consider the implications for neuroscience. Neuroscientists have become interested in the specific states of consciousness deemed "mystical" here. (It is odd that there is more interest in mystical experiences in academia today in neuroscience than in the humanities.) Should mystical experiences cause us to revise our understanding of the brain? Are these experiences like high-energy physics that caused physicists to revise Newtonian physics, as Alan Wallace suggests (2003: 167)? Or are introvertive experiences with differentiated content merely cases of subconscious material flowing into the conscious mind, and can the depth-mystical experience be ignored as simply a worthless feedback effect that occurs when the mind has no material to work with? Should these experiences affect the status of the normal baseline state of consciousness? William James famously said,

> Our normal waking consciousness, rational consciousness as we call it, is but one special type of consciousness, whilst all about it, parted from it by the filmiest of screens, there lie potential forms of consciousness entirely different. We may go through life without suspecting their existence; but apply the requisite stimulus, and at a touch they are there in all their completeness, definite types of mentality which probably somewhere have their

field of application and adaptation. No account of the universe in its totality can be final which leaves these other forms of consciousness quite disregarded. How to regard them is the question—for they are so discontinuous with ordinary consciousness. Yet they may determine attitudes though they cannot furnish formulas, and open a region though they fail to give a map. At any rate, they forbid a premature closing of our accounts with reality. Looking back on my own experiences, they all converge towards a kind of insight to which I cannot help ascribing some metaphysical significance. ([1902] 1958: 298)

Do the ASCs in fact have such "metaphysical significance"? How do we tell?

When we turn from mystical experiences and ASCs themselves to the cultural phenomena of mysticism—that is, the rest of a mystical ways of life—once again we find something important to study. We can see that the clichés about mysticism are not helpful. There is a diversity of mysticisms and a diversity of accounts of mystical experiences within those mysticisms. Such diversities raise the problem of whether any highly ramified account can capture the nature of what was experienced. The felt phenomenology of any type of mystical experience does not dictate any one ontological interpretation. Is "union with God" just our general description of any lessening of the sense of self or of conceptual barriers in extrovertive mystical experiences? Is the unified conscious state of the depth-mystical experience "union with God," or is the experience merely interpreted after the event that way by theists who see no other options? Evelyn Underhill's classic definition of mysticism as "the art of union with Reality" ([1915] 1961: 23) shows how mysticism has been misconstrued over the years: mysticism is more than mystical experiences; the experiences do not involve a unification of two separate realities; and what is ultimate "Reality" differs in different mystical traditions and need not be transcendent in the case of extrovertive mysticism. Samkhya-Yoga has multiple independent transcendent centers of consciousness and a separate realm of matter, not one Reality. "Ultimate reality" is not necessarily a personal god, nor is realizing Brahman or the Dao a matter of union, since they are already operating in us. And today there are now naturalist options to understanding the significance of all mystical experiences.

The modern psychologization of mysticism as a matter of only mystical experiences misrepresents classical mysticism. Traditionally, mysticism is not about cultivating ASC experiences as ends in themselves. These altered states are necessary to classify a person or tradition as "mystical," but classical mysticism is about transforming one's whole inner life in accordance with reality (as defined by one's metaphysics) free from a sense of a separate phenomenal self. Not all mystics fit the caricature of world-hating ascetics or other-worldly escapists, morally indifferent and concerned only with themselves, sitting blissed out in the forest in a trance. In fact, most mystical belief systems grant the temporal world and human beings sufficient reality that concern for others' welfare is possible, and mystical experiences and the activities of many mystical ways of life enable social activity and moral action.

Generalizations that all mystics are, for example, disengaged and nonmoral or are loving do not reflect the diverse history of mysticism. Mystics may be hermits or may be social leaders. They may be pacifists or warriors. They may be unconcerned with anything worldly or energetically helping people with their existential and physical suffering. Selfless enlightened mystics usually follow their society's religious duties and do not butt heads with religious and civil authorities. Even those who see themselves as "beyond good and evil" may remain engaged with society at large and not indulge in antinomian actions. The sense of unity in these ASCs can change one's perspective: in themselves, these experiences do not give new ethical precepts, but they can lead to a sense of selflessness and thereby lessen the sense of self-centeredness and any desire for self-assertion—this selflessness can be filled with a moral concern for others. It can lead to a strict impartiality that eliminates giving priority to oneself or one's family. Seeing that we all have fundamentally the same needs can lead to a more disinterested point of view and to a greater concern for the suffering of others.

The social dimension and the social effects of mystical ways of life also should be studied. The future effect of mysticism upon society will depend on our collective judgment of the value of mystical experiences and mystical ways of life. The vitality of a religious component to a society also depends upon that judgment. Many agree with William Inge that mystical experiences are the "raw material of all religion" (1899: 5). Louis Dupré claims, "The drive toward mystical union is the vital principle of all religious life. Without it religion withers away in sterile ritualism or arid moralisms" (quoted in Stoeber 2017: 3). The Catholic theologian Karl Rahner predicted that the Christian of the future will be a mystic—that is, one who has experienced God—or he or she will not exist at all in our increasingly secular world (1984: 22). Late in his life the Protestant theologian Paul Tillich stated that the question for his time was this: "Is it possible to regain the lost dimension, the encounter with the Holy, the dimension that cuts through the world of subjectivity and objectivity and goes down to that which is not world but is the mystery of the Ground of Being?" (quoted in Smith 2000a: 32). Many people today have a thirst for transcending the mundane world, the mundane self, and the materialistic worldview that the rituals and doctrines of conventional religions do not satisfy. Even among many of the religiously unaffiliated—the "none's"—there is a desire for a sense of meaning and for experiences of transcendence. This makes mystical experiences attractive as ends in themselves.

Mystical experiences may be the most intense and important experiences for the religious, but a mystocentrism that reduces religion to merely having mystical experiences is also faulty—mysticism was never the whole of religion even in early or classical times. And several apologists for the religious use of psychedelic drugs—Huston Smith, William Barnard, and William Richards—question whether a religious institution that centers itself solely on psychedelic experiences could survive; they argue only that psychotropic substances are capable of enabling mystical states of consciousness and might enhance the religious life if the experiences are contextualized within a genuine faith and discipline that approaches them with spiritual reverence and trust (Stoeber 2017: 20). However, if religion has no place for experiences of transcendence and is reduced to social actions and rituals, it may become a relic in today's increasingly secular culture in the West.

However, much of the growing interest in mindfulness and meditation is secular in nature and does not touch upon embracing a mystical way of life or adding mysticism to religion more generally. Meditation, psychedelic drugs, and mystical experiences today do not appear to be leading to a new Renaissance or a new evolutionary development of the human mind—a pervading "cosmic consciousness"—as New Age enthusiasts hope. Most people today see mysticism as an outdated, medieval practice and frame of mind. Our era can be defined by "a loss of faith in transcendence, in a reality that encompasses but surpasses our quotidian affairs" (quoted in Smith 2000b: 655). We live on the surface of things: we see the shadows on the walls of Plato's cave and accept them as all of reality—we do not even entertain the possibility of asking about our ultimate condition or cosmic setting. In classical mysticism, mysticism was a way to return an ontological depth to our surface reality. ASC mystical experiences turned this world upside down, shattering the sense of an individual self and revealing what is real behind appearances. But in an era of spiritual decline perhaps the immediate future of mystical experiences lies in the secular realm: the value of mystical experiences enabled by meditation and psychedelic drugs will be seen only in terms of their secular benefits for the experiencer, not the alleged cognition fostered by classical mystical ways of life. Naturalists can accept any such demonstrated benefits and that mystical experiences may help us overcome any sense of isolation from the rest of reality by helping us realize that we are thoroughly connected to the natural world and to each other without endorsing more.

Whether religion declines as a cultural factor or not, greater understanding of mystical altered states of consciousness will nevertheless aid our understanding of consciousness, the human mind, and the sense of "self" and its transcendence. In addition, studying classical mystical ways of life will help us to expose our preconceptions and judgments of what is of value and significance in life. This exploration can lead to personal growth, if not a mystical transformation. In sum, the study of mysticism can lead to understanding and perhaps revising our view of ourselves and our place in the web of reality.

Notes

Chapter 1

1. I will not add the word "alleged" in front of every mystical knowledge-claim. Rather, the mystics' claims will be accepted for purposes of exposition and the philosophical issues reserved for later (see chaps. 11–13; Jones 2016).

2. Surveys suggest that mystical experiences are much more common than usually supposed (e.g., Hardy 1983). Perhaps one third of Americans have had intense spiritual experiences. However, how many of these experiences are *mystical* in the sense used here is not clear—what a participant means by "mystical" may differ from the meaning of more technical definitions. For example, for many people feeling "lifted out of oneself" may apply to any religious experience. Or any emotional state in a religious setting may be taken as "union with God." Some Christians may feel "one with God" every Sunday morning in a church service. Hence the need for detailed surveys and in-depth interviews by researchers knowledgeable about the variety of mystical and other types of ASC experiences to get past canned cultural rhetoric. One survey (Hardy 1983) initially found 65 percent of respondents were aware of or influenced by a "presence or power," but the number dropped to 29.4 percent in follow-up interviews (20.2 percent had dualistic numinous experiences, and 9.2 percent had a sense of union). But sophisticated questionnaires (such as Ralph Hood's) have been devised.

3. "Experience," "consciousness," and "awareness" have proven remarkably hard to define in philosophy (as have "reality" and "existence"). "Altered states of consciousness" involve, in Charles Tart's definition, a qualitative shift in the stabilized pattern of mental functioning from our baseline state that maintains a unique configuration despite changes in input and small changes in subsystems (1969: 1). Stanley Krippner (1972) delineates twenty different states of consciousness. The "baseline" state of consciousness is actually a conglomeration of states—we have various states during the day when we are awake (e.g., daydreaming). So too, unlike giving up a sense of self, not all ASCs are unusual or a major shift in consciousness—some are

quite familiar and easy to achieve (e.g., some illnesses, dreaming, or being drunk). But for most in our culture, the alert, sober state of ordinary awareness is taken to be the baseline state of consciousness and necessary for all cognitive matters.

4. A "mystical experience" may involve phases or a series of episodes in different ASCs, not a single event, although it may seem singular to the experiencer.

5. Today even the distinction between mystical experiences and nonmystical dualistic "numinous" experiences (such as revelations or visions) is falling out of favor in religious studies. The distinction is being replaced by one category—"religious experiences"—as if all religious experiences were the same in nature and whatever is said about any of them applied equally to all. Lumping together significantly different types of experiences reflects a growing lack of interest in the "subjective" in religious studies today in favor of texts and observable sociological and historical phenomena (as discussed in chapter 14).

6. Emphasizing knowledge does not mean that emotions are not a prominent part of mystical ways of life but only that classical mystics are more likely to consider mystical experiences to be primarily *cognitive* rather than *affective*.

7. Hollenback believes that paranormal phenomena are not peripheral to mysticism (1996: 276–300) and so includes psychics such as D. D. Home as mystics but excludes the Buddha's realization of *nirvana* as mystical. (However, he would include the Buddha for his paranormal powers.) But paranormal powers and experiences are not central to mystical quests to align oneself with reality and can be a source of attachment and distraction.

8. Teresa had inner "intellectual visions" but no "external" visions (*Interior Castles* 6.9.4). She says that although she used the word "vision," the soul does not *see* anything—it is not an "imaginative vision" but an "intellectual vision" in which she saw how God has things in himself (6.10.2).

Chapter 2

1. Wainwright points out that any typology must be taken with a grain of salt—e.g., there may be borderline cases that cannot be subsumed neatly under a typology's categories (1981: 38). Typologies based on *theological reasons* rather than the study of the history of mysticism end up being a Procrustean bed that distorts mystical claims. For example, to make Buddhism fit his typology, R. C. Zaehner had to tell Buddhists what they really experience—an eternal self (*atman*)—even though they themselves explicitly reject that notion. He later admitted that Zen experiences did not fit his typology.

2. This is paradoxical if one believes that realities must be either entirely transcendent or only part of the natural universe—emanationism and any immanence of a transcendent reality in the natural world are then deemed impossible.

3. This raises a question of terminology. Is anyone who has had a mystical experience a mystic even if the experience did not affect his or her life? Or must one be a continuing altered state of consciousness? Or is anyone engaged in a mystical way of life a mystic even if he or she has not had a mystical experience?

4. This living totally in the present moment is not like suffering from Korsakoff's syndrome in which one greets each moment with no memory: the mystic still has memories that provide structure. Only in a case of "pure" mindfulness would such structure disappear.

5. How can one remain centered in a transcendent reality while maintaining the commotion of everyday activities? How can two layers of consciousness (the depth and the surface) operate at once? Think of carrying on a conversation while driving a car: our focus is always on the road, but we can still talk to the passenger. Meister Eckhart gave another analogy: a thirsty man can do other things besides drink and can turn his mind to other thoughts, but he never loses the thought that he needs something to drink (2009: 491–92). But one's attention is split, and so one is not solely engaged in the worldly activity.

6. As discussed in chapter 13, this spontaneity does not mean that mystics act free of values and beliefs: in their enlightened state, mystics have internalized values and beliefs from their tradition and thus usually acts without reflecting on their beliefs and values.

Chapter 3

1. In the Middle Ages, few Christian ascetic male saints engaged in mystical practices and vice versa (Kroll & Bachrach 2005: 217). In the late Middle Ages, the rate of extreme asceticism among *women* saints was much greater than among men saints (215).

2. Intercessory prayer and prayers of gratitude do not fall into this characterization of meditation, but they can lead to forms of praying that do—e.g., the chanting of *dhikr* in Sufism, *japa* in Hinduism, and the Jesus Prayer of Eastern Orthodox Christianity.

3. Concentrative meditation requires stilling the body, and so sitting is ultimately necessary. Sitting in a steady posture (such as the lotus position) also helps to minimize the sensory input and thus is useful for long sessions of meditation.

4. Taxonomies of meditative techniques usually involve the methods employed in different meditative practices or states of consciousness enabled, but today scientists are also beginning to classify types of meditation in other ways (e.g., Nash & Newberg 2013).

5. The problem with such tactics in mystical practices is that they can become expected and thus lose their effectiveness as enlightenment techniques. Here, koans

became standardized, and books with answers were produced. But any answer that disciples give is not as important as *how they give it*, thereby revealing their attitude toward concepts. That is, disciples must demonstrate to their master that they have insight, not merely parrot back some memorized answer.

6. Philosophical texts certainly have some philosophical substance to be studied, but the effect of hearing or even simply reciting some texts may have mind-altering effects. In Plato's *Symposium* (216a–d), Alcibiades speaks of how Socrates's speech induced in him a trance similar to ones induced by the Corybants playing flutes. Treating mystical texts such as the *Enneads* as simply delivering positions on metaphysical issues misses the effect in oral cultures of the actual sounds and rhythms of the words in potentially transforming the consciousness of a listener. The written texts were meant to be read out loud for the same effect as oral teaching. Parts of the *Koran* may have been composed for that effect as well.

Chapter 4

1. The term "infinite" comes up in mystical discourse, but calling a transcendent reality "infinite" means that it is *totally other* than finite phenomenal realities, not that it is an *infinite amount* of the stuff of the natural realm. That is, it is *nonfinite* and thus unlike anything *finite*.

2. Those who argue that ultimately doctrines do not matter to classical mystics cite the Buddhist analogy of the raft: the Buddhist doctrine (*dharma*) is only a means to the other shore (i.e., escape from rebirths), and once one has reached that shore the raft should not be clung to but abandoned (*Majjhima Nikaya* I.22). However, if one reads the Buddha's address to his disciples in which the analogy is set, one finds that nothing in it suggests that the Buddhist doctrines are incorrect or do not inform the Buddhist enlightened way of life but only that precepts designed for *the path to enlightenment* should be let go. So too, once one is enlightened, there is no need to consult and reflect on the doctrines. In addition, the Buddha employed a "graduated" teaching method of teaching different things to different listeners depending on their capacity to understand (e.g., *Anguttara Nikaya* I.10, III.182–84), but this does not mean that what he taught to his advanced disciples was not the final truth.

3. One caveat: most mystics, like most people, may well not be interested in doctrinal matters—they simply accept their tradition's account as the best depiction of the nature of things. Mysticism, after all, is a matter of practices and how one lives, and mystics may want to get on with that without reflecting very much on doctrines. Of course, the fact that mystics believe that they have *experienced* something fundamental may make mystics more interested than most people in examining their beliefs, and there have been mystics who were also philosophers. But the important point is that mystics need to have a sense that they understand the nature of what they experienced in the scheme of things, even if they hold their beliefs only tacitly.

4. Other parts of a mystic's implicit belief-framework also are important for how they act. For example, if Buddhists did not believe in a chain of rebirths, then they need do nothing to end the existential problem of suffering—it would be cured with our death. Adopting a way of life of meditation and restrictions to end desires would not be needed.

5. The doctrine of nonduality in Shankara's version of Advaita Vedanta constantly leads to an obvious problem: Advaitins have to admit that the ontological nature of the phenomenal world is ultimately indescribable (*anirvachaniya*) in their metaphysics, since it is neither real nor unreal. Without a doctrine of emanation or creation, the assertion of Brahman as the only true reality is hard to maintain—why the world even appears at all is inexplicable, since only Brahman is actually real.

6. Differentiated introvertive experiences of love or of anything suggesting personhood would still not per se support a triune Christian interpretation or any other highly ramified theory. Theologians and other religious theorists cannot cite low-ramified descriptions of mystical experiences as supporting their theory over others.

7. We are not aware of an experiencing self during the vast majority of our everyday experiences—we sense things, not sense that we are aware of things. But during or after an ordinary experience, we can become aware that there is something distinct from the objects that were sensed that does the sensing, but this does *not alter our state of consciousness*. Not so with mystical experiences.

8. Paul Marshall (2005: 60–64) delineates four types of unity in extrovertive mysticism: being an integral part of the whole, immersion, identity, and incorporation into the whole.

9. To use another analogy: consider the Being (*ousia*) from the One as *red*, and each soul as *purple* (a mixture of the red of pure Being common to all things and the blue produced by its individuality). The soul does not gain the red from this experience but has it already. When the One and a soul are "one'd," the One never takes on the blue color to become purple, and the individual soul never loses the blue to become red (pure Being). Thus, the soul is overlaid but distinguishable.

10. In the West, the Christian Richard Fishacre in the thirteenth century made a similar claim to explain how God could be omnipresent without being spatial: since God transcends the universe, he transcends any sense of spatiality; being spaceless, God can exist in toto in every segment of space—i.e., what is nondimensional can be present in each portion of the three-dimensional world, just as a transcendent timeless god is present in all times, or a dreamer is entirely present in each portion of a dream. But this idea never gained traction in any Western theism.

Chapter 5

1. The *Showings* by English anchorite Julian of Norwich (1342–ca. 1416) related her visions of Jesus. The differences between her earlier short accounts of her experiences and her later more elaborate ones show how mystics may change their

view of their experiences over time. She felt "one'd" or "fastened" to God—"alike in kind and substance"—but upon later reflection she concluded that "God is God, and our substance is a creature in God."

2. Buber's example also shows the difficulty of determining the phenomenological content of an experience or what realities may have been experienced when the experiencers use canned cultural descriptions such as "union with God." Different mystics may use the same cultural lexicon even when different types of mystical experiences are involved. Any account of a mystical experience may be heavy with highly-ramified theological terminology from the experiencer's own culture, and such culturally determined expressions may not reflect the experience but the experiencer's postexperiential understanding. And whether such high-level conceptualizations penetrate the experiences themselves is an issue: even if all experiences have some low-level structuring ("I saw a bright light"), more interpretative beliefs ("I saw Christ in all his glory") may still be distinguishable from the experiences themselves as Jamesian "over-beliefs."

3. The issue in the sociology of knowledge of the general construction of *knowledge-claims* goes back to Friedrich Nietzsche's claim that there are no facts but only interpretations. But constructivism in the study of mysticism has been a matter of the construction of mystical *experiences*. That we construct the world and our sense of "self" from our perceptions and nonconscious mental processes is generally accepted; but meditation *inhibits* this process (Goleman & Davidson 2018: 148–49, 153–55).

4. Walter Stace concurred (1960a: 203). Katz later qualifies this in light of Sallie King's example of drinking coffee: all experiences except those on the "the most brutish, infantile, and sensate level" are culturally constructed (1988: 755).

5. Meditation upon a specific image or concept (e.g., a deity or compassion) would be replacing mental content with other content and thus providing content that could be constructed. But this does not hold for all types of meditation.

6. Mystical experiences have less control over interpretations than do sense-experiences (which can at least be indirectly tested by other observations by oneself and others), and thus more interpretations are possible. This is especially true of the depth-mystical experience if it is empty of any differentiated content. For strong constructivists, what is experienced in the end completely falls out of the picture (since prior cultural beliefs totally control the content of belief-content), but for others mystical experiences enter the pool of experiences and cultural beliefs out of which mystical beliefs are derived.

7. Like other postmodernists, constructivists have a basic problem regarding truth: if everyone (including postmodernists themselves) are subject to cultural constraints, their claims are limited to one culture and cannot transcend it—yet they take their claim that "all truth-claims are limited to only the culture from which they arise" (which is generated and defended from a particular cultural perspective)

itself to be universal and thus independent of particular cultures. Katz's example of Édouard Manet painting some of Notre Dame's archways in the wrong style that can be objectively seen to be in error (1978: 30) does suggest that there are standards of truth that transcend cultural conceptions. Either postmodernists have transcended their cultural restrictions (in which case others can too), or their claims are limited to only those who endorse their premises (and so their claims cannot be taken to be universal)—either way, they have a problem.

8. Most classical mystics did not see themselves as innovators but merely as commentators explicating the original knowledge given in their tradition's fundamental scriptures, even though their ideas seem innovative to us. Innovation was condemned within Hinduism, since the complete knowledge was seen as given at the beginning of time. In Buddhism, commentators claimed that they were expounding the true meaning of the Buddha's teaching.

9. As noted in chapter 1, the consensus among philosophers and students of religion is that all consciousness is intentional—i.e., that consciousness is always consciousness *of* something. Thus, consciousness is always related to an object—without an object, there is no consciousness. Even self-awareness is awareness *of* something—awareness of being aware. Constructivists believe that all consciousness has an object, but nonconstructivists reject this: consciousness may still be "on" even if one is not aware of an object—only after the experience can one realize that one was aware and determine what was experienced. It may seem empty or contentless, but consciousness itself is the content of the event. However, this is realized only *after the event is over*, and only then can it be given different ontological interpretations reflecting a mystic's beliefs.

10. One extrovertive state of consciousness in particular may also be free of all conceptualizations: a "pure" mindfulness involving sensory differentiations unmediated by any conceptualizations—i.e., sensations not structured into perceptions.

11. Teresa did not understand how it was possible that the experiencer could remember the "intellectual vision" when there were no images or understanding during the experience itself, but nevertheless the experience gave certitude (*Interior Castle* VI.4.5–8). She also was willing to accept how the learned within the Catholic Church interpreted these experiences "even though they have never experienced these things" themselves because she believed that God had enlightened the church (V.1.6).

12. Katz rightly notes that the "no self" experience in Buddhism cannot be the same experience of an intense, loving intimate relationship between substantial selves (God and a soul) in Jewish mysticism (1978: 38–40) and that the Buddhist term "*nirvana*" does not the same refer to the same experience as the Jewish term *devekut* ("cleaving" to God) (38; Katz 2013: 9). However, he takes this as evidence of the differences in the *construction* of the one mystical experience. Rather, it is more clearly evidence of *different types of mystical experiences*—introvertive and extrovertive, undifferentiated and differentiated, nonpersonal and personal. In short, they are

not the same experience except for differing structuring elements. Merely because scholars refer to "*the* mystical experience" should not mislead us into believing that all mystical experiences are of one type.

13. Katz's examples are limited to historical texts, but Forman uses both historical texts and examples of current experiencers (1990), including himself (2011). Constructivists would respond that we are still limited to "texts"—i.e., the accounts given by these experiencers after their experiences are over—and so we cannot get to the experiences themselves. But we can interview contemporary experiencers about the phenomenology of their experiences and through questions perhaps determine if their experiences were free of highly ramified concepts (e.g., Chen et al. 2011a; Chen et al. 2011b; also see Sullivan 1995).

14. Not all levels of theory affect perceptions or scientific observations. Differing conceptions affect Gestalt figures—e.g., seeing a vase or two faces—but it is hard to argue that the differing Ptolemaic and Copernican cosmologies affected Ptolemy's and Copernicus's *perceptions* of the sun, moon, and stars. Constructivists have to show how mystical experiences must be more like Gestalt experiences than theoretical understandings of what was allegedly experienced that do not affect the experiences themselves.

Chapter 6

1. Thus, a mystic's *description* of a mystical experience (whether explicit or entailed by the mystic's doctrinal statements) should be distinguished from that mystic's own *explanation* of the experience in terms of his or her tradition, and those explanations must be distinguished from *explanations* from outside that mystic's traditions. An explanation from outside of the mystic's traditions does not have to be acceptable to the mystic to be valid, unlike a scholar's descriptive account of a mystic's beliefs.

2. Theologians who impose a theological understanding on all mystical experiences also may feel no need to study the experiences of mystics in other traditions, or indeed in their own, since they believe that they know what is really going on in all mystical experiences.

3. The reductionism/antireductionism issue is only one polarity in the study of mysticism and religion. Others include experience versus interpretation, human versus divine, transcendent realism versus naturalism, mind versus matter, surface versus depth, identity versus difference, and healthy versus unhealthy.

Chapter 7

1. As discussed in chapter 14, postmodernists raise objections to the idea that there may be any "objective" history or whether outsiders can understand and present another culture's point of view.

2. Devotional mystics are more positive in their characterization of what is experienced (and utilize more sexual imagery); wisdom mystics rely more on the *via negativa*. It is worth noting that wisdom traditions usually began first, and devotional mysticism became more dominant around the world early in the second millennium CE, appearing even in Buddhism.

3. Psychedelic substances may have evolved as a defense mechanism for plants since they are toxic to most animals, but hominids evolved in a way that could utilize them (Winkelman 2014: 334–44).

4. Each soul is identical to the Nous in the way that each character in a dream is identical to the dreamer.

5. "Humility" in theistic mysticism generally means not modesty about one's accomplishments but something more extreme: realizing that we have no reality without God—we do not exist without God and cannot achieve enlightenment by our own effort but must rely on God's action. The context is our total dependence on God.

6. Some mystics advocated doctrines and practices that got them into trouble and would cause controversy today—for example, Julian of Norwich and William Law saw no hell and believed all people, including non-Christians, would be saved. Some early Christian desert hermits advocated the doctrine of rebirth: human beings had to pass through all types of human existence before reaching heaven. And, as in Judaism and Islam, there were antinomians.

7. Not all mystical options espoused in history have survived. Buddhist and Advaita texts discuss doctrines from schools that no longer exist. Huston Smith regards the world's existing religions as "the winnowed wisdom of the human race, with a lot of dross" (2005: 123).

8. Suffering (*duhkha*) in Buddhism does not mean that all experiences are painful—that there are pleasures and joys in life is not denied—but that even pleasurable experiences are only transitory, and we realize that if we are reborn indefinitely even the happiest of lives is only temporary and ultimately frustrating and disappointing. Such dissatisfaction is ingrained into the very fabric of life. The only way to end suffering completely is to get out of the chain of rebirth that keeps us in the realm of suffering.

9. In Buddhism, the creator god Brahma was considered delusional: he was the first reality emanated from Brahman in each new world-cycle and mistakenly thinks that he creates the emanations that follow.

10. At the turn of the twentieth century, Richard M. Bucke saw "cosmic consciousness" as the "first beginnings of a new race" ([1901] 1969: 384).

11. A personal observation: Over the years when I have told people of my interest in mysticism and philosophy, some have told me of their own ASC experiences, some of which qualify as mystical in the sense used here (although many were uncomfortable with the label). But few identify themselves as "mystics," and the few who do call themselves "mystics" have all been pompous and very full of themselves—they are absolutely certain about their beliefs and will brook no

questioning of them or listen to problems or alternative interpretations or explanations. Their mystical experiences certainly did not give them humility but only an arrogance about claiming to know all there is to mystical knowledge.

Chapter 8

1. Bertrand Russell also saw mysticism as a matter of emotion—a certain intense and deep feeling regarding what is believed about the universe ([1935] 1997: 186–87). It is an emotional attitude toward scientific truths, but since mysticism is only emotional it is only subjective and not cognitive and thus cannot add any new truths. Treating mystical experiences as matters primarily or exclusively of emotion, with no cognitive element, has remained common in psychological studies (e.g., Laski [1961] 1990 on religious and secular ecstasy). Ecstatic joy does accompany some cases of mystical insight—others are greeted with calm serenity—but that does not mean the insight is grounded in our emotions. I started out as a math major in college and can remember dancing in my dorm room with joy after seeing the solution to a particularly difficult problem, but my seeing that the solution touched off joy does not mean that the mathematical intuition leading to seeing the solution was grounded in the emotions rather than in the mind's cognitive functions. And the same seems to apply to mystical insights, since joy is not a part of every mystical experience—joy can accompany it without joy being its cause or substance. Today a cognitive component to emotion is also gaining attention.

2. Rolland's own extrovertive mystical experience did not lead him to giving up his denial of life after death and his denial of the existence of a personal god. But he wanted a space for a "mystical psychoanalysis," not simply the secular cure of the soul that Freud was attempting (Parsons 1999: 167).

3. From what I have read (and it is not remotely exhaustive), psychologists have tended to reduce the diversity of mystical experiences to only one type and usually have had a simplistic interpretation of them based on perennial philosophy. They tend to take Asian mystical ideas uncritically, often based on poor translations.

4. If mystical experiences did involve memories of any of these events, one would expect "mother" symbolism to be the most prevalent symbolism in all cultures.

5. Mystics may change their social state by becoming cloistered monks and nuns, and they may withdraw from society as part of their training on the path, but seclusion or isolation is usually temporary—inner mystical detachment from the personal repercussions of their actions does not require mystics to live separately from the social world.

6. The condemnation of visions and voices was not a modern notion, nor was it done by nonmystics alone. Jantzen acknowledges that medieval mystics such as Meister Eckhart, Jan van Ruusbroec, and the author of the *Cloud of Unknowing* decried these alleged communications from God (1995: 325). Paranormal bodily experiences were also considered suspect.

7. As discussed, mysticism encompasses more than having mystical experiences, nor can the examination of mystical experiences be isolated from the mystic's cultural context. But this does not mean mystical experiences and ASCs are not themselves a legitimate topic for examination. Nor, as noted in chapter 14, should the study of mysticism be limited only to our current interests. Nor should earlier mystics be read only in light of today's interests—scholars should not impose their own contemporary perspectives on past mystics.

8. Feminists tend to adopt constructivism and contextualism (e.g., Jantzen 1995: 12–25, 337–38). Beverly Lanzetta rejects both nonconstructivism and essentialism (2005). But whether the cultural influences occur after the experiences or penetrate the experiences themselves has not yet been studied (see Jacobs 1992).

9. There is a long tradition in Christianity of treating the soul and wisdom (*sophia*) as feminine. Since the soul is considered female, there is often imagery that is taken to be homoerotic in men's "bridal mysticism." This also occurs in other traditions—e.g., in Hindu Bhakti, men have written songs with the man longing for Krishna as a wife longs for her husband (modeled on Krishna's wife Radha) or as the Gopi milkmaids longed for him.

Chapter 9

1. The cognitive scientific study of religious phenomena is a multidisciplinary field combining neuroscience, cognitive psychology, philosophy, systems theory, and other approaches. But in religious studies it has not yet been applied specifically to mysticism.

2. Meditation does appear to have a measurable effect on the body, but the claims of physical and psychological *benefits* from meditation—e.g., lowering stress or blood pressure or lessening the effects of aging—have to be examined carefully. They may be exaggerated: there may be an early spike in well-being when these practices are adopted that has little to do with the meditation itself but may be due only to a "vacation effect" of leaving everyday problems behind (Goleman & Davidson 2018: 72–73, 187). There may be more benefits in some areas simply from exercising (195–97). Different meditative practices produce different types of results—e.g., mindfulness meditation may help to calm and relieve stress, but concentrative meditation does not (68–69). However, scientific studies often do not identify the method uses in a meditative study or lump together different types of meditation (68–69; Nash & Newberg 2013). Factors such as how experienced in meditation the participants are or the quality of the sessions often are not specified (Goleman & Davidson 2018: 68–69). Often researchers implicitly assume that all meditative techniques are really the same and that there is only one state of consciousness achieved. Beginners and advanced meditators are lumped together. So too, meta-analyses typically do not make these distinctions. Thus, despite the hype little can be said with certainty about meditation's alleged health benefits (187).

3. The drugs also enable synesthesia, perhaps by connecting and integrating parts of the brain that are not normally connected.

4. While the research is suggestive of meditation's effects on the brain, the claims to altering the brain, as with the claims of the benefits of meditation, must be taken with caution (Fox et al. 2014). For example, factors such as behavior outside of meditation or lifestyles that may affect brain structures are not considered (68). While meditation has positive effects on cognitive and emotional processes, the effects in altering anatomical structures in several brain regions appear comparable to roughly medium effects of other behavioral, educational, and psychological interventions (69).

5. In their "neurotheology," d'Aquili and Newberg refer to what was experienced as the "Absolute Unitary Being," although they admit no experiencer referred to that (1999: 116). Michael Winkelman's neurotheology is in terms of shamanism (2016: 369–70).

6. The psychiatrist Arthur Deikman (2000) offers an explanation of at least extrovertive mystical experiences in terms of the "deautomatization" of the mental structuring array that blocks or ignores some sensory input from our awareness.

7. Empirical studies of meditators also suggest that the nonlinguistic centers of the brain are attuned to beingness, and thus the states of consciousness in which the use of language is possible removes us from the proper state of mind to experience beingness.

8. An underlying problem is the lack of consensus today in cognitive science on what *consciousness is*—views run the gamut from consciousness being the primary (or indeed the only) reality to it being an irreducible fundamental property of matter to it not existing at all. In a conference titled "Toward a Science of Consciousness" held in Tucson, Arizona, in 1994, the attendees' views on anomalous phenomena (which included mystical experiences) apparently were divided into three groups: one-third thought that anomalous phenomena did not really exist, one-third thought that they did exist but could be explained at least in principle in physical terms, and one-third thought that not only did they exist but that consciousness was the primary reality (Baruss & Mossbridge 2016: 28).

9. Various types of "first-person sciences," "altered state sciences," and "neurophenomenology" that would complement current neuroscience through experiencers' investigation of their own psychedelic or meditative ASCs have been proposed (see Varela & Shear 1999). These approaches bracket the issue of what realities may or may not be involved in a mystical experience—the focus is on the experience's phenomenological content alone. The objective of phenomenology is to get at the experiences themselves as they are presented to consciousness prior to reflection and explanations. First-person introspection by qualified observers of different types of mystical experiences may help neuroscientists create a better map of the brain and how it works. But the basic issue here is whether the very process of critically examining an ASC changes the *content* of a mystical experience: can we

examine the *experience* without mentally distancing ourselves from the experience and making it into an *object*, thereby disrupting and ending a mystical ASC? Isn't what is observed not the lived experience itself? So too can experiencers look back at their experiences objectively or read them only in light of their philosophical beliefs?

10. Experienced meditators carry their psychological changes resulting from mystical experiences (and thus perhaps changes in neural activity) into their life outside of their session in the lab, and the changes can become enduring traits. But one problem with determining long-term effects of meditation is that most subjects who are studied by neuroscientists are self-selected participants who are members of particular religious traditions already seeking these experiences. For example, the participants of the famous 1962 "Good Friday" experiment were theological students (Pahnke 1966; Doblin 1991). This would predispose the participants toward a religious understanding and a lasting religious impact. Thus, it is difficult to determine if any changes in values or ways of living are the results of neural changes or of their religious beliefs and their prior or continuing training—do the lasting effects result from new brain conditioning or from a mixture of a memory of the mystical experience and the mystic's beliefs? Participants in drug studies also may adjust their impressions of the realness of spiritual experiences over time (Yaden et al. 2017a: 59). The long-lasting effects of these experiences on one's character may result not from new states of the brain but from the impact of an *experience* on how the experiencer decides to live. There may be no lingering chemical effect of the drugs on the brain. Rather, changes in character as a result of the experience would have to account for the increase in some positive effects over time. That volunteers in drug experiments are usually self-selected and are people already looking for a religious experience would skew the findings toward the religious—that is, the percentage of participants having mystical experiences may not reflect the population as a whole.

11. It may also be that different dosages of a given drug produce different neurochemical states of the brain that ground different experiences. That a person may experience more than one state of consciousness during a psychedelic or meditative session complicates the issue.

12. The loss of a sense of an individual phenomenal self is central to mystical experiences, and connections have been made to theories such as that of Daniel Dennett in which the "self" is only an artifice generated by the brain as the center of narratives (e.g., Hood 2017).

13. Other triggers have different degrees of effectiveness in enabling mystical experiences, but none approach producing mystical experiences 100 percent of the time. These include different types of meditation, prayers, music, contemplating the beauty of nature, dancing, recreation, illness, stress, despair, near-death experiences, sleep deprivation, silence or chanting, sex or celibacy, sensory deprivation or sensory overload, giving birth, and intense physical or emotional dangers or trauma—anything that disrupts our baseline state of consciousness can sometimes enable extrovertive or introvertive mystical experiences. (But it appears that only

meditation can induce a state of mindfulness.) Arthur Koestler had a mystical experience in a concentration camp while contemplating a mathematical problem (Kelly & Grosso 2007: 509–10). The question for scientists is whether or not all triggers create the same brain conditions.

14. Set and setting may also apply to meditation. For example, the experiences may differ and the effects of meditation on the brain may differ if the meditator's *intention* is to strive for a spiritual goal rather than merely to relieve stress or some other limited health-related goal. So too, a spiritual framework for understanding meditation may be more effective in reducing stress and increasing tolerance to pain than secular meditation (see Wachholtz & Pargament 2005). But a mystical way of life will not lead to a life free of physical pain. For example, Teresa of Avila points to the physical suffering that a person may endure—indeed, one's entire body may ache—even while one's soul is at rest in its innermost chamber (*Interior Castle* 7.2.9–11). Suffering is part of the imitation of the life of Jesus, and increases the closer one gets to God (7.4.4–5).

15. The term "entheogen" ("generating God within") was coined in 1979 for any substance that, when ingested, catalyzes or generates an altered state of consciousness deemed to have spiritual significance to replace both "psychedelic" ("mind-opening") because of its negative cultural baggage and also the pejorative "hallucinogen" ("generating hallucinations"). But the term "psychedelic" has returned to respectability in science.

16. The placebo effect holds for psychedelic drugs: once we learn a response, we can be given what we think is the drug (when in fact it is a placebo) and an ASC will occur. Conversely, we can unknowingly ingest the active ingredient and no change in consciousness occurs. This effect makes it harder to relate states of consciousness to brain states.

17. Many in the fields of the scientific study of meditation and psychedelics are drawn to perennial philosophy or at least its terminology (e.g., Richards 2016: 211; Hood 2013: 301). For their interests, mystical doctrines are not important. Saying "God (or whatever your favorite noun for ultimate reality may be)" (Richards 2016: 211) is easier than studying the details of different doctrines in different mystical traditions. So too, the scientists may not intend the full emanationist metaphysics of perennial philosophy but merely mean only that all introvertive mystics have the same experiences or experience the same reality. Nevertheless, it must be remembered that classical mystics live according to their tradition's specific doctrines—including their understanding of what transcendent reality was experienced in mystical experiences—not according to "whatever you want to call it." In sum, these scientists may be too busy to study mystical doctrines and philosophical issues, but they should realize that, while mystics who have had introvertive mystical experiences may well all have experienced *the same reality* or had *similar experiences* (within different types), their full *understanding* of what is real is what guides their lives, not modern perennial philosophy. Nor should the scientists' use one perennialist claim be taken as empirical scientific support for the perennialists' full theory.

18. Zaehner tried mescaline and ended up with only an upset stomach (1957: 212–26). This points again to the issue of a proper dosage and a supportive mental set and setting. He did later admit that some drug-enabled experiences had a sense of sacredness. But he rightly criticized Aldous Huxley (and other perennialists) for equating an extrovertive experience of nature with an introvertive theistic "Beatific Vision."

19. Religious individuals from theistic traditions tended to score lower on the mystical experience measure of the study than did atheists (Yaden et al. 2017b: 349).

20. That disease can radically impair our thinking does not show that the mind is merely the brain. Dualists can respond that disease or damage in the brain merely adversely affects our reception of a transcendent consciousness, like damage to a radio affects receiving a signal—but just as the radio does not generate the programming that it receives, neither does the brain generate consciousness. The effect of drugs and illness on our state of consciousness does establish that the brain and the mind are associated, but one's final verdict on whether the brain causes mental events or receives them rests on a metaphysical choice on the nature of the mind. A similar problem occurs in the case of other paranormal experiences. For example, does the fact that scientists can stimulate parts of the brain and an "out of body" experience is induced mean that this experience is merely a brain-generated subjective event, or does the stimulation merely disrupt the brain conditions and sever the connection of the soul to the body?

Chapter 10

1. Albert Einstein remarked that "the cosmic religious feeling is the strongest and noblest motive for scientific research" and that "the most beautiful emotion we can experience is the mystical. It is the power all true art and science" (see Jones 2011–2012: 2:71–74). These remarks have led many to claim that Einstein was a mystic, but he scoffed at the idea. These and similar remarks he made are about being humble before the *awe and wonder of the natural order of the universe*, not before a transcendent reality. Einstein had a profound sense of the mystery of reality that he thought reason would never fully penetrate. But the mystery for him was always part of the natural universe—nothing transcending the natural realm was involved—and he approached that part of nature as an analytical scientist rather than as a contemplative mystic. (He used the word "mystical" to denote the *mystery* of things.) In sum, "cosmic religious feeling" for him did not involve a transcendent god (whom he did not believe in) but a "deep faith in the rationality of the structure of the world"—i.e., faith in a purely *natural deep order to the universe* even if the analytical mind cannot fully comprehend it.

2. On scientific analysis not necessarily being *reductive*, see Jones 2013: 53–92.

3. With a more expansive view of "mysticism" that includes paranormal powers, it is possible that mystics might provide new scientific information about

the world: mystics might find paranormal structures (if they exist) that scientists miss. An expansive view of mysticism that includes alchemy and Renaissance occultism would also expand mysticism's role in the history of science. The possibility of "first-person" sciences that would incorporate the phenomenology of mystical experiences into a new form of neuroscience also cannot be ruled out. (The problem of consciousness will be noted below.)

4. So too, the word for world—"*loka*"—relates only to our experience, not the "objective" world per se: the phenomenal world is "*kama-loka*," the "realm of desire." The higher realm of form (*rupa*) and formless realm (*arupa*) relate to meditative attainments.

5. Some Indian mystical traditions do have a concept for "matter." Samkhya has *prakriti* or *pradhana*, which also encompasses many mental processes that we consider "mind." Jainism has six eternal ingredients or substances (*dravyas*), one of which is matter (*pugdala*) consisting of permanent and indestructible bits of matter (*pramanus*).

6. Nature's laws, forces, and constants (e.g., the speed of light) may be eternal or permanent (if they in fact do not change over time), but such a permanence does not affect the Buddhist picture of reality any more than does the permanence of the law of *karma*—the Buddhist view is about the *impermanence of things that we experience* in the world of interacting laws, not anything about the nature of lawful structures. Whatever scientists find about the permanence of laws, the world we actually experience still appears impermanent and constantly changing, and this is what Buddhist mindfulness is about.

7. "String" theorists postulate that elementary particles are different vibrations of fantastically tiny strings existing in five or more dimensions. This might seem like a return to the Advaitin Gaudapada's theory that the visible realm is a vibration of the consciousness (*chitta-spandita*) that is Brahman. But it is only in the abstract that they converge—they are still different things that are taken to be vibrating and different levels of reality (quantum realm versus the surface world). So too with mystical and nonmystical notions of harmony, motion, rhythm, and the "music of the spheres."

8. Ironically, Capra himself became disenchanted with "Eastern mysticism" and shifted his focus to Christian mysticism because he found that "many Eastern spiritual teachers . . . [are] unable to understand some crucial aspects of the new paradigm that is now emerging in the West" ([1975] 2000: 341). Why this should be so would be hard for him to explain since he believes that the new paradigm is simply the expression of the essence of all Asian mystical traditions.

9. See Jones (2011–2012: 1:79–136) for the notion of religious "control beliefs" in science.

10. Ideas for scientific hypotheses can come from any source, including mysticism. Some of the great ideas in philosophy and science have come from nonmystical ASC experiences. Two prominent examples: the chemist Dmitri Mendeleev saw the

periodic table first in a dream; while dozing in front of a fire; August Kekulé came up with the benzene ring in a dream of two snakes with their tails in each other's mouth. Of course, the initial ideas were worked out into scientific hypotheses and examined in the baseline state of consciousness after the ASC experiences were over, and the initial hunches that came from ASC experiences themselves did not figure in support for the new theories.

11. Physicists are now beginning to speculate that the fundamental processes of nature lie beyond the natural realm of time and space and that space-time emerges from a hologram-like reality. This and other speculations have led to the charge that physicists are no longer doing science but have entered the field of metaphysics (see Jones 2018a: 103–4). On the most basic issues, physicists may have exhausted current data and may have to wait until a new generation of empirical data is generated by more energy to return to testable claims. Currently, elegant mathematics alone seems to be leading the theorizing in basic physics.

12. For a fuller reconciliation along these lines, see Jones 2015: 261–78. Stumbling blocks include whether consciousness should be treated as a nonmaterial reality, whether a sense of self is necessary to be human, whether any mystical experiences are in fact cognitive of transcendental realities, and any interventions by transcendent realities (such as a theistic god) into the natural realm. Many conflicts are more a matter of the metaphysics of religions than mysticism per se.

Chapter 11

1. As noted in chapter 5, constructivists (and other postmodernists) believe truth-claims are confined to different cultures and so cannot be compared—in fact, mystics in different cultures experience different realities and live in different "mystical worlds" (Penner 1983: 93; Katz 1978: 50–52). Thus, for them there are no cross-cultural universal mystical truth-claims. Furthermore, even within a culture "no veridical propositions can be generated on the basis of mystical experience" (Katz 1978: 22).

2. Mystics do often make claims about having paranormal powers, but even if scientists can establish claims of paranormal power (e.g., clairvoyance), this would not help establish mystics' basic cognitive mystical claims. Such a confirmation cannot be transformed to other claims even if it somehow helps establish mystics' general credibility.

3. Shankara took our basic *self-awareness* as being an eternal and permanent transcendent conscious reality (Brahman) (*Brahma-sutra-bhashya* 2.1.14, 2.3.7) while René Descartes took the same awareness as confirming only the existence of the embodied mind of one individual. For Descartes, it was obvious and not in need of any further argument that the consciousness belonged to an individual alone. Shankara believed it was obvious that the consciousness transcends any individual.

Buddhists accept temporary episodes of consciousness while denying a phenomenal self. This shows the difficulty in taking internal experiences by themselves as establishing a basic claim about our nature: we may know a "pure consciousness" in the depth-mystical experience, but its ontological nature is not given there—the Advaitin claim that it is a consciousness that constitutes all of reality is not given but is a matter of reflection on the experience and must be defended as such. Metaphysics and values affect the matter. This problem also exists for all mystical experiences.

4. This does not happen only in classical mystical traditions. For example, Huston Smith believed that in his first psychedelic drug experience he was "experiencing the metaphysical theory known as emanationism" that was part of the perennial philosophy he had been espousing for years; he was now *seeing* what previously had only been conceptual theories for him; his experience "supported the truth of emanationists of the past" (2000a: 11). The experience "experientially validated my world-view that was already in place" (2005: 227), and he felt "incomparably fortunate to have that validation" (234). In short, he was being shown what he already believed to be true. This indicates an element of suggestibility in these experiences that would impact the issue of whether the experiences are cognitive.

5. Here the issue is the question of the validity of the *mystical experiences*, but it must be remembered that even if theories of what is experienced are all "over-beliefs," they are still essential to *mysticism* since mystics themselves must have some understanding of their own experiences in order to lead their ways of life in accord with how they see reality.

6. *Brahma-sutra-bhashya* 2.1.11. In this passage, Shankara also noted the objection that this is itself an instance of reasoning, but he still asserted that the Vedas, being eternal, provide the necessary true knowledge. The standard of knowledge is certainty, and only revealed texts provide that. But he also insisted that even the Vedas needed *interpretation* when the literal meaning of passages did not conform to his nondualism.

7. Some Protestants theologians who oppose the idea that God is experienceable through mysticism have actually *reversed* this and used the universality of mystical experiences as evidence that such experiences are *not* experiences of God: that mystical experiences are common among theists *and nontheists* alike points to them being only subjective brain-generated events and nothing more.

8. Rationality does not require the certitude that mystics typically claim. It is rational to hold, for instance, "I believe I experienced God even though I know I might be mistaken."

9. Establishing true epistemic equality may be impossible. And of course, mystics in one tradition may not accept mystics in other traditions as their peers—but mystics in other traditions may claim the same.

10. If rationality is the only standard for accepting beliefs, "prima facie" justification may well satisfy most believers in most religions: in practice, there will not be any overriding arguments against them—there can be no new experiential

evidence concerning alleged mystical realities that could be forthcoming that would refute a claim (unlike in science) but only more of the same mystical experiences, and any new reasoned arguments will be accepted or rejected depending on the underlying metaphysics that a person accepts.

Chapter 12

1. Nonmystical theologians may use the *via negativa* as only a *complement* to positive attributions, but mystical theorists usually do not treat them as equals—the *via negativa* surpasses the *via positiva* as a mystical method.

2. Of course, we can be so absorbed in the moment in any activity that stopping to reflect on the experience snaps us out that experience. Normally this does not change our *state of consciousness*, but in the case of ASC mystical experiences and some ASC mystical states of consciousness, stopping to reflect disrupts the altered state of consciousness.

3. If a mystic's metaphysics is that God or Brahman is all that is real and ultimately we are nothing, his or her language may be confusing: they may claim "I am everything" (since our being is one with Brahman) or "I am nothing" (since we have no existence apart from God) or "I am both" or "I am neither" or "I am beyond both." But the metaphysics can be stated consistently.

4. Not all mystics consider language "conventional" and "provisional." Many Hindu mystical schools treat Sanskrit as divine. Many Jewish mystics do the same for Hebrew. Basic scripture in the Abrahamanic traditions are considered the literal word of God. In Hinduism, the Vedas are authorless but eternal and fixed.

5. In principle, Buddhist "conventional truths" can be restated in the ultimately correct ontology of the *dharmas*. But as Nagarjuna states (*Mulamadhyamakakarikas* 24.10), even ultimate truths cannot be stated without resorting to conventional terms. And Buddhists may be no more successful in describing reality in ontologically correct terms of *dharmas* than were logical positivists in restating scientific statements in terms of sense-experiences. That failure would affect what Buddhists must accept in their ontologies.

6. Some "paradoxes" result only from bad translations (see Jones 2012b: 172–96 on the Buddhist *Diamond-Cutter Sutra*).

7. Paradoxes can also be used for soteriological purposes to help people break the hold of the conceptualizing mind. Zen *koans* are a prime example. Employing paradox would not be an effective tool if people thought the mystics were merely speaking gibberish.

8. Mystics are not always any more consistent than most people. Mystics' general reliance on metaphors and images also complicates their presentation and reasoning. John Rist also points out that Plotinus was "not a stickler for exact terminology" (1967: 95), and the same can be said of many other well-known mystics, including some with a philosophical bent, such as Eckhart and Shankara. Many

mystics, like most people, may not care about the consistency of doctrines and may be more interested in the practices of their way of life. Often basic beliefs are not explicitly defended or even articulated but only tacitly assumed and only revealed by the questions a person asks and what is acceptable as an answer.

9. Augustine noted that God cannot be called "ineffable" because this claim makes a statement *about him*. Anything that is experienced is not literally ineffable—the mere fact that it can be labeled "ineffable" trivially means that it is something in some sense that can be experienced. If a reality were not experienceable at all and thus absolutely unknown, or if nothing were retained from a mystical experience, mystics would have nothing to name and would have no experiential basis to state that something is "unknowable" or "ineffable." But, despite what is often claimed by philosophers, there is no "paradox of ineffability" here—i.e., if the nature of a transcendent reality is inexpressible, then that fact cannot itself be expressed without producing paradox. The statement of ineffability is about what can be *said* about transcendent realities, not about the *realities themselves*. That is, that statement is a second-order claim about first-order claims of the nature of transcendent realities: pointing out that nothing can be said about the nature of those realities is not itself a first-order claim about their nature. One can affirm without contradiction that "No *phenomenal attributes* apply to transcendent realities," since that claim is not itself a phenomenal attribute, and the same principle applies more generally.

10. Ineffability in the modern sense becomes urgent in philosophy because philosophers tend to assume that only what can be encoded in language is real—language determines what can appear as real to our mind.

11. Nontheists may treat their scripture more skeptically since they would not have to be questioning the alleged word of God. For example, Shankara believed that the Vedas gave only an indirect indication of the nature of Brahman, not a direct one. It is worth noting that the Upanishads are the only basic religious texts in the world religions that proclaim their earlier revealed texts—the Vedic hymns—to be only a matter of *lower* knowledge (*apara-vidya*) (*Mundaka Upanishad* 1.1.4–6; also see *Chandogya Upanishad* 7.1.4).

12. The prohibition against such images was originally not because God was understood to be *incorporeal*—it was assumed he had a body or could assume one—but only because of our *inability* to depict it.

Chapter 13

1. Mysticism shares this inner concern with morality. That the early Buddhists defined action (*karma*) in terms of personal *intention* (*chetana*) (*Anguttara Nikaya* 3.207, 3.415) points to the centrality of the inner life in mystical cultivation.

2. For more on the factual presuppositions of morality, see Jones 2004: 25–27.

3. The Samkhya-Yoga's and Jaina's doctrine of totally separate transcendent persons (*purushas*, *jivas*) also eliminates the agent or target of moral concern since

it does not act nor can be affected. However, the world is deemed real and the *embodied selves* can be affected and led to enlightenment. Thus, the enlightened mystics in these traditions can be moral. It is Advaita's doctrine of the final *unreality* of anything individual that is the problem.

4. Mystics' enlightened ways of life are shaped by the beliefs of their culture about the nature of reality: their actions may be selfless and moral but still *misguided* if those factual beliefs are wrong. But a mystic can overcome personal suffering through emotional detachment regardless of the tradition's factual beliefs.

5. The language of morality is based on the assumption of an *actor*. But this can be treated as only a "conventional truth," and not a correct depiction of what is actually real, without undercutting morality.

6. As Danto noted (1987: 17), the will and freedom of the will are not major issues in traditional Asian philosophy. But the doctrine of *karma* is not deterministic: it gives those within its sanction the free will to choose actions—otherwise, once one is under the power of *karma*, liberation from it would be impossible. We are dealt a hand of cards, as it were, but we are free to play the hand as we choose. If predestination in Western theism means our choices are predetermined, it is a far greater problem to free will than anything in the major Asian traditions. So too the doctrine of God's omnipotence denies that any creature could have free will or control, since any such power would be contrary to God's absolute power.

7. Bodhisattvas also represent a change in the doctrines of *karma* and rebirth reflecting the new valuation: one can now become enlightened and still remain in the cycle of rebirth for others' welfare. For Theravadins, even the Buddha was gone after his final death—he had no choice. Belief in karmic effects and rebirth also show how factual beliefs can affect moral decisions. For example, in the ninth century a Buddhist monk assassinated a Tibetan king for *the king's own good*: the king was karmically harming himself by persecuting Buddhists—his actions would lead to bad future rebirths leading away from enlightenment. And the monk who did the "killing" was karmically *rewarded* with a rebirth in a heaven for his selfless act of risking karmic damage to himself to help another, since no real "person" was killed.

8. See Versluis 2011 for a contemporary defense of the Daoist village society of *Daodejing* chapter 80 with its opposition to technology.

9. There is antinomian behavior by some mystics in all traditions. In Japan, "wild Zen" was exemplified by Ikkyu in the fifteenth century: he spent long periods as a hermit in the mountains, but when he came to town he frequented sake shops and brothels. But it is mainly the *theistic traditions* that treat God as acting through a person that led to the antinomian conclusion. (Tantrism combines theistic and nontheistic elements.)

10. This claim is often overstated in works on Zen, since even the enlightened may need to reflect on alternative courses of action at some points. They cannot respond selfishly, but the right course of action to help others may not be obvious even to the enlightened. Compassion and a set of Buddhist factual beliefs will have been completely internalized, but they may not entail one course of action.

11. Actually three senses of "quietism" can be distinguished: quiet forms of sitting meditation, the denial that any other form of training is necessary, and moral quietism in one's actions. Zen masters can affirm quiet sitting while still insisting that physical labor such as cooking and cleaning a monastery is a necessary part of the discipline—as Baizhang Huaihai put it, "A day of no working is a day of no eating." To distinguish sitting meditation (*zazen*) from the rest of the Zen way of life sets up a duality that the enlightened do not see. But quietism in mystical practices does not entail moral quietism in a mystic's actions toward others: a mystic may still be active helping others outside of periods of quiet meditation. So too, being "selfless" or free of self-will should not be equated with being *antinomian*—one can be free of a sense of an individual self and still endorse orthodox practices. Nullifying a sense of a real self will not lead to moral indifference or inaction if the mystic is aligning his or her will to the will of a moral god or to another other-regarding principle. Thus, the practice and ethical issues should not be conflated.

12. A life dedicated solely to mystical cultivation raises an existential and moral issue: Would a life dedicated solely to meditation be a meaningful life? What would be the point of sitting alone in a cave meditating for fifty years even if the meditator were blissfully happy? Would such a happy but empty life be the way we should live? Would such a life be worth living? Would it be moral to live such a life?

Chapter 14

1. The phenomenology of religious phenomena should not be confused with the philosophical phenomenology of experiences arising from the work of Edmund Husserl and Maurice Merleau-Ponty. Both share bracketing questions of what is experienced and whether claims are true or not, but philosophical phenomenology is about describing the "lived" subjective consciousness of experiences—to present the "givenness" of felt experiences—while religious phenomenology studies observable phenomena. The former involves describing the experiences themselves as they are presented to our consciousness prior to reflection and explanations, while the latter focuses on the observed public phenomena. (For hybrid proposals, see Pike 1992 and Steinbock 2007.) Problems with incorporating phenomenology into science were noted in chapter 9. A philosophical phenomenology of mystical experiences would be more like the approach that Frits Staal wanted: it would present the basic structure of different types of mystical experiences after collecting different first-person descriptions from contemporary subjects of the felt experiences free of doctrinal interpretations. (Separating low-ramified accounts of the experiences themselves from doctrinal understandings is an issue.) The experiences can then be redescribed in terms of the shared structure in a way that the experiencers can accept. If mysticism consisted only of experiences (rather than understanding reality and aligning one's life with reality), mystical practices for inducing experiences and

a phenomenology of different types of mystical experiences would be all there is to the study of mysticism.

2. Scholars' own religious faith becomes an issue for religious study. Many scholars believe that scholars should not themselves espouse any religious faith—a professional scholar of religion's job is not to believe. Others disagree. According to Jeffrey Kripal, it is "as if taking the sacred seriously is equivalent to surrendering one's intellect and critical faculties to the faith claims" of a religious tradition (2010: 26). But religious studies has become, in B. Alan Wallace's words, "the only academic field in which it is commonly assumed that those who neither believe in nor practice their subject matter are better able to understand it and teach it than those who do" (2003: 170).

3. That ASC experiences are part of the defining feature of mysticism does not mean that mystics talk only about their experiences. Some scholars (such as Denys Turner and Michael Sells) make the mistake that if a text does not explicitly discuss mystical experiences then such experiences do not inform the text at all. But as discussed in chapter 3, classical mystics are interested in the realities experienced and thus more often discuss *realities* and *knowledge*, not their own experiences. They value the *enlightened way of life* in accord with a fundamental reality, and thus they can say to "let go" or "abandon" experiences leading to that state once the necessary knowledge and the enlightened state are achieved, but this does not disparage the experiences or deny the need for them to gain a participatory knowledge. Mystical texts must not be assumed to be only matters of autobiography: the absence of the discussion of one's own experiences does not mean that mystical experiences did not inform the text.

4. The term "text" can be construed broadly to include art, music, and any other cultural artifice, but in the case of most mystics it is a matter of written texts.

5. To nonpostmodernists, viewing mysticism as simply a category of literature is like viewing music as "an activity that produces sheet music"—the latter is true, but it misses the whole point of music. Indeed, trying to understand the sheet music as a "form of writing" while ignoring the music itself would be pointless. Those not under the sway of postmodernism think the same way with regard to mystical literature and mystical experiences—we cannot analyze discourse about experiences while ignoring the experiences. The fact that we can never get into the mind of other people and see their experiences does not mean that those experiences do not play an important role in people's lives. Mystics seldom give a straightforward phenomenological account of their experiences—usually they are discussing the reality that they believe they experienced or other doctrinal matters. But that does not mean that ASC experiences are irrelevant in shaping beliefs and actions—it is the lived experiences, not discourse about them, that affects mystics' lives. Only postmodernists who deny the experiences occur or for whom (like extreme constructivists) there is no difference in the end to having or not having these experiences would disagree.

6. Some anthropologists have come to question the postmodernist approach emphasizing only differences—indeed, the total otherness and the self-containment of each culture—and have renewed the idea of cross-cultural commonalities and even cultural universals (e.g., Brown 1991).

7. Postmodernists also raise the same issues for the term "religion," denying that there is such a thing as "religion." But some in religious studies are pushing back against the current consensus and arguing that recent European terms do not create or impose new, extraneous, colonial configurations on non-European cultures and that the idea of "religion" as a separate category of culture is not a modern Western conception (see Casadio 2016).

8. Some scholars want to restrict the term "mysticism" to only Christianity since that is the tradition the term arose in. But if so, we would have to invent another term that encompasses the various experiences and phenomena in different cultures that are now labeled "mystical." But postmodernists would point out that if a new term is invented, it too would be a modern Western one and would still be imposed on other cultures, and they would raise the same objections as with "mysticism"—it would perhaps be free of colonial connotations, but its use would still be a matter of Western intellectual imperialism.

9. Using umbrella terms such as "mystical experience" and "enlightenment" as *translations* for different culturally embedded terms may obscure ideas specific to a culture. Also, terms change their meaning over the years. For example, the meaning of "God" has changed over the centuries, and we may well read back our own understanding into earlier Western and Eastern theists' use of the term. Thus, postmodernists who confine terms to specific eras could not study the history of even their own culture. However, the total configurations of terms in a specific culture's discourse show their meaning in a translation.

10. That the words "mysticism" and "mystic" have so many different meanings today also affects this issue: with the absence of one set meaning to the terms, there is the danger of outside connotations being read into any particular usage specified by a scholar.

11. However, if terminology is limited to only the tradition from which came, any commonalities perceived in different religions would be impossible to discuss or perhaps even to notice. Any perceived commonalities would have to be expressed in terms transcending each religion—e.g., "*A* in Christianity is like *B* in Buddhism because they are both *x*." Such a cross-cultural framework can come from outside any one specific tradition even if the terminology originally arose in one tradition.

Chapter 15

1. A few theologians have attempted to present the beliefs of other religions objectively since at least the Franciscan Ramon Llull in the thirteenth century. In

his *Book of the Gentile and the Three Wise Men*, a Christian, a Jew, and a Muslim tell a nonbeliever their doctrines, and in the end it is not clear which religion the nonbeliever chose.

2. Throughout most of the twentieth century Christian theology in general showed little interest in mysticism. The Catholic philosopher Jacques Maritain, whose wife had mystical experiences, was an exception. Most Protestants argued that God is "wholly other" and so could not be experienced. Paul Tillich, on the "ground of being," was an exception, but he saw mysticism as opposed to revelation.

3. But mystics' interfaith cordiality should not be construed as agreement on doctrinal matters: mystics may be less likely to dispute others over matters of doctrine concerning mystical experiences because they accept doctrines to be tentative due to the "ineffability" of the experiences—it is hard to be dogmatic with a negative theology—or otherwise not contentious. (And it must be noted that throughout history mystics very often did dispute other mystics' doctrines, sometimes violently, even within their own tradition.) Instead, they may be interested only in comparing notes on practices or in understanding the doctrines of others.

4. Inclusivism existed long before twentieth-century Christianity. For example, for the Vedantist Ramanuja, all deities derive their authority from Vishnu—Shaivites actually worship Vishnu, not Shiva, who is the "inner controller" (*antaryamin*) of Shiva. Many Hindus agree that all mystics experience God or Brahman, but they often dispute the understanding of those outside (and sometimes inside) their own traditions, and question whether outsiders with their erroneous understanding have escaped the cycle of rebirths. And there is more *exclusivism* in Indian history than Westerners influenced by Neo-Vedanta think. For example, there is a story that the theist Madhva advised a king to have thousands of Jainas impaled on stakes. More typically, groups (e.g., most Shaivite schools) teach that one must ultimately convert to that group in some lifetime to become enlightened.

5. Beliefs and practices may be borrowed between traditions. However, mystical traditions are organic wholes: they can have some grafting and still grow, but there are limits.

6. The danger of theologians distorting the thought of mystics in other traditions is always present. A recent example is the Catholic theologian Bradley Malkovsky (2001) writing on Shankara's idea of Brahman: Malkovsky sees grace—the self-disclosure of Brahman—as necessary to bring about enlightenment. He does this by taking Shankara's language voiced from a conventional point of view, despite the fact that Shankara ultimately rejected any dualisms with regard to Brahman (as an act of disclosure to a person would involve) and insisted that from the ultimately correct point of view Brahman does not act or change in any way—nor is Brahman personal in nature or concerned with persons (*jivas*) in the phenomenal world. Malkovsky also makes the world a dependent creation, another view Shankara rejects: creation is a dualistic misreading of the one reality, Brahman.

References and Further Reading

1. General

Bharati, Agehananda. 1976. *The Light at the Center: Context and Pretext of Modern Mysticism*. Santa Barbara, CA: Ross-Erickson.

Bouyer, Louis. 1980. "Mysticism: An Essay on the History of the Word." In *Understanding Mysticism*, edited by Richard Woods, 42–55. Garden City, NY: Doubleday.

Bucke, Richard M. (1901) 1969. *Cosmic Consciousness: A Study in the Evolution of the Human Mind*. New York: Dutton.

de Certeau, Michel. 1992. *The Mystic Fable: The Sixteenth and Seventeenth Centuries*. Translated by Michael B. Smith. Chicago, IL: University of Chicago.

Ellwood, Robert S., Jr. 1999. *Mysticism and Religion*. 2nd ed. San Francisco, CA: Seven Bridges Press.

Forman, Robert K. C. 2011. *Enlightenment Ain't What It's Cracked Up to Be*. Washington, DC: O-Books.

Hardy, Alister. 1983. *The Spiritual Nature of Man: A Study of Contemporary Religious Experience*. Oxford: Clarendon Press.

Harmless, William. 2008. *Mystics*. New York: Oxford University Press.

Hollenback, Jess Byron. 1996. *Mysticism, Experience, Response, and Empowerment*. University Park: Pennsylvania State University Press.

Idel, Moshe, and Bernard McGinn, eds. 1996. *Mystical Union in Judaism, Christianity, and Islam: An Ecumenical Dialogue*. New York: Continuum.

Inge, William Ralph. 1899. *Christian Mysticism: Considered in Eight Lectures Delivered before the University of Oxford*. London: Methuen.

———. 1947. *Mysticism in Religion*. New York: Hutchinson's University Library.

James, William. (1902) 1958. *The Varieties of Religious Experience: A Study of Human Nature*. New York: New American Library.

Johnston, William. 1981. *The Mirror Mind: Spirituality and Transformation*. San Francisco, CA: Harper & Row.

Jones, Rufus. 1909. *Studies in Mystical Religion*. London: Macmillan.

Katz, Steven T. 2013. *Comparative Mysticism: An Anthology of Original Sources*. New York: Oxford University Press.
Komjathy, Louis, ed. 2015. *Contemplative Literature: A Comparative Sourcebook on Meditation and Contemplative Prayer*. Albany: State University of New York Press.
Kripal, Jeffrey J. 2010. *Authors of the Impossible: The Paranormal and the Sacred*. Chicago, IL: University of Chicago Press.
Krippner, Stanley. 1972. "Altered States of Consciousness." In *The Highest State of Consciousness*, edited by John White, 1–5. New York: Doubleday.
Marshall, Paul. 2005. *Mystical Encounters with the Natural World: Experiences and Explanations*. New York: Oxford University Press.
McGinn, Bernard, ed. 1978–. *Classics of Western Spirituality*. New York: Paulist Press.
———. 1994. "The Modern Study of Mysticism." In *The Foundations of Mysticism: Origins to the Fifth Century*, 265–343. New York: Crossroad.
———. 2008. "Mystical Consciousness: A Modest Proposal." *Spiritus* 8 (Spring): 44–63.
Nelstrop, Louise, Kevin Magill, and Bradley B. Onishi. 2009. *Christian Mysticism: An Introduction to Contemporary Theoretical Approaches*. Burlington, VT: Ashgate.
Parsons, William B., ed. 2011. *Teaching Mysticism*. New York: Oxford University Press.
Russell, Bertrand. 1917. *Mysticism and Logic and Other Essays*. London: George Allen & Unwin.
Schmidt, Leigh Eric. 2003. "The Making of Modern 'Mysticism.'" *Journal of the American Academy of Religion* 71 (2): 273–302.
Staal, Frits. 1975. *Exploring Mysticism: A Methodological Essay*. Berkeley: University of California Press.
Stoeber, Michael. 2017. "The Comparative Study of Mysticism." Oxford Research Encyclopedia of Religion. DOI: 10.1093/acrefore/9780199340378.013.93.
Underhill, Evelyn. (1915) 1961. *Practical Mysticism*. New York: E. P. Dutton.
———. (1911) 1990. *Mysticism: A Study in the Nature and Development of Man's Spiritual Consciousness*. 12th ed. New York: Image Books.
Wildman, Wesley J. 2011. *Religious and Spiritual Experiences*. New York: Cambridge University Press.
Woods, Richard, ed. 1980. *Understanding Mysticism*. Garden City, NY: Doubleday.

2. Philosophy

A. General

Almond, Philip C. 1982. *Mystical Experience and Religious Doctrine: An Investigation of the Study of Mysticism in World Religions*. New York: Mouton.
Alston, William. 1991. *Perceiving God*. Ithaca, NY: Cornell University Press.

Franks Davis, Caroline. 1989. *The Evidential Force of Religious Experience*. New York: Oxford University Press.
Gellman, Jerome. 2001. *Mystical Experience of God: A Philosophical Inquiry*. Burlington, VT: Ashgate.
Hick, John. 1989. *An Interpretation of Religion: Human Responses to the Transcendent*. New Haven, CT: Yale University Press.
Jones, Richard H. 2016. *Philosophy of Mysticism: Raids on the Ineffable*. Albany: State University of New York Press.
Lewin, David, Simon D. Podmore, and Duane Williams, eds. 2017. *Mystical Theology and Continental Philosophy: Interchange in the Wake of God*. New York: Routledge.
Maritain, Jacques. 1959. *Distinguish to Unite, or, The Degrees of Knowledge*. 4th ed. Translated by Gerald B. Phelan. New York: Charles Scribner's Sons.
Pike, Nelson. 1992. *Mystic Union: An Essay in the Phenomenology of Mysticism*. Ithaca, NY: Cornell University Press.
Stace, Walter Terrence. 1960a. *Mysticism and Philosophy*. New York: Macmillan.
———. 1960b. *The Teachings of the Mystics*. New York: New American Library.
Steinbock, Anthony J. 2007. *Phenomenology and Mysticism: The Verticality of Religious Experience*. Bloomington: Indiana University Press.
Wainwright, William. 1981. *Mysticism: A Study of Its Nature, Cognitive Value, and Moral Implications*. Madison: University of Wisconsin Press.

B. Mysticism and Science as Ways of Knowing

Capra, Fritjof. (1975) 2000. *The Tao of Physics: An Exploration of the Parallels between Modern Physics and Eastern Mysticism*. 4th ed. Boston, MA: Shambhala Press.
Goswami, Amit, with Maggie Goswami. 1997. *Science and Spirituality: A Quantum Integration*. New Delhi: Project of History of Indian Science, Philosophy and Culture.
Gyatso, Tenzin (His Holiness the XIVth Dalai Lama). 2005. *The Universe in a Single Atom: The Convergence of Science and Spirituality*. New York: Morgan Road Books.
Gyatso, Tenzin, and Daniel Goleman. 2003. "On the Luminosity of Being." *New Scientist* 178 (2396 [May 24]): 42–43.
Halbfass, Wilhelm. 1988. *India and Europe: An Essay in Understanding*. Albany: State University of New York Press.
Jones, Richard H. 1986. *Science and Mysticism: A Comparative Study of Western Natural Science, Theravada Buddhism, and Advaita Vedanta*. Lewisburg, PA: Bucknell University Press. Paperback ed., BookSurge, 2008.
———. 1993a. "Concerning Joseph Needham on Taoism." In *Mysticism Examined: Philosophical Inquiries into Mysticism*, 127–46. Albany: State University of New York Press.

———. 2011–2012. *For the Glory of God: Positive and Negative Roles of Christian Doctrines in the Rise and Development of Modern Science*. 2 vols. Lanham, MD: University Press of America.

———. 2013. *Analysis and the Fullness of Reality: An Introduction to Reductionism and Emergence*. New York: Jackson Square Books.

———. 2015. *Piercing the Veil: Comparing Science and Mysticism as Ways of Knowing Reality*. Rev. edition. New York: Jackson Square Books / Createspace.

———. 2018a. *Mystery 101: The Big Questions and the Limits of Human Knowledge*. Albany: State University of New York Press.

———. 2019. "Mysticism in the New Age: Are Mysticism and Science Converging?" In *Mysticism and Meaning: Multidisciplinary Perspectives*, edited by Alex S. Kohav, 247–77. St. Petersburg, FL: Tree Pines Press.

Kaiser, David. 2011. *How the Hippies Saved Physics: Science, Counterculture, and the Quantum Revival*. New York: W. W. Norton.

Kohn, Livia. 2016. *Science and the Dao: From the Big Bang to Lived Perfection*. St. Petersburg, FL: Three Pines Press.

Lopez, Donald S., Jr. 2008. *Buddhism and Science: A Guide for the Perplexed*. Chicago, IL: University of Chicago.

Malin, Shimon. 2001. *Nature Loves to Hide: Quantum Physics and the Nature of Reality, A Western Perspective*. New York: Oxford University Press.

Mansfield, Victor N. 2008. *Tibetan Buddhism and Modern Physics: Toward a Union of Love and Knowledge*. West Conshohocken, PA: Templeton Foundation Press.

Ricard, Matthieu, and Trinh Xuan Thuan. 2001. *The Quantum and the Lotus: A Journey to the Frontiers Where Science and Buddhism Meet*. New York: Crown Publishers.

Wallace, B. Alan. 1989. *Choosing Reality: A Contemplative View of Physics and the Mind*. Boston, MA: Shambhala New Science Library.

———, ed. 2003. *Buddhism and Science: Breaking New Ground*. New York: Columbia University Press.

Weber, Renée. 1986. *Dialogues with Scientists and Sages: The Search for Unity*. New York: Routledge & Kegan Paul.

Wilber, Ken, ed. 1984. *Quantum Questions: Mystical Writings of the World's Great Physicists*. Boulder, CO: Shambhala New Science Library.

Zukav, Gary. (1977) 2001. *The Dancing Wu Li Masters: An Overview of the New Physics*. New York: HarperCollins.

C. Language

Keller, Carl A. 1978. "Mystical Literature." In *Mysticism and Philosophical Analysis*, edited by Steven T. Katz, 75–100. New York: Oxford University Press.

Kukla, André. 2005. *Ineffability and Philosophy*. New York: Routledge.

Sells, Michael A. 1994. *Mystical Languages of Unsaying*. Chicago, IL: University of Chicago Press.

D. Art

Brennan, Marcia. 2012. *Curating Consciousness: Mysticism and the Modern Museum.* Cambridge, MA: MIT Press.

Gombrich, Carl. 2008. "Expressions of Inexpressible Truths: Attempts at Descriptions of Mystical and Musical Experiences." *World of Music* 50 (1): 89–105.

Khan, Hazrat Inayat. 1996. *The Mysticism of Sound and Music.* Boston, MA: Shambhala.

Nelstrop, Louise, and Helen Appleton, eds. 2018. *Art and Mysticism: Interfaces in the Medieval and Modern Periods.* New York: Routledge.

Soltes, Ori Z. 2005. *Our Sacred Signs: How Jewish, Christian, and Muslim Art Draw from the Same Source.* Cambridge, MA: Westview Press.

———. 2020. "Words and Images of a Transcendent Inner *Mysterion*: Mysticism in Contemporary Western Literature and Art." In *Mysticism and Experience: Twenty-First Century Approaches,* edited by Alex Kohav, 93–116. Lanham, MD: Lexington Books.

Steer, Maxwell, ed. 1996. *Music and Mysticism.* 2 vols. Amsterdam: Harwood Academic Publishers.

Underhill, Evelyn. 1980. "The Mystic as Creative Artist." In *Understanding Mysticism,* edited by Richard Woods, 400–414. Garden City, NY: Doubleday.

E. Rationality

Biderman, Shlomo, and Ben-Ami Scharfstein, eds. 1989. *Rationality in Question: On Eastern and Western Views of Rationality.* New York: E. J. Brill.

Gupta, Bina. 2009. *Reason and Experience in Indian Philosophy.* New Delhi: Indian Council of Philosophical Research.

Hansen, Chad. 1983. *Language and Logic in Ancient China.* Ann Arbor: University of Michigan Press.

Matilal, Bimal Krishna. 1977. *The Logical Illumination of Indian Mysticism.* New York: Oxford University Press.

———. 1998. *The Character of Logic in India.* Albany: State University of New York Press.

Staal, Frits. 1975. *Exploring Mysticism: A Methodological Essay.* Berkeley: University of California Press.

F. Morality

Barnard, G. William, and Jeffrey J. Kripal, eds. 2002. *Crossing Boundaries: Essays on the Ethical Status of Mysticism.* New York: Seven Bridges.

Danto, Arthur C. 1987. *Mysticism and Morality: Oriental Thought and Moral Philosophy.* 2nd ed. New York: Columbia University Press.

Jones, Richard H. 2004. *Mysticism and Morality: A New Look at Old Questions.* Lanham, MD: Lexington Books.

G. Social Change

Pollard, Alton B. 1992. *Mysticism and Social Change: The Social Witness of Howard Thurman*. New York: Peter Lang.

Rakoczy, Susan. 2006. *Great Mystics and Social Justice: Walking on the Two Feet of Love*. New York: Paulist Press.

Thurman, Howard. 1961. *Mysticism and the Experience of Love*. Wallingford, PA: Pendle Hill.

Versluis, Arthur. 2011. *The Mystical State: Politics, Gnosis, and Emergent Cultures*. Minneapolis, MN: New Cultures Press.

H. Constructivism

Buber, Martin. 1947. *Between Man and Man*. Translated by Maurice Friedman. New York: Routledge & Kegan.

Chen, Zhuo, et al. 2011a. "Common Core Thesis and Qualitative and Quantitative Analysis of Mysticism in Chinese Buddhist Monks and Nuns." *Journal for the Scientific Study of Religion* 50 (4): 654–70.

Chen, Zhuo, et al. 2011b. "Mystical Experience among Tibetan Buddhists: The Common Core Thesis Revisited." *Journal for the Scientific Study of Religion* 50 (2): 328–38.

Forman, Robert K. C., ed. 1990. *The Problem of Pure Consciousness: Mysticism and Philosophy*. New York: Oxford University Press.

———, ed. 1998. *The Innate Capacity: Mysticism, Psychology, and Philosophy*. New York: Oxford University Press.

———. 1999. *Mysticism, Mind, Consciousness*. Albany: State University of New York Press.

Gimello, Robert M. 1983. "Mysticism in Its Contexts." In *Mysticism and Religious Traditions*, edited by Steven T. Katz, 61–88. New York: Oxford University Press.

Hood, Ralph W., Jr. 2004. "Conceptual and Empirical Consequences of the Unity Thesis." In *Mysticism: A Variety of Psychological Perspectives* (edited by Antoon Geels and Jacob A. Belzen, 17–54. International Series in the Psychology of Religion, no. 13. Amsterdam: Rodopi.

———. 2006. "The Common Core Thesis in the Study of Mysticism." In *Where God and Science Meet: How Brain and Evolutionary Studies Alter Our Understanding of Religion: The Psychology of Religious Experience,* edited by Patrick McNamara, 119–38. Vol. 3. Westport, CT: Greenwood Press.

———. 2017. "Self-Loss in Indigenous and Cross-Cultural Psychologies: Beyond Dichotomies?" *Research in the Social Scientific Study of Religion* 28:112–32.

Jones, Richard H. 2020. "On Constructivism in the Philosophy of Mysticism." *Journal of Religion* 100(1): 1–41.

Katz, Steven T., ed. 1978. *Mysticism and Philosophical Analysis*. New York: Oxford University Press.

———, ed. 1983. *Mysticism and Religious Traditions*. New York: Oxford University Press.
———, ed. 1992. *Mysticism and Language*. New York: Oxford University Press.
———, ed. 2000. *Mysticism and Sacred Scripture*. New York: Oxford University Press.
———. 2014. "Analyzing Mystical Experience." Address given to Conference on Contemporary Philosophy of Religion in Teheran, Iran, January 14, 2014.
Katz, Steven T., Huston Smith, and Sallie B. King. 1988. "On Mysticism." *Journal of the American Academy of Religion* 56 (4): 751–61.
King, Richard. 1999. *Orientalism and Religion: Post-Colonial Theory, India, and "The Mystic East."* New York: Routledge.
King, Sallie B. 1988. "Two Epistemological Models for the Interpretation of Mysticism." *Journal of the American Academy of Religion* 56 (2): 257–79.
Moore, Peter. 1978. "Mystical Experience, Mystical Doctrine, Mystical Technique." In *Mysticism and Philosophical Analysis*, edited by Steven T. Katz, 101–31. New York: Oxford University Press.
Penner, Hans. 1983. "The Mystical Illusion." In *Mysticism and Religious Traditions*, edited by Steven T. Katz, 89–116. New York: Oxford University Press.
Smart, Ninian. 1965. "Interpretation and Mystical Experience." *Religious Studies* 1 (1): 75–87.
Smith, Huston. 1987. "Is There a Perennial Philosophy?" *Journal of the American Academy of Religion* 55 (3): 553–66.
Stoeber, Michael. 1992. "Constructivist Epistemologies of Mysticism: A Critique and a Revision." *Religious Studies* 28 (1): 107–16.

I. Attribution Theory

Barnard, G. William. 1992. "Explaining the Unexplainable: Wayne Proudfoot's *Religious Experience*." *Journal of the American Academy of Religion* 60 (2): 231–57.
Proudfoot, Wayne. 1985. *Religious Experience*. Berkeley: University of California Press.
Taves, Ann. 2009. *Religious Experience Reconsidered: A Building-Block Approach to the Study of Religion and Other Special Things*. Princeton, NJ: Princeton University Press.

3. Social Sciences

A. Psychological Approaches

Belzen, Jacob A., and Antoon Geels, eds. 2003. *Mysticism: A Variety of Psychological Perspectives*. International Series in the Psychology of Religion, no. 13. New York: Rodopi.
Cattoi, Thomas, and David M. Odorisio, eds. 2018. *Depth Psychology and Mysticism*. New York: Palgrave MacMillan.

Coward, Harold. 1985. *Jung and Eastern Thought*. Albany: State University of New York Press.
Ferrer, Jorge N. 2002. *Revisioning Transpersonal Theory: A Participatory Vision of Human Spirituality*. Albany: State University of New York Press, 2002.
Ferrer, Jorge N., and Jacob H. Sherman, ed. 2009. *The Participatory Turn: Spirituality, Mysticism, Religious Studies*. Albany: State University of New York Press.
Freud, Sigmund. (1930) 2010. *Civilization and Its Discontents*. Edited and translated by James Strachey. New York: W. W. Norton.
Grof, Stanislav. 1998. *The Cosmic Game: Explorations of the Frontiers of Human Consciousness*. Albany: State University of New York Press.
Hood, Ralph W., and G. N. Byrom. 2010. "Mysticism, Madness, and Mental Health." In *The Healing Power of Spirituality: How Faith Helps Humans Thrive*, edited by J. Harold Ellens, 171–91. Vol. 3. Santa Barbara, CA: Praeger.
James, William. (1902) 1958. *The Varieties of Religious Experience: A Study of Human Nature*. New York: New American Library.
Jones, Richard H. 1993b. "Concerning Carl Jung and Asian Religious Traditions." In *Mysticism Examined: Philosophical Inquiries into Mysticism*, 169–83. Albany: State University of New York Press.
———. 2000. *Reductionism: Analysis and the Fullness of Reality*. Lewisburg, PA: Bucknell University Press.
Kelly, Edward F., and Michael Grosso. 2007. "Mystical Experience." In *Irreducible Mind: Toward a Psychology for the Twenty-First Century*, edited by Edward F. Kelly et al., 495–575. Lanham, MD: Rowman & Littlefield.
Kripal, Jeffrey J. 1995. *Kali's Child: The Mystical and the Erotic in the Life and Teachings of Ramakrishna*. 2nd ed. Chicago, IL: University of Chicago Press.
Kroll, Jerome, and Bernard Bachrach. 2005. *The Mystic Mind: The Psychology of Medieval Mystics and Ascetics*. New York: Routledge.
Laski, Marghanita. (1961) 1990. *Ecstasy in Secular and Religious Experiences*. New York: St. Martin's Press.
Leuba, James H. (1929) 2000. *The Psychology of Religious Mysticism*. Rev. ed. New York: Routledge.
Maslow, Abraham H. 1964. *Religions, Values, and Peak Experiences*. New York: Penguin.
Maven, Alexander. 1972. "The Mystic Union: A Suggested Biological Interpretation." In *The Highest State of Consciousness*, edited by John White, 429–35. Garden City, NY: Anchor Books.
Neumann, Erich. 1968. "Mystical Man." In *The Mystic Vision: Papers from the Eranos Yearbooks*, edited by Joseph Campbell, 375–415. Vol. 6. Princeton, NJ: Princeton University Press.
Parnas, Josef, and Mads Gram Henriksen. 2016. "Mysticism and Schizophrenia: A Phenomenological Exploration of the Structure of Consciousness in the Schizophrenia Spectrum Disorders." *Consciousness and Cognition* 43:75–88.

Parsons, William. 1999. *The Enigma of the Oceanic Feeling: Revisioning the Psychoanalytic Theory of Mysticism*. New York: Oxford University Press.
Vergote, Antoine. 2003. "Plying between Psychology and Mysticism." In *Mysticism: A Variety of Psychological Perspectives*, edited by Jacob A. Belzen and Antoon Geels, 81–107. New York: Rodopi.
Washburn, Michael. 2003. *Embodied Spirituality in a Sacred World*. Albany: State University of New York Press.
Wulff, David M. 2013. "Mystical Experience." In *Varieties of Anomalous Experience: Examining the Scientific Evidence*, edited by Etzel Cardeña, Steven J. Lynn, and Stanley C. Krippner, 397–440. 2nd ed. Washington, DC: American Psychological Association.

B. Eroticism

Cattoi, Thomas, and June McDaniel, eds. 2011. *Perceiving the Divine through the Human Senses: Mystical Sensuality*. New York: Palgrave.
Feuerstein, Gerog. 2003. *Sacred Sexuality: The Erotic Spirit in the World's Great Religions*. Rochester, VT: Inner Traditions.
Hanegraaff, Wouter J., and Jeffrey J. Kripal, eds. 2008. *Hidden Intercourse: Eros and Sexuality in the History of Western Esotericism*. Boston, MA: Brill.
Idel, Moshe. 2005. *Kabbalah and Eros*. New Haven, CT: Yale University Press.
Kripal, Jeffrey J. 2001. *Roads of Excess, Palaces of Wisdom: Eroticism and Reflexivity in the Study of Mysticism*. Chicago, IL: University of Chicago.
———. 2017. *Secret Body: Erotic and Esoteric Currents in the History of Religions*. Chicago, IL: University of Chicago Press.
Wolfson, Elliot. 2005. *Language, Eros, Being: Kabbalistic Hermeneutics and Poetic Imagination*. New York: Fordham University Press.

C. Sociological and Anthropological Approaches

Gombrich, Richard F. 2006. *Theravada Buddhism: A Social History from Ancient Benares to Modern Colombo*. 2nd ed. New York: Routledge.
Greeley, Andrew. 1975. *The Sociology of the Paranormal: A Reconnaissance*. Beverly Hills, CA: Sage.
Hood, Ralph W., Jr., and Zhuo Chen. 2017. "The Social Scientific Study of Christian Mysticism." In *The Wiley-Blackwell Companion to Christian Mysticism*, edited by Julia Lamm, 577–91. New York: Wiley Blackwell.
Leach, Edmund. 1954. *Political Systems of Highland Burma*. London: Bell.
Lewis, I. M. 1989. *Ecstatic Religion: An Anthropological Study of Spirit Possession and Shamanism*. 2nd ed. London: Routledge.
Preston, David. L. (1988) 2012. *The Social Organization of Zen Practice: Constructing Transcultural Reality*. New York: Cambridge University Press.

Samuel, Geoffrey. 1995. *Civilized Shamans: Buddhism in Tibetan Societies.* Washington, DC: Smithsonian Institute Press.
Sosteric, Mike. 2017. "The Sociology of Mysticism." *ISA e-Forum.* http://www.sagepub.net/isa/resources/ebulletin_pdf/EBulSostericJul2017.
Spickard, James V. 1993. "For a Sociology of Religious Experience." In *A Future for Religion? New Paradigms for Social Analysis,* edited by Willian H. Swatos, Jr., 109–28. Thousand Oaks, CA: Sage.
Spiro, Melford E. 1982. *Buddhism and Society: A Great Tradition and Its Burmese Vicissitudes.* 2nd ed. Berkeley: University of California Press.
Troeltsch, Ernst. (1912) 1981. *The Social Teachings of the Christian Church.* 2 vols. Chicago, IL: University of Chicago.
Wexler, Philip. 2013. *Mystical Sociology: Toward Cosmic Social Theory.* New York: Peter Lang.

D. Gender Studies

Bostic, Joy. 2013. *African American Female Mysticism: Nineteenth Century Religious Activism.* New York: Palgrave.
Brunn, Emilie Zum, and Georgette Epiney-Burgard, eds. 1989. *Women Mystics in Medieval Europe.* Translated by Shelia Hughes. New York: Paragon House.
Giles, Mary E. 1982. *The Feminist Mystic and Other Essays on Women and Spirituality.* New York: Crossroad.
Hollywood, Amy. 2002. *Sensible Ecstasy: Mysticism, Sexual Difference, and the Demands of History.* Chicago, IL: University of Chicago.
Jacobs, Janet L. 1992. "Religious Experiences among Women and Men: A Gender Perspective on Mystical Phenomena." *Research in the Social Scientific Study of Religion* 4 (2): 261–79.
Jantzen, Grace M. 1994. "Feminists, Philosophers, and Mystics." *Hypatia* 9 (4): 186–206.
———. 1995. *Power, Gender, and Christian Mysticism.* Cambridge: Cambridge University Press.
Lanzetta, Beverly. 2005. *Radical Wisdom: A Feminist Mystical Theology.* Minneapolis, MN: Fortress Press.
Mercer, Calvin, and Thomas W. Durham. 1999. "Religious Mysticism and Gender Orientation." *Journal for the Scientific Study of Religion* 38 (1): 175–82.
Raphael, Melissa. 1994. "Feminism, Constructivism and Numinous Experience." *Religious Studies* 30 (4): 511–26.
Soelle, Dorothee. 2001. *The Silent Cry: Mysticism and Resistance.* Translated by Barbara Rumscheidt and Martin Rumscheidt. Minneapolis, MN: Fortress Press.
Wawrytko, Sandra A. 1995. "The 'Feminine' Mode of Mysticism." In *Mysticism and Mystical Experience: East and West,* edited by Donald H. Bishop, 195–229. London: Associated University Press.

4. Science

A. Neuroscientific Study of Meditators

d'Aquili, Eugene G., and Andrew B. Newberg. 1999. *The Mystical Mind: Probing the Biology of Religious Experience*. Minneapolis, MN: Fortress Press.

Austin, James H. 1998. *Zen and the Brain: Toward An Understanding of Meditation and Consciousness*. Cambridge, MA: MIT Press.

Barrett, Frederick S., and Roland R. Griffiths. 2018. "Classic Hallucinogens and Mystical Experiences: Phenomenology and Neural Correlates." In *Behavioral Neurobiology of Psychedelic Drugs*, edited by Adam L. Halberstadt, Franz X. Vollenweider, and David E. Nichols, 393–430. New York: Springer.

Barušs, Imants, and Julia Mossbridge. 2016. *Transcendent Mind: Rethinking the Science of Consciousness*. Washington, DC: American Psychological Association.

Benson, Herbert, and Miriam Z. Klipper. 2000. *The Relaxation Response*. New York: HarperCollins.

Bradford, David T. 2013. "Emotion in Mystical Experience." *Religion, Brain & Behavior* 3 (2): 103–18.

Byrd, Kevin R., Delbert Lear, and Stacy Schwenka. 2000. "Mysticism as a Predictor of Subjective Well-Being." *International Journal for the Psychology of Religion* 10 (4): 259–69.

Deikman, Arthur J. 2000. "A Functional Approach to Mysticism." *Journal of Consciousness Studies* 7 (11/12): 75–92.

Devinsky, Orrin, and George C. Lai. 2008. "Spirituality and Religion in Epilepsy." *Epilepsy & Behavior* 12 (4): 636–43.

Dewhurst, Kenneth, and A. W. Beard. 1970. "Sudden Religious Conversions in Temporal Lobe Epilepsy." *British Journal of Psychiatry* 117 (November): 497–507.

Dunn, Bruce R., Judith A. Hartigan, and William L. Mikulas. 1999. "Concentration and Mindfulness: Unique Forms of Consciousness." *Applied Psychophysiology and Biofeedback* 24 (3): 147–65.

Fingelkurts Alexander A., and Andrew A. Fingelkurts. 2009. "Is Our Brain Hardwired to Produce God, Or is Our Brain Hardwired to Perceive God?" *Cognitive Processing* 10 (4): 293–326.

Fox, Kieran C. R., et al. 2014. "Is Meditation Associated with Altered Brain Structure? A Systematic Review and Meta-Analysis of Morphometric Neuroimaging in Meditation Practitioners." *Neuroscience and Biobehavioral Reviews* 43:48–73.

Goleman, Daniel, and Richard J. Davidson. 2018. *Altered Traits: Science Reveals How Mediation Changes Your Mind, Brain, and Body*. New York: Avery.

Goleman, Daniel, and Robert A. F. Thurman, eds. 1991. *MindScience: An East-West Dialogue*. Boston, MA: Wisdom.

Griffiths, Roland R., et al. 2006. "Psilocybin Can Occasion Mystical-Type Experiences Having Substantial and Sustained Personal Meaning and Spiritual Significance." *Psychopharmacology* 187 (3): 268–83, 284–92.

Griffiths, Roland R., et al. 2008. "Mystical-Type Experiences Occasioned by Psilocybin Mediate the Attribution of Personal Meaning and Spiritual Significance 14 Months Later." *Journal of Psychopharmacology* 22 (3): 621–32.

Griffiths, Roland R., et al. 2011. "Psilocybin Occasioned Mystical Type Experiences: Immediate and Persisting Dose Related Effects." *Psychopharmacology* 218 (4): 649–65.

Harrington, Anne, and Arthur Zajonc, eds. 2006. *The Dalai Lama at MIT*. Cambridge, MA: Harvard University Press.

Hood, Ralph W., Jr. 2001. *Dimensions of Mystical Experiences: Empirical Studies and Psychological Links*. Amsterdam: Rodopi.

———. 2013. "Theory and Methods in the Psychological Study of Mysticism." *International Journal for the Psychology of Religion* 23 (4): 294–306.

Johnson, Matthew W., et al. 2019. "Classic Psychedelics: An Integrative Review of Epidemiology, Mystical Experience, Therapeutics, and Brain Network Function." *Pharmacology & Therapeutics* 197 (May): 83–102.

Jones, Richard H. 2018b. "Limitations on the Neuroscientific Study of Mystical Experiences." *Zygon: Journal of Science and Religion* 53 (4): 992–1017.

Lebedev, Alexander V., et al. 2015. "Finding the Self by Losing the Self: Neural Correlates of Ego-Dissolution under Psilocybin." *Human Brain Mapping* 36:3137–53.

Lindahl, Jared R., et al. 2017. "The Varieties of Contemplative Experience: A Mixed Methods Study of Meditation Related Challenges in Western Buddhists." *PLOS ONE* 12 (5): e0176239.

McNamara, Patrick. 2009. *The Neuroscience of Religious Experience*. Cambridge: Cambridge University Press.

Newberg, Andrew B., Eugene d'Aquili, and Vince Rause. 2002. *Why God Won't Go Away: Brain Science and the Biology of Belief*. New York: Ballantine Press.

Newberg, Andrew B., and Mark R. Waldman. 2016. *How Enlightenment Changes Your Brain: The New Science of Transformation*. New York: Penguin Random House.

Nour, Matthew M., and Robin L. Carhart-Harris. 2017. "Psychedelics and the Science of Self-Experience." *British Journal of Psychiatry* 210:177–79.

Ospina, Maria B., et al. 2007. "Meditation Practices for Health: State of the Research." *U.S. Department of Health and Human Services: AHRQ Publication No. 07-E010*.

Persinger, Michael A. 1987. *Neuropsychological Bases of God Beliefs*. New York: Praeger.

Picard, Fabienne, and Florian Kurth. 2014. "Ictal Alterations of Consciousness during Ecstatic Seizures." *Epilepsy & Behavior* 30:58–61.

Ricard, Matthieu, Antione Lutz, and Richard J. Davidson. 2014. "The Mind of the Meditator." *Scientific American* (November): 39–45.

Saver, Jeffrey L., and John Rabin. 1997. "The Neural Substrates of Religious Experiences." *Journal of Neuropsychiatry and Clinical Neurosciences* 9 (3): 498–510.
Schmidt, Stefan, and Harald Walach, eds. 2014. *Meditation: Neuroscientific Approaches and Philosophical Implications.* New York: Springer.
Searle, John R. 1992. *The Rediscovery of Mind.* Cambridge, MA: MIT Press.
Smith, Allan L., and Charles T. Tart. 1998. "Cosmic Consciousness Experience and Psychedelic Experiences: A First-Person Comparison." *Journal of Consciousness Studies* 5 (1): 97–107.
Sullivan, Philip R. 1995. "Contentless Consciousness and Information-Processing Theories of the Mind." *Philosophy, Psychiatry & Psychology* 2 (March): 51–59.
Tang, Yi Yuan, Britta K. Hölzel, and Michael I. Posner. 2015. "The Neuroscience of Mindfulness Meditation." *Nature Reviews Neuroscience* 16 (18 March): 213–25.
Valentine, Elizabeth R., and Philip G. Sweet. 1999. "Meditation and Attention: A Comparison of the Effects of Concentrative and Mindfulness Meditation on Sustained Attention." *Mental Health, Religion & Culture* 2 (1): 59–70.
Varela, Francisco J., and Jonathan Shear. 1999. "First-Person Methodologies: What, Why, How?" *Journal of Consciousness* 6 (2–3): 1–14.
Wachholtz, Amy B., and Kenneth I. Pargament. 2005. "Is Spirituality a Critical Ingredient of Meditation? Comparing the Effects of Spiritual Meditation, Secular Meditation, and Relaxation on Spiritual, Psychological, Cardiac, and Pain Outcomes." *Journal of Behavioral Medicine* 28 (4): 369–84.
Yaden, David B., et al. 2017a. "The Noetic Quality: A Multimethod Exploratory Study." *Psychology of Consciousness: Theory, Research, and Practice* 4 (1): 54–62.

B. Psychedelic Drugs

Doblin, Rick. 1991. "Pahnke's 'Good Friday Experiment': A Long-Term Follow-Up and Methodological Critique." *Journal of Transpersonal Psychology* 23 (1): 1–28.
Jones, Richard. 2019a. "Limitations on the Scientific Study of Drug-Enabled Mystical Experiences." *Zygon: Journal of Science and Religion* 54 (3): 756–92.
Pahnke, Walter N. 1966. "Drugs and Mysticism." *International Journal of Parapsychology* 8 (Spring): 295–414.
Pahnke, Walter N., and William A. Richards. 1966. "Implications of LSD and Experimental Mysticism." *Journal of Religion and Health* 5 (July): 175–208.
Richards, William A. 2016. *Sacred Knowledge: Psychedelics and Religious Experiences.* New York: Columbia University Press.
Smith, Huston. 2000a. *Cleansing the Doors of Perception: The Religious Significance of Entheogenic Plants and Chemicals.* New York: Penguin Putnam.
———. 2005. "Do Drugs Have Religious Import? A Forty Year Follow-Up." In *Higher Wisdom: Eminent Elders Explore the Continuing Impact of Psychedelics*, edited by Roger Walsh and Charles S. Grob, 223–39. Albany: State University of New York Press.

Tart, Charles T. 1969. *Altered States of Consciousness: A Book of Readings.* New York: Wiley.
Yaden, David B. et al. 2017b. "Of Roots and Fruits: A Comparison of Psychedelic and Nonpsychedelic Mystical Experiences." *Journal of Humanistic Psychology* 57 (4): 338–53.

5. History

A. General

Jones, Richard H. Forthcoming. *History of Mysticism.*

B. Prehistory: Shamanism

Brown, Joseph Epes. 1991. *The Spiritual Legacy of the American Indians.* New York: Crossroad.
Eliade, Mircea. (1951) 1972. *Shamanism: Archaic Techniques of Ecstasy.* Princeton, NJ: Princeton University Press.
Harner, Michael J. 1980. *The Way of the Shaman: A Guide to Power and Healing.* New York: Bantam Books.
Lewis, I. M. 1989. *Ecstatic Religion: An Anthropological Study of Spirit Possession and Shamanism.* 2nd ed. London: Routledge.
Rossano, Matt J. 2007. "Did Meditation Make Us Human?" *Cambridge Archeological Journal* 17 (1): 47–58.
Walsh, Roger N. 1990. *The Spirit of Shamanism.* Los Angeles, CA: Jeremy P. Tarcher.
Winkelman, Michael. 2010. *Shamanism: A Biological Paradigm of Consciousness and Healing.* 2nd ed. Santa Barbara, CA: Praeger.

C. Prehistory: Psychedelic Drugs

Badiner, Allan, and Alex Grey, eds. 2015. *Zig Zag Zen: Buddhism and Psychedelics.* 2nd ed. Santa Fe, NM: Synergetic Press.
Devereux, Paul. 1997. *The Long Trip: A Prehistory of Psychedelia.* New York: Penguin Books.
Ellens, J. Harold, ed. 2014. *Seeking the Sacred with Psychoactive Substances: Chemical Paths to Spirituality and to God.* 2 vols. Santa Barbara, CA: Praeger.
Hillman, D. C. A. 2008. *The Chemical Muse: Drug Use and the Roots of Western Civilization.* New York: St. Martin's.
Huxley, Aldous. 1954. *The Doors of Perception.* New York: Harper & Row.
———. 1955. *Heaven and Hell.* New York: Harper & Row.

McKenna, Terence. 1992. *Food of the Gods: The Search for the Original Tree of Knowledge*. New York: Bantam.

Merkur, Dan. 2001. *The Psychedelic Sacrament*. Rochester, VT: Park Street Press.

Partridge, Christopher. 2018. *High Culture: Drugs, Mysticism, and the Pursuit of Transcendence in the Modern World*. New York: Oxford University Press.

Roberts, Thomas. 2013. *The Psychedelic Future of the Mind: How Entheogens Are Enhancing Cognition, Boosting Intelligence, and Raising Values*. Rochester, VT: Part Street.

Strassman, Rick. 2001. *DMT—The Spirit Molecule: A Doctor's Revolutionary Research into the Biology of Near-Death and Mystical Experiences*. Rochester, VT: Park Street Press.

Wasson, R. Gordon, et al. 1986. *Persephone's Quest: Entheogens and the Origins of Religion*. New Haven, CT: Yale University Press.

Weil, Andrew. 1986. *The Natural Mind: An Investigation of Drugs and the Higher Consciousness*. Boston, MA: Houghton Mifflin.

Winkelman, Michael. 1999. "Altered States of Consciousness and Religious Behavior." In *Anthropology of Religion: A Handbook*, edited by Stephen D. Glazier, 393–428. Westport, CT: Greenwood Press.

———. 2014. "Evolutionary Views of Entheogenic Consciousness." In *Seeking the Sacred with Psychoactive Substances: Chemical Paths to Spirituality and to God*, edited by J. Harold Ellens, 341–64. Vol. 1. Santa Barbara, CA: Praeger.

———. 2016. "Shamanism and the Brain." In *Religion: Mental Religion*, edited by Niki Kasumi Clements, 355–72. New York: Macmillan Reference.

———. 2017. "The Mechanisms of Psychedelic Visionary Experiences: Hypotheses from Evolutionary Psychology." *Frontiers in Neuroscience* 11:1–17.

———. 2021. "Anthropology, Shamanism, and Hallucinogens." In *Handbook of Medical Hallucinogens*, edited by Charles S. Grob and Jim Grigsby, 46–67. New York: Guilford.

Zaehner, Robert C. 1957. *Mysticism Sacred and Profane: An Inquiry into Some Varieties of Praeternatural Experience*. New York: Oxford University Press.

———. 1972. *Zen, Drugs, and Mysticism*. New York: Pantheon Books.

D. Greece

Armstrong, A. H. 2000. *Plotinus*. 7 vols. Cambridge, MA: Harvard University Press.

Bussanich, John. 1994. "Mystical Elements in the Thought of Plotinus." *Aufstieg und Niedergang der Römischen Welt* 2 (36): 5300–30.

———. 1999. "Socrates the Mystic." In *Traditions of Platonism: Essays in Honour of John Dillon*, edited by John J. Cleary, 29–51. London: Ashgate.

Hadot, Pierre. 1993. *Plotinus or The Simplicity of Vision*. Translated by Michael Chase. Chicago, IL: University of Chicago.

———. 1995. *Philosophy as a Way of Life: Spiritual Exercises from Socrates to Foucault.* Translated by Michael Chase. Oxford: Blackwell.
Harris, R. Baine, ed. 1982. *Neoplatonism and Indian Thought.* Norfolk, VA: International Society for Neoplatonic Studies.
Kingsley, Peter. 1995. *Ancient Philosophy, Mystery, and Magic: Empedocles and Pythagorean Tradition.* New York: Oxford University Press.
MacKenna, Stephen, trans. 1991. *Plotinus: The Enneads.* Abridged ed. New York: Penguin Books.
Rist, J. M. 1967. *Plotinus: The Road to Reality.* New York: Cambridge University Press.
———. 1989. "Back to the Mysticism of Plotinus: Some More Specifics." *Journal of the History of Philosophy* 27 (2): 183–197.
Ruck, Carl A. P. 2006. *Sacred Mushrooms of the Goddess and Secrets of Eleusis.* Oakland, CA: Ronin Publishing.
Stróżyński, Mateusz. 2008. *Mystical Experience and Philosophical Discourse in Plotinus.* Poznan, Poland: Pozna / Society for the Advancement of the Arts and Sciences.
Ustinova, Yulia. 2009. *Caves and the Ancient Greek Mind: Descending Underground in the Search for Ultimate Truth.* Oxford: Oxford University Press.
Yount, David J. 2017. *Plato and Plotinus on Mysticism, Epistemology, and Ethics.* New York: Bloomsbury.

E. Jewish Mysticism

Afterman, Adam. 2016. *"And They Shall Be One Flesh": On the Language of Mystical Union in Judaism.* Boston, MA: Brill.
Buber, Martin. 1970. *I and Thou.* Translated by Walter Kaufmann. New York: Charles Scribner's Sons.
Dan, Joseph. 1998–99. *Jewish Mysticism.* 4 vols. Northvale, NJ: Jason Aronson.
Idel, Moshe. 1988. *Kabbalah: New Perspectives.* New Haven, CT: Yale University Press.
Kohav, Alex. 2013. *The Sôd Hypothesis: Phenomenological, Semiotic, Cognitive, and Noetic Literary Recovery of the Pentateuch's Embedded Inner Core Mystical Initiation Tradition of Ancient Israelite Cultic Religion.* Denver, CO: MaKoM.
Laenen, J. H. 2001. *Jewish Mysticism: An Introduction.* Translated by David E. Orton. Louisville, KY: Westminster John Knox Press.
Lancaster, Brian L. 2005. *The Essence of Kabbalah.* Edison, NJ: Chartwell Books.
Matt, Daniel. 1995. *The Essential Kabbalah: The Heart of Jewish Mysticism.* San Francisco, CA: Harper.
Mayse, Ariel Evan, ed. 2014. *From the Depth of the Well: An Anthology of Jewish Mysticism.* New York: Paulist Press.
Scholem, Gershom G. 1961. *Major Trends in Jewish Mysticism.* New York: Schocken Books.

Wolfson, Elliot R. 1995. "Varieties of Jewish Mysticism: A Typological Analysis." In *Mysticism and the Mystical Experience East and West*, edited by Donald H. Bishop, 133–69. Selinsgrove, PA: Susquehanna University Press.

F. Christian Mysticism

Dupré, Louis. 1981. *The Deeper Life: An Introduction to Christian Mysticism*. New York: Crossroad.

Dupré, Louis, and James A. Wiseman, eds. 2001. *Light from Light: An Anthology of Christian Mysticism*. 2nd ed. New York: Paulist Press.

Eckhart, Meister. 2009. *The Complete Mystical Works of Meister Eckhart*. Edited and translated by Maurice O'C. Walshe. Revised by Bernard McGinn. New York: Crossroad.

Fanning, Steven. 2001. *Mystics of the Christian Tradition*. New York: Routledge.

Harmless, William. 2004. *Desert Christians: An Introduction to the Literature of Early Monasticism*. New York: Oxford University Press.

Johnston, William, ed. 1973. *The Cloud of Unknowing and the Book of Privy Counseling*. Garden City, NY: Image Books.

Kavanaugh, Kieran, ed. 1987. *John of the Cross: Selected Writings*. New York: Paulist Press.

Lamm, Julia A., ed. 2017. *The Wiley-Blackwell Companion to Christian Mysticism*. New York: Wiley Blackwell.

Lossky, Vladimir. 1957. *The Mystical Theology of the Eastern Church*. London: Clark.

Louth, Andrew. 1981. *The Origins of the Christian Mystical Tradition: From Plato to Denys*. New York: Oxford University Press.

McGinn, Bernard. 1994–. *The Presence of God: A History of Western Christian Mysticism*. New York: Crossroad.

———. 2001. *The Mystical Thought of Meister Eckhart: The Man from Whom God Hid Nothing*. New York: Crossroad.

———, ed. 2006. *The Essential Writings of Christian Mysticism*. New York: Random House.

Ruusbroec, John. 1985. *The Spiritual Espousals and Other Works*. Translated by James A. Wiseman. New York: Paulist Press.

Teresa of Avila. 1979. *The Interior Castle*. Translated by Kieran Kavanaugh and Otilio Rodriguez. Mahwah, NJ: Paulist Press.

Walsh, James. 1981. Translated and edited by *The Cloud of Unknowing*. Mahwah, NJ: Paulist Press.

G. Islamic Mysticism

Abrahamov, Binyamin. 2003. *Divine Love in Islamic Mysticism: The Teachings of al-Ghazâlî and al-Dabbâgh*. New York: Routledge Curzon.

Aminrazavi, Mehdi. 1995. "Antinomian Tradition in Islamic Mysticism." *Bulletin of the Henry Martyn Institute of Islamic Studies* 14 (January–June): 17–24.
Andrae, Tor. 1987. *In the Garden of Myrtles: Studies in Early Islamic Mysticism*. Albany: State University of New York Press.
Chittick, William C. 1983. *The Sufi Path of Love: The Spiritual Teachings of Rumi*. Albany: State University of New York Press.
———. 1989. *The Sufi Path of Knowledge: Ibn al-'Arabi's Metaphysic of Imagination*. Albany: State University of New York Press.
———. 2000. *Sufism: A Beginners' Guide*. London: Oneworld.
Ernst, Carl W. (1997) 2011. *Sufism: An Introduction to the Mystical Tradition of Islam*. Boston, MA: Shambhala.
Ghazali, Abu Hamid. 1998. *The Niche of Lights*. Translated by David Buchman. Provo, UT: Brigham Young University Press.
Green, Nile. 2012. *Sufism: A Global History*. Malden, MA: Wiley Blackwell.
Knysh, Alexander. 2000. *Islamic Mysticism: A Short History*. Boston, MA: E. J. Brill.
Lewis, Franklin D. 2008. *Rumi Past and Present, East and West: The Life, Teachings, and Poetry of Jalal al-Din Rumi*. London: Oneworld.
Rumi, Jalal al-din. 1926–1934. *The Mathnawi*. 3 vols. Translated by R. A. Nicholson. London: Luzac.
———. 1968. *Mystical Poems of Rumi*. Translated by A. J. Arberry. Chicago, IL: University of Chicago Press.
Schimmel, Annemarie. 2011. *Mystical Dimensions of Islam*. 2nd ed. Chapel Hill: University of North Carolina Press.
Sells, Michael A. 1995. *Early Islamic Mysticism: Sufi, Qur'an, Mi'raj, Poetic, and Theological Writings*. New York: Paulist Press.

H. Hindu Mysticism

Carman, John B. 1974. *The Theology of Ramanuja*. New Haven, CT: Yale University Press.
Deussen, Paul. (1907) 1966. *The Philosophy of the Upanishads*. New York: Dover.
Deutsch, Eliot, and Rohit Dalvi, eds. 2004. *The Essential Vedanta: A New Source Book of Advaita Vedanta*. Bloomington, IN: World Wisdom.
Edgerton, Franklin. 1942. "Dominant Ideas in the Formation of Indian Culture." *Journal of the American Oriental Society* 62 (September): 151–56.
Eliade, Mircea. 1970. *Yoga: Immortality and Freedom*. Princeton, NJ: Princeton University Press.
Feuerstein, Georg. 1996. *The Philosophy of Classical Yoga*. Rochester, VT: Inner Traditions.
———. 1998. *Tantra: The Path of Ecstasy*. Boston, MA: Shambhala.
Flood, Gavin. 1996. *An Introduction to Hinduism*. New York: Cambridge University Press.

———. 2004. *The Ascetic Self: Subjectivity, Memory and Tradition*. New York: Cambridge University Press.
———. 2006. *The Tantric Body: The Secret Tradition of Hindu Religion*. New York: Palgrave Macmillan.
Jones, Richard H., trans. 2014a. *Early Indian Philosophy*. New York: Jackson Square Books / Createspace.
———, trans. 2014b. *Early Advaita Vedanta Philosophy* Vol. 1. New York: Jackson Square Books / Createspace.
Klostermaier, Klaus K. 2010. *A Survey of Hinduism*. 3rd ed. Albany: State University of New York Press.
Kripal, Jeffrey J. 1995. *Kali's Child: The Mystical and the Erotic in the Life and Teachings of Ramakrishna*. 2nd ed. Chicago, IL: University of Chicago Press.
Lutyens, Mary. 1991. *Krishnamurti: His Life and Death*. New York: St. Martin's Press.
Miller, Barbara Stoler, trans. 1986. *The Bhagavad-Gita: Krishna's Counsel in Time of War*. New York: Columbia University Press.
———. 1998. *Yoga: Discipline of Freedom*. New York: Bantam Books.
Olivelle, Patrick, trans. 2008. *Upanisads*. New York: Oxford University Press.
Padoux, André. 2017. *The Hindu Tantric World: An Overview*. Chicago, IL: University of Chicago Press.
Potter, Karl. 1963. *Presuppositions of India's Philosophies*. Englewood Cliffs, NJ: Prentice-Hall.
———, ed. 1983–. *Encyclopedia of Indian Philosophies*. Delhi: Motilal Banarsidass.
Ramanujan, A. K. 1973. *Speaking of Siva*. Baltimore, MD: Penguin.
White, David Gordon. 2003. *Kiss of the Yogini: Tantric Sex in Its South Asian Context*. Chicago, IL: University of Chicago Press.
———. 2009. *Sinister Yogis*. Chicago, IL: University of Chicago Press.

I. Indian and Tibetan Buddhist Mysticism

Bronkhorst, Johannes. 1993. *Two Traditions of Meditation in Ancient India*. 2nd ed. Delhi: Motilal Banarsidass.
Garfield, Jay. 1995. *The Fundamental Wisdom of the Middle Way: Nagarjuna's Mulamadhyamakakarika*. New York: Oxford University Press.
Gyatso, Tenzin (His Holiness the XIVth Dalai Lama). 2005. *Essence of the Heart Sutra*. Somerville, MA: Wisdom.
Harvey, Peter. 2013. *An Introduction to Buddhism: Teachings, History, and Practices*. 2nd ed. Cambridge: Cambridge University Press.
Hopkins, Jeffrey. 1983. *Meditation on Emptiness*. Boston, MA: Wisdom.
Jones, Richard H., 2011. *Indian Madhyamaka Buddhist Philosophy after Nagarjuna*. Vol. 1. New York: Jackson Square Books / Createspace.
———. 2012a. *Indian Madhyamaka Buddhist Philosophy after Nagarjuna*. Vol. 2. New York: Jackson Square Books / Createspace.

———. 2012b. *The Heart of Buddhist Wisdom: Plain English Translations of the Heart Sutra, the Diamond-Cutter Sutra, and Other Perfection of Wisdom Texts.* New York: Jackson Square Books / Createspace.

———, trans. 2014c. *Nagarjuna: Buddhism's Most Important Philosopher.* Rev. and expanded ed. New York: Jackson Square Books / Createspace.

King, Winston L. 1980. *Theravada Meditation: The Buddhist Transformation of Yoga.* University Park: Pennsylvania State University Press.

Komarovski, Yaroslav. 2015. *Tibetan Buddhism and Mystical Experience.* New York: Oxford University Press.

Long, Jeffrey D. 2009. *Jainism: An Introduction.* New York: I. B. Tauris.

Nanamoli, Bhikkhu. 1991. *The Path of Purification (Visuddhimagga): The Classic Manual of Buddhist Doctrine and Meditation.* 5th ed. Kandy, Sri Lanka: Buddhist Publication Society.

Nhat Hanh, Thich. 1988. *The Heart of Understanding: Commentaries on the Prajñaparamita Heart Sutra.* Berkeley, CA: Parallax Press.

———. 2010. *The Diamond That Cuts Through Illusion: Commentaries on the Prajñaparamita Diamond Sutra.* Berkeley, CA: Parallax Press.

Obeyesekere, Gananath. 2012. *Awakened Ones: Phenomenology of Visionary Experience.* New York: Columbia University Press.

Powers, John. 2007. *Introduction to Tibetan Buddhism.* Ithaca, NY: Snow Lion.

Queen, Christopher S., and Sallie B. King, eds. 1996. *Engaged Buddhism: Buddhist Liberation Movements in Asia.* Albany: State University of New York Press.

Rahula, Walpola. 1974. *What the Buddha Taught.* Rev. and expanded ed. New York: Grove Press.

Shaw, Sarah, ed. 2014. *Spirit of Buddhist Meditation.* New Haven, CT: Yale University Press.

Thurman, Robert A. F. 1977. *The Holy Teaching of Vimalakirti.* University Park: Pennsylvania State University Press.

———. 1991. *The Central Philosophy of Tibet: A Study and Translation of Jey Tsong Khapa's Essence of True Eloquence.* Princeton, NJ: Princeton University Press.

———. 1995. *Essential Tibetan Buddhism.* New York: HarperCollins.

Wayman, Alex, trans. 1978. *Calming the Mind and Discerning the Real: Buddhist Meditation and the Middle View from the Lam rim chen mo of Tsonkhapa.* New York: Columbia University Press.

Williams, Paul, and Anthony Tribe, and Alexander Wynne. 2012. *Buddhist Thought: A Complete Introduction to the Indian Tradition.* 2nd ed. New York: Routledge.

J. Chinese Mysticism

1. GENERAL

Chan, Wingtsit. 1963. *A Source Book in Chinese Philosophy.* Princeton, NJ: Princeton University Press.

Creel, Herrlee G. 1953. *Chinese Thought from Confucius to Mao-Tse-Tung.* Chicago, IL: University of Chicago Press.
Nisbett, Richard E. 2003. *The Geography of Thought: How Asians and Westerners Think Differently . . . and Why.* New York: Free Press.
Schwartz, Benjamin. 1985. *The World of Thought in Ancient China.* Cambridge, MA: Harvard University Press.

2. DAOISM

Ames, Roger T., ed. 1998. *Wandering at Ease in the Zhuangzi.* Albany: State University of New York Press.
Coutinho, Steve. 2014. *An Introduction to Daoist Philosophies.* New York: Columbia University Press.
Csikzentmihalyi, Marc, and Philip J. Ivanhoe, eds. 1999. *Religious and Philosophical Aspects of the Laozi.* Albany: State University of New York Press.
Eno, Robert. 1996. "Cook Ding's Dao and the Limits of Philosophy." In *Essays on Skepticism, Relativism, and Ethics in the Zhuangzi,* edited by Paul Kjellberg and Philip J. Ivanhoe, 127–51. Albany: State University Press of New York.
Graham, Angus C., trans. 1981. *Chuang-tzu: The Seven Inner Chapters and Other Writings from the Book of Chuang-tzu.* London: George Allen & Unwin.
Henricks, Robert. 2000. *Lao Tzu's Tao Te Ching: A Translation of the Startling New Documents Found at Guodian.* New York: Columbia University Press.
Kjellberg, Paul, and Philip J. Ivanhoe, eds. *Essays on Skepticism, Relativism, and Ethics in the* Zhuangzi. Albany: State University of New York Press.
Kohn, Livia. 2009. *Readings in Daoist Mysticism.* Dunedin, FL: Three Pines Press.
Komjathy, Louis. 2014. *Daoism: A Guide for the Perplexed.* New York: Bloomsbury.
LaFargue, Michael. 1992. *The Tao of the "Taoteching."* Albany: State University of New York Press.
Mair, Victor H., trans. 1990. *"Tao Te Jing": The Classic Book of Integrity and the Way.* New York: Bantam Books.
———. 2000. *Wandering on the Way: Early Taoist Tales and Parables of Chuang Tzu.* Honolulu: University of Hawaii Press.
———, ed. 2010. *Experimental Essays on Chuang-tzu.* Dunedin, FL: Three Pines.
Miller, James. 2003. *Daoism: A Beginner's Guide.* Oxford: Oneworld.
Robinet, Isabelle. 1997. *Taoism: Growth of a Religion.* Translated by Phyllis Brooks. Stanford, CA: Stanford University Press.
Roth, Harold D. 1999. *Original Tao: Inward Training (Nei-Yeh) and the Foundations of Taoist Mysticism.* New York: Columbia University Press.
———. 2000. "Bimodal Mystical Experience in the Qiwulun of *Chuang Tzu.*" *Journal of Chinese Religions* 28 (1): 1–20.
Slingerland, Edward G. 2004. *Effortless Action: Wuwei as Conceptual Metaphor and Spiritual Ideal in Early China.* New York: Oxford University Press.

Waley, Authur. 1958. *The Way and Its Power: A Study of the "Tao Tĕ Ching" and Its Place in Chinese Thought*. New York: Grove Press.
Watson, Burton. 1968. *The Complete Works of Chuang-tzu*. New York: Columbia University Press.

3. BUDDHISM IN CHINA AND JAPAN

Cleary, Thomas. 2005. *Classics of Buddhism and Zen*. 5 vols. Boston, MA: Shambhala.
Dumoulin, Heinrich. 2005. *Zen: A History*. 2 vols. Rev. and expanded ed. Translated by James W. Heisig and Paul Kittner. Bloomington, IN: World Wisdom.
King, Winston Lee. 1993. *Zen and the Way of the Sword: Arming the Samurai Psyche*. New York: Oxford University Press.
Masunaga, Reiho, trans. 1971. *A Primer of Soto Zen: A Translation of Dogen's Shobogenzo Zuimonki*. Honolulu, HI: East-West Center Press.
Miller, David. 2003. "It's More Than a Zen Thing: The Mystical Dimension in Japanese Religion." In *Mysticism East and West: Studies in Mystical Experience*, edited by Christopher Partridge and Theodore Gabriel, 3–18. Carlisle: Paternoster.
Victoria, Brian. 2006. *Zen at War*. 2nd ed. New York: Rowman & Littlefied.
Waddell, Norman. 2002. *Wild Ivy: The Spiritual Biography of Zen Master Hakuin*. Boston, MA: Shambhala.
Yampolsky, Philip B. 1967. *The Platform of the Sixth Patriarch*. New York: Columbia University Press.
Zücher, Erik. 1972. *The Buddhist Conquest of China: The Spread and Adaptation of Buddhism in Early Medieval China*. 2 vols. Leiden: E. J. Brill.

4. NEO-CONFUCIANISM

Chan, Wingtsit. 1963. *Instructions for Practical Living and Other Neo-Confucian Writings by Wang Yangming*. New York: Columbia University Press.
———. 1989. *Chu Hsi: New Studies*. Honolulu: University of Hawaii Press.
Ching, Julia. 1976. *To Accumulate Wisdom: The Way of Wang Yang-ming*. New York: Columbia University Press.
De Bary, Wm. Theodore. 1989. *The Message of the Mind in Neo-Confucianism*. New York: Columbia University Press.
Huang, Xiuji. 1999. *Essentials of Neo-Confucianism: Eight Major Philosophers of the Song and Ming Periods*. Westport, CT: Greenwood Press.
Keenan, Barry C. 2011. *Neo-Confucian Self-Cultivation*. Honolulu: University of Hawai'i Press.

K. Mysticism Today

1. GENERAL

Cupitt, Don. 1998. *Mysticism after Modernity*. Oxford: Blackwell.

Gunnlaugson, Olen, et al. eds. 2014. *Contemplative Learning and Inquiry across Disciplines*. Albany: State University of New York Press.
Harris, Sam. 2014. *Waking Up: A Guide to Spirituality without Religion*. New York: Simon & Schuster.
Horgan, John. 2003. *Rational Mysticism: Dispatches from the Border between Science and Spirituality*. Boston: Houghton Mifflin.
Jäger, Willigis. 2006. *Mysticism for Modern Times: Conversations with Willigis Jäger*. Edited by Christoph Quarch. Translated by Paul Shepherd. Liguori, MO: Liguori/Triumph.
Johnston, William. 1978. *The Inner Eye of Love: Mysticism and Religion*. New York: Harper & Row.
———. 2000. *Arise, My Love: Mysticism for a New Era*. Maryknoll, NY: Orbis Books.
Keating, Thomas. 2006. *Open Mind, Open Heart*. New York: Continuum.
King, Ursula. 1980. *Towards a New Mysticism: Teilhard de Chardin and Eastern Religions*. London: Collins.
Komjathy, Louis. 2018. *Introducing Contemplative Studies*. New York: Wiley-Blackwell.
Osto, Douglas. 2016. *Altered States: Buddhism and Psychedelic Spirituality in America*. New York: Columbia University Press.
Roth, Harold D. 2006. "Contemplative Studies: Prospects for a New Field." *Teachers College Record* 108 (9): 1187–215.
Sheldrake, Philip. 2014. *Spirituality: A Guide for the Perplexed*. New York: Bloomsbury.
Wallace, B. Alan. 2003. *The Taboo of Subjectivity: Toward a New Science of Consciousness*. New York: Oxford University Press.
Wasserstrom, Steven M. 1999. *Religion after Religion: Gershom Scholem, Mircea Eliade, and Henry Corbin at Eranos*. Princeton, NJ: Princeton University Press.

2. MEDITATION

Eifring, Halvor, ed. 2013. *Meditation in Judaism, Christianity, and Islam: Cultural Histories*. New York: Bloomsbury.
———. 2014. *Hindu, Buddhist, and Daoist Meditation: Cultural Histories*. Keysville, VA: Hermes Publishing.
———. 2016. *Asian Traditions of Meditation*. Honolulu: University of Hawai'i Press.
Goleman, Daniel. 1988. *The Meditative Mind: The Varieties of Meditative Experience*. New York: Tarcher/Putnam.
Goodenough, Ursula. 1998. *The Sacred Depths of Nature*. New York: Oxford University Press.
Heller, Rick. 2015. *Secular Meditation: Thirty-Two Practices for Cultivating Inner Peace, Compassion, and Joy*. Novato, CA: New World Library.
Kabat-Zinn, Jon. 2005. *Wherever You Go, There You Are: Mindfulness Meditation in Everyday Life*. New York: Hachette Books.

Kelsey, Morton. 1976. *The Other Side of Silence: A Guide to Christian Meditation.* Paramus, NJ: Paulist Press.

Kohn, Livia. 2008. *Meditation Works: In the Daoist, Buddhist, and Hindu Traditions.* Magdalena, NM: Three Pines Press.

Laird, Martin. 2006. *Into the Silent Land: A Guide to the Christian Practice of Contemplation.* New York: Oxford University Press.

Nash, Jonathan D., and Andrew B. Newberg. 2013. "Toward a Unifying Taxonomy and Definition of Meditation." Article no. 806. *Frontiers in Psychology* 4 (November).

Shear, Jonathan, ed. 2006. *The Experience of Meditation: Experts Introduce Major Traditions.* New York: Paragon House.

Tart, Charles. T. 1994. *Living the Mindful Life: A Handbook for Living in the Present Moment.* Boston, MA: Shambhala.

3. NEW AGE

Boslough, John. 1985. *Stephen Hawking's Universe.* New York: Quill.

Chopra, Deepak. 1989. *Quantum Healing.* New York: Bantam Books.

Chopra, Deepak, with Menas Kafatos. 2017. *You Are the Universe.* New York: Harmony Books.

Cohen, Andrew Z. 2011. *Evolutionary Enlightenment: A New Path to Spiritual Awakening.* New York: Select Books.

Feuerstein, Georg. 1991. *Holy Madness: The Shock Tactics and Radical Teachings of Crazy-Wise Adepts, Holy Fools, and Rascal Gurus.* New York: Penguin Arkana.

Fox, Matthew. 1991. *Creation Spirituality: Liberating Gifts for the Peoples of the Earth.* San Francisco, CA: HarperOne.

Hanegraaff, Wouter J. 1998. *New Age Religion and Western Culture: Esotericism in the Mirror of Secular Thought.* Albany: State University of New York Press.

Heelas, Paul, and Linda Woodhead. 2005. *The Spiritual Revolution: Why Religion Is Giving Way to Spirituality.* Malden, MA: Blackwell.

Jones, Richard H. 1986. *Science and Mysticism: A Comparative Study of Western Natural Science, Theravada Buddhism, and Advaita Vedanta.* Lewisburg, PA: Bucknell University Press. Paperback ed., BookSurge, 2008.

———. 2015. *Piercing the Veil: Comparing Science and Mysticism as Ways of Knowing Reality.* Rev. ed. New York: Jackson Square Books / Createspace.

———. 2019b. "Mysticism in the New Age: Are Mysticism and Science Converging?" In *Mysticism and Meaning: Multidisciplinary and Perspectives*, edited by Alex S. Kohav, 247–77. St. Petersburg, FL: Tree Pines Press.

Storr, Anthony. 1996. *Feet of Clay—Saints, Sinners, and Madmen: A Study of Gurus.* New York: Free Press.

Teasdale, Wayne. 1997. "The Inter-Spiritual Age: Practical Mysticism for the Third Millennium." *Journal of Ecumenical Studies* 34 (1): 74–91.

———. 2001. *The Mystic Heart: Discovering a Universal Spirituality in the World's Religions*. Novato, CA: New World Library.
Tolle, Eckhart. 1999. *The Power of Now: A Guide to Spiritual Enlightenment*. Novato, CA: New World Library.
Watts, Alan. 1962. *The Joyous Cosmology: Adventures in the Chemistry of Consciousness*. New York: Vintage Books.
———. 1966. *The Book: On the Taboo against Knowing Who You Are*. New York: Vintage Books.
Wilbur, Ken. 2007. *The Integral Vision: A Very Short Introduction to the Revolutionary Integral Approach to Life, God, the Universe, and Everything*. Boston, MA: Shambhala Press.

6. Comparative Approaches

A. Religious Studies

Bronkhorst, Johannes. 2017. "Can Religion Be Explained? The Role of Absorption in Various Religious Phenomena." *Method and Theory in the Study of Religion* 29 (1): 1–30.
Bush, Stephen S. 2012. "Are Religious Experiences Too Private to Study?" *Journal of Religion* 92 (2): 199–223.
Casadio, Giovanni. 2016. "Historicizing and Translating Religion." In *The Oxford Handbook of the Study of Religion*, edited by Michael Stausberg and Steven Engler, 33–51. New York: Oxford University Press.
Clarke, J. J. 1997. *Oriental Enlightenment: The Encounter between Asian and Western Thought*. New York: Routledge.
Eliade, Mircea. 1958. *Patterns in Comparative Religion*. Translated by Rosemary Sheed. New York: Meridian Books.
Flood, Gavin. 2013. *The Truth Within: A History of Inwardness in Christianity, Hinduism, and Buddhism*. New York: Oxford University Press.
Idinopulos, Thomas A., Brian C. Wilson, and James C. Hanges, eds. 2006. *Comparing Religions: Possibilities and Perils?* Boston, MA: Brill.
Izutsu, Toshihiko. 1983. *Sufism and Taoism: A Comparative Study of Key Philosophical Concepts*. Tokyo: Iwanami Shoten.
McDaniel, June. 2018. *Lost Ecstasy: Its Decline and Transformation in Religion*. New York: Palgrave MacMillan.
Neville, Robert Cummings, ed. 2001. *Ultimate Realities: A Volume in the Comparative Religious Ideas Project*. Albany: State University of New York Press.
Otto, Rudolf. 1932. *Mysticism East and West: A Comparative Analysis of the Nature of Mysticism*. Translated by Bertha L. Bracey and Richenda C. Payne. New York: Macmillan.

Paden, William E. 1994. *Religious Worlds: The Comparative Study of Religion*. Boston, MA: Beacon Press.

———. 2016. *New Patterns for Comparative Religion: Passages to an Evolutionary Perspective*. New York: Bloomsbury Academic.

Patton, Kimberley C., and Benjamin C. Ray, eds. 2000. *A Magic Still Dwells: Comparative Religion in the Postmodern Age*. Berkeley, CA: University of California Press.

Roy, Louis. 2003. *Mystical Consciousness: Western Perspectives and Dialogue with Japanese Thinkers*. Albany: State University of New York Press.

Sharf, Robert H. 1995. "Buddhist Modernism and the Rhetoric of Meditative Experience." *Numen* 42 (3): 228–83.

———. 1998. "Experience." In *Critical Terms in Religious Studies*, edited by Mark C. Taylor, 94–116. Chicago, IL: University of Chicago Press.

———. 2000. "The Rhetoric of Experience and the Study of Religion." *Journal of Consciousness Studies* 7 (11–12): 267–87.

Sharma, Arvind. 2005. *Religious Studies and Comparative Methodology: A Case for Reciprocal Illumination*. Albany: State University of New York Press.

Sharpe, Eric J. 1986. *Comparative Religion: A History*. 2nd ed. London: Duckworth.

Smart, Ninian. 1996. *Dimensions of the Sacred: An Anatomy of the World's Beliefs*. San Francisco, CA: HarperCollins.

Smith, Jonathan Z. 1982. "In Comparison a Magic Dwells." In *Imagining Religion: From Babylon to Jonestown*, 19–35. Chicago, IL: University of Chicago Press.

———. 1990. "On Comparison." In *Drudgery Divine: On the Comparison of Early Christianity and the Religions of Late Antiquity*, 36–53. Chicago, IL: University of Chicago Press.

Stausberg, Michael. 2011. "Comparison." In *The Routledge Handbook of Research Methods in the Study of Religion*, edited by Michael Stausberg and Steven Engler, 21–29. New York: Routledge.

Streng, Frederick. 1991. "Mysticism: A Popular and Problematic Thematic Course." In *Tracing Common Themes: Comparative Courses in the Study of Religion*, edited by John B. Carman and P. Stephen Hopkins, 127–38. Atlanta: Scholars Press.

Taylor, Mark C., ed. 1998. *Critical Terms in Religious Studies*. Chicago, IL: University of Chicago Press.

Wildman, Wesley J. 2006. "Comparing Religious Ideas: There's Method in the Mob's Madness." In *Comparing Religions: Possibilities and Perils?*, edited by Thomas A. Indinopulos, Brian C. Wilson, and James C. Hanges, 77–113. Boston, MA: Brill.

B. Postmodernism

Brown, Donald. 1991. *Human Universals*. New York: McGraw-Hill.

Cupitt, Don. 1998. *Mysticism after Modernity*. Oxford: Blackwell.

Smith, Huston. 2000b. "Postmodernism's Impact on the Study of Religion." *Journal of the American Academy of Religion* 58 (4): 653–70.
Turner, Denys. 1995. *The Darkness of God: Negativity in Christian Mysticism*. Cambridge: Cambridge University Press.

C. Perennial Philosophy

Abhyananda, Swami. 2012. *History of Mysticism: The Unchanging Testament*. Fallsburg, NY: Atma Books.
Ferrer, Jorge N. 2000. "The Perennial Philosophy Revisited." *Journal of Transpersonal Psychology* 32 (1): 7–30.
Huxley, Aldous. 1945. *The Perennial Philosophy*. New York: Harper & Row.
Jones, Richard H. 2021. "Perennial Philosophy and the History of Mysticism." *Sophia* 60 (2): 1–20.
Lings, Martin, and Clinton Minnaar, eds. 2007. *The Underlying Religion: An Introduction to Perennial Philosophy*. Bloomington, IN: World Wisdom.
Nasr, Seyyed Hossein. 1981. *Knowledge and the Sacred*. New York: Crossroad.
———. 1993. "The *Philosophia Perennis* and the Study of Religion." In *The Need for a Sacred Science*. Albany: State University of New York Press, 53–68.
Schuon, Frithjof. 1975. *The Transcendent Unity of Religions*. Translated by Peter Townsend. New York: Harper & Row.
Shear, Jonathan. 1994. "On Mystical Experiences as Support for the Perennial Philosophy." *Journal of the American Academy of Religion* 62 (2): 319–42.
Smith, Huston. 1976. *Forgotten Truth: The Primordial Tradition*. New York: Harper & Row.
———. 1987. "Is There a Perennial Philosophy?" *Journal of the American Academy of Religion* 55 (3): 553–66.
Smith, Huston, and Henry Rosemont, Jr. 2008. *Is There a Universal Grammar of Religion?* Chicago, IL: Open Court.
Stoddart, William. 2005. "Mysticism." In *Ye Shall Know the Truth: Christianity and the Perennial Philosophy*, edited by Mateus Soares de Azevedo, 57–69. Bloomington, IN: World Wisdom.

D. Theology

Carrette, Jeremy, and Richard King. 2004. *Selling Spirituality: The Silent Takeover of Religion*. New York: Routledge.
Clooney, Francis X. 1993. *Theology after Vedanta: An Experience of Comparative Theology*. Albany: State University of New York Press.
———. 2010a. *Comparative Theology: Deep Learning across Religious Borders*. New York: Wiley-Blackwell.

———, ed. 2010b. *The New Comparative Theology: Voices from the New Generation*. New York: Continuum.

Cousins, Ewert. 1985. *Global Spirituality: Toward the Meeting of Mystical Paths*. Madras, India: University of Madras (Radhakrishnan Institute for Advanced Study in Philosophy).

Fredericks, James. 2004. *Buddhists and Christians: Through Comparative Theology to Solidarity*. Maryknoll, NY: Orbis Books.

Gyatso, Tenzin (His Holiness the XIVth Dalai Lama). 2010. *Toward a True Kinship of Faiths: How the World's Religions Can Come Together*. New York: Three Rivers Press.

Hart, Kevin, and Barbara Wall, eds. 2005. *The Experience of God: A Postmodern Response*. New York: Fordham University Press.

Hedges, Paul, and Alan Race, eds. 2008. *Christian Approaches to Other Faiths*. London: SCM.

Johnston, William. 1989. *The Still Point: Reflections on Zen and Christian Mysticism*. New York: Fordham University Press.

Keenan, John P. 1989. *The Meaning of Christ: A Mahayana Christology*. Maryknoll, NY: Orbis Books.

Knitter, Paul. 2002. *Introducing Theologies of Religion*. Maryknoll, NY: Orbis Books.

Locklin, Reid B., and Hugh Nicholson. 2010. "The Return of Comparative Theology." *Journal of the American Academy of Religion* 78 (2): 477–514.

Malkovsky, Bradley J. 2001. *The Role of Divine Grace in the Soteriology of Samkaracarya*. Boston, MA: Brill.

Martin, Craig. 2016. "Experience." In *The Oxford Handbook of the Study of Religion*, edited by Michael Stausberg and Steven Engler, 525–40. New York: Oxford University Press.

McIntosh, Mark Allen. 1998. *Mystical Theology: The Integrity of Spirituality and Theology*. Malden, MA: Blackwell.

Merton, Thomas. 2003. *The Inner Experience: Notes on Contemplation*. Edited by William H. Shannon. New York: HarperOne.

Nicholson, Hugh. 2011. *Comparative Theology and the Problem of Religious Rivalry*. New York: Oxford University Press.

Panikkar, Raimon. 2014. *Mysticism and Spirituality*. 2 vols. Maryknoll, NY: Orbis Books.

Rahner, Karl. 1984. *The Practice of Faith: A Handbook of Contemporary Spirituality*. New York: Crossroad.

Schmidt-Leukel, Perry, and Andreas Nehring, eds. 2016. *Interreligious Comparisons in Religious Studies and Theology*. New York: Bloomsbury.

Spencer, Daniel. 2021. "The Challenge of Mysticism: A Primer from a Christian Perspective." *Sophia* 60 (1): 1–18.

Thomas, Owen C. 2000. "Interiority and Christian Spirituality." *Journal of Religion* 80 (1): 41–60.

Tillich, Paul. 1952. *The Courage to Be*. New Haven, CT: Yale University Press.

Index

Abhyananda, Swami, 72
Advaita Vedanta, 33, 36, 38, 42, 46, 49, 67, 89, 90, 102, 136, 138, 156, 158, 160–61, 166, 169, 194, 195, 196, 203, 205, 241n5, 245n7, 252n7, 254n3, 257n3. *Also see* Shankara
Alston, William, 165–66
altered states of consciousness (ASC), 3–8 passim, 12, 13, 19, 20, 21, 24, 28, 37, 42, 43, 44, 53, 67, 71, 78–79, 80, 82, 90, 96, 99, 115–16, 118, 127, 131, 143, 146, 150, 151, 152, 154, 170, 183, 186, 211, 231–36 passim; 237nn2–3, 238n4, 249n9, 250n16, 252n10, 255n2; altered state sciences, 248n9, 255n2
antinomianism, 52, 85, 91, 162, 190–91, 196, 199, 202, 204, 234, 245n6, 257n9, 258n11
approaches in the study of mysticism, 63–76; relation of approaches, 108–10
Aquinas, Thomas, 2, 172
art, 183–84
asceticism, 7, 27–28, 79, 103, 125, 191, 229, 234, 239n1
attribution theory, 53–54
Augustine, 172, 203, 256n9

Barnard, G. William, 191, 235
Basho, 203
Beguines, 106
Benson, Herbert, 95, 111, 115
Berger, Peter, 105
Bergson, Henri, 43
Bernard of Clairvaux, 2, 45, 198
"beyond good and evil," 202–204
Bhagavad-gita, 89, 196, 198, 201, 203
Bhakti Hinduism, 17, 23, 46, 52, 89, 108, 247n9
Bharati, Agehananda, 190
Bonaventure, 2, 84
Bradford, David, 126
Broad, C. D., 42
Bronkhorst, Johannes, 213
Buber, Martin, 48, 52–53, 214, 242n2
Bucke, Richard M., 13, 35, 55, 197, 245n10
Buddhism, 12, 14, 20, 21, 22, 25, 26, 27, 28, 29, 30, 31, 36, 37, 47, 48, 68, 71, 78, 90–91, 93–94, 100, 102, 104, 105, 109, 114, 115, 121, 129, 131–32, 134–35, 137–39, 140, 141, 142–43, 156, 158–59, 161, 163, 166, 171, 172, 175–76, 183, 184, 185, 186, 188, 190, 192, 194, 195, 197, 198, 199, 203, 205, 210–11, 215, 222, 226, 228, 238,

291

Buddhism *(continued)*
  238n2, 238n1, 240n2, 241n4, 243n8, 243n12, 245n2, 245nn7–9, 252n6, 254n3, 255nn5–6, 256n1, 257n7, 286n1
Bynum, Caroline Walker, 107

Campbell, Joseph, 101
Capra, Frithjof, 129, 134, 136, 140–41, 143, 252n8
Catherine of Siena, 106, 125
Chesterton, G. K., vii
Chew, Geoffrey, 144
Chinese mysticism. *See* "Dao and Daoism"
Chomaky, Noam, 225
Christianity, 1, 2, 17, 26, 36, 45, 48, 52, 61, 64, 68, 77, 80, 81–82, 82, 83–86, 103, 105, 105–108, 115, 124, 125, 156, 161, 162, 174, 183, 191, 192, 193, 198, 203, 209, 210, 215, 218–19, 223, 226–30, 239nn1–2, 241n6, 241n10, 245n6, 247n9, 261n2, 261n4
Clifford, James, 215
Cloud of Unknowing, 246n6
cognitivity, issue of, 6, 7–8, 8, 11, 22, 40, 43, 53, 55–56, 57, 58, 74–75, 95, 98, 99, 112, 145, 146, 147–68, 181, 182, 201, 212, 213, 232, 238n6, 246n1, 248n4, 253n2; science, 126–28, 149–55; pragmatic grounds, 154–55, 162–63; limitations, 163–65
comparative approaches, 207–23
comparativism, 219–22, 228
complementarity, 143–44
conflicting claims, 155–59, 161–63
constructivism and nonconstructivism, 53, 54–60, 61–62, 73, 212, 216, 220, 226, 242n3, 242nn6–7, 243n9, 244nn13–14, 247n8, 253n1, 259n5

contextualism, 57, 61, 62, 73, 214, 219, 224, 226, 235
Copernicus, Nicholaus, 61–62, 164, 244n14
creating mystical agreement, 160–61
cross-cultural study, 69–71
Cupitt, Don, 54

Danto, Arthur, 193–94, 199, 200, 257n6
Dao and Daoism, 4, 12, 35, 38, 47, 67, 70–71, 79, 91–94, 104, 132, 169, 183, 192–93, 198, 200, 201, 202, 214, 222, 233, 257n8
d'Aquili, Eugene, 114–15, 118, 248n5
Dass, Ram, 204
Davis, Caroline Franks, 161
Deikman, Arthur, 248n6
Dennett, Daniel, 195, 249n12
depth-mystical experience, 17–18, 39–40
Derrida, Jacques, 212
Descartes, René, 253n3
detachment, 21, 23, 25, 27, 30, 81, 89, 94, 101, 121, 198, 199–202, 247n5, 257n4
Deussen, Paul, 195, 196
dimensions of reality, mystical and scientific, 133–37
Dogen, 139
Dupré, Louis, 235

Eastern Orthodox Christianity, 82, 174, 183, 239n2
Eckhart, Meister, 17, 25–26, 26, 42, 43, 45, 57, 66, 85, 86, 106, 107, 148, 158, 170–71, 172, 199, 200, 201, 204, 210, 239n5, 246n6, 255n8
Edgerton, Franklin, 195
Einstein, Albert, 251n1
Eliade, Mircea, 99, 209, 210

Ellens, J. Harold, 119
Emerson, Ralph Waldo, 207
entheogens, 79, 121, 250n15
epileptic microseizures, 125–26
essentialism, 60–62, 77, 100, 212, 214, 225, 226, 229, 247n8
ethics. *See* morality

Fingarette, Herbert, 99
Fishacre, Richard, 241n10
Forman, Robert, 4, 44, 56, 58, 59, 60, 118, 244n13
Francis of Assisi, 125, 203
Free Spirits, 191
Freud, Sigmund, 98–99
Fromm, Erich, 99

Gandhi, Mohandas, 104, 187–88, 198
Gellman, Jerome, 149
gender studies, 105–108
Gerson, Jean, 2
Gimello, Robert, 55
Goswami, Amit, 136
Graham, Aelred, 227
Greek mysticism, 79–82, 84, 240n6
Greeley, Andrew, 105
Griffiths, Bede, 228
Guénon, René, 224
Gyatso, Tenzin (His Holiness the XIVth Dalai Lama), 15, 112, 139, 141–43

Hadot, Pierre, 80
Hakuin, 29
Halbfass, Wilhelm, 138
Hasidism. *See* Jewish mysticism
Hawking, Stephen, 129
Hick, John, 56
Hildegard of Bingen, 106
Hinduism, 17, 52, 68, 77, 88–90, 91, 103, 105, 108, 121, 129, 166, 183, 190, 195–96, 215, 216, 228, 239n2, 243n8, 247n9, 255n4, 261n4
history of mysticism, 77–96
Hollenback, Jess Byron, 7, 238n7
Home, D. D., 238n7
Hood, Ralph, W., Jr., 122, 217n2
Huaihai, Baizhang, 258n11
Huxley, Aldous, 183, 224, 230, 251n18

Ignatius of Loyola, 86
Ikkyu, 257n9
illusion, 15, 36, 37–38, 40, 41, 45, 81, 82, 84, 88–89, 100, 129, 136, 154, 170, 175, 194
inclusivism, 261n4
ineffability, 2, 11, 55, 83, 170, 178, 181–82, 186, 212, 256nn9–10, 261n3
Inge, William, 2, 61, 103, 234
Islamic mysticism. *See* Sufism

Jäger, Willigis, 229
Jainism, 3, 40, 44, 89, 162, 203, 252n5, 256n3
James, William, 2, 34, 42, 60, 71, 74, 98, 125, 156, 160, 161, 162, 167, 183, 209, 223, 232–33, 242n2
Janzten, Grace, 106, 215, 246n6
Jewish mysticism, 23, 45, 52–53, 82–83, 84, 85, 98, 102, 156, 192, 204, 214, 243n12, 255n4
John of the Cross, 7, 26, 39, 45, 85, 183
Johnston, William, 182, 229
Josephson, Brian, 129
Julian of Norwich, 106, 241n1, 245n6
Jung, Carl, 69, 99, 100

Kabat-Zinn, Jon, 30
Kabbalah. *See* Jewish mysticism
Kakar, Sudhir, 101

Kant, Immanuel, 42, 53, 148
Katz, Steven, 54–56, 59, 61, 123, 220, 224, 242n4, 243n7, 243n12, 244n13
Keenan, John, 228
Kekulé, August, 253n10
King, Sallie, 242n4
Knitter, Paul, 229
Koestler, Arthur, 250n13
Kohn, Livia, 28
Kripal, Jeffrey, 7, 102, 259n2
Krippner, Stanley, 237n3
Krishnamurti, Jiddu, 104

Lancaster, Brian, 52
language, 169–86, 215–19; enlightened use, 184–85
Lanzetta, Beverly, 107, 247n8
Laozi, 67, 104, 169
Law, William, 245n6
Le Saux, Henri, 228
Leach, Edmund, 109
Leuba, James, 98
Lewis, I. M., 104
Lilly, John, 111
Llull, Ramon, 260n1
Lotus Sutra, 139

Madhva, 57, 89, 261n4
Maimonides, 82
Malkovsky, Bradley, 261n6
Manet, Édouard, 243n7
Mansfield, Victor, 135, 140
Manson, Charles, 190
Maritain, Jacques, 261n2
Marshall, Paul, 241n8
Maslow, Abraham, 99
Masson, Jeffrey, 101
McDaniel, June, 211
McGinn, Bernard, 4, 56
meditation, 14–15, 16, 20, 25, 26–27, 28–30, 111, 239nn3–4, 242n5; techniques, 11, 28, 29, 79, 95, 100, 112, 114, 114–15, 190, 239nn3–4, 247n2
Mendeleev, Dmitri, 252n10
Merton, Thomas, 198, 227
metaphysics, 35–43; depth-mystical, 40–41
mindfulness, vii, 9, 10, 13–16, 18, 20, 24, 27, 38, 47, 66, 78, 91, 95, 111, 113, 114, 118, 122, 127, 131, 136, 139, 184, 235, 239, 243n10, 247n2, 249n13, 252n6
morality, 187–206; nature of, 187; presuppositions, 193–94; and wholeness, 196–98; mystical selflessness, 204–206
Müller, Friedrich Max, 207, 209
music, 183
mystical enlightenment, 18–24
mystical experience, 3–5, 30–31; extrovertive, 9–10, 11–16; introvertive, 10–11, 16–18; theistic introvertive, 17; types, 9–24
mystical knowledge claims, 31–49, 51–62; knowledge by participation, 33; and science, 129–46
mystical paths, 25–31
mysticism, nature of, 1–8, 51–53; history of the word, 1–2; contemporary, 8, 94–96; study of, 231–36

Nagarjuna, 15, 71, 155, 255n5
naturalism, viii, 8, 22, 32, 36, 40, 41, 42, 53, 74–75, 94, 115, 122, 145, 146, 150, 151, 152, 154, 155, 157, 159, 160, 161, 163, 164, 166, 168, 213, 229, 232, 233, 236
Needham, Joseph, 70
Neo-Buddhism, 141–42
Neo-Vedanta, 129, 261n4
Neumann, Erich, 99

neuroscience, viii, 7, 9, 54, 59, 65, 74, 75, 111–28, 141–42, 149–53, 211, 213, 217, 232, 247n1, 248n9, 249n10, 252n3
neurotheology, 248n5
New Age, 19, 70, 94, 99, 129–46 passim, 150, 230, 235
Newberg, Andrew, 114–5, 248n5
Nhat Hanh, Thich, 199
Nicholas of Cusa, 184
Nietzsche, Friedrich, 242n3
nonduality, 12, 13, 15, 24, 30, 36, 34, 37, 40, 46, 47, 49, 65, 88, 89, 102, 159, 160, 179, 186, 194, 195, 241n5, 255n6

Otto, Rudolph, 209, 210
Owen, Richard, 215–16

Pahnke, Walter, 27, 119
Panikkar, Raimon, 227
pantheism, 36, 52, 84, 87, 94; versus panentheism, 36
paradox, 27, 29, 33, 67, 85, 118, 174–76, 178, 179, 180, 238n2, 255nn6–7, 256n9
paranormal phenomena, 7, 78, 238n7, 247n6, 251n20, 251n3, 253n2
Parsons, William, 97
pathology, 26–27, 97–99, 101, 124–26, 132, 152, 251n20
Paul of Tarsus, 125
Penner, Hans, 61
perennial philosophy, 37, 50, 60, 63, 72–73, 76, 77, 100, 160, 212, 218, 224–26, 246n3, 250n17, 251n18, 254n4
Persinger, Michael, 111, 125
phenomenological approach, 63, 209, 210, 248n9, 258n1
Philo Judaeus, 83
Pike, Nelson, 160

placebo effect, 250n16
Plato, 80, 235, 240n6
Plotinus, 18, 31, 43, 46, 57, 58, 66, 80–82, 170, 171, 172, 176, 180, 204, 255n8
Porete, Marguerite, 107
positive characterizations, 170–72
postmodernism, 54, 60, 61, 70, 104, 210, 211, 212, 213–19, 219–22 passim, 226, 242n7, 244n1, 253n1, 259n5, 260nn6–9
prayer, 3, 66, 86, 87, 103, 120, 122, 156, 169, 204, 239n2, 249n3
Protestantism, 52, 229, 234, 254n7, 261n2
Pseudo-Dionysius the Areopagite, 1–2, 148, 173
psychedelic drugs, vii, ix, 5, 8, 63, 65, 78, 95, 100, 109, 111, 112, 118–24, 127, 150–52, 235, 245n3, 250nn15–17, 254n4
psychological approaches, 97–102
psychotherapy, 95, 98, 100, 155
Ptolemy, 61–62, 164, 244n14
pure consciousness event, 117–18

quietism, 52, 203, 258n11

Rahner, Karl, 228, 235
Ramanuja, 57, 89, 261n4
rationality, 80, 143, 165–67, 177, 180, 189, 197, 209, 213, 215, 254n8, 254n10
reductionism and antireductionism, 73–75, 98–99, 101–102, 116, 122, 124–35, 130, 133, 160, 195, 211, 251n2
reliability of mystical experiences, 159
religious studies, viii, 208–11, 238n5; disparagement of religious experiences, 210–13
Richards, William, 96, 118, 235

Rinpoche, Chogyam Trungpa, 190
Rist, John, 255n8
Roland, Romain, 98, 246n2
Rolle, Richard, 48
Roth, Harold, 211
Russell, Bertrand, 146, 246n1
Ruusbroec, Jan van, 17, 85, 86, 193, 246n6

Samkhya-Yoga, 3, 35, 44, 46, 88, 89, 90, 156, 194, 233, 252n5, 256n3
Santayana, George, 51
schizophrenia. *See* pathology
Schleiermacher, Friedrich, 209
Schuon, Frithjof, 72
science, nature of, 130–31; reconciling science and mysticism, 144–46
scientific method and mysticism, 137–39
scientific theories and mystical knowledge–claims, 139–43
Searle, John, 117
secular mysticism, 8, 37, 64, 77, 94–96, 155, 235–36, 250n14
self, sense of, 5, 7, 12, 13, 14, 15, 18, 19–21, 24, 25, 27, 30, 31, 41, 44, 78, 86, 91, 94 95, 99, 100–101, 107, 112, 113, 119, 126, 145–46, 150, 154, 155, 163, 190, 192, 194, 201, 204, 233, 237n3, 253n12
selflessness, 19, 28–29, 115, 117, 146, 163, 187, 190, 192, 193–95, 198, 200, 201, 202, 203–206, 234
Sells, Michael, 259n3
Sengcan, 202
sense-perception analogy, 149
set and setting, 101, 119, 121–24 passim, 150, 250n14, 251n18
shamanism, 78–79, 104, 248n5
Shankara, 36, 38, 42, 46–47, 57, 89, 138, 145, 158, 161, 171–72, 173, 180, 191–92, 200, 210, 241n5, 253n3, 254n6, 255n8, 256n11, 261n6
Sharf, Robert, 210–11, 212
Smart, Ninian, 65
Smith, Huston, 119, 123, 208, 225, 235, 245n7, 254n4
Smith, Jonathan, 216
social action, 198–99
sociological approaches, 102–105
socioscientific approaches, 97–105, 151
Soelle, Dorothee, 107
Spencer, Daniel, 230
Spickard, James, 105
Spinoza, Baruch, 42
Staal, Frits, 65, 210, 258n1
Stace, Walter, 9, 123, 189–90, 192, 193, 242n4
Stoeber, Michael, 219
Sufism, 23, 26, 28, 45–46, 52, 79, 82, 86–88, 103, 136, 174, 176, 183, 191, 215, 227, 239n2, 245n6
Sullivan, Philip, 117
surveys, 237n2
symbolism, 79, 183–84, 186

Tantrism, 47, 79, 89, 90, 91, 102, 108, 183, 190–91, 257n9
Tart, Charles, 237n3
Taves, Ann, 211
Teresa of Avila, 7, 20, 30, 45, 58, 86, 106, 107, 125, 162, 201, 238n8, 243n11, 250n14
theism, 16–18, 39–41, 48–49, 122–24, 160–61, 257n9
theology, 2, 209, 224–30, 238n1, 244n2, 255n1, 261n6
Theosophical Society, 207
Therese of Lisieux, 106
Thomas à Kempis, 229
Tillich, Paul, 234–35, 261n2
Toynbee, Arnold, 13
Troeltsch, Ernest, 105

transcendentalism, 2, 207
triggers, 8, 9, 11, 28, 119, 122, 123, 126, 150, 249n13
Turner, Denys, 259n3

Underhill, Evelyn, 2, 233
understanding and explaining, 73–76
understanding mystical claims, 64–69, 176–79
union, mystical, 2, 43–48, 58, 78, 83, 85, 87, 92, 185, 233, 237n2, 242n2
unknowing, 5, 25, 26, 56, 92
Upanishads, 38, 46, 57, 88, 89, 109, 171–72, 174, 181, 191, 195–96, 256n11

via negativa, 81, 85, 172–74, 239, 245n2, 255n1
visions, 3, 4, 7–8, 31, 49, 58, 78, 79, 82, 106, 107, 111, 119, 120, 121, 122, 124, 125, 238n5, 238n8, 241n1, 243n11, 246n6, 251n18

Wainwright, William, 8, 238n1

Waldman, Mark, 68
Wallace, B. Alan, 138, 232, 259n2
Walsh, Roger N., 78
Wawrytko, Sandra, 108
Weber, Max, 67
Whitehead, Alfred North, 42, 143
Whitman, Walt, 12
Wilber, Ken, 101
Wilson, Edward O., 146
Winkelman, Michael, 248n5
Wittgenstein, Ludwig, 42, 181, 219
Wordsworth, William, 12

"you are that (*tat tvam asi*)," 46, 88, 195–96

Zaehner, R. C., 99, 123, 238n1, 251n18
Zen Buddhism, 21, 23–24, 24, 26, 29, 94, 99, 105, 139, 175, 183, 185, 199, 202, 203, 227, 229, 238n1, 255n7, 257nn9–10, 258n11
Zhuangzi, 43, 193, 214
Zukav, Gary, 129